Modern Alchemy

Occultism and the Emergence of Atomic Theory

MARK S. MORRISSON

UNIVERSITY PRESS

2007

OXFORD
UNIVERSITY PRESS

Oxford University Press, Inc., publishes works that further
Oxford University's objective of excellence
in research, scholarship, and education.

Oxford   New York
Auckland   Cape Town   Dar es Salaam   Hong Kong   Karachi
Kuala Lumpur   Madrid   Melbourne   Mexico City   Nairobi
New Delhi   Shanghai   Taipei   Toronto

With offices in
Argentina   Austria   Brazil   Chile   Czech Republic   France   Greece
Guatemala   Hungary   Italy   Japan   Poland   Portugal   Singapore
South Korea   Switzerland   Thailand   Turkey   Ukraine   Vietnam

Copyright © 2007 by Oxford University Press, Inc.

Published by Oxford University Press, Inc.
198 Madison Avenue, New York, New York 10016

www.oup.com

Oxford is a registered trademark of Oxford University Press

All rights reserved. No part of this publication may be reproduced,
stored in a retrieval system, or transmitted, in any form or by any means,
electronic, mechanical, photocopying, recording, or otherwise,
without the prior permission of Oxford University Press.

Library of Congress Cataloging-in-Publication Data

Morrisson, Mark S.
Modern alchemy : occultism and the emergence of atomic theory / Mark S. Morrisson.
   p. cm.
ISBN 978-0-19-530696-5
1. Alchemy—History.   2. Occultism—History.   3. Nuclear chemistry.   4. Alchemy in
literature.   I. Title.
QD13.M67   2007
540.1'12—dc22   2006029629

9 8 7 6 5 4 3 2 1

Printed in the United States of America
on acid-free paper

*To Laura, Devin, and Ciara,
Marilyn and Clovis Morrisson,
and Mary von Ahnen—again*

Acknowledgments

Several scholars and institutions have been instrumental in helping me launch and research this project. I am especially grateful to Philip Jenkins, without whose encouragement, support, and voluminous knowledge of the world of occultism this book would not have realized its full potential, and to Cynthia Read, my editor at Oxford University Press, for her unflagging support of a project that crosses so many disciplinary lines. I owe an immense debt of gratitude to Linda Dalrymple Henderson, whose constant encouragement and detailed research on the intersections between science and occultism in the modernist period have inspired much of my work. M. E. Warlick's vast knowledge of alchemy and its twentieth-century manifestations in the arts has likewise moved my thinking along at several sessions of the Society for Literature, Science, and the Arts. Indeed, the project benefited greatly from the cross-disciplinary testing ground provided by the SLSA. Susan Squier, Wenda Bauchspies, and other members of the science studies reading group at Penn State University helped clarify the aims of this project in its early stages. I am grateful to Michael Gordin, whose meticulous reading of my manuscript challenged me to reconsider some of my assumptions and deepened my knowledge of occult appropriations of nineteenth- and early-twentieth-century science. I am also greatly indebted to the anonymous second reader of the manuscript for a number of key suggestions that enhanced the final project. I also wish to thank Lynn Allan Kauppi for his careful yet speedy copyediting.

I also wish to thank the Bodleian Library at Oxford University for permission to do research in the Frederick Soddy Papers in their Modern Manuscripts collections, and the Museum of the History of Science, Oxford University, for permission to work with Soddy's lecture notes and papers in their archives. I thank University College London, Special Collections, for permission to do research in the Sir William Ramsay Papers. I also thank the special collections librarians at the University of Illinois, Urbana-Champaign, for access to H. G. Wells's papers, and the University of Texas at Austin Harry Ransom Humanities Research Center for access to Edith Sitwell's papers. Frances Soar of the Geographical Association, the administrators of the Frederick Soddy Trust, and Maxwell Wright and Gwen Huntley of Bunkers Solicitors generously helped me in my efforts to track down an estate for Frederick Soddy's unpublished writings. And I wish to thank Mark Smithells and the Smithells family in New Zealand for permission to quote from Arthur Smithells's unpublished manuscript in the Frederick Soddy Papers.

Penn State University provided me a sabbatical, a Faculty Research Grant from the Research and Graduate Studies Office, and a semester as a Resident Scholar at the Institute for the Arts and Humanities that provided the time away from teaching and administrative duties and the travel support that facilitated the completion of this book. I owe special thanks to my department head, Robert Caserio, for his extraordinary commitment to this project, and Deborah Clarke, Janet Lyon, Robin Schulze, and Sanford Schwartz for helping me keep the project moving at crucial stages. My undergraduate research assistants Greg Jones and Elizabeth Parfitt provided invaluable help with their careful exploration of many years of Theosophical and occult periodicals, newspapers, and popular science journals. Likewise, the hardworking Interlibrary Loan staff at the Penn State Pattee Library graciously handled my seemingly endless requests for obscure periodicals.

Finally, I wish to thank my wife, Laura Reed-Morrisson, for her support and her careful readings and insightful suggestions on every draft of the manuscript, and I thank my son Devin and daughter Ciara for their willingness to endure the long hours I spent at work on this project.

Contents

Introduction, 3

1. From the Golden Dawn to the Alchemical Society, 31

2. Occult Chemistry, Instrumentation, and the Theosophical Science of Direct Perception, 65

3. Chemistry in the Borderland, 97

4. Atomic Alchemy and the Gold Standard, 135

Epilogue, 185

Appendix A: Boundary-Work, Border Crossings, and Trading Zones, 195

Appendix B: Occult Interest Books by Alchemical Society Members, 205

Appendix C: A Partial List of Alchemical Society Members, 207

Notes, 209

Works Cited, 235

Index, 253

Modern Alchemy

Introduction

Stories of the Birth of Modern Alchemy

For many in the twenty-first century, the word "alchemy" conjures up images of medieval zealots rummaging through ancient books and scrolls in dark hot basements, seeking the secrets of transmutation in the dim firelight of brick furnaces and archaic laboratory equipment with strange names—athanor, horn of Hermes, cucurbite. The occult wisdom forged by these alchemists was intended to bring them immense wealth, great longevity, and spiritual purification. In spite of Enlightenment attacks upon alchemy as unscientific superstition, or merely the foolish pursuit of the self-deluded, it is now clear that alchemy was a scientifically and spiritually serious pursuit from antiquity through the Middle Ages, with roots in Egyptian metallurgy, Aristotelian philosophy of matter and form, and Jewish, Arabic, early Christian, and Hermetic sources.

Alchemy was not a monolithic practice, but virtually all versions of it involved destroying the nature of a "base" metal—lead or mercury, for instance—thus reducing it to a *prima materia* without the specific characteristics of any element. Then, the powder of the prized "Philosopher's Stone" or some other process would instill a "nobler" essence into the substance, transmuting it into gold or silver. The physical processes of alchemy involved several stages in which the base metal would be altered through heating, distilling, and the addition of various chemicals (saltpeter, alcohol, nitric acid, and sulphuric acid, for example). These stages were often known by specific colors that would appear during their successful execution. An intricate and seemingly mysterious set of images and symbols emerged, too, in the Greek, Arabic, and medieval literatures of alchemy. These included the tail-eating serpent, Ouroboros, symbolizing the unity of the cosmos, and various images representing the stages of the "Great Work" of alchemy (e.g., the black raven for the *nigredo* stage or the white dove for the *albedo*). Alchemy moved in pharmacological directions as well, using the logic of the purification of matter to seek chemical cures for ailments—and even for aging, which would be vanquished by the fabled Elixir of Life. Just as alchemy represented the chemistry of the Middle Ages, figures such as Paracelsus (1493–1541) helped direct alchemical thinking toward the practice of medicine.

By the eighteenth century, though, alchemy was under assault and largely dismissed by those supporting the rigorous scientific method and new ways of understanding matter that laid the groundwork for modern chemistry. Eighteenth- and nineteenth-century scientists pronounced alchemy's methods of reasoning and experimentation nonscientific. But, perhaps most important, they rejected alchemy's understanding of the nature of matter. Alchemy held that all the elements could be reduced to a *prima materia,* and then transmuted into other elements. But modern chemistry, as it emerged during the Enlightenment, came to the opposite view of the nature of matter. Culminating in John Dalton's field-defining 1808 treatise, *A New System of Chemical Philosophy,* modern chemistry held that atoms were the smallest particles, both indivisible and unalterable. An atom of each element was a fundamental, distinct particle (Keller 1983, 9–10). The material basis for alchemy was thus seen as nothing more than a long-held intellectual mistake, now relegated to the realm of superstition and pseudoscience.

Alchemy was to reassert itself with a vengeance, though, in a most unanticipated arena at the beginning of the twentieth century. In an often quoted exchange between chemist Frederick Soddy (1877–1956) and physicist Ernest Rutherford (1871–1937) in their lab at Canada's McGill University in 1901, when they discovered that radioactive thorium was transforming into an inert gas, "Soddy recalled, 'I was overwhelmed with something greater than joy—I cannot very well express it—a kind of exaltation.' He blurted out, 'Rutherford, this is transmutation!' 'For Mike's sake, Soddy,' his companion shot back, 'don't call it *transmutation*. They'll have our heads off as alchemists'" (Weart 1988, 5–6). Indeed, within a decade of the 1896 discovery of radiation by French physicist Henri Becquerel (1852–1908), the newly emerging science of radioactivity routinely generated comparisons to alchemy. The transformation that radioactive elements underwent into other elements—Rutherford and Soddy's discovery—was frequently figured as alchemical transmutation. Some even imagined the highly radioactive element radium, only discovered in

1898 by the Curies, to be a modern-day Philosopher's Stone. Moreover, the little understood effects of mysterious radiation on living tissue evoked the alchemical Elixir of Life for many. By the 1920s, atomic physics and radiochemistry were regularly called "modern alchemy" in the press. Multiple textbooks on the new subject took that name.[1] Though Rutherford was initially wary of alchemical comparisons, as the above conversation attests, even he titled his last book *The Newer Alchemy* (1937).

But what were the origins of this alchemical emphasis? Why would rigorously trained scientists such as Soddy, Sir William Ramsay, and others, working in the most modern laboratories available to chemistry and physics, have so quickly turned to alchemy to imagine the nature and implications of the changes they witnessed in radioactive elements? Investigating why the latest in cutting-edge science was cast in terms of a discredited earlier knowledge, one seemingly reduced to the status of a pre-Enlightenment occult relic, offers fascinating insights into the boundaries between science, religion, and other areas of culture at the beginning of the twentieth century. Indeed, to understand how the science of radioactivity came to be so tied to alchemical tropes and images, we must turn to an apparently unscientific phenomenon: the major fin-de-siècle revival of interest in alchemy and esoteric religion. Stunning landmarks of atomic science occurred alongside an efflorescence of occultism that ascribed deep significance to questions about the nature of matter and energy. And perhaps more surprisingly, the broad alchemical revival had an impact on the way some scientists understood and portrayed their research programs.[2] This book will explore the ways in which the alchemical revival in occult circles obliquely helped inform, and was in turn profoundly shaped by, the emerging science of radioactivity and radioactive transformation.

Stories of Modern Alchemy

But how should we tell such a story? As with most narratives, the history of the birth of modern atomic science could be told in any number of ways. Historians of science generally tell it by chronicling key discoveries and the experiments and theoretical imperatives that produced them. Such an account tends to emphasize theoretical breakthroughs and laboratory triumphs, and, in outline, would unfold something like this. In November 1895, while passing electric current through a cathode ray tube (a glass tube evacuated of most of its air) shielded by heavy black cardboard, German physicist Wilhelm Röntgen (1845–1923) discovers mysterious rays that can pass through flesh and wood, even producing photographic images of the bones inside his wife's hand. He names them "X-rays" because of their unknown nature. A few months later, in February 1896, Becquerel finds, quite by chance, that the uranium potassium sulphate crystals that he had placed on photographic plates in a drawer give off rays of their own. Marie Curie (1867–1934) soon names this phenomenon "radioactivity." Marie and her husband Pierre Curie (1859–1906) show that thorium, too, is radioactive, and go on to discover new radioactive elements—including the highly radioactive radium in 1898. Becquerel and the Curies share the Nobel Prize in physics in 1903, initiating a long series of Nobel Prizes to be awarded to the pioneers of atomic physics.

In 1897, at the Cavendish Laboratory at Cambridge University, British physicist J. J. Thomson (1856–1940) seeks to explain the workings of those cathode ray tubes that preoccupied Röntgen and several other physicists. Thomson shows that the mysterious cathode rays are, in fact, made of negatively charged particles, for which he uses a name coined by physicist Johnstone Stoney: electrons. In February 1897 before his colleagues at Cambridge, and in April before the Royal Institution of Great Britain (the oldest independent research institution in the world), Thomson strikingly argues against the Daltonian understanding of atoms of each element as fundamental particles. Atoms are not indivisible, but, he argues, have negatively charged particles, called electrons, that can be torn from them. These particles all have the same mass and charge, and they have less than a thousandth of the mass of a hydrogen atom, the least massive atom. In 1904, Thomson goes on to propose his "plum pudding" model of the atom, in which negatively charged electrons dwell in a positively charged fluid orb.

Meanwhile, in a lab at Canada's McGill University, Rutherford, who had studied with Thomson at Cambridge, and Soddy, a young Oxford-trained chemist, reveal the mechanism of radioactivity in 1901 and 1902. They show that the radioactive elements disintegrate, releasing radioactivity and transforming into other elements in the process. Several years later, back in England at the University of Manchester, Rutherford observes the scattering of alpha particles (consisting of two protons and two neutrons, essentially a helium nucleus, emitted by uranium or radium) bombarding thin foils. From this experiment, he develops a model of the atom: a positively charged nucleus around which electrons orbit. Stunningly, Rutherford's model suggests that atoms are overwhelmingly composed of empty space.

In 1913, the Danish physicist Niels Bohr (1885–1962) sees problems in Rutherford's model and refines it to suggest that electrons exist only in specific states. He uses Planck's constant, formulated by German physicist Max Planck, to explain the stability that these states confer on atoms. In 1919, Rutherford—now director of the Cavendish Lab at Cambridge—discovers the positively charged particle, the proton, in the atom's nucleus. But his assistant director at the Cavendish, James Chadwick, is troubled by the discrepancy between the atomic number of an atom (the number of protons in the nucleus) and its atomic mass. In 1932, Chadwick discovers the neutron, a neutral particle that contributes to an atom's mass but not to its atomic number.

Meanwhile, in 1923 and 1924 the French physicist Louis de Broglie (1892–1987) uses Einstein's theory that photons (the basic entities of electromagnetic radiation) exhibit properties of both waves and particles, to suggest that electrons, too, have the same dual properties. De Broglie argues that electrons should not be thought of as localized particles in space around a nucleus, but rather as something like a cloud of negative charge. Following de Broglie's theories, Austrian physicist Erwin Schrödinger (1887–1961) develops an equation allowing him to predict the future behavior of electrons. German physicist Max Born (1882–1970) uses the wave function of electrons to calculate the possibility of finding a particle at a specific region at a specific time. Niels Bohr and German physicist Werner Heisenberg (1901–1976) begin working on quantum mechanics in 1924, and, in 1927, Heisenberg propounds his uncertainty principle—the theory that one cannot simultaneously know a particle's exact position and velocity.

An outline of discoveries like this provides one view of the nascence of nuclear physics and quantum mechanics. We could extend the narrative through the early twenty-first century to describe the ever-expanding stable of subatomic particles (many predicted by theory and then confirmed by particle accelerators), the emergence of high-energy particle physics, the birth of atomic warfare and atomic energy in civilian life, the advent of string and super-string theory, and more. Writing the history of science in this way would draw particular attention to a chain of problem-solving physicists, each of whom constructed successful experiments to explain a physical phenomenon or to correct problems in another physicist's formulation. (Rutherford's nuclear model of the atom corrected Thomson's plum pudding model, for instance, just as Bohr's atom solved problems in Rutherford's. Notably, each of these two cases represents a student's correction of his former teacher.)

A more lengthy study would add greater complexity to the simplified narrative above. It would go into the details of the experiments themselves, the history of fields of scientific inquiry—such as electromagnetism and ether physics—that led up to the discoveries of the 1890s, the importance of international exchanges among scientists and their working partnerships, and the theoretical necessities or inconsistencies that sparked revisions of theories and further laboratory experiments.[3] It would also show that not everyone working in the field was a physicist. Chemist Sir William Crookes's 1875 experiments with cathode rays showed that they were deflectable by a magnet, and hence were not light. Frederick Soddy, along with Rutherford, made crucial contributions to work on radioactive transformation. He also originated our basic understanding of isotopes, for which he won the 1921 Nobel Prize in chemistry. This more extensive narrative of scientific progress in the field would discuss the importance of chemist Sir William Ramsay's discovery of helium (which he and Soddy definitively identified as the mystery gas produced in radioactive decay) and other inert atmospheric gases, which earned *him* the Nobel in chemistry in 1904. Such a history of nuclear physics would be enhanced by an account of the role of its key instruments—the Geiger counter, scintillation counter, cloud chamber, cyclotron, bubble chamber, and the like—that Peter Galison has offered in *Image and Logic: A Material Culture of Microphysics* (1997). The strength of the standard history of science based upon key discoveries, experiments, and theoretical innovations is the clarity with which it can portray the relations among successful experiments and breakthroughs that advanced the science.

The history of atomic science might also be approached through the cultural history of its public reception. This kind of study would rely not on the annals of scientific journals and laboratory experiments but instead on the images atomic science inspired in popular culture and in scientists' aspirations for it. Spencer Weart's sweeping volume *Nuclear Fear: A History of Images* (1988) presents just such a cultural history. It plumbs the archives of newspapers, science fiction pulp magazines, popular science journals, government propaganda, and other sources to trace the history of images from nuclear physics' early years through the Cold War. Weart charts a complicated terrain of fears and hopes for nuclear energy that run from the "white city of the future," the alchemical Elixir of Life and Philosopher's Stone, and other positive images to their opposite: horrific doomsday fears, anxieties about monsters, rays, dangerous scientists, and, of course, nuclear annihilation.

Yet the resurrection of alchemical tropes at the birth of modern atomic science demands a third version of the story. Weart notes that the word "transmutation" offered "a clue that could help explain almost every strange image that would later appear in nuclear energy tales" (6). In order to understand fully the relationships between alchemical transmutation and the science of radioactivity, I take a path that branches off from both the traditional history of scientific discovery and the image history that Weart provides. In *Modern Alchemy*, I reconstruct the history of how scientific knowledge was produced and how it was elaborated in a broader cultural and spiritual context. That is, I look at science, its public elaboration, and its spiritual[4] dimensions as mutually interacting realms, and tell a story of how science and occultism were entwined.

Modern Alchemy offers the first sustained exploration of the relationships between a thriving occult alchemical revival and what by the 1920s had widely come to be known as the "modern alchemy" of atomic science. It chronicles the surprisingly inter-connected pursuits of occultists and atomic scientists around the emergence of radiochemistry and nuclear physics as new scientific fields. Let me make the limits of my argument clear from the beginning, though. I am not arguing for a symmetrical influence between occultists and the scientists who created modern atomic science. Other than Sir William Crookes, none of the scientists whose work I explore were members of occult groups—not even Ramsay or Soddy, who contributed the most to the alchemical figuration of the early discoveries in the field of radioactivity (though Ramsay was a member of an organization that investigated what we would now call paranormal phenomena). While occultists were carefully scanning scientific journals and books for information on radioactivity and subatomic particles to support their claims for occult alchemy, there is no evidence that the chemists (again, other than Crookes) were reading the occult periodicals. Instead, I will show that the broad revival of interest in alchemy in the late nineteenth and early twentieth centuries (that included occultists, non-occult historians of chemistry, educators, journalists, and scientists alike) gave chemistry a trope that influenced its public reception and its sense of its own identity and that contributed to its early understanding and portrayal of radioactivity's significance.

The chapters focus on key moments in the developing relationship between occultism and the science of atomic transmutation primarily in the Anglophone West. Though the work that launched the fields of nuclear physics and radiochemistry spanned several countries, many crucial early discoveries about the transmutability of the elements were made in Britain, Canada, and the United States. Rutherford and Soddy's 1901–1902 experiments demonstrating radioactive "transmutation" at McGill were central to the emerging importance of alchemical tropes, as were Soddy and Ramsay's confirmations in London that helium was created in the transmutation. Ramsay's own efforts to transmute an element artificially, first published in 1907, initiated a frenzy of alchemical aspirations, as did Rutherford's 1919 successful artificial transmutation of nitrogen at the Cavendish Lab. Ernest O. Lawrence's early work with cyclotrons at the University of California at Berkeley in the 1930s was also crucial. Ramsay and Soddy's lectures, books, and articles aimed at the broader public made alchemical interpretations of the new science of intense interest in Britain and the United States. Moreover, Britain and America both had thriving occult movements during the period that positioned alchemy as one of the most important Hermetic sciences. Their translations and numerous publications of key alchemical texts helped launch new histories of chemistry that included chapters on alchemy and fueled the broader public interest in the subject. Thus, while *Modern Alchemy* explores international dimensions of its subject, it focuses specifically on Britain and America, where boundaries carefully erected between the sciences and occultism across the nineteenth century became more noticeably permeable. Even boundaries between the sciences of chemistry and physics, and between those sciences and economics, were blurred by the presence of alchemy as a trope or even as a religious belief guiding the new understanding of matter and energy.[5]

In chapter 1, the interests of occult alchemists and mainstream chemists combine in the founding of the Alchemical Society in London in 1912. The mid-nineteenth-century occult understanding of alchemy as primarily about spiritual transformation (so-called spiritual alchemy) and not material transmutation was supplanted by an increasing certitude that ancient and medieval alchemy had always been a material process, though one with spiritual implications. Reciprocally, scientists in the Alchemical Society came to see the relevance and even spiritual significance of alchemy to modern atomic science. Chapter 2 tells how the close relationship between Theosophical theories of matter and the new atomic science led Theosophists to launch, in 1895, a decades-long research program of "clairvoyant chemistry." (This research continued across the twentieth century: It has even occupied recent and contemporary scientists with doctoral degrees in chemistry and physics.) In chapter 3 I describe a "transmutational gold rush" between 1904 and the 1920s. Academic chemists, portraying their work in terms provided by the alchemy revival, attempted to transmute elements—and, yes, even to make gold. By the 1920s, these blendings of atomic science and occult alchemy begin to affect still other domains of knowledge, particularly those of economics and monetary policy, eventually inspiring concerns about the gold standard in the 1920s and '30s. Chapter 4 traces the influence of alchemy on debates over monetary theory. It also charts the rise of science fiction that imagined the dire economic consequences of synthetic gold during Britain's arguments over the gold standard and during the banking and currency reforms of the first FDR administration in America.

Scientists and science writers did not merely turn to occult notions to help describe or even inspire their research. As *Modern Alchemy* demonstrates, during the period from the turn of the century to just before World War II, the trajectories of science and occultism briefly *merged*. The stories told here document how and why the nature of matter was so newly important to both scientists and occultists—and they uncover the spiritual and ethical implications of the new material science of radioactivity.

The Alchemical Revival and the "Modern Alchemy" of Radioactivity

Alchemy played a crucial role in the practice and beliefs of Hermetic societies, such as the now famous Hermetic Order of the Golden Dawn and its various international offshoots. It also permeated the teachings of the Theosophical Society, with its merging of Eastern and Western occult traditions and religious beliefs. In short, the West witnessed an alchemical renaissance in the 1880s that gained momentum by the turn of the century. As we shall see in chapter 3, histories of alchemy—and histories of chemistry that took alchemy as a starting point, even if they dismissed it as science—began to proliferate during this period. But at the same time, and not coincidentally, the occult revival privileged alchemy as a source of deep spiritual and even scientific wisdom.

Alchemical texts began to circulate in every conceivable form. Handwritten alchemical treatises were secretly copied and passed among initiates of the Golden Dawn and similar Hermetic orders. Limited-circulation and commercially unviable books were written or translated by occultists and mystics such as A. E. Waite, whose alchemical translations and publications with the publisher James Elliott during the mid-1890s were bankrolled by Fitzherbert Edward Stafford-Jerningham, Lord Stafford, who had taken a great interest in alchemy. Broader circulation books were published by occult publishers such as Rider and Sons and Phillip Wellby in Britain, David McKay in America, and the Theosophical Publishing House in Madras. Books on alchemy brought out by mainstream publishers such as Longmans, Green in the United Kingdom, and Appleton in the United States reached even larger audiences. Moreover, a flourishing occult periodical press, including dozens of Theosophical and Hermetic journals across Europe and North America, published numerous articles on alchemy. Tellingly, Waite launched his eclectic occult journal *Unknown World* in 1894 with an article on alchemy. Even the mass market newspapers began to run stories on efforts at alchemical transmutation, and their books pages reviewed new histories of alchemy. Societies dedicated to exploring alchemy also began to emerge, including La Société Alchimique de France in Paris, which was run by the practicing alchemist François Jollivet-Castelot. The Alchemical Society in London was headed by H. Stanley Redgrove, an academic chemist with a degree from the University of London, and John Ferguson, the Regius Professor of Chemistry at the University of Glasgow.

But until the discovery of radioactive "transmutation" by Rutherford and Soddy, many outside of occult circles were content to view alchemy as simply an interesting, unscientific, and wrongheaded ancestor of chemistry. Even occultists often emphasized that alchemy was really a process of spiritual development, of self-transmutation. The chemical symbols and processes described in ancient and medieval alchemical texts, they asserted, secretly stood for nonphysical processes. After Rutherford and Soddy's 1902 publication, such attitudes changed dramatically. Even religious skeptics began to wonder if the alchemists might have understood something about the nature of matter that nineteenth-century scientists had missed. Could radium have been the fabled Philosopher's Stone, capable of causing transmutations, or perhaps the legendary Elixir of Life, which could rejuvenate living tissue and extend life for hundreds or even thousands of years? Fellows of the Royal Society and Nobel Prize-winning scientists turned to alchemical tropes to emphasize the mutability of the elements, and, for some, to bring a spiritual dimension to their works. Scientific certitude about the fundamental composition of the material world was put to the test; the origins of scientific hypotheses and scientific authority were scrutinized anew. The Daltonian foundation of chemistry was, of course, antithetical to the alchemical premise that the elements were transmutable. But the new science of radioactivity had superseded Dalton and began to suggest, even to scientists, that the bases of alchemy and those of the new chemistry were not mutually exclusive.

Occultists, then, increasingly focused on alchemy as a material science validated by the new atomic chemistry and physics, even if it was a science with spiritual implications. Many occult phenomena now began to be explained in terms of radiation and material particles as occultists turned to scientists to validate their belief.[6] Never had modern occultism been so much concerned with the nature of matter—that is, the nature of material change. To understand this development in the relationship between occultism and material science, we must first briefly rehearse the history of the broad occult movement beginning half a century earlier.

Setting the Scene: The Occult Revival

By the 1840s, Western Europe and North America were seeing the beginnings of what would become a major revival of interest in Western esotericism and occultism. Though many of the key ideas of the revival were centuries old, they took on modern guises. Even the phrase "Western esotericism" only dates from the beginning of the nineteenth century (Faivre 1994, 5), and "occultism" appeared even later, perhaps first in Jean-Baptiste Richard de Randonvilliers' *Dictionnaire des mots nouveaux* (1842). French magus Éliphas Lévi popularized the term in his *Dogme et ritual de la haute magie* from 1856. In 1875 H. P. Blavatsky, the founder of the Theosophical Society and a key conduit of Eastern religious ideas into Western esotericism, spread the word through English-speaking countries (Hanegraaff 2005, 887). These new words helped key figures of the revival create new syntheses of ideas from the past (or the imagined past).

Antoine Faivre has usefully identified four characteristics intrinsic to Western esotericism: (1) a belief in "symbolic and real correspondences... among all parts of the universe, both seen and unseen"; (2) a sense of a "Living Nature," of all nature as animated by a life energy or divinity; (3) an understanding that the religious creative imagination can explore unknown realms between the material world and the divine; and (4) a belief in the "experience of transmutation," of the spiritual transmutation of the inner man, who is connected with the divine (Faivre 1994, 10–14). Beyond these four characteristics, two others are often present that were highly significant to the occultists of the fin de siècle: (1) a belief in the "praxis of concordance," the fundamental concordance between multiple spiritual traditions—that is, a "primordial Tradition"—and (2) an emphasis on the careful passing on of knowledge suggesting that "an esoteric teaching can or must be transmitted from master to disciple following a preestablished channel, respecting a previously marked path" (14).

While one would not want to reduce Western esotericism to Faivre's schema, it is clear that by the mid-nineteenth century, much of the West was experiencing a revival of beliefs like those described by Faivre—beliefs that might previously have been relegated to the dustbin of pre-Enlightenment history. This revival of interest in all things occult took many different forms. But by the turn of the century, many recognizable manifestations of Western esotericism flourished on both sides of the Atlantic. Mesmerism and spiritualism were two early progenitors of the occult revival, and, by later in the century, Theosophy and a number of secret (or not so secret) Hermetic and Rosicrucian societies dedicated to alchemy and ritual magic had become significant cultural forces.

Mesmerism

Mesmerism had been conceived by the German physician Franz Anton Mesmer (1734–1815) as a medical practice. He attempted to use magnets and then simply his own hands and will to amplify what he saw as a kind of "fluid" that connects all beings and things to each other. He also tried to heal disease by increasing this fluid's circulation in the patient's body and by transferring his fluid to his patient via an act of his own will. (He named his discovery "animal magnetism.") While the popularity of mesmerism had waned by the late eighteenth century, it was reborn in France after 1815 through the work of the Marquis de Puységur, and it remained prominent in the eighteenth and nineteenth centuries in Germany. It spread to Britain and the United States in the 1830s, enjoying considerable interest through the 1860s.

Yet mesmerism was not just a phenomenon of psychological and physiological healing. Its altered state of consciousness—or somnambulistic trance—also was seen by many to confer such occult faculties as clairvoyance, the ability to speak with the dead, and the power to predict the future. From the 1830s through the 1850s, many examples of such feats became press sensations. Mesmerized clairvoyants searched for the lost British explorer John Franklin. Prominent Victorian writer Harriet Martineau experimented with mesmerism, and her landlady's nineteen-year-old niece, Jane Arrowsmith, under mesmeric trance, described a shipwreck hundreds of miles away that was thought to have occurred simultaneously with her clairvoyant feat. The phenomenon of table turning, during which participants would harness mysterious forces to cause tables to turn as they placed their hands on them, was highly popular in major European cities in 1851. The table turning was deemed to be the result of human magnetic or electrical forces, or even evidence of the supernatural, as it was sometimes connected to spiritualistic séances.[7] The famous "Seeress of Prevorst," a Bavarian peasant and invalid named Friederike Hauffe (1801–1829), remained in a semi-permanent trance state and evidenced clairvoyant and prophetic talents as well as the ability to carry on an ongoing conversation with the spirits of the dead. Justinus Kerner (1786–1862), the Swabian poet and physician who mesmerized her, published *Die Seherin von Prevorst* in 1829. Its translation into English in 1845 widened its impact. Other cases of mesmerized invalid women gaining extraordinary powers began to occur in the West.[8]

Spiritualism

Those who claimed the ability under mesmerism to speak with the dead helped merge mesmerism with what was to become a major component of the occult revival: spiritualism. In Hydesville, New York, in 1848, Kate and Margaret Fox, daughters of a fairly poor family, began to communicate with a spirit that had been haunting their wooden house for some time. They communicated by an alphabetical code that the spirit knocked out for them.[9] News of the "Hydesville knockings" rapidly spread, making celebrities of the Fox girls and helping launch a frenzy of séances and other spiritualist activity that would peak after the Civil War as Americans sought to contact their dead family members. By the 1880s spiritualism had waned and come under considerable attack in both America and Britain. (In the late 1880s, Margaret Fox confessed that the Hydesville knockings were nothing more than a "horrible deception" carried out by the sisters.) It revived again in the aftermath of the First World War.[10] As Janet Oppenheim explains: "In an atmosphere prepared by widespread interest in mesmerism and phrenology, religious unorthodoxy, mysticism, and social utopianism, spiritualism found a ready audience in numerous American communities. As spiritualism steadily moved westward across the United States, expansion to the east, across the ocean, was only a matter of time" (Oppenheim 1985, 11). Peter Washington links spiritualism to other "alternative" activities. It was seen as akin to "vegetarianism, feminism, dress reform, homeopathy and every variety of social and religious dissent" (Washington 1995, 11).

Britain welcomed mediums from America such as Daniel Dunglas Home, who arrived in London in the spring of 1855 and performed séances for upper-class British for almost two decades.[11] Home also helped promote spiritualism in Russia with a trip in 1859 and a second in the early 1870s, during which he performed a successful séance for Tsar Alexander II (Gordin 2004, 84). Spiritualism caught the interest of Russian nobles, including Aleksandr Nikolaevich Aksakov, who sponsored mediums visiting from outside Russia, published on spiritualism, and even convinced one of Russia's most respected chemists, A. M. Butlerov, of the validity of spiritualism (Gordin 84–85). In Britain, the intense interest in spiritualist communication with the dead spread across class lines, though, from upper-class homes to the professional middle class and working class (from which most of the mediums themselves came). Working-class audiences avidly attended the tours of traveling mediums and received the same kinds of messages from the other world that the aristocrats were receiving in their own private séances (Oppenheim 28–29).

Theosophy

In 1875, spiritualist circles in New York helped launch the Theosophical Society, another major component of the occult revival. The Society was founded by H. P. Blavatsky (1831–1891) and Colonel Henry Steel Olcott (1832–1907). Blavatsky, who was born in the Russian Ukraine, claimed to have studied for seven years under Hindu mahatmas and even to have traveled in Tibet at a time when few Westerners were permitted into the country. Olcott had worked in the Navy Department during the Civil War; he had even been one of three members of the special commission to investigate the assassination of Abraham Lincoln. Both Olcott and Blavatsky had been drawn to spiritualism, and Blavatsky had worked as a spirit medium. But the organization and worldview they created was a synthesis of Western Hermeticism and Eastern religion (primarily Hinduism and Buddhism) that Blavatsky elaborated in her major works, *Isis Unveiled* (1877) and the two-volume *Secret Doctrine* (1888). Blavatsky claimed to have been instructed by the Great White Brotherhood of Masters (or mahatmas), which, she claimed, had included the religious leaders and occult adepts of the past (Jesus, Buddha, Lao Tzu, Jacob Boehme, Confucius, Moses, Plato, Roger Bacon, and Francis Bacon, to name but a few [Washington 34–36]).

Maria Carlson has aptly identified Theosophy's importance to modern European culture:

> First, it offered to resolve the contradiction between science and religion, knowledge and faith, thereby curing the post-Enlightenment psychic schizophrenia that had led directly to the crisis of culture and consciousness. Second, it dispensed with alienating materialism by simply terming it "illusory," and offered modern man an eternal, spiritual life instead. Third, it replaced a waning Christianity's threat of unendurable and eternal torment in hell (or its modern alternative, pessimistic existentialism) with the more soothing concepts of karma and reincarnation, thus extending the existence of the soul and providing a world that is cosmically fair and just. (Carlson 1993, 12–13)

Theosophy's synthesis of Eastern and Western religious ideas offered as scientific knowledge and the notion of a secret brotherhood of adepts living in the world appealed to a widespread audience.

Blavatsky organized the Society around lodges, following a Masonic model. She moved the Society's headquarters in 1882 to Adyar, near Madras, India (where it remains today). As Washington notes, "Throughout the 1880s the Theosophical Society steadily recruited members. By 1885, 121 lodges had been chartered—106 of them in India, Burma and Ceylon, where the Society had the bulk of its membership. Within a decade of Theosophy's foundation that membership was running into thousands, and distinguished converts included the poet Ella Wheeler Wilcox, Darwin's collaborator Alfred Russel Wallace and the inventor Thomas Edison" (68). The Theosophical Society also created a publishing house to bring out its books, and it spawned dozens of Theosophical journals across Europe and America and from far-flung regions of Russia, Norway, and India.

Hermetic and Rosicrucian Orders

Yet another element in the occult revival, one still influential today, was the emergence of many Hermetic and Rosicrucian orders—some secret, some not. Hermeticism refers to a religious worldview that emphasizes the interrelationship between God, humanity, and the cosmos. Everything enjoys a fundamental unity because it derives from God. The Hermetic literature of antiquity and of the Middle Ages and Renaissance is based around the fictional Hermes Trismegistus. In reality, the Hermetic corpus consisted of texts written by Neo-Platonists and Greek Gnostics of the second and third centuries C.E. that were believed during the Renaissance to have been written by a real person, Hermes Trismegistus, who was an ancient Egyptian sage.[12] He can be seen as a human composite figure possessing characteristics of the Egyptian god Thoth and the Greek god Hermes. In the late Greco-Roman period, he was styled as an Egyptian sage with vast knowledge of the interconnected material and spiritual world. The Hermetic literature emerging from antiquity through the Middle Ages articulates a vast knowledge of astrology, medicine, alchemy, divination, and natural magic.

Rosicrucianism dates to the early seventeenth century, and in many ways, it derived from renaissance Hermetic ideas. Between 1614 and 1620, texts began to appear in Germany telling of a fifteenth-century German nobleman who had traveled east, to Damascus and then to Damcar in present-day Yemen, to learn occult wisdom. The traveler, Christian Rosenkreuz (purportedly 1378–1484), or Rosycross, stayed with a group of wise men who taught him occult secrets, mathematics, and science. (They also improved his Arabic.) Rosycross then returned to Germany and established a "Fraternity of the Rosie Cross" of four persons, each of whom was initiated into the magical secrets Rosycross brought back with him. The initiates were to cure the sick and to pass on their magical knowledge to chosen successors. They were to remain undistinguished from normal society in dress and reputation and would only know each other by the letters R.C. The fraternity was to remain completely secret for one hundred years. The pamphlets narrate the finding of the Tomb of Christian Rosycross in a secret Vault of Seven Sides discovered in the fraternity's headquarters. The vault contained the uncorrupted body of Rosycross as well as magical lamps, mirrors, books, and details of a vast knowledge of the universe—all dedicated to the glory of God.[13]

Like Hermes Trismegistus and his supposed writings, Christian Rosycross was also a fabrication of a later period. The story and the writings were a product of the early seventeenth-century manifestoes. As Frances Yates was to argue some thirty years ago, "the leading themes of the Rosicrucian manifestos, Magia, Cabala, and Alchymia united in an intensely religious outlook which included a religious approach to all the sciences of number." This synthesis very much bore the stamp of Renaissance Hermetic philosopher John Dee, who had influenced the religious politics of Bohemia and Germany during the reign of Queen Elizabeth I (Yates 1972, 39). Indeed the heavy alchemical emphasis was central to Rosicrucianism and wedded to the Renaissance Hermetic-Kabbalist tradition that preceded it.

In the second half of the nineteenth century, a number of orders dedicated to Rosicrucian and Hermetic wisdom sprang up in the West. They were often modeled on ceremonies and initiation structures of Masonic lodges and Rosicrucian visions of initiates guarding secret knowledge. While terms like "Rosicrucian" and "Hermetic" had become conflated by the turn of the century, in the earlier nineteenth century, "Rosicrucian" was often favored over "Hermetic" because of its stronger associations with Christianity and the Holy Land (as opposed to the Egyptian and polytheistic associations with "Hermeticism"). Later in the century, "Hermetic" seemed to privilege Western esotericism over the Indian and other Asian roots of Theosophy, though the founders of Hermetic societies often were also members of Theosophical lodges.[14] Many members of these orders had been influenced by the writings of Éliphas Lévi, whose *Dogme et rituel de la haute magie* (Dogma and Ritual of High Magic, 1856) and *L'Histoire de la magie* (History of Magic, 1860) had envisioned an ancient wisdom found in alchemy, Kabbalah, tarot, and other occult knowledge that had survived in secrecy over the centuries. In *Dogme et ritual,* for instance, Lévi forged for modern occultism a crucially important, if fanciful, connection between the Kabbalah and the tarot (McIntosh 148), and he argued that scientists had ignored this arcana to the detriment of the Enlightenment. In England, the Rosicrucian order Knights of the Red Cross of Rome and Constantine was founded in 1865. More significantly, the Societas Rosicruciana in Anglia (or S.R.I.A.) was founded in London in 1867 by Robert Wentworth Little (1840–1878). Its members studied the Kabbalah and the knowledge of Hermes Trismegistus, used Masonic systems of initiation into grades, and had each initiate choose a motto as his or her official S.R.I.A. name (such names were often Latin phrases). The S.R.I.A. spawned two still-extant American orders: the Societas Rosicruciana in Civitatibus Foederatis and the Societas Rosicruciana in America.

Philip Jenkins has pointed out that German settlers in seventeenth-century Pennsylvania brought Rosicrucianism with them to America—but modern Rosicrucianism was a more recent invention (Jenkins 2000, 82). The American spiritualist and occult writer Paschal Beverly Randolph (1825–1875) traveled to Britain and to Europe in the 1850s, teaching about spiritualism, magical mirrors, mesmerism, and Rosicrucianism. (He is believed to have met significant figures in the British occult world, including Edward Bulwer-Lytton, Hargrave Jennings, Frederick Hockley, and K. R. H. Mackenzie, as well as Baron Dupotet de Sennevoy, the most prominent French mesmerist of the day.) In the 1860s, Randolph founded the Rosicrucian Fraternity in the United States. Reuben Swinburne Clymer (1878–1966), who had published a history of Rosicrucianism in 1902, eventually founded his own Fraternitas Rosae Crucis, following Randolph's teachings.[15] And in 1915 Harvey Spencer Lewis (1883–1939) in New York founded the Ancient and Mystical Order Rosae Crucis (AMORC), which still exists today.

France was fertile ground for Rosicrucianism in the later nineteenth century. Stanislas de Guaita (1861–1897), Gérard Encausse (known as Papus, 1865–1916), and Joséphin Péladan (1858–1918) founded a major Rosicrucian order, the Kabbalistic Order of the Rose Cross, in Paris in 1887. Alchemy was crucial to the French Rosicrucian scene, and Papus's friend Albert Poisson was a major practitioner (McIntosh 204). In spite of eventual fractures among these founders, Rosicrucianism and occultism in general were so well established in France that Blavatsky's Theosophical movement had some trouble taking root there.[16]

Back in Britain, the most famous order to emerge from the S.R.I.A. was the Hermetic Order of the Golden Dawn, founded in March 1888 by three S.R.I.A. members: William Wynn Westcott, a London coroner; William Robert Woodman, the Supreme Magus of the S.R.I.A.; and Samuel Liddell Mathers. Chapter 1 of this volume examines the Golden Dawn in some detail, but its synthesis of Hermeticism, Kabbalah, and other occult wisdoms and its novel emphasis on the actual practice of magic within a structure of initiation has loomed large over Western occultism. Its highest magical secrets were preserved for an "Inner Order" called the "Rosae Rubeae et Aureae Crucis" (or R.R. et A.C.), which consisted of the Adepts. The Golden Dawn founded a number of temples, including the Isis-Urania Temple in London, the Horus Temple in Bradford in Yorkshire, the Osiris Temple at Weston-Super-Mare in Somerset, the Ahathoor Temple in Paris, and the Amen-Ra Temple at Edinburgh.

Several Golden Dawn initiates were prominent in the world of literature and drama, including the Irish poet W. B. Yeats, actress Florence Farr, Abbey Theatre patron Annie Horniman, and actress and political agitator Maud Gonne. Some even came from the sciences: Sir William Crookes joined several chemists in the Golden Dawn. But the order fragmented during infighting in the early twentieth century—and splinter groups and imitators followed. One notorious Golden Dawn member, whom we will encounter in chapter 1, was

Aleister Crowley (1875–1947). Crowley founded his own magical order, the A.A., in 1909. He also went on in 1912 to create the British branch of the Ordo Templi Orientis (OTO)—an order founded by the German journalist, occultist, ex-opera singer, and political radical Theodor Reuss (1855–1923) and the wealthy Austrian paper chemist and industrialist Carl Kellner (1850–1905) to espouse occult teachings and the practice of sexual magic. Several other successor orders influenced by the Golden Dawn emerged in London and elsewhere in the early twentieth century, such as R. W. Felkin's Stella Matutina. In 1903, prominent Golden Dawn member A. E. Waite moved the Isis Urania Temple of the Golden Dawn away from magic and toward Christian mysticism in his new order, the Independent and Rectified Rite. After its collapse in 1915, he created yet another order, the Fellowship of the Rosy Cross, that initiated novelist Charles Williams. There were several others. A Hermetic Order of the Golden Dawn styled as the Outer Order of The Rosicrucian Order of Alpha+Omega still exists today. It even boasts "the first Internet-based temple for Golden Dawn members at a distance."[17] A Golden Dawn Temple in Paris and a later American version of the Order—the Builders of the Adytum, founded by Paul Foster Case (1884–1954)—are still active.

Contested Science

Occult writings often derided mechanistic science and rationality, and many scholars have seen the occult revival as a response to the scientific materialism of the nineteenth century and the waning of institutionalized Christianity. Yet it would be wholly inaccurate to see the occult revival as simply anti-scientific. Historical work on the scientific revolution of the seventeenth century has dispelled the notion that scientific rationality explicitly excluded the occult from early modern science.[18] Similarly, historians of the nineteenth-century occult revival have begun to emphasize that occultism's relationship to science was not a simple rejection. Alison Winter has shown that mesmerism, for example, grew from medical discourse and continued to challenge emerging institutions of scientific validation. Far from being a marginalized pseudoscience, "mesmerism became the occasion for contests over authority in science, medicine, and intellectual life alike, and these contests revealed the location and character of such authority to have been more insecure than historians appreciate" (Winter 1998, 4). During the 1830s and 1840s, as mesmerism swept through Britain, Winter shows that new institutions and written texts attempted to structure the sciences, establishing boundaries and relationships among them.[19] (Even then, definitions of science were never clear or absolute, and mesmerism could still garner widespread interest and support.) Spiritualism might at first glance appear most antithetical to Victorian science, and spiritualists blamed modern science itself for an extreme materialism that undermined Christianity (Oppenheim 2). Yet it, too, was animated by the impulse toward scientific explanation. As Alex Owen puts it, "Many believers argued that spiritualism provided scientific evidence for the spirit's survival after death, and did not perceive science as inimical to spiritualist beliefs. Indeed, early adherents held out the fervent hope that science would prove their case, and sought to establish both the survival of the spirit and its materiality through strict adherence to the empirical method" (Owen 1989, xv–xvi). Spiritualism elicited a scientific response in the Society for Psychical Research (SPR) and like organizations. Spiritualists were convinced of the validity of séances, but many psychic researchers approached demonstrations of psychic powers and individual séances with critical minds. Their mission, though, was to use scientific data-gathering methods to prove immortality and to probe the powers of the human mind.[20]

The SPR was founded in 1882 by professors at Trinity College, Cambridge, including Henry Sidgwick and Frederick Myers. It was hardly the first such organization. In 1875, Dmitrii Mendeleev had convened a Commission within the recently founded Russian Physical Society and St. Petersburg University to position professional scientists as the arbiters of the validity of spiritualism at a moment when it had increased in popularity. The Commission invited the pro-spiritualist Aksakov and Butlerov in as consultants, and proceeded during 1875 and 1876 to test mediums brought in from Britain and elsewhere by Aksakov. The skeptics and believers quickly fell out over methods of scientific testing. Mendeleev, for instance, insisted upon experimental devices to produce scientific data during the séances, and the believers argued against them (Gordin 97–98), and the pro-spiritualists decried the negative findings of the Commission as biased (Gordin 87–111).

British predecessors to the SPR included the Cambridge Association for Spiritual Inquiry, or "Ghost Society," as it was known, which was founded around 1850; the Oxford Phasmatological Society lasted from 1879 to 1885. Sidgwick, the first president of the Society for Psychical Research, had been a member of the Ghost Society when an undergraduate at Cambridge (Oppenheim 123). The SPR aimed to use scientific principles to explore mediums, apparitions, telepathy, mesmerism, and other such phenomena. An American branch opened in 1885.

The research of the SPR was most geared toward sciences of the mind and understandings of immortality. (Myers and William James were its most famous psychologist presidents.) But some of its members came from physics and chemistry just as those disciplines were reconsidering their understanding of the relationship between matter and energy. Nobel Prize-winning chemists and physicists in the SPR included Marie Curie (who was an honorary member before the First World War), Lord Rayleigh and J. J. Thomson (successive Cavendish Professors of Experimental Physics at Cambridge, and both part of the skeptical wing of the SPR), and Sir William Ramsay, who will figure prominently in this book. Other famous scientists included the chemist Sir William Crookes and the ether physicist Sir Oliver Lodge, who unequivocally proclaimed the survival of the personality after death. Crookes's five years of active psychic research between 1870 and 1875 harmed his reputation as a scientist. He famously upheld the reality of the spirit Katie King, whom a notorious medium, Florence Cook, helped materialize (Oppenheim 340–41). Nevertheless, his career recovered, and he went on to do groundbreaking work with cathode rays and in many other areas. He eventually became president of several societies, including the Chemical Society, the British Association for the Advancement of Science, the SPR, and the Royal Society, and he earned a knighthood in 1897 and the Order of Merit in 1910.

Most British scientists ignored the phenomena that the SPR took so seriously. As Oppenheim concludes, "All the fundamental questions that the SPR addressed, and all the major assumptions of spiritualism, were neither definitively provable nor falsifiable by any conceivable test. For these reasons, the models of the physical sciences—whether those of physics or of biology—never really applied to the efforts of the SPR before World War I, and even less to the pursuits of the spiritualist associations throughout the country" (394). The Royal Society and the British Association both eschewed psychical research as fundamentally nonscientific. Yet the occult societies and orders at the heart of the occult revival often viewed their practices and knowledge as explicitly scientific. Some magical movements or organizations that we will explore in the following chapters, such as Aleister Crowley's Scientific Illuminism, sought to style magical experimentation as a scientific research program.[21]

Radioactivity and the New Occult Materiality
in Popular Fiction

This scientific sea change in the understanding of occultism was apparent even in popular fiction. For example, the most famous literary influence on the mid-Victorian occult revival was Edward Bulwer-Lytton's novel *Zanoni* (1842). Bulwer-Lytton (1803–1873) was a successful politician—serving as a Whig MP, and then as a Tory MP, and as Secretary for the Colonies—and a thriving novelist. Though he himself is not thought to have belonged to any secret society or occult group,[22] he was involved in research into spiritualism, mesmerism, astrology, and geomancy from the 1840s through the 1860s. He also influenced Éliphas Lévi, whom he befriended upon Lévi's first trip to England in 1854 (McIntosh 1972, 101). Bulwer-Lytton's immense effect upon the occult revival in America and Europe was primarily due to novels and short stories such as *Zanoni,* "The Haunted and the Haunters," *A Strange Story,* and *The Coming Race.* These fictions explored Rosicrucianism, alchemy, ceremonial magic, spirit mediums, mesmerism, psychic energies, and even notions of a hollow earth inhabited by a super race.

Zanoni provided a powerful vision of the adept as someone possessing hidden Hermetic knowledge that had been passed on, in secret, for centuries. Set during the French Revolution and the Terror, *Zanoni* portrays the two surviving Chaldean initiates of an ancient order—far older and wiser than its successors, the Rosicrucians and medieval alchemists. The two adepts, Zanoni and Mejnour, have learned powerful secrets and extended their lives through the Elixir of Life. Zanoni is the younger of the two, being only 5000 years old. Both have rejected earthly passions and attachments in order to pursue their wisdom, but Zanoni eventually chooses to reenter the world of human emotions and mortality, gaining the two things that Mejnour has rejected—love and, at the hands of the revolutionaries, death.

Zanoni portrays several aspects of occult knowledge in the early Victorian period, but one major strand of the novel involves a young neophyte called Clarence Glyndon (himself the descendant of an alchemist who successfully developed the elixir). Glyndon pursues Zanoni's secrets, and his efforts at initiation raise questions about the relationship of occult knowledge to the natural world, the world of science. Bulwer-Lytton writes of Glyndon that "it would have only disappointed his curiosity to find the supernatural reduced to Nature" (Bulwer-Lytton 102). But Mejnour tells Glyndon that "Nature supplies the materials; they are around you in your daily walks. In the herbs that the beast devours and the chemist disdains to cull; in the elements from which matter in its meanest and its mightiest shapes is deduced; in the wide bosom of the air; in the black abysses of the earth; everywhere are given to mortals the resources and libraries of immortal lore" (209). Indeed, Mejnour argues that "All that we profess to do is but this—to find out the secrets of the human frame, to know why the parts ossify and the blood stagnates, and to apply continual preventives to the effects of Time. This is not Magic; it is the Art of Medicine rightly understood" (232).

Despite Mejnour's claims, the magical universe in *Zanoni* would be unrecognizable to a scientist in 1842. Mejnour explains that to prevent the knowledge's falling into evil hands, initiates must survive "tests that purify the passions and elevate the desires. And Nature in this controls and assists us: for it places awful guardians and insurmountable barriers between the ambition of vice and the heaven of the loftier science" (233). These guardians are portrayed as actual spirit beings, not simply the almost inscrutable forces of nature. Indeed, the novel describes the occult universe as a supernatural one inhabited by different levels of spirit beings, including a being named Adon-Ai (from whom Zanoni learns his wisdom) and a "Dweller of the Threshold" whom Zanoni and Glyndon must both overcome. Glyndon fails to follow the ascetic rigors prescribed to him before his ordeal of initiation. He takes the elixir prematurely—and Bulwer-Lytton jumps directly into the spiritual and supernatural. Glyndon hears ghostly echoes of voices and music, and then sees apparitions, which finally are replaced by the demonic Dweller of the Threshold, a creature with "a human head, covered with a dark veil, through which glared with livid and demoniac fire, eyes that froze the marrow of his bones.... 'Thou hast entered the immeasurable region. I am the Dweller of the Threshold. What wouldst thou with me? Silent? Dost thou fear me?... Wouldst thou be wise? Mine is the wisdom of the countless ages. Kiss me, my mortal lover'" (258–59). Bulwer-Lytton does not take a scientific perspective on the materiality of the elixir or its effects on the body. Instead, the magical vision of *Zanoni* is one of human contact with spirit beings that can either be controlled through ascetic and occult rigor, in the case of Zanoni and Mejnour, or not, in the case of Glyndon. Scientific explanation seems almost beside the point.

Yet compare the role of nature and science in this early occult classic to that of popular occult-themed novels of the period immediately following the discovery of X-rays and radioactivity. In 1903, the year after Rutherford and Soddy's major publications elucidating the mechanism of radioactivity essentially as transmutation, Bram Stoker published his classic of Egyptian Hermetic lore and occult horror—his "mummy novel," *The Jewel of Seven Stars* (*JSS*). This tale, about an Egyptologist's efforts to use ancient occult sciences to resurrect an Egyptian queen and magus (the 5000-year-old Tera), takes up many of the occult themes explored by *Zanoni* sixty-one years earlier. It addresses Hermetic alchemical knowledge, astrology, spiritualism, astral travel, ritual magic, control over the will of others, and the like, and it, too, locates them in the ancient Middle East. Queen Tera learned black magic and the control of the Old Gods in order to dominate the unruly priests who had attempted to usurp her power. Invoking spiritual and magical rebirth through a motif central to alchemy, Rosicrucianism, and Hermetic orders such as the Golden Dawn, Stoker writes that Tera "had won secrets from nature in strange ways; and had even gone to the length of going down into the tomb herself, having been swathed and coffined and left as dead for a whole month" (*JSS* 161–62). (So impressive was *The Jewel of Seven Stars* as a Hermetic novel that J. W. Brodie-Innes, a central figure in the Amen-Ra Temple of the Golden Dawn and its successor Alpha and Omega Temple, claimed in a letter to Stoker that the novel shed "clearer light on some problems which some of us have been fumbling in the dark after for long enough" [quoted in Glover 1996, 81]).

The plot of the novel, though, revolves not around a modern Hermetic adept but around the Egyptologist Abel Trelawny and other representatives of Victorian science and professionalism. Among these figures are a medical doctor, a lawyer, and a trained scientist with multiple PhDs in fields such as science, Oriental languages, and philosophy. (He is similar to the Van Helsing figure in *Dracula*.) The group, to which Trelawny's daughter Margaret also belongs, seeks to resurrect the Queen in order to benefit modern science— that is, to enhance *modern* science by recovering *ancient* science. Notably, Trelawny rationalizes his decision to put the lives of his friends and daughter in jeopardy in terms of the Hermetic "Great Work," but he gives it a scientific valence by referring to it as the "Great Experiment." And the goal of this experiment in resurrecting the Queen, restoring ancient occult knowledge, knowledge from the world "before what is called 'the Flood,'" is specifically a *scientific* goal:

> But life and resurrection are themselves but items in what may
> be won by the accomplishment of this Great Experiment. Imagine
> what it will be for the world of thought—the true world of human
> progress—the veritable road to the Stars, the *itur ad astra* of the
> Ancients—if there can come back to us out of the unknown past one
> who can yield to us the lore stored in the great Library of Alexandria,
> and lost in its consuming flames. Not only history can be set right,
> and the teachings of science made veritable from their beginnings;
> but we can be placed on the road to the knowledge of lost arts, lost
> learning, lost sciences, so that our feet may tread on the indicated
> path to their ultimate and complete restoration.... If indeed this
> resurrection can be accomplished, how can we doubt the old
> knowledge, the old magic, the old belief! (Stoker 268)

Indeed, the Queen herself is described as a scientist wresting secrets from nature.

Bulwer-Lytton might have seen something of his Mejnour in the Queen, who uses the secrets of nature for purposes of immortality. But Stoker goes further, attempting to bring the ancient science into line with cutting-edge modern atomic science. He locates the source of Queen Tera's incredible powers in atomic energy—in radium's radiation. Invoking the names of Crookes, Curie, and Ramsay, Trelawny twice speculates about the mysterious powers of the magic coffer that is to be part of the resurrection proceedings. Does it work by Röntgen's X-rays, cathode rays, Becquerel rays, or the emanations from radium? Does the aerolite from which the coffer is made contain, perhaps, an unknown element with hidden powers, such as radium in pitchblende (the ore in which radium is found) (276)?

The narrator, a lawyer named Malcolm Ross, even wonders for an entire chapter about possible scientific explanations of the Queen's seemingly magical powers. In one chapter, "Powers—Old and New," Ross is wary of the "Great Experiment." He thinks, "could we realize what it was for us modern mortals to be arrayed against the Gods of Old, with their mysterious powers gotten from natural forces, or begotten of them when the world was young" (231). But for Ross, the powers of the "Old Gods" are indeed scientific powers. Invoking Röntgen and other modern work on new types of light, he speculates that "The time may not be far off when Astrology shall be accepted on a scientific basis" (234). He even imagines that an Egyptian hieroglyph that looks like a "Flagellula" hints that some Egyptians may have had the "knowledge of microscopy" (235). But, above all, he speculates that "The discoveries of the Curies and Laborde, of Sir William Crookes and Becquerel, may have far-reaching results on Egyptian investigation. This new metal, radium—or rather this old metal of which our knowledge is new—may have been known to the ancients. Indeed it may have been used thousands of years ago in greater degree than seems possible to-day" (236). Though pitchblende had not been found in Egypt, he argues that

> it is more than probable that radium exists in Egypt. That country has perhaps the greatest masses of granite to be found in the world; and pitchblende is found as a vein in granite rocks.... it is possible that here and there amongst these vast granite quarries may have been found not merely veins but masses or pockets of pitchblende. In such case the power at the disposal of those who knew how to use it must have been wonderful. The learning of Egypt was kept amongst its priests, and in their vast colleges must have been men of great learning; men who knew well how to exercise to the best advantage, and in the direction they wished, the terrific forces at their command. (237)

He concludes that "These scientific, or quasi-scientific discussions soothed me. They took my mind from brooding on the mysteries of the occult, by attracting it to the wonders of nature" (238). This notion that an ancient advanced civilization might have controlled the powers of radiation and that such powers were the source of a seemingly occult tradition was to become a powerful fantasy of the period immediately following the discovery of radiation. Even scientists were not immune to it, as we shall see in Frederick Soddy's speculations in his scientific tour de force, *The Interpretation of Radium* (1909).

While Ross holds up a reassuring nature against occultism, the import of his thoughts and Trelawny's is really quite the opposite—that occultism *is*, in fact, natural. It has a basis in material science. One recent critic perceptively sees the ending of the 1903 novel (the 1912 rewrite had a much less threatening, more sentimental ending) as unusual for Stoker, in that it shows nature triumphing over science (Senf 2002, 91). But one might slightly revise this reading to suggest that in the novel, ancient science vanquishes modern science—or, more specifically, the progressive underpinnings of modern science. Trelawny has always assumed that the Queen will willingly convey her ancient scientific knowledge to her modern resurrectors. But the novel ends horribly, with the return of the Queen and the slayings of all the key figures other than the narrator, who unwittingly helps the Queen from the thick black smoke in the resurrection chamber.

Other key works of occult or gothic fiction in the years immediately following the radioactivity revolution similarly hinted at new scientific explanations for previously "magical" forces. While the marvelous powers of Rider Haggard's 2,000-year-old Ayesha (aka "She Who Must Be Obeyed") in his 1887 blockbuster novel *She* were ascribed by the narrator to chemistry,[23] there is never any effort at real scientific explanation. Like Zanoni and Queen Tera, Ayesha's powers derive from ancient Egyptian and other knowledge combined with her own investigations. Ayesha evinces a range of occult feats common to the emerging stable of Hermetic lore during the occult revival: mirror scrying (on a bowl of still water), ritual curses on her ancient rival, powers to heal diseases progressed beyond modern medicine's capabilities, powers to strike down foes with a mere gaze, and the like. But after the discovery of radium in 1898, and Rutherford and Soddy's 1902 paper on atomic transformation, Haggard's 1904–1905 sequel, *Ayesha: The Return of She*, provided a specific explanation for Ayesha's immense power, and for her alchemical transmutations to create gold. The source of the powerful "Fire of Life" she harnesses in her volcanic mountain home, Kôr, turns out (not surprisingly) to be radium emanations, and Ayesha's powers only reveal the ability of an even more advanced science to harness them.[24] Or, in *War in Heaven* (1930), the first novel by Charles Williams (1886–1945)—one of the so-called "Inklings" group, along with J. R. R. Tolkien and C. S. Lewis, and at one time a member of the Salvator Mundi Temple of the Fellowship of the Rosy Cross, an offshoot of the Hermetic Order of the Golden Dawn—Williams portrays the magically powerful Holy Grail as if it were essentially a radioactive atom, a "storehouse of power" "encompassed" by "radiations," a "material centre" that could be "dissipated" (141). The occult warfare described in the novel largely consists of directed energies: "fine arrows of energy" (141), "shaft[s] of direct power" (241) and "stream[s] of energy" (242) that were wholly familiar to readers by 1930 as the province of atomic physics. One could go on at great length enumerating examples. Within a decade of its discovery, radium had invaded almost every subgenre of fiction—including science fiction, occult, adventure, western, detective, and romance fiction, and even children's novels. Again, after the discovery of radioactive transmutation, tales inspired by the occult revival sought to ground occult phenomena in the science of radioactivity rather than simply leave them as unexplained supernatural events.

Disenchantment and Re-enchantment

Rather than seeing the occult revival as a simple rejection of science, we must come to a more nuanced understanding. An influential interpretation of modernity's relationship to religious worldviews has been that the modern West has become ever more secularized. In 1917, German sociologist Max Weber identified this secularization as a phenomenon of the rationalization and intellectualization of modern life, and he famously argued that this process had resulted in the "disenchantment of the world." By "disenchantment," Weber meant that the rational scientific worldview of modernity had emptied the world of the mysteries and magical forces once believed to have controlled it. The spiritual and ethical meanings offered by religion, then, fell in the face of a rational rejection of the supernatural.[25]

The nineteenth century did indeed see figures such as John Tyndall (1820–1893) use writings and public addresses and his position as Superintendent of the Royal Institution in London to advance the intellectual position and prestige of science in Victorian England by demarcating it clearly from religion.[26] Many who urged the independence of science from religious thinking and authority offered precise definitions of science that would exclude other forms of thought and feeling. Typical narratives of the advance of science portray secularization, in fact, as a natural consequence of the triumph of scientific rationality.

Yet while there clearly was a decline of organized Christianity's authority across the nineteenth century, historians have recently challenged or complicated this "secular" narrative. Alex Owen, for example, has shown in *The Place of Enchantment: British Occultism and the Culture of the Modern*, that the "new occultism" she identifies at the turn of the century "was attractive partly because it offered a spiritual alternative to religious orthodoxy, but one that ostensibly operated without the requirement of faith . . . [T]he occultism that underwrote this movement was intrinsic to a contemporary shift in ideas about what might constitute belief and unbelief or mark the limits of the sacred and profane" (2004, 12). Owen sees in fin-de-siècle Hermetic and ritual magic practices a kind of enchantment—or, one might say, re-enchantment—of the modern world.

Other rebellions against Weber's hypothesis—that one must either be out of step with modern rationality or be resigned to a disenchanted world—occurred in Germany in the fields of biology and psychology. As Anne Harrington has shown, the nineteenth-century German efforts by Hermann von Helmholtz, Emil Du Bois-Reymond, and Rudolf Virchow to integrate physiology and physics to forge a highly mechanistic science met with a backlash at the turn of the century. The early twentieth-century vitalist biology of Hans Driesch, and the emphasis by Adolf Meyer-Abich and Ludwig von Bertalanffy on the inadequacy of mechanistic models to explain the workings of living organisms, led to a kind of "re-enchantment" of physiology and psychology, to a "holistic" science of life and mind (Harrington 1996, xvi–xvii).[27]

As we shall see, the "modern alchemy" that emerged from the alchemical revival of the fin de siècle meant different things to different people or groups. For many, it was an effort to re-enchant chemistry and physics, the most materialistic sciences of all. The boundary-disturbing and scientifically and spiritually stimulating work of the trope of alchemy remained potent until World War II. Hiroshima and Nagasaki ushered in a new era, a Cold War understanding of nuclear energy and physics that left transmutation behind for much grimmer alternatives.

If magic and the occult had been explained in terms of the science of matter and energy, the science of matter and energy was also, during the period from 1895 to 1939, invested with the tropes and concerns of the occult. It is to the story of the Alchemical Society of London, a fertile ground for reciprocally rethinking both atomic science and occultism, that we must now turn.

I

From the Golden Dawn to the Alchemical Society

Mapping the Occult Boundaries of Atomic Theory

In William Butler Yeats's 1897 story "Rosa Alchemica," the narrator tells of a mysterious visit from his old friend Michael Robartes, who comes upon the narrator in his Dublin home as he is conducting alchemical experiments. They engage in a late-night conversation replete with exotic incense and strange visions. Robartes then convinces the narrator to join his Order of the Alchemical Rose and takes him to a secluded seashore, where the Order secretly houses its initiates and its large alchemical library. After preparing for a magical initiation ritual, the narrator relates:

> I stopped before a door, on whose bronze panels were wrought great waves in whose shadow were faint suggestions of terrible faces. Those beyond it seemed to have heard our steps, for a voice cried, "Is the work of the Incorruptible Fire at an end?" and immediately Michael Robartes answered, "The perfect gold has come from the athanor." The door swung open, and we were in a great circular room, and among men and women who were dancing slowly in crimson robes. Upon the ceiling was an immense rose wrought in mosaic; and about the walls, also in mosaic, was a battle of gods and angels, the gods glimmering like rubies and sapphires. (Yeats 1897, 287)

Beyond the exotic splendor Yeats imagined, his evocation of the Order emphasizes two key components of the Hermetic and

Rosicrucian orders of the late nineteenth and early twentieth centuries: the secrecy of their practices and the centrality of alchemical symbolism to their rituals. Only those spiritually purified—as the base metals are physically purified in the athanor during alchemical transmutation—are allowed access to the order's secret spiritual life and aesthetic wealth. (As we shall see, for many alchemists the purification of metals in alchemical transmutation was matched by a purification of the soul, a kind of self-transmutation in the Hermetic Great Work.) Yeats and Aleister Crowley—who created a similar vision of the white lodge in his *Moonchild*—based their fictional orders upon ideals of initiation, magic, and alchemy in the Hermetic Order of the Golden Dawn. The Golden Dawn became the most famous and enduringly influential Hermetic society of the fin de siècle, but it was only one of several such orders active during the period.

The Golden Dawn's influence upon the history of twentieth-century occultism has been enormous. (Accounts of the Order and its various splinter groups are legion, so I will not rehearse that convoluted narrative in detail here.[1]) In 1887 three freemasons and S.R.I.A. members—a coroner for the Crown, Wynn Westcott, his friend Samuel Liddell MacGregor Mathers, and W. R. Woodman (the Supreme Magus of the S.R.I.A.)—founded the Order. They based it upon supposedly ancient ritual manuscripts (written on nineteenth-century paper) and a correspondence with a fictitious German Rosicrucian adept.[2] Golden Dawn historian Ellic Howe summarizes its achievement:

> In the G. D.... we encounter an important reservoir of "hidden knowledge" based upon an ingenious construction of arbitrary relationships between different symbolical systems, e.g. the Cabbalistic Tree of Life, astrology, alchemy, the Tarot trumps and so on....
> Those who joined the G. D. during the 1890s had access to a store of "hidden" or "rejected" knowledge ... that had no contemporary counterpart in the west. It was certainly far more elaborately codified than anything the Theosophical Society could offer. (Howe 1972, xxii–xxiii)

Among the "hidden" knowledge in the Golden Dawn's synthesis of symbolic systems, alchemy was crucial. It represented a link to the past, to a world in which the processes of nature bowed to the spiritual power of purification practiced both by and upon the alchemist.

Infighting by its members had fragmented the Golden Dawn by around 1903. A number of offshoots then appeared, each run along similar lines of initiation and secret ritual. But within a decade of the Golden Dawn's dissolution, some of its key members had become part of a very different kind of order: the Alchemical Society. Founded in late 1912 in London, the Alchemical Society diverged markedly in three ways from the Golden Dawn's approach to alchemy. It conducted its explorations in a stridently public forum that imitated turn-of-the-century scientific societies. It brought occultists into direct dialogue with mainstream scientists. And it insistently analyzed alchemical thinking by engaging specific cutting-edge scientific research on atomic structure and radioactivity. Joining a number of scientists in the Alchemical Society were occult devotees, including at least three Golden Dawn members—Isabelle de Steiger, W. T. Horton, and A. E. Waite. (De Steiger wrote widely on mysticism and Hermeticism for occult publications. Waite was a major translator of alchemical texts who had been the editor of *Unknown World* and a regular columnist for the *Occult Review*. And even as Waite and de Steiger served as vice presidents of the Alchemical Society, Waite simultaneously acted as the chief of the Isis-Urania Temple in London—a successor of the original Golden Dawn temple.) Several other occult luminaries with significant public roles in the occult revival joined the Alchemical Society as well. The Honorable Ralph Shirley (1865–1946), the younger brother of the eleventh Earl Ferrers, was the owner of the key occult publishing house Rider & Co. and the founder and editor of the *Occult Review* (founded in 1905). Daniel Nicol Dunlop (1868–1935), the Irish Theosophist, edited *The Path* and helped organize Theosophical summer schools. Philip Sinclair Wellby published occult books under his own imprint from 1901 to 1908 and then worked for Rider. The prominent astrologer Walter Gorn Old, who published under the pseudonym "Sepharial," had once been a member of H. P. Blavatsky's inner circle in London.[3]

How could some of the most committed members of secret societies like the Golden Dawn play central roles in the highly visible and publicly promoted Alchemical Society, which included many members of the legitimated scientific community and grappled with current scientific theories? What changed in the world of science between the 1887 creation of the Golden Dawn and the 1912 founding of the Alchemical Society? The most remarkable scientific events—those that help us interpret the strange marriage of science and occultism in the Alchemical Society—were the discoveries of radiation, radium, and radioactive "transmutation." The material world, in the form of radioactive matter, had decidedly intervened in the theoretical debates of both atomic science and occultism. No scientific theory of matter that could not account for the strange properties of radioactive elements could still be taken as valid. During these early years of the science of radioactivity, theories that seemed to offer insight into radioactive transformation included those of Rutherford, Soddy, Thomson, and Ramsay—but, for some, also included those of Paracelsus, Flamel, Lully, and Vaughan.

The emergence of the Alchemical Society in London in late 1912 marks a significant moment in the histories both of alchemy and of atomic science in the twentieth century—one that illustrates the fertile interchange between the two domains of knowledge. Quite simply, it signals the moment at which the trajectories of science and occultism merged. The rich relationship between occultism and mainstream science exhibited by the Society during the nascence of modern particle physics complicates our understanding of the boundaries between occultism and science. The Alchemical Society redirected alchemy toward spiritualizing the scientific future rather than simply reconstructing a lost spiritual past. Indeed, it offered what might be seen as a "re-enchantment" of science.

A common explanation for the occult revival of the late nineteenth and early twentieth centuries is that it was a reaction against an increasingly rationalized, scientific world—against what sociologist Max Weber called the "disenchantment" of Western society. Typifying this interpretation is historian Francis King's assessment of the roots of the Golden Dawn: "Its foundation came at a time when many people were beginning to be dissatisfied with the pathetically over-confident materialism of the nineteenth-century science on one hand, and the fatuous pietism of fundamentalist religion on the other" (King 1970, 34). But the degree of occult engagement with science during the period, as we will see, challenges the simple explanation of the occult revival as a reaction *against* a scientific culture.

Hermetic and Rosicrucian circles such as the Golden Dawn began to engage more publicly with science after the discoveries of radiation, radioactive transformation, and radium. In a case like that of the Alchemical Society, two subjects, alchemy and radiation,[4] allowed the groups from sharply different social worlds—those of mainstream science and occultism—to interact. These interactions also contributed to the popular press's "alchemical understanding" of the newly emerging discourse of atomic physics.

The Golden Dawn's Alchemical Negotiations with Science

The complicated public engagement with science by the Alchemical Society stands in marked contrast to the practices and ideals of the Golden Dawn from a few decades before. The secrecy of the Golden Dawn obviously prevented it from engaging in high-profile public challenges to the boundaries between science and occultism, and it constructed its identity largely for internal consumption. The Golden Dawn had officially disseminated alchemical knowledge to its members through specific manuscripts, such as the now famous Z2 manuscript, written by Westcott, upon which the higher-grade adepts were examined. A few unofficial subgroups formed to discuss and interpret alchemical writings on their own. Rev. W. A. Ayton's small circle of alchemists, for example, exchanged and hand-copied alchemical manuscripts. But though some devotees of occultism proclaimed the scientific nature of occultism in published writings, they did not engage with the science of the day in a sustained way. And while the Golden Dawn's members did begin some study of chemistry and tried some actual alchemical laboratory experiments, for the most part, they followed an interpretation of alchemy grounded in the occult classic *A Suggestive Inquiry into the Hermetic Mystery* (1850) by Mary Anne Atwood. Atwood's book convinced members to see the goal of alchemy as more a spiritual than a physical and scientific quest. It took the discovery of radiation and radioactive transformation to shift the occult understanding of the nature of alchemy to a more insistently scientific basis. In fact, the new physics greatly augmented occultists' engagement with science in general and their efforts to validate their work as scientific.

Early Positioning through "Spiritual Alchemy"

While the Theosophical Society had from the start thrived upon and courted publicity, from the late nineteenth century through the first few decades of the twentieth, groups exploring alchemical practices and esoteric rituals often remained deliberately removed from public scrutiny. Secret occult societies, many of them sprung from the Golden Dawn, were numerous in London and Paris at this time.[5] But, as Golden Dawn historian R. G. Torrens notes, "the general public and the student had very little hope of obtaining knowledge from this body, and in any case the public did not know of its existence until 1901, when the Horos scandal hit the headlines... [and] the rituals of the Golden Dawn were quoted by the prosecution as evidence of black magic" (Torrens 1972, 17).[6] Though Golden Dawn rituals involved a number of occult systems and were not confined to alchemy, the secrecy of the Order was certainly in keeping with alchemical history. The arcane and complex symbols of alchemical writing were widely viewed during the period, for instance, as a method of shielding key secrets from the uninitiated and unworthy.

As noted above, the alchemical text that most left its mark on the Golden Dawn in the pre-radioactivity era was Atwood's *Suggestive Inquiry*. The circumstances of its publication and immediate withdrawal in 1850 probably helped seal its reputation as a desirable occult work. It was much sought after by collectors, not being reprinted until 1918, after the author had died. Mary Anne South (who later became Atwood by marriage) was the daughter of Thomas South, a "gentleman of leisure" who studied and collected a large library of Hermetic texts in rural Hampshire. After much research, he wrote a long poem on alchemy while his daughter wrote *Suggestive Inquiry*, which she published anonymously with a London house. Immediately, the story goes, both father and daughter feared that she had revealed too much about the Hermetic mystery. They burned all the remaining copies of the book on their lawn, even tracking down as many of the hundred or so copies that had already been sold as they could, buying them back to destroy them. With such an aura of mystery and forbidden knowledge surrounding the destruction of the book, many occultists waded through it in the British Library and ascribed it tremendous authority.

Suggestive Inquiry was the source of two powerful ideas that pervaded Golden Dawn thinking about alchemy in the '80s and '90s. First, Atwood argued that the writings of the alchemists were deliberately cryptic and obscure in order to prevent the uninitiated and unworthy public from misusing their wisdom. As Atwood put it, "the records of Alchemy are, above all, calculated to mislead those who have gone abroad thoughtlessly seeking for that perfection which was to be found only by experimentally seeking at home within themselves" (1850, 162). Second, she asserted that the true subject of alchemy was not the transmutation of metals but rather the transmutation of man's nature from the profane and carnal to the divine. The focus of some alchemists on the elements was simply a debasement of the true Hermetic project. Atwood explained that man "is the true laboratory of the Hermetic art; his life the subject, the grand distillatory, the thing distilling and the thing distilled, and Self-Knowledge to be at the root of all Alchemical tradition" (162). The great secret that Atwood had revealed was that the Hermetic practice involved a kind of mesmerism, a magnetic trance state that allowed for self-purification and mystical union with God. All the lower realms, beginning with the mineral and on through the vegetable and animal, also were subject to such transmutation. Hence the properly trained adept could indeed transmute the metals, advancing them to their most pure state. But only the "pseudo-alchemist," who had never been on the proper Hermetic path in the first place, would see this as a goal. All the chemical language and symbolism in the process was ultimately in the service of self-transmutation:

> In the last operation the union of the Philosophic Stone is said to be finally cemented, in its component parts agreeing and having

relation to the external world; which union or consummation of its transmutative virtue is called Fermentation. Mark the harmonious mystery—that which in the Kabalah is denominated the union of man, reduced to the simplicity of the Monad, with God, that in metaphysico-chemistry is called Fermentation. The most pious and experienced amongst the Adepts do not demur either to compare the phenomena of their work to the Gospel tradition of the Life of Christ and our human redemption. (520)

Atwood certainly did not attempt to validate occultism by ascribing scientific validity to it or by discussing it in scientific terms. Quite the opposite. She made certain to *disentangle* alchemy from science, to make their boundaries more rigid, not to assert the scientific nature of alchemy. The apparatus of reference and allusion that sustains the roughly 600 pages of the *Suggestive Inquiry* is built upon texts from classical philosophy, Christianity, and medieval and early modern alchemy. While Atwood occasionally nodded in the general direction of modern science, she did not mention specific scientists or provide a coherent picture of any mid-Victorian science. One can only discern faint glimmerings of knowledge of ether physics and of physiology in popular forms.[7] More typically, though, she attempted to separate alchemy definitively from any hint of modern science. "No modern art or chemistry, notwithstanding all its surreptitious claims," Atwood averred, "has any thing in common to do with Alchemy, beyond the borrowed terms, which were made use of in continuance chiefly to veil the latter; not from any real relation, either of matter, method, or practical result" (143).

The thesis of Atwood's rare and much-sought-after volume appealed to many Golden Dawn members and, I would argue, augmented the importance of alchemical symbolism in the ceremonies aimed at spiritual self-transformation. Indeed, the Rosicrucian legend itself was read as an alchemical myth in the late nineteenth century. Alchemical rebirth imagery was given a particularly powerful, mystical valence in Atwood's work and in the Golden Dawn rituals.

A (Subordinate) Place for Science

Though secret societies like the Golden Dawn would not attempt a wholesale *public* negotiation of the boundaries between occult alchemy and modern science, some members of the group nevertheless engaged in a modest effort to garner some of the legitimacy of scientific knowledge for occultism. At the same time, they asserted that occult wisdom was superior, *as science*, to conventional materialist scientific thought. In this respect they sought to maintain Atwood's emphasis on spirituality but also to suggest a place for science within alchemical thinking. Occultists even outside Theosophical circles aligned themselves from time to time with the rigor of experimental science. French occultist Éliphas Lévi published material on magic and ritual and inspired many in the British and American occult revival of the second half of the century. Waite, who had schooled himself in Lévi's work beginning in 1881 and published English translations of his major writings, valued Lévi's attempt to "establish harmony between religion and science" (quoted in Gilbert 1987, 89).

Waite engaged in similar, if limited, challenges to the boundaries drawn to exclude occultism from science during the lifetime of the first Golden Dawn group through both his books and his fascinating (if short-lived) periodical, *The Unknown World* (1894–95). Gilbert notes that Waite had long dreamed of producing a "non-sectarian occult journal (i.e. one that was not devoted solely to the glories of either Spiritualism or Theosophy)" (81). *The Unknown World* accomplished this goal with such broadly based content that it serves as a sampler of the range of "occult sciences" and mysticisms at the close of the century.[8] In spite of this eclecticism, Waite emphasized the scientific rigor of the new occultism as he launched the journal. His opening editorial, "In the Beginning," quickly used the journal's title to evoke an intellectual explorer: "the belt of mystery is continually receding before the persistence of intellectual adventure; and even in the remotest paths, where most men shrink from penetrating, the voices of a few daring pioneers are crying to us in the darkness, encouraging us to advance intrepidly, for there is firm ground before them, and they descry light in the distance" (1894b, 1). But it became clear in the first few pages of the new journal that Waite more specifically envisioned the occult explorer as a *scientific* pathbreaker. Attempting to appropriate the cognitive authority of science for the world of occultism, Waite argued that the journal intended to explore "whatsoever is unachieved in science" and to provide "material for a reconciliation, not only of Eastern and Western wisdom, but of spiritual and physical science, in other words, of religion and modern thought" (2–3). Fending off the charge leveled by many scientists against occultism, and trying to one-up the position of current science in Victorian society, Waite summed up the purpose of the journal: "In a word, the UNKNOWN WORLD will be devoted to the 'superstitions' of the past, or, more correctly, to the science of the future" (2). This rhetorical redemption of alchemy from a tainted past and its positioning as the ultimate progress, the science of the future, became common in the work of occultists. And alchemy, as the most rigorously experimental and seemingly most "scientific" of the occult sciences, would take pride of place in the journal, whose first paper after Waite's leader was his article "What Is Alchemy?" (1894c, 7–11).

Of course, Waite at this time was still influenced by Atwood's spiritual reading of alchemy. In "What Is Alchemy?" Waite argued for the validity of accounts of transmutation in the past (1894c, 8), for alchemy's broad inclusion of all aspects of Hermetic and transcendental thought (7), and for a vision of alchemy's "strange symbols" and veiled wisdom as a "spiritual achievement" (10), "mystically of far higher import than a mere secret science of the manufacture of precious metals" (11). Waite had begun to move away from Atwood's position, however, while he studied Paracelsus during the 1890s. He had firmly rejected it by the time of the Alchemical Society after radioactive transmutation had been discovered.

Other Golden Dawn initiates also tried to merge Atwood's spirituality with some version of modern science as well. Several were involved in the translation and republication of key alchemical treatises of the medieval and classical periods. Golden Dawn founder Wynn Westcott, a noted authority on alchemy, published his pamphlet *The Science of Alchymy: Spiritual and Material* (1893) under his Golden Dawn motto/pseudonym, "Sapere Aude" ("dare to be wise"). Westcott used the tract to engage in the same mild boundary negotiation that Waite would attempt in *Unknown World* the next year. In it, Westcott argues that alchemy "must be regarded as a science uniting ancient chemistry with a religious basis" (4). He ventures the claim that historians of chemistry were soon to make: "Chemistry, the modern science which investigates the constitution of material substances, is the lineal descendant of Mediæval and Ancient Al-Chymy" (5). But unlike more mainstream historians of science, Westcott rejects the modern chemist's distaste for his progenitor: "No modern science has shown more intolerance towards its ancestors than the chemistry of our era has shown to the discoveries of those Egyptian, Arabian and Mediæval sages who were the founders of chemistry in the dim and distant past" (8).

Westcott then adopts what was to become a common strategy for occultists who hoped to renegotiate the boundaries of science and occultism. He attempts to revive alchemy not as an outmoded predecessor to modern chemistry, but as a source of ancient wisdom that anticipated the discoveries of the most modern chemists. In the 1880s and early 1890s, that cutting-edge chemistry was Sir William Crookes's effort to challenge the discipline's emphasis on irreducible elements. (Again, while Crookes had joined the Theosophical Society and was secretly a Golden Dawn initiate, to the broader British public he was known as a preeminent researcher and decorated chemist.) After explicating the alchemical doctrine of the First Matter, the primordial foundation of all substance, Westcott turns to the much-vaunted modification of William Prout's concept of the protyle (to which Theosophists had also harkened with great interest) that, as we shall see in chapter 2, Crookes had explained with great flair in an address to the Royal Institute in 1887. Westcott claims it as simply a modern restatement of alchemical doctrine. Alchemy thus becomes not the embarrassing ancestor but the future of modern chemistry:

> The discovery of the Elements has been *the* grand achievement of modern chemistry, and sure and certain renown has for half a century been granted to any chemist who has added a new Element to the existing catalogue. But if we may trust one of the most eminent chemists of the day, Professor Crookes, the future will change all this system, and a niche in the Temple of Fame will in the future be allotted by preference to one who succeeds in dividing one of our present elements into its constituents. The Chemistry of the Future is to destroy the present theory, and to gain the power of reducing all compounds, and all the Elements to one primordial matter, to be named PROTYLE. In other words the most ancient chemical doctrine of the ... FIRST MATTER, is to become paramount. This, then, is the Reconciliation of the Future.
>
> No sooner is the modern Doctrine of Elements laid aside, than the discoveries of the Primordial Matter, the Transmutation of Metals, and the Elixir of Life reappear and once more enter the range of the possible. (9)

Indeed, Westcott cites Crookes and the venerable Faraday as sources for alchemical thinking, quoting a statement that sounds very much like those that Soddy himself would make a few years later: "Profs. Crookes and Faraday now say, 'To decompose the metals, to re-form them, to change one into another, and to realise that once absurd notion of transmutation, are the problems given to the chemist of the future for solution'" (11). We shall see in chapter 3 how significant Faraday's earlier nineteenth-century claim was to later chemists.

Citing such important scientists, noting their professorial status, and enlisting them to affirm the scientific prescience of the alchemists rhetorically strengthens alchemy's claim to scientific validity. Westcott augments this strategic validation by reaching for the authority of another cutting-edge science that would soon set Soddy thinking about atomic transmutation: the spectroscopic work of Sir Norman Lockyer. As early as 1873, Lockyer's spectroscopic studies of stars suggested the "dissociation hypothesis" to him—that at extreme heats in stars, elements broke down into constituent parts. Indeed, after his December 12, 1878 talk to the Royal Society propounding this hypothesis that the chemical elements are compound bodies, Lockyer was ridiculed as an "alchemist" by the popular press and some colleagues (Brock 1985, 189). In a typically Victorian flourish, Westcott proclaims that science is based upon progress. But he then argues that scientists must recognize when science has gone astray from the path of progress and must choose a new path. In this case, the new path is an ancient one. Westcott asserts, "It seems then that a true and ancient doctrine of Occult Science has been once more recognized, and bids fair to be the dogma of the future" (12).

Applied Occultism

Westcott was important to the Golden Dawn's alchemical synthesis in that he had translated key alchemical writings in his 10-volume *Hermetica Collectanea* (1893–1911) and, perhaps most important, in his edition of *Aesh Mezareph or Purifying Fire* (1894), which Ithell Colquhoun sees as a key source of alchemical inspiration for the Golden Dawn (Colquhoun 1975, 272). But Colquhoun's account downplays the role of two men whose alchemical knowledge, I believe, was crucial to the Golden Dawn: W. A. Ayton and A. E. Waite. Ayton (1816–1909), whom Yeats called "my alchemist" in letters to Lady Gregory (Howe in Ayton 1985, 109), was the Vicar of Chacombe in the Diocese of Oxford during the beginnings of the Golden Dawn. He was considerably older than the other key Golden Dawn members, and he was introduced to Yeats by Mathers, who said of him, "He unites us to the great adepts of the past" (quoted by Howe in Ayton 9). He was seventy-two when he joined the Golden Dawn in 1888, having taken his BA at Cambridge in 1841. For many years he had been involved in alchemy and occultism in general. He was a friend of H. P. Blavatsky, a staunch supporter of Theosophy (though he was suspicious of Annie Besant), and an occasional Freemason (Howe in Ayton 10–11). He knew earlier generations of British occultists, including Frederick Hockley, and he may even have met Lévi in the 1860s.

Ayton's correspondence between 1886 and 1905 to fellow Golden Dawn member F. L. Gardner reveals a paranoid man who believed that the Black Brethren or B.B. (i.e., the Jesuits) were out to destroy England and make it bow to papal authority through devious occult tricks and sinister plots. Ayton also feared the power of gnomes and ghosts and claimed to have successfully created the Elixir of Life half a century earlier. (He left it to take later in his life, but found it had dried out.) But the letters also reveal that his advice about the practical workings of alchemy—from texts to furnace types—was frequently sought by other Golden Dawn members, who valued his knowledge of alchemy. Ayton published little other than a translation of Thomas Smith's *Life of John Dee* (Theosophical Publishing Society, 1908). But he secretly circulated and hand copied alchemical manuscripts with fellow Golden Dawn initiates Percy Bullock and Gardner, and with a friend, Julius Kohn, whose publications included a volume of Paracelsus's writings (Ayton 77).

Ayton advocated what one might call "applied occultism," and in a letter of 5 April 1895, he praised the Golden Dawn for the fact that it "gives you much more of the practical working of the occult than the T[heosophical] S[ociety]" (81), which he saw as more theoretical. Indeed, in an undated letter of 1889, Ayton specifically recommended the Golden Dawn as a means by which Gardner could gain alchemical knowledge: "They teach what the T S never has done, and never will. You get all the Alchemical first principles" (29). Though in a letter of 27 March 1890 Ayton suggested that Gardner take a look at the British Library's copy of Atwood's *Suggestive Inquiry* (Ayton 50), most of Ayton's advice to Gardner involved the practical experience of alchemy he had gained in his own working laboratory. (He had hidden his lab beneath his house so that the bishop would not find it.) He frequently assigned to Gardner not only alchemical texts but also works such as *Watts Dictionary of Chemistry*, *Thorpe's Dictionary of Applied Chemistry* (50), and Andrew Ure's 1823 *Dictionary of Chemistry* (29). (Indeed, *Watts Dictionary of Chemistry* and works by Thorpe were still being assigned in mainstream chemistry courses such those taken by Frederick Soddy at University College of Wales, Aberystwyth, and at Merton College, Oxford, in the mid to late 1890s.[9])

Ayton clearly understood alchemy as a physical process as much as a spiritual one. In a letter of 17 May 1890, he noted, "I have just had a letter from my most learned friend [presumably Kohn], saying that he is more and more convinced that one must first attain to *spiritual* Adeptship, before you can get to the Physical Adeptship of [alchemical] Transmutation. I think I have evidence to the contrary" (56). Others in the Golden Dawn were also involved in alchemical research as a physical project. Many members were doctors and a few were even working chemists.[10] Aleister Crowley himself was brought into the Golden Dawn by two chemists who were also conducting alchemical experiments, Julian Baker and George Cecil Jones. (More on Baker, Jones, and Crowley in a moment.)

Of course, by far the most prolific and influential historian and proponent of alchemy—indeed, the most significant source of alchemical information in the Golden Dawn—was A. E. Waite. As noted above, Waite was one of the foremost authorities of his age on alchemy and mysticism, though he did not involve himself in laboratory experiments. Despite his ponderous writing style (for which Crowley savaged him in the figure of Edwin Arthwaite in *Moonchild*), he published dozens of books on various occult subjects and several translations of key Hermetic works. It was Waite who provided many of the major alchemical texts and studies that late-nineteenth- and early-twentieth-century occultists could mine for information on the Great Work. He had already been a part of the explosion of books on alchemy in the 1880s and early 1890s, publishing a number of works—including his influential edition of the *Lives of the Alchemystical Philosophers* (1891)—with the occult publisher George Redway in London. In 1891, Fitzherbert Edward Stafford-Jerningham, who became the eleventh Baron Stafford in 1892, wrote to beg his advice with his Hermetic researches into transmutation and arranged with him to translate some alchemical texts. With the financial support of Lord Stafford and the publishing house of James Elliott (which, as Gilbert puts it, "existed for the sole purpose of disseminating the wit and wisdom of Arthur Edward Waite" [81]), from 1893 to 1895 Waite published six major alchemical works. He began with *The Hermetic Museum Restored and Enlarged* and went on to publish one of the major alchemical books of his lifetime, the two-volume *Hermetic and Alchemical Writings of Paracelsus*.

Waite's introduction to *Lives of the Alchemystical Philosophers* and much of his thinking on alchemy in the early to mid-1890s had been profoundly influenced by Atwood's *Suggestive Inquiry*, and he was a major conduit for Atwood's influence on the Golden Dawn in its early years. Waite later came to reject Atwood's interpretation of alchemy as entirely a spiritual process, and he would play a crucial role in the Alchemical Society, as we will see. But Atwood's vision of "spiritual alchemy" allowed the Golden Dawn's rituals and symbolism to idealize an alchemical self-transformation of initiates even in the absence of an accomplished laboratory transmutation. While Colquhoun notes that "a Ritual for Transformation formed part of the GD magical corpus and was intended for practical working" (272),[11] alchemical laboratory practice had been sporadic and had largely ceased in the Golden Dawn by around 1900.[12] The *Suggestive Inquiry* had, in fact, circumscribed the Golden Dawn's engagement with science. (It continued to appeal to the progeny of the original Golden Dawn across the twentieth century, most powerfully in the work of Israel Regardie, as we shall see.) It would take the discovery of radioactive "transmutation" to reenergize interest in alchemy as a science of the *material* world and to spur the second and very different alchemical revival that is the subject of this book, the birth of "modern alchemy." The transition of Golden Dawn attitudes toward scientific engagement can be seen in the post-Golden Dawn career of Aleister Crowley, the man whom many felt had betrayed the order when he published its rituals in *The Equinox*, his new journal of "scientific illuminism."

Crowley's Scientific Illuminism

The strategy of positioning an ancient wisdom as the future culmination of scientific progress was greatly intensified by some Golden Dawn members after the atomic discoveries at the century's turn. The post-Golden Dawn occult career of Aleister Crowley demonstrates the degree to which the workings of a Hermetic society could be fashioned as a cutting-edge "new" science, one that predated all existing scientific knowledge by centuries. Indeed, the connection between modern chemistry and alchemy in Crowley's introduction to the Golden Dawn and Hermeticism in general is quite striking. Crowley's biographers have noted that he had been brought into the Golden Dawn in November 1898 by two active chemists (who were also practicing alchemists) specifically *because* of Crowley's interest in alchemy. He had studied at Trinity College, Cambridge, from 1895 until July 1898, at which time he left without sitting the degree examinations. His university career traversed a number of subjects, but Robert Anton Wilson claims that he had majored in organic chemistry (Wilson 1999, xv). He had certainly passed a special examination in chemistry in 1897 (Booth 2000, 49).

Before matriculating at Cambridge, Crowley had spent a year as a nonmatriculated student at King's College, University of London, studying medicine and natural sciences. He had enrolled in September 1894 and remained through the end of the spring 1895 term. While at King's, he attended lectures by Sir William Ramsay, who would later be awarded a Nobel Prize in chemistry, and John Norman Collie, Ramsay's assistant (Booth 43–44). Crowley was an avid and accomplished alpine mountaineer, and he went on a number of climbs with Collie, one of the foremost mountaineers of his day. At London, Crowley also met and began climbing with Morris Travers, Collie's demonstrator in chemistry at the University of London, who would go on to work with Ramsay on inert gases and become his biographer after Ramsay's death. Collie even did Crowley the honor of proposing him for membership in the Alpine Club in London (which, as Booth notes, was the first society of its kind in the world [55]).

But Crowley gained more in his year at London with Ramsay and Collie—and his mountain climbing with Collie and Travers—than improved mountaineering skills. I would suggest that it was through Ramsay and Collie that Crowley developed his interest in both chemistry and alchemy, and he began to see occult "sciences" and modern experimental science as invaluable to each other. Ramsay was one of the foremost laboratory experimenters of his day. As we shall see in chapter 3, he also had been teaching alchemy as part of the history of chemistry and using occult press sources for alchemical knowledge in his chemistry teaching as far back as at least 1885 at the University of Bristol.

And in 1896 (and possibly even the year before, when Crowley had attended his lectures), Ramsay had asked his class to think of themselves as medieval students of alchemy. He asked them to imagine him as the alchemist Basil Valentine as he read to them one of Valentine's discourses on alchemy in class. Ramsay and Collie both would be at the center of what, in chapter 3, I shall call the "transmutational gold rush"—when academic chemists, beginning around 1904 and following Ramsay's lead, attempted to use radiation to transmute the elements and specifically saw this practice in alchemical terms.

Crowley's biographers are clear on what happened after Crowley went down from Cambridge in July 1898. In order to train for a trip to the Himalayas, he went to Switzerland to live in a tent on the Schönbühl glacier below Dent Blanche with his mountaineering friend Oscar Eckenstein. Eckenstein was a railway engineer who had studied chemistry at universities in London and Bonn (Booth 69). But Crowley's health declined, forcing him off the glacier and back to Zermatt to recover. What happened next has become a celebrated incident in the history of British Hermeticism. Crowley was in a bar, lecturing the bar's patrons on alchemy, when he was approached by another British climber, Julian L. Baker, who was "an analytical chemist, a student of magic and a real practising alchemist who claimed he had 'fixed mercury'" (Booth 81–82). Baker discussed alchemy with Crowley and promised to introduce him to Hermeticists. Back in London, Baker brought Crowley to George Cecil Jones, who, as Booth notes, "was an industrial chemist with a laboratory in central London . . . [who] was also widely read in the subject of magic, which he studied with scientific curiosity and exactitude" (Booth 82). Crowley and Jones became good friends, and Jones put Crowley forward for membership in the Golden Dawn and introduced him to Mathers (Booth 85). Crowley's introduction to the Hermetic practices of the Golden Dawn—and even before that, to alchemy as a science that related to modern chemistry—was largely effected, therefore, by academically trained London chemists.[13] I would argue that this path into alchemy and the occult led to the specific scientific vision of occultism that Crowley would articulate fully in the "scientific illuminism" of his own Hermetic order, the A.A.

Crowley joined the Golden Dawn in November 1898 and had left it by the spring of 1900, having participated in much of the internal dissension that drove the order apart (Howe 192). In 1907 Crowley went on to create the A.A., which he based largely on Golden Dawn rituals and grade structures.[14] Crowley caused a crisis in Golden Dawn circles when he published the rituals of its Outer Order in the second issue of his magazine, *The Equinox: The Official Organ of the A.A.: The Review of Scientific Illuminism*, which began publication in March 1909. Moreover, after a legal battle from Mathers, he published the rituals of the R.R. et A.C. in the third issue (King 91). In 1912 Crowley joined the Ordo Templi Orientis, an order founded at the beginning of the century by the German freemason and occultist Karl Kellner that was devoted to a kind of sexual magic/illuminism that couched its principles in alchemical terms (King 96). Crowley created the Mysteria Mystica Maxima (a British chapter of the O.T.O.) in 1912. He ended the group workings of the A.A. in 1914 and left for America, emerging as head of the O.T.O. in 1922. Historians have primarily focused on Crowley's synthesis of sex magic and Golden Dawn practices. But of equal significance, I would argue, is the degree to which Crowley ascribed scientific rigor to the occult practices of the A.A. and O.T.O. and claimed his scientific illuminism as modern science. Or, perhaps in a more fitting description of the nature of his project, Crowley claimed modern science *for* scientific illuminism.

Crowley's lead editorial in the first issue of *The Equinox* introduced the public to the A.A. with typical Crowleyian hyperbole: "With the publication of this REVIEW begins a completely new adventure in the history of mankind" (1909a, 1). But Crowley went to great pains to make this "new adventure" clearly conform to the trappings of scientific experiment. He presented the A.A. as a now publicly announced hidden experimental society: "It is the intention of the Brothers of the A.A. to establish a laboratory in which students may be able to carry out ... experiments" (3). Following the strategies by now familiar to readers of Westcott, Waite, and others who had claimed scientific authority for ancient occult wisdom that had been kept alive by secret societies, Crowley asserted that "this school of wisdom has been for ever most secretly hidden from the world, because it is invisible and submissive solely to illuminated government.... Through this school were developed the germs of all the sublime sciences, which were first received by external schools, then clothed in other forms, and hence degenerated" (1909b, 11).

Yet Crowley went significantly beyond the claim to scientific validity made by his immediate predecessors in the Golden Dawn and positioned the A.A. as a kind of official sanctioning body for experimental validity and for scientific training. Crowley laid down a set of numbered rules governing experiments, proclaiming, for example:

1. It is absolutely necessary that all experiments should be recorded in detail during, or immediately after, their performance.
2. It is highly important to note the physical and mental condition of the experimenter or experimenters.
3. The time and place of all experiments must be noted; also the state of the weather, and generally all conditions which might conceivably

have any result upon the experiment either as adjuvants to or causes of the result, or as inhibiting it, or as sources of error. (1909c, 25)

Noting that "the written record should be intelligibly prepared so that others may benefit from its study" (26), Crowley urged readers to examine a sample from an advanced student published in the same issue of *The Equinox*. He boldly asserted that "the more scientific the record is, the better" (26). He also cautioned that "The A.A. will not take official notice of any experiments which are not thus properly recorded" (25). The vision of scientific method that Crowley expressed in *The Equinox* would certainly have conformed to his own education in scientific research under Ramsay and Collie at London and at Cambridge. For Crowley, scientific illuminism would be characterized by meticulous and objective record keeping of laboratory experiments, a concern about possible "sources of error," the broader research community's access to other scientists' research results, and the sanctioning of practices by an authorizing body.

Crowley's vision of a Hermetic society dedicated to scientific research found fictional representation in Crowley's most famous novel, *Moonchild* (1929). A major figure in the Order proclaims, "The Order to which I belong . . . does not believe anything; it knows, or it doubts, as the case may be; and it seeks ever to increase human knowledge by the method of science, that is to say, by observation and experiment" (24). In addition to settling scores with Golden Dawn rivals (Yeats, Waite, Westcott, and Mathers are brutally parodied), *Moonchild* involves an experiment to incarnate the soul of a spirit being in a human baby. Crowley portrays the wedding of ancient magical practice to modern scientific canons of experimental accuracy and measurement. He explains occult phenomena, such as the existence of supernatural beings, by invoking new theories about atomic structure from particle physics.[15] Indeed, he turns to recent discoveries like X-rays and radioactivity to explain that magic is a science like other physical sciences:

> The laws of magick are closely related to those of other physical sciences. A century or so ago men were ignorant of a dozen important properties of matter; thermal conductivity, electrical resistance, opacity to the X-ray, spectroscopic reaction, and others even more occult. Magick deals principally with certain physical forces still unrecognized by the vulgar; but those forces are just as real, just as material—if indeed you can call them so, for all things are ultimately spiritual—as properties like radio-activity, weight and hardness. The difficulty in defining and measuring them lies principally in the subtlety of their relation to life. Living protoplasm is identical with dead protoplasm in all but the fact of life. (150)

Using the word "occult" to describe recently discovered energies like X-rays, of course, invokes both its meaning as "hidden from view" and its supernatural connotation. Moreover, it aligns the kind of "occult" forces Crowley describes in *Moonchild* with any other physical energy or force known to mainstream science, and draws upon the still scientifically debated theories of a "life force" posited by turn-of-the-century vitalism.

To further destabilize the opposition between science and occultism, the narrator, who speaks fairly directly in Crowley's own voice, argues:

> The fundamental difference between ancient and modern science is not at all in the field of theory. Sir William Thomson was just as metaphysical as Pythagoras or Raymond Lully, and Lucretius quite as materialistic as Ernst Haeckel or Büchner.
>
> But we have devised means of accurate measurement which they had not, and in consequence of this our methods of classification are more quantitative than qualitative. The result has been to make much of their science unintelligible; we no longer know exactly what they meant by the four elements, or by the three active principles, sulphur, mercury, and salt. Some tradition has been preserved by societies of wise men, who, because of the persecutions, when to possess any other book than a missal might be construed as heresy, concealed themselves and whispered the old teaching one to another. The nineteenth century saw the overthrow of most of the old ecclesiastical tyranny, and in the beginning of the twentieth it was found once more possible to make public the knowledge. The wise men gathered together, discovered a student who was trustworthy and possessed of the requisite literary ability; and by him the old knowledge was revised and made secure; it was finally published in a sort of periodical encyclopædia (already almost impossible to find, such was the demand for it) entitled *The Equinox*. (186)

Of course, Crowley is positioning himself and his journal as the repository of the ancient knowledge. (The idea that Crowley was "trustworthy" must have rankled Golden Dawn members to no end.) But beyond the narcissism so characteristic of Crowley's writing, the efforts by which scientific illuminism attempted to blur the boundaries of science depended on the assertion that ancient occult knowledge could be used with modern scientific rules of experiment, verification, and accurate measurement because it in fact *was* an extension of the physical sciences.

Even beyond Crowley, the later followers of the Golden Dawn across the twentieth century could no longer ignore atomic physics in their espousal of alchemy. Decades after work on subatomic particles had become firmly grounded in physics, rather than in chemistry, Colquhoun naturally emphasized that alchemy "is not chemistry of any kind, not even so-called Hyperchemistry [referring to the laboratory work of François Jollivet-Castelot]; it is rather an aspect of nuclear physics, and its well-attested transmutations result from nuclear reaction brought about by a still-unknown process" (270).[16] The intervention both of the material world of radioactive elements and the paradigm shift in chemistry and physics permanently changed the way Golden Dawn initiates viewed alchemy, and that process of change became apparent in the brief history of the Alchemical Society.

The Alchemical Society

In late 1912, the rapprochement between occultism and modern science culminated in the formation of an unprecedented institution in the occult revival—the Alchemical Society. In regular meetings over the next three years, occultists and academically sanctioned chemists used conceptions of alchemy and radioactivity to renegotiate the disciplinary boundaries between occultism and science and to frame questions about the cosmological, spiritual, and ethical conclusions to be drawn from the burgeoning field of atomic science. These discussions helped shape the popular perception of atomic science during at least the first third of the twentieth century. The Alchemical Society's choice of the professional society or civic club as its model, rather than the secret Hermetic society, enabled the press to treat its discussion of alchemy seriously. (Recall that the Golden Dawn had only come to the attention of the press during the Horos trials in 1901, and the publicity had been entirely negative.) But the key challenge to scientists like H. Stanley Redgrove, John Ferguson, F. H. Loring, Joseph Mellor, and others was to reconceive alchemy scientifically and science alchemically, yet still preserve the cognitive authority of science. In order to maintain the legitimating status of science, the scientists routinely downplayed any claims that alchemy in its medieval form was itself a modern science that could be validated and verified through laboratory work—the very project in which Ayton, Gardner, and other Golden Dawn members had been engaged. Instead, they salvaged alchemy through the back door of history, portraying it as having possessed scientific legitimacy during its own historical period. Most significantly, they also envisioned alchemy as possessing a wisdom that is born out *experimentally* by modern science—a philosophical position from which to interpret modern science, to spiritualize its implications. The academic credentials of the scientist members of the Alchemical Society lent legitimacy to claims that occultists also had advanced, with little success, in the period following the discovery of radioactive transmutation.

The shared interest in alchemy and radioactivity did more than simply allow scientists and occultists to work together. It also disrupted the boundaries previously drawn by both fields to separate themselves from one another. The papers presented before the Society and the ensuing discussions of them gradually hashed out a vision of the new atomic physics refracted through alchemical ideals. The Society thus conceptualized atomic physics as a science that complicated scientific materialism and privileged the unity of the cosmos in a spiritually and ethically invigorating way. The discussions opened up new ways of understanding energy that moved beyond eighteenth- and nineteenth-century ideals of efficiency and worked toward something approaching the arcane mysteries of the Philosopher's Stone.

The Public Aspirations of the Alchemical Society

The Golden Dawn and other secret societies that explored alchemy had largely hidden themselves from public view, only engaging established modern science in an occasional published essay. By comparison, the short-lived Alchemical Society at its inception already *was* part of that scientific establishment—but only just barely. It existed in a kind of borderland, neither entirely of the occult world nor of mainstream science. The institutional choices the Society made—from its organizational model, its meeting place, and the publisher for its journal to the kinds of press notice it sought—allowed it a public voice that was recognizably scientific. But its occult membership and focus were outside the normal boundaries of scientific discourse. Similarly, its scientist members and its institutional choices noticeably distinguished it from the Hermetic orders from which it also drew members.

The Alchemical Society was founded in late 1912 by H. Stanley Redgrove (1887–1943), a Fellow of the Chemical Society who earned a BSc from the University of London in 1907, not only the year that Crowley began the A.A. and scientific illuminism but, above all, the very year that Ramsay published in *Nature* his stunning claims to have caused artificial transmutations. As we shall see in chapter 3, Ramsay's announcement set off a host of transmutation efforts by Collie and others. While Redgrove was earning his degree, Ramsay was performing the experiments that led up to his 1907 claims. Transmutation, as we shall see, was very much in the air in scientific London because of the work by Ramsay, Collie, and others. Redgrove likely attended lectures by Ramsay and Collie, just as Crowley had, but *after* their involvement with radioactivity and transmutation experiments had begun. Redgrove taught chemistry at the London Polytechnic and then at West Ham Municipal Institute (which had only been founded in 1898). The Society began its general meetings in January 1913 in London, and continued until roughly the end of 1915, when the war made it impossible to continue. The *Journal of the Alchemical Society*, edited by Redgrove, reported on its monthly general meetings and its annual meetings. It also published the talk given each month at the general meeting, provided an abstract of the discussion that followed it, and included reviews of books and journals deemed of interest to its members. In spite of the fact that members of the Society were prominent occult publishers and editors, the Society did not publish its journal with an occult press. (Rider would have been an obvious choice, as Ralph Shirley, its owner, was a member.) Instead, it chose to emphasize its credentials in mainstream science by selecting H. K. Lewis, a popular science publisher who also ran a "Technical and Scientific Circulating Library."[17]

In spite of the Alchemical Society's significant constituency of key occultists, its aims, membership, mission, public self-representation, and organizational structure were completely different from those of a secret Hermetic society such as the Golden Dawn, or even those of the more public Theosophical Society. Rather than meeting in private residences, or in anything resembling the cloistered vaults of the Hermetic orders, the Society conducted itself in a fashion more akin to a professional society or social club. The Society availed itself of office space at Rider for its headquarters. But it held its monthly meetings at a non-occult location: the International Club on Regent Street, S.W.[18] It conducted meetings by parliamentary procedure, and it created a written constitution and by-laws featuring a full slate of officers, financial auditors, council members, and stipulations for monthly general meetings and regular annual meetings. Its members were all officially elected into the club, as was the case in many social clubs and professional societies, and it charged an annual membership fee.

The Alchemical Society passed over secret vaults and initiation rituals, instead relying on a modest advertising budget and word-of-mouth exhortations to expand its membership and public profile. Names of new members were announced at each general meeting, and the secretary commented on the state of the membership at each annual meeting. At the first annual meeting, in May 1913, the secretary—astrologer Walter Gorn Old—articulated the Society's goals of a larger active membership: "It is gratifying to observe that, from the inception of this Society and its formal inauguration on January 10th, 1913, the membership has been steadily increasing and at this date the Society constitutes a body of some strength, having representatives in many centres of intellectual activity throughout the world. Doubtless, as the aims and objects of our Society come more generally to be known and appreciated, there will be a further influx of members and a corresponding increase in our activities" (Old 1913, 66). Old imagined a larger society whose increased membership would allow it to obtain a permanent residence of its own and create a library of alchemical literature for its use (66–67). Emphasizing the open-minded yet scientific nature of the Society, Old concluded that "the aims and objects of the Society are sufficiently inclusive to give place to many and varied aspects of scientific and speculative thought, and the fullest scope is provided for the expression of every kind of thought that is pertinent to the main subject of our enquiry. This attitude of the Society should certainly prove attractive and, if more generally voiced by members, will no doubt lead to a considerable increase in membership" (67). This tone of boosterism continued in the secretarial addresses of Old's successor, Sijil Abdul-Ali, and membership building remained a top priority through the life of the Society.[19]

The Alchemical Society's self-promotional efforts resulted in public notice of its activities in a variety of intellectual and popular periodicals, suggesting that the broader journalistic media viewed the Society as relevant to contemporary science. The daily *Westminster Gazette* published reviews of the Alchemical Society's meetings. And on the more intellectual end of the spectrum, a venerable weekly review, the *Athenæum*, reviewed the first issue of the *Journal of the Alchemical Society* in its March 8, 1913 issue. The *Athenæum* went on to publish detailed reports of eleven of the Alchemical Society's meetings in the "Societies" section of its "Science" columns, putting it on par with groups like the Meteorological Society, the Mathematical Society, the Historical Society, and the Philological Society.[20] Moreover, reports of the Society's activities in the *Athenæum* were included among numerous articles on radium and radiation as well as reviews of Soddy's *Interpretation of Radium* and Rutherford's *Radio-active Substances and Their Radiations*.[21] The alchemy trope clearly guided the reviewer's understanding of radioactivity, as he especially remarked on Rutherford's response to "Sir William Ramsay's 'transmutation' hypothesis."[22]

Accounts of the Alchemical Society's meetings and publications also appeared in major scientific periodicals, including *Nature* and *The Chemical News*, and in popular scientific journals including *The English Mechanic* and *Knowledge*. *Nature*, a leading scientific periodical then as it is now, included respectful notices of four of the meetings of the Alchemical Society in its "Notes" section. Like the *Athenæum*, *Nature* situated the Alchemical Society's meetings among those of other scientific societies and similar events.[23]

Scientists of the Alchemical Society

The Alchemical Society's ability to position itself in the borderland between science and occultism enabled it to attract a number of serious scientists into its ranks. Unlike the Theosophical lodges and Hermetic temples, the Alchemical Society's membership was as scientific as it was occult. The Society's Honorary President was Professor John Ferguson (1837–1916), who held an MA from Glasgow and an LL.D. from St. Andrews and was a Fellow of the Institute of Chemistry, a Fellow of the Chemical Society, and, most significantly, the Regius Professor of Chemistry at Glasgow University from 1874 until 1915. He had credentials as a historian of alchemy, having published books on alchemical collections and books of secrets. But as his obituary in *Nature* noted, Ferguson was best known as the man who greatly expanded the chemistry laboratories at Glasgow and created separate departments of organic chemistry, metallurgical chemistry, and physical chemistry. He had taught "many distinguished chemists, including Prof. Millar Thomson, Sir William Ramsay, Sir J. J. Dobbie, Carrick Anderson, Profs. Henderson, Boyd, Long, and Parker, and A. W. Stewart" (*Nature*, 1915: 192). Ramsay, of course, became a leading proponent of modern alchemy, and Ferguson may well have inspired his interest in medieval alchemy. Though Ferguson himself, unlike Ramsay, is not considered a pioneer of modern atomic science, he presided over the department at Glasgow while Frederick Soddy taught and researched there as the first lecturer in physical chemistry and radioactivity at Glasgow. Soddy later asserted "quite definitely that the decade at Glasgow from the year 1904 to the outbreak of the first world war ranks as my most productive period" (quoted in Howorth 1958, 142). These years saw his publication of *The Interpretation of Radium* (1909), his major effort to lay out his theories of radioactivity and relate them to alchemy. In spite of the distance between Glasgow and London, Ferguson presided over some meetings of the Alchemical Society and even delivered a paper before it.

Because of the asymmetry of power between science and occultism, and the ever-growing public faith in the authority of science, the members of a borderland institution like the Alchemical Society had to work self-consciously to solidify its public perception as a scientific society. But the subject of the Society—alchemy—already enjoyed considerable prestige in the occult community. So the Alchemical Society used the impressive scientific and educational credentials of its membership as part of its self-validation in the eyes of the scientific world and the broader public. Most formal mentions by the *Journal* of its members (either as authors of papers or as participants in the meetings or in the Society's governance) proudly displayed their educational credentials and their membership in prestigious societies. Of the forty-two members of the Society mentioned by name in the *Journal*'s accounts of its meetings, the Society could boast that three held BSc degrees, two held an MA, four held doctoral degrees (one DSc, two PhDs, and a DD), one may have been a medical doctor (he was simply referred to as "Dr."), two held LLBs, and one held a JB (see Appendix C). Several had been elected as Fellows of scientific societies: Two were Fellows of the Chemical Society, one was a Fellow of the Institute of Chemistry, one was a Member of the Institute of Civil Engineers, one was a Fellow of the Royal Geographical Society, one a Fellow of the Zoological Society, and one (who was listed as a visitor and may not have joined) was a Fellow of the Linnean Society.

At least four members were professional chemists with successful careers and significant scientific publications—Ferguson, Redgrove, F. H. Loring, and Joseph Mellor. Redgrove, Loring, Mellor, and engineer Herbert Chatley (1885–1955) were regularly publishing in two key scientific publications of the day, *Nature* (edited by Sir Norman Lockyer) and *The Chemical News* (edited by Sir William Crookes). Redgrove published books on occult subjects, many of them with Rider—including *Matter, Spirit and the Cosmos* (1910), *Alchemy: Ancient and Modern* (1911, 1922), *A Mathematical Theory of Spirit* (1912), *Bygone Beliefs* (1920), *Joseph Glanvill* (1921), *Roger Bacon* (1920), *Purpose and Transcendentalism* (1920), and *Joannes Baptista Van Helmont, Alchemist, Physician and Philosopher* (1922). But he also authored scientific, mathematical, and philosophical books, including *On the Calculation of Thermo-Chemical Constants* (1909), *Experimental Mensuration* (1913), *The Magic of Experience: A Contribution to the Theory of Knowledge* (1915), and *Industrial Gases* (1916). In later life he went on to work on the chemistry of cosmetics, and he published many books and articles on the subject.[24] During his years as acting president of the Alchemical Society and editor of its journal, he published four articles in *Chemical News* (three of them lead articles), mostly on thermodynamics and on the relationships of matter, mass, and weight. His *Experimental Mensuration* and *The Magic of Experience* were reviewed positively in the journal.

Loring published chemistry books—*Studies in Valency* (1913), *Atomic Theory* (1921), *Definition of the Principle of Equivalence* (1922), and *The Chemical Elements* (1923). During the brief existence of the Alchemical Society, he published twenty articles (eight of them lead articles) in *Chemical News* on such subjects as atomic weight, the radio-atoms, the evolution of chemical elements, and a five-part "Introduction to the Theory of Relativity." He also published seven correspondences in the journal, and *Chemical News* reviewed his *Studies in Valency* positively.

Mellor ran the Stoke-on-Trent Pottery School beginning around 1905 and oversaw the opening of the laboratories of the New Central Schools of Science and Technology at Stoke-on-Trent. His *Modern Inorganic Chemistry*, first published in September 1912, was revised and republished even beyond the author's death, at least as late as the 1960s. Several of his other chemistry books during the period, including *Higher Mathematics for Students of Chemistry and Physics* (1902), *Chemical Statics and Dynamics* (1904, published in Sir William Ramsay's Textbooks of Physical Chemistry series), and *A Comprehensive Treatise on Inorganic and Theoretical Chemistry* (1922), and his books on the chemistry of pottery went through numerous editions. During the life of the Alchemical Society, Mellor published an article and three reviews in *Nature*, and *Nature* positively reviewed several of his books, calling his *Modern Inorganic Chemistry* "one of the most original of the textbooks that have been published in recent years" (T. M. L. 1913, 669). Several of his books were also reviewed in *Chemical News* during the same period.[25]

Chatley was an engineer working and teaching at Tangshan Engineering College, North China, at the time. He published on Chinese alchemy for the Alchemical Society but also published articles in *Nature* during the same period. (Moreover, *Nature* reviewed a work of his appearing in *Knowledge*.) Chatley's prolific career, his work on silts and currents in China, and his general polyglot cultural sensibility were lauded in obituaries in *Engineer* and *Engineering*. Other members of the Alchemical Society were degreed professionals in different fields. Two were clergy holding doctoral degrees (including the Venerable J. B. Craven, Archdeacon of Orkney). Two were retired military men—a colonel and a lieutenant-colonel who held a Volunteer Officer's Decoration, or VD—who had gone on to practice law.

The Permeability of Discourse Boundaries

As Sharon Traweek (1992) has argued, borderlands are not simply powerless margins. They can sometimes generate surprising advantages. Members of the Alchemical Society found a strategic value to its strange meeting of scientists and occultists. The Society was able to serve as a forum in which occultists interested in science and scientists interested in alchemy could hammer out an understanding of the uses of alchemical thinking in a modern atomic age. No other such forum existed at the nascence of modern atomic theory. These debates self-consciously raised issues of the spiritual implications of science, the unity of nature, and the uses of analogy in the production of scientific understanding. They never affirmed a simple, straightforward use of alchemy as an analogy for atomic science. Instead, they revealed a complex sense of the permeable boundaries of scientific discourse.

The subjects of alchemy and radioactivity allowed groups from radically different social worlds to work together (see Appendix A). But they also helped to break down the boundary between the discourses of science and occultism, rather than simply allowing disparate discourses and purposes to coexist within the same organization. The meetings aired a number of points of view about the validity of alchemy *as* science, about the veracity of alchemical texts' claims of transmutation, about the extent to which a knowledge of alchemical texts might shape an understanding of the goals and nature of modern physics and chemistry, and even about the very nature of alchemy. These debates and some of their key voices may well have had an impact on the kinds of uses to which alchemical tropes were put in the press. They shaped a vision of modern physics and chemistry that could draw from some of the strengths of alchemical discourse, and which is not, in fact, so very far from the direction toward the unification of theories that much atomic science has taken since the early twentieth century.

John Ferguson may have initially seen the Alchemical Society as answering a need for histories of chemistry and pharmaceutics. He had advanced this claim in the introduction to the work for which he is now most famous, the two-volume *Bibliotheca Chemica* (1906), which has served as one of the major descriptive bibliographies of alchemical texts. But by 1913, many members of the Alchemical Society felt the subject was important as more than simply part of the early history of those disciplines. Indeed, almost every paper and discussion at the Society's meetings urged that alchemy should not be consigned to the vaults of history. The Society quickly moved beyond some early historical quibbling about whether any medieval alchemist had actually effected the transmutation of lead into gold (most thought not, though a few disagreed and cited examples affirmed by scientists such as van Helmont). Throughout the life of the Society, members valued a nuanced historical understanding of alchemy, but found the uses of that history for modern science far more compelling.

Differences of opinion even on the nature of the alchemical project proliferated in the papers read to the Society and the discussions that followed. The lines of inquiry and interpretation often involved using alchemy to interrogate scientific reasoning (weighing inductive versus deductive reasoning, for instance) and to explore the significance of scientific "abstraction." Science speaks in symbols and analogies, as members observed, especially when, as in the case of subatomic particles, it addresses the invisible and intangible. Alchemy raised questions about the interpretation of alchemical symbols and modes of reasoning, just as modern scientific modes of reasoning came under similar scrutiny. Indeed, the intangibility of the new subatomic particles and the murky interrelationships (or even interchangeability) of matter and energy in the new science were foremost in the minds of many occultists as they approached the subject. In the year the Society was founded, William R. Moore wrote in *The Occult Review* that "we have to consider that science has now reached a stage at which the tangible realities seem to melt gradually into the abstract, and at which visible phenomena will not admit of a physical explanation" (1912, 73).[26]

Within the Society, there were five major interpretations of alchemy. Redgrove—who carried much weight as the Society's acting president, a chemist, and a scholar of alchemy—argued that alchemists were indeed some of the foremost scientists of their day, but they based their chemical explorations upon deductive rather than inductive reasoning. They applied tenets of mystical theology and philosophy to their experimental data—essentially providing experimental confirmation of their starting assumptions. Redgrove averred that their methods would not hold up to the inductive rigor of modern science. Yet, as he noted in a talk before the Society, "recent developments in physical and chemical science seem to indicate that the alchemists were not so utterly wrong in their concept of nature, as has formerly been supposed—that, whilst they certainly erred in both their methods and their interpretations of individual phenomena, they did intuitively grasp certain fundamental facts concerning the universe" (1913a, 2).[27] He concluded, "As for the basic concepts of Alchemy themselves, such as the fundamental unity of the Cosmos and the evolution of the elements, in a word, the applicability of the principles of mysticism to natural phenomena; these seem to me to contain a very valuable element of truth—a statement which, I think, modern scientific research justifies me in making,—though the alchemists distorted this truth and expressed it in a fantastic form" (14). Redgrove's bedrock assumption that alchemical thinking was relevant to contemporary science became widely held within the Society by members with scientific backgrounds and those from occult circles.

Waite, the most significant occultist scholar of alchemy in the Society, argued against the spiritual alchemy thesis of Atwood's *Suggestive Inquiry* that had so dominated occult thinking (and shaped his own) before the discovery of radioactive transformation. Waite affirmed Atwood's suggestion that alchemical writings were in a secret code designed to protect them from profane minds. Indeed, he argued that research for such decoding should be the major work of the Society.[28] But unlike Atwood, he argued that it largely protected "in the ordinary sense of the word a metallic secret," even if it was a secret "belonging to the spiritual order" (1913, 23–24). By the advent of the Alchemical

Society, Waite clearly saw alchemy as a chemical science with spiritual dimensions. Waite was in agreement with Redgrove on most issues, including his portrayal of medieval alchemy and his argument that alchemy was relevant to contemporary science—although he might have phrased it that contemporary science was relevant to alchemy. He also provided some correction to some of the historical nuances of Redgrove's account.[29] While Redgrove brought a formidable knowledge of contemporary science to his writings on alchemy, Waite brought an immense store of alchemical and occult knowledge to his understanding of modern chemistry. In other words, this strain of thinking within the Society was almost identical to Redgrove's, but with an emphasis on the occult.

On the other hand, Isabelle de Steiger followed the spiritual alchemy path set out by her friend, the recently deceased Atwood. De Steiger argued that the chemical language was entirely symbolic. The true subject of alchemy was the science of redeeming man from the Fall and perfecting his soul through the use of a special process of mesmerism (1907, 21–22). Updating Atwood with the new science, she claimed that the "nearest demonstrated analogy" to the action of this mesmerism "is no doubt to be found in the phenomena of radioactivity" (23). De Steiger's position was also referred to as "transcendental alchemy." De Steiger remained loyal to Atwood's spiritual alchemy thesis and helped facilitate the 1918 first reprinting of the *Suggestive Inquiry* about a decade after Atwood's death. But Redgrove and Ferguson both weighed in with papers that criticized the *Suggestive Inquiry* thesis, arguing that alchemy was indeed about physical substances, and not simply symbolic (Ferguson, 1913, 16; Redgrove, 1913a, 3).

Echoing de Steiger's (and Atwood's) argument that chemical terms conceal a project of transformation enacted upon the alchemist, early psychoanalyst Elizabeth Severn subtly shifted the emphasis away from mesmerism and mysticism to psychological and spiritual self-development. Severn held a doctoral degree from Chicago and published many books on psychotherapy. She even went through an analysis with Sándor Ferenczi. Severn and others grafted the language of alchemy onto that of psychoanalysis, seeing alchemy as a kind of transmutational operation upon the self, even a kind of "character-building" (Severn 1914, 110). The phrase "spiritual alchemy" was often invoked by the proponents of this view (and also sometimes by those of the Atwood interpretation).[30] But Severn's psychoanalytic emphasis differed from that of Atwood and de Steiger. It was a significant precursor to Jung's psychoanalytic interpretation of alchemy and Regardie's synthesis of ritual magic and clinical psychoanalysis.

A fifth position on alchemy held by Wellby and others—though a decidedly minority one—held that the alchemists had indeed effected transmutation of metals, created the elixir of life, and achieved other medical feats. Some believed that the adept achieved the spiritual and psychic power to transmute metals using only mental energy. Members of the Alchemical Society, including Waite, generally dismissed this idea (*Journal of the Alchemical Society* 1913a, 32).

Though several understandings of alchemy had emerged in the Society's debates, the members took one another's positions seriously. And these emerging positions themselves show how permeable the boundaries between science and occultism had become. Even de Steiger, who defended Atwood's thesis, had argued for it by analogy to radioactivity—a use of contemporary science to clarify her Hermetic thesis that Atwood herself certainly would not have made. Indeed, the discussions after each talk recorded in the *Journal of the Alchemical Society* demonstrate not simply an ongoing dialogue between science and occultism, but rather a blurring of the boundaries between the two domains.

Atomic Alchemy and a Return to Spirituality

But another set of questions rapidly moved beyond these ongoing arguments about the nature of alchemy—questions concerning the relationship of medieval and ancient alchemy to the exciting new experimental and theoretical breakthroughs made by Soddy, Rutherford, Ramsay, and others in the realm of atomic physics and chemistry. In addition to alchemy, radiation quickly became a subject that allowed the productive meeting of the disparate worlds of science and occultism in the borderland. Both alchemy and radiation caused considerable disruption of these domains of knowledge, however. The ensuing strategic maneuvering by members of the Society advanced their understanding of the "modern alchemy" in surprising directions, leading to a re-enchantment of science that remained with us in some form across the twentieth century.

From the first meeting of the Alchemical Society, recent theories in atomic chemistry and physics immediately entered the discussions. Redgrove's paper, mentioned above, brought up the subject. Walter Gorn Old raised Crookes's theory of the protyle as an essentially alchemical notion. Sijil Abdul-Ali discussed the resemblance of properties of the Philosopher's Stone to those of the ether (*Journal of the Alchemical Society.* 1913a, 15–16). The early meetings of the Alchemical Society coincided, in fact, with enormous press attention to Ramsay's latest assertions that he had effected transmutation using modern chemistry (the subject of chapter 3). Waite himself raised the subject of alchemy's relationship to the new physics and chemistry after presenting his paper in the second meeting. This meeting, on Friday evening, February 14, 1913, was held just over a week after the February 6 meeting of the Chemical Society in which Ramsay, and then Collie and Hubert Patterson, announced that they had transmuted various elements. This meeting of the Chemical Society, discussed in chapter 3, represents the apex of a transmutational "gold rush" among academic chemists that was portrayed in alchemical terms by Ramsay himself. Indeed, young chemists such as Redgrove, Loring, and Mellor must have been following in the pages of *Nature,* the *Journal of the Chemical Society,* and other scientific journals the transmutation efforts leading up to the February 1913 Chemical Society meeting. The heightened scientific emphasis on transmutation among chemists might well even have been an inspiration for creating the Alchemical Society.

The occultists were following the chemists' efforts closely too. Waite had read a press account of Ramsay's announcement, and he must have seen Collie and Patterson's paper from the meeting and J. J. Thomson's response to it in the February 13, 1913, issue of *Nature.* In the Alchemical Society meeting the next day, a meeting that was a virtual extension of the Chemical Society's meeting, Waite addressed the chemists' claims:

> It is only yesterday that we heard of a discovery by Sir William Ramsay and other scientists—working, I believe, independently— which may mean the transmutation of one chemical element into another—subject, of course, to the validity of Prof. Sir J. J. Thomson's alternative contention. We must seek to know more of the trend of recent discovery in this direction, and we need to be informed by someone who has an eye to the efforts of the past, but also a complete disregard of any *a priori* reasonings which actuated those efforts.
> (1913, 20)

The response to Waite's call for a paper on the subject came at the very next meeting. Abdul-Ali's March 1913 talk, "An Interpretation of Alchemy in Relation to Modern Scientific Thought," juxtaposed alchemical concepts with modern scientific thought. Abdul-Ali engaged science ranging from Norman Lockyer's spectroscopic work on the evolution of elements in stars, Rutherford's new model of electrons orbiting a positively charged particle, and Crooke's protyle theory to contemporary discussions of energy, incandescence, and ether.[31] He did not suggest that alchemists were transmuting lead into gold using radium as a kind of Philosopher's Stone (a hypothesis that Wellby later ventured, but that received little support). Rather, he underscored the relevance of alchemical thinking and its vision of an interconnected universe to modern scientific thought. Indeed, Abdul-Ali saw alchemy as a philosophical system that extended beyond the bounds of scientific inquiry. Alchemy could lend science just such a substratum of philosophical and spiritual implication. Abdul-Ali asserted that "inasmuch as the fundamental doctrines of Alchemy were philosophical rather than scientific, and applicable to man rather than to matter, any purely scientific interpretation of the literature must necessarily be inadequate" (45).

In the discussion that followed, Redgrove affirmed the direction of Abdul-Ali's thought. He argued that the alchemists were often not scientific and had never effected transmutation, but had intuitively grasped something about the nature of matter that had been missed by modern science since Dalton—namely, that there were no irreducible elements, but instead energies and particles that were configured differently to make up a multiplicity of substances (*Journal of the Alchemical Society* 1913c, 46). Over the last few years, Redgrove had come to see alchemy as a philosophical, or even spiritual, corrective to the narrow focus of modern science, even as science gave accuracy to alchemical aspirations. As he had put it in *Alchemy: Ancient and Modern* in 1911: "If I were asked to contrast Alchemy with the chemical and physical science of the nineteenth century I would say that, whereas the latter abounded in a wealth of much accurate detail and much relative truth, it lacked philosophical depth and insight; whilst Alchemy, deficient in such accurate detail, was characterised by a greater philosophical depth and insight; for the alchemists did grasp the fundamental truth of the Cosmos" (Redgrove 1922, xii–xiii). The science of the twentieth century, then (in opposition to that of the nineteenth and the alchemy of the middle ages), would be a modern alchemy with both scientific accuracy and philosophical depth. Modern alchemy would not represent a retreat to religion in the face of an overly scientific culture, but rather would be a science that could temper its empirical successes with spiritual insight.

Indeed, many Alchemical Society members came to see value in alchemy's insistence on the unity not only of nature but also of soul and body. This ethical imperative did not challenge the methods of modern science, but rather emphasized a worldview by which legitimate scientific understandings of nature could be held to have spiritual implications. The Society had clearly moved well away from Atwood's spiritual alchemy, which had little need for science at all. While Alchemical Society members, such as J. W. Frings, certainly noted the continuation of secret alchemical groups essentially practicing alchemy as religion (Frings 1913, 23), what most came to affirm instead was a goal of perceiving modern science spiritually through an alchemical lens.

Some authors used radiation as a metaphor for various spiritual or physical processes of alchemy. Others used alchemy as a metaphor for various aspects of modern scientific theory. Still others insisted on a less metaphorical connection. Ramsay's alleged transmutations using radioactive bombardments were discussed at great length. But as the debates progressed over the three years of the Society's existence, the subject of transmutation came to be less significant. W. de Kerlor read a paper on the alchemical research of the contemporary French alchemist Jollivet-Castelot (who was an honorary member of the Society, as some members of the Society were honorary members of Jollivet-Castelot's French alchemical society), claiming that Jollivet-Castelot had effected transmutations using modern chemical processes. But several members criticized the paper and Jollivet-Castelot's research as not throwing any light on the Hermetic alchemy of the middle ages, thus being ultimately beside the point for the Alchemical Society's concerns. As Redgrove noted:

> in the case of many members of the Alchemical Society, their studies had led them to a point where, paradoxical though it might seem to say so, metallic transmutation was not of prime importance to Alchemy. [Redgrove] was not especially referring to those who regarded the subject as a veiled mysticism. But... it was not the fact (if fact it be), but the method and reason of transmutation that were of prime importance. It was possible to conceive of metallic transmutation being effected in such a manner as to leave the whole question of Alchemy—of Hermetic philosophy—untouched. (*Journal of the Alchemical Society* 1914, 11)

As deliberations shifted away from the topic of transmutation, they turned to what ultimately became the most significant topic to emerge in the early atomic years: energy. While some members, such as the scientifically rigorous B. Ralph Rowbottom,[32] cautioned against seeing earlier ages as possessing modern atomic knowledge, others, such as Lt.-Col. Jasper Gibson, actually argued that alchemists must have possessed modern concepts of energy. Gibson suggested that electricity, heat, and radioactivity corresponded to the alchemical concepts of mercury, sulphur, and salt, and that the Philosopher's Stone that Edward Kelly had claimed to possess was radioactive material. What the alchemist had was essentially the ability to manipulate energy (Gibson 1914, 17–25). As unconvincing as Gibson's argument was, it does highlight something that was emerging in the use of alchemical tropes and alchemical thinking in relationship to modern science—that is, a greater emphasis on the control of energies than on the creation of gold. Indeed, Soddy's *Interpretation of Radium* (1909) channeled discussions in this direction—even asserting a possibility much like that advanced by Gibson, that ancient humans might have been able to control matter and energy through atomic knowledge of radioactivity. Moreover, H. G. Wells's novel *The World Set Free* (1914), which Redgrove reviewed in the *Journal of the Alchemical Society*, made a similar leap into energy. In the novel, gold becomes an incidental and common byproduct of the creation of atomic energy. The control (and abuse, through atomic weaponry) of atomic energy, dressed in alchemical terms, becomes the dominant issue (see chapter 4).

Alchemical thinking helped lead the Society to interpret the implications of modern atomic theory in a way that emphasized the unity of matter (and even of energy); that saw oneness, rather than disunity and distinctness, as a major substratum of atomic theory; and that pushed to spiritualize this principle. This grasping for ever simpler and more basic unity is, of course, not so uncommon an impulse in twentieth-century physics. (Consider unified field theories, and even the Theory of Everything in more recent physics.) Alchemy allowed the scientists and Hermeticists of the Alchemical Society to re-enchant science by positing the origins of the modern scientific push for unity in ancient Hermetic spirituality.

Moreover, another kind of unity was a main feature of alchemical thinking—that of the living world and the inorganic. This strand of occult thinking raised the issue of alchemy's medicalization for the Society. The "Elixir of Life" was said by alchemists to purify not only metals but also the body, causing it to live to a great age. This dimension of alchemy was also closely wrapped up in the discussions of radium's effect on cells and vitality. (Radium was already being used to treat cancer by around the turn of the century.) In 1922, at the end of the "Modern Alchemy" chapter that concluded the second edition of *Alchemy: Ancient and Modern*, Redgrove invoked a 1904 Ramsay article on radium for *Harper's* in which Ramsay referred to the possible regenerative effect on cells that radium might have in terms of a Philosopher's Stone and the *elixir vitæ*. Redgrove concluded his book by citing Ramsay's efforts at transmutation and Rutherford's successful transmutation of 1919: "Whatever may be the final verdict concerning [Ramsay's] own experiments, those of Sir Ernest Rutherford, referred to in the Preface to the present edition, demonstrate the fact of transmutation; and, it is worth noticing how many of the alchemists' obscure descriptions of their Magistery well apply to that marvelous something which we call Energy, the true 'First Matter' of the Universe. And of the other problem, the *Elixir Vitæ*, who knows?" (141).

Indeed, as we shall see in chapter 3, Ramsay's experiments in chemistry labs in London had failed to demonstrate transmutation. But in 1919, Rutherford's work at the physics laboratory at Cambridge had finally conclusively proven that the elements could be artificially transmuted. The press immediately proclaimed Rutherford's accomplishment the achievement of the alchemist's dream of transmutation. Throughout the 1920s and 1930s, nuclear physics became "modern alchemy" in textbooks and press accounts. That phrase in itself marks the hybrid cultural nature of the new science born of both stunning achievements by scientists and the imaginative spiritual synthesis of occultism and science propounded by occultists and scientists alike. For a time, the Alchemical Society provided a literal meeting place for exchanges that had been happening in print since the discovery of radiation. The occult alchemical revival had helped set an agenda of transmutation for modern science and helped provide a philosophical and religious dimension to its laboratory work. Conversely, the new science had infused occultism with more rigorously scientific aims and methods. But it had also focused occultists' attention on the developing notions of matter and energy in atomic science, rather than simply grounding their work in Hermetic texts. The Friday meetings of the Alchemical Society had effectively helped recast both modern science and modern occultism.

But no account of occultism's engagement with modern atomic science could be even adequate without addressing the "occult chemistry" of one of the most successful occult institutions of the late-nineteenth and early twentieth centuries—the Theosophical Society. It is to Annie Besant and C. W. Leadbeater's efforts to ground Theosophical knowledge in a "scientific" research program that we must now turn.

2

Occult Chemistry, Instrumentation, and the Theosophical Science of Direct Perception

From the late nineteenth century through the first quarter of the twentieth, clamoring voices debated the fundamental nature of matter. Theories proliferated from various corners of the scientific and the occult worlds, and, as we have seen in the history of the Alchemical Society, their theories could even be brought into line with each other. Dalton's indivisible fundamental particles—the elemental atoms of nineteenth-century chemistry—found themselves vying with theories from ether physics, such as Kelvin's suggestion that an atom might simply be a vortex in the ether. William Prout's early nineteenth-century theory that all the elements were made up of differing numbers and configurations of hydrogen atoms, and his concept of the "protyle," gave way in the later nineteenth century to Sir William Crookes's own elaboration of a matter from which all the elements were ultimately formed (see Brock 1985). Yet Prout's and Crookes's theories could easily find confirmation by occult alchemists, who saw the protyle merely as a current scientific elaboration of the alchemical *prima materia*. Discoveries about the nature of radioactivity further complicated scientific and occult understandings of the relationships between matter and energy and of the nature of atoms.

One theme in this cacophony emerged from Theosophists who attempted to propound an "occult chemistry." (More about Theosophy below.) Such a "science" was an effort, much like that of the Alchemical Society, to seek a material science that could bridge the apparent divide between mechanistic science and spirituality. Occult chemistry, like the spiritual alchemy espoused by many Theosophists and some Hermeticists, explicitly addressed the role of the will and the mind of the spiritually purified adept in manipulating the matter of the physical world. The project (and its efforts at scientific validation) of necessity addressed what has become a major component of atomic science across the twentieth century: the role of instruments in gleaning information about an invisible subatomic world.

With the transformation of natural philosophy into *experimental* natural philosophy around 1650 (Le Grand 1990, xi), instrumentation began to play a central part in the practice of chemistry and physics—and has since been crucial to the emergence of new theories of matter.[1] The alchemical laboratory, of course, featured its own array of instruments, including the athanor, bain-marie, alembic, retort, balneum, and pelican. By the late nineteenth and early twentieth centuries, though, these machines and vessels had long been relegated to the colorful prehistory of chemistry. Scientists had adopted far more sophisticated devices for manipulating and probing the material world. Given the invisibility of subatomic particles to human vision, a variety of detectors confirmed the existence of a particle or the occurrence of an event by examining an effect of that event. The spectroscope, cathode ray tube, electrometer, spinthariscope, cloud chamber, and ionization chamber, for example, allowed turn-of-the-century scientists to detect signs of an otherwise imperceptible atomic world.

C. T. R. Wilson's 1895 invention of the cloud chamber and Donald Glaser's 1952 invention of the bubble chamber allowed major breakthroughs in, respectively, low-energy and high-energy particle physics. These instruments allowed investigators to "see" particles by seeing their trails in condensation lines or bubble lines. (Both Wilson and Glaser won Nobel Prizes for their inventions.) But these chambers represent only one direction in instrumentation. Peter Galison has identified contrasting traditions of experimentation in twentieth-century physics: "One embraced the visual detectors, such as the cloud chamber and the bubble chamber, which etched onto film the fine details of individual events. Quite another tradition formed around electronic detectors.... Only in the early 1980s [did] these two traditions merge when electronic detectors [became] capable of producing computer-constructed images that [were] so well resolved that individual events [acquired] significance" (1987, 248–49). Both varieties of detectors presuppose the value of perception, of literal observation, in the development of scientific theory and participate in a tradition extending back through Comtian positivism and British empiricism (Galison 1997, 11). The image detectors, though, with their privileging of mimesis—of the "golden event" that showed the forms of the subatomic world—were key to many of the breakthrough discoveries in physics from 1895 through the 1930s.

The possibility of visually experiencing an invisible world aligned the emerging physics of the 1890s and early twentieth century with the Theosophical Society, one of the major institutions of the late Victorian occult revival. Just as the Hermetic societies explored in chapter 1 argued that the emerging sciences of radioactivity and subatomic particles revealed the validity of alchemical theory—and that the alchemical worldview could productively shape modern science—the Theosophical Society, too, carefully followed the experimental and theoretical work of scientists such as Crookes, Ramsay, Röntgen, Thomson, Soddy, Rutherford, and the Curies. Theosophists believed that the new science validated both the theories of medieval alchemists and, of course, the wisdom of Theosophical adepts, including the founders of the Society, H. P. Blavatsky and Colonel Henry Olcott, and their Theosophical heirs, especially Annie Besant (1847–1933) and Charles Webster Leadbeater (1854–1934). Even more remarkably, Theosophical engagements with authorized science helped confirm the emerging "image orientation" of the new atomic science from the outset.

For the first two decades of the Theosophical Society's existence, Theosophy's written attempts to legitimate itself as a science (to "sanitize" its occultism, to borrow Roy Wallis's apt term) consisted of frequently citing scientific works and adopting scientific terms. But in 1895, the year in which Wilson built his first cloud chamber and Röntgen discovered X-rays, Besant and Leadbeater, both rising stars in the Theosophical firmament, shifted the terms of Theosophical sanitization and launched a series of direct experiments into the nature of the chemical elements. The results of these August 1895 investigations into the subatomic structure of hydrogen, oxygen, nitrogen, and a fourth gas—which, they claimed, had not yet been discovered by chemists— were published in *Lucifer,* the major Theosophical journal founded by Blavatsky in 1887. The experiments were resumed in 1907 with work on fifty-nine more elements. In the intervening years, of course, the discoveries of radioactivity, radium and other radioactive elements, the electron, and radioactive transformation had radically altered the field of atomic science. Indeed, on the very day (July 18, 1907) that Sir William Ramsay published his remarkable claims in *Nature* to have transmuted elements, Sir William Crookes replied to his friends, Besant and Leadbeater, who had requested a large selection of sample elements. (Lithium, chromium, selenium, titanium, vanadium, boron, and beryllium he could supply, whereas scandium, gallium, rubidium, and germanium, he warned, were almost impossible to get in a pure state [Besant and Leadbeater 1951, 2].) Leadbeater and Besant continued their experiments that summer during a vacation in Weisser-Hirsch near Dresden, and they made use of the mineral specimens in a Dresden museum. The reinvigorated investigations continued intermittently until the deaths of Besant in 1933 and Leadbeater in 1934, and they resulted in a volume entitled *Occult Chemistry* that went through three editions (1908, 1919, and 1951) and remains in print today.[2] Like much turn-of-the-century alchemical writing on chemistry, *Occult Chemistry* echoed Victorian scientists who had argued that Dalton's chemical elements must be composed of something simpler and unitary. As noted above, alchemists had called it the *prima materia,* or "first matter," while Kelvin had called it the vortex atom and Prout and Crookes had called it the protyle. Besant and Leadbeater called it the ultimate physical atom, or "anu" (from Sanskrit).

Their experiments marked a significant shift from revelation to experimentation as a source for the scientific basis of Theosophy—a move intended to garner the validation of scientific method and the prestige of experimental science in that period. But the experiments were remarkable for another reason: They were conducted clairvoyantly. Besant and Leadbeater claimed that direct perception of subatomic structure was superior to the scientific data that could be gleaned from instrumentation. Or, to put it slightly differently, they posited the human observer as a kind of occult detection instrument. It is easy to be dismissive of these experiments. As Washington notes, "though the authors made several of their chemical discoveries while sitting on a bench in the Finchley Road, as so often in scientific research the right materials were not always to hand and Leadbeater had to make several astral visits to glass cases in museums where the rarer metals and minerals were housed" (Washington 1995, 120). Yet Besant and Leadbeater saw these experiments as important enough to continue across almost the last forty years of their lives and to bring out in multiple book editions and journal articles. The significance of their clairvoyant forays into the subatomic world cannot be dismissed so easily. They speak to a number of important issues—including the relationship between spirituality and the materialist science of the period's emerging chemistry and physics.

As the new atomic science, through ever more sophisticated detectors, opened a realm that could not be directly perceived by the physical senses, occult chemistry offered an alternative, a mode of scientific experimentation that could attempt to claim legitimacy through its scientific writing, charts, and visual illustrations of data while it also connected the human psyche to the subatomic world through a direct form of perception—that is, clairvoyance. (Theosophists argued that clairvoyance was indeed a sense faculty.) The conception of alchemy that supported such a vision was the "spiritual alchemy" we have seen in chapter 1 espoused by some members of the Golden Dawn, and for a while, of the Alchemical Society. Not surprisingly, Theosophists asserted that transmutation was effected directly by the spiritually purified adept. Both Besant and Leadbeater claimed the ability to break down chemical compounds into their constituent elements and then to break apart subatomic structures merely by the power of their trained and purified minds.

The material realm of the subatomic world thus became available to sensuous—and even sensual—encounters. The unseen world was portrayed voluptuously; even subatomic particles were seen not only as animate but also as sexed. The perceiving body became, in Theosophical conceptions, an instrument of scientific knowledge production rather than simply the subject of it. And, as this chapter will show, the elements themselves essentially were used by two competing groups, mainstream scientists and occult investigators, to gain a better understanding of the nature of the material world and to strengthen their own methods' claims to validity. As I have argued about the Hermetic explorations of the Alchemical Society scientists, such experiments—and the Theosophical worldview in general—should not be seen as a rejection of science in response to the West's disenchantment of the world. Rather, we should see Theosophical experimentation as an attempt to re-enchant science itself.

Theosophy and the Boundaries of Physical Science

The Theosophical Society, with its formal governance structure, its open and regular meetings, its public self-promotion, and its vast publishing industry, was a very different sort of occult enterprise from the secret Hermetic societies like the Golden Dawn and played a more prominent role in the public perception of occult subjects. The Society had been founded in New York in 1875 by Helena Petrovna Blavatsky, a daughter of Russian nobility who had made a living in her wanderings as a spirit medium (among other colorful occupations), and by Colonel Henry Olcott, a Civil War veteran who had served as Special Commissioner to the War Department and as a member of the three-man panel investigating Abraham Lincoln's assassination. Olcott had become an ardent spiritualist in the 1870s. Theosophy was initiated by Blavatsky's book, *Isis Unveiled* (1877). Blavatsky claimed that the book was the work of the Masters, adepts of a secret international Great White Lodge, who precipitated the manuscript onto the desk in Blavatsky's study or used her body to write it out directly. Of course most reviewers were openly skeptical, calling it "discarded rubbish" or "a large dish of hash" (quoted in Washington

52), and they were equally dismissive of her magnum opus, *The Secret Doctrine* (1888). Nevertheless, Blavatsky, Olcott, and the early members of the Theosophical Society in America, Britain, and India (where the two founders moved in 1878) created a flourishing spiritual movement and publishing industry.

Theosophy posited seven interpenetrating planes, each consisting of successively more rarified matter, with the material plane of our everyday existence and perceptions being the most dense. But all matter, in the Theosophical cosmos, is essentially living and spiritual and participates by emanation in a Universal Spirit. Moreover, all life forms and worlds are going through an evolutionary process, with the lower life forms' evolution being directed by more highly evolved spiritual beings.

The Theosophical movement built upon the energies of mid-nineteenth century spiritualism and the later Victorian occult revival. It also called upon the prestige of Victorian science and thrived on the cultural controversies caused by that science. Much of its success stemmed from Blavatsky's imaginative synthesis of Western occultism and Eastern religions, especially Buddhism, and her efforts to situate the new religion as essentially an ancient science.[3] In *Isis Unveiled*, Blavatsky challenged what she saw as the narrow materialism of Darwin, Huxley, and recent science, but she also rejected the dogmas of Christianity and called for a wisdom that would unite science and religion.

In the early years of Theosophy during Blavatsky's lifetime, the modern science that most occupied the movement was, without doubt, the theory of evolution rather than Victorian discoveries in physics and chemistry.[4] While Blavatksy in *Isis Unveiled* and *Secret Doctrine* grappled in a limited way with modern physics and chemistry, she engaged much more fully with the work of alchemists, especially that of Paracelsus. Her defense of alchemical transmutation was based not upon contemporary science—though she asked of transmutation, "Is the idea so absurd as to be totally unworthy of consideration in this age of chemical discovery"? (*Isis* 1:503)—but rather upon the exalted reputation of medieval and early modern scientists and alchemists who claimed to have witnessed transmutation (1:503–504). Moreover, the major events that launched modern particle physics—the discoveries of X-rays, the electron, radiation, radium, and radioactive decay—all occurred after Blavatsky died in 1891.

If Blavatsky meant to make Theosophy a science whose ultimate goal was spiritual wisdom, her methods of scientific engagement were beginning to show their limitations within a few years after her death. Her oracular style in

The Secret Doctrine allowed her to give precise details of the religious and philosophical tenets she was amassing from Buddhism, Hinduism, and Western occult traditions, yet her characterizations of the modern science that supposedly supported such thinking were always vague. She thus seemed persuasive primarily to those who already affirmed her occult authority. She usually offered direct quotations from works by scientists sympathetic to spiritual views of science. In *Isis Unveiled,* for instance, she drew from Balfour Stewart and P. G. Tait's *Unseen Universe* (1875), a book in which two eminent figures in the development of classical thermodynamics found religious doctrine supported by the physics of energy and ether. (Victorian physics presupposed a physical, but massless, medium, the ether, through which electromagnetic waves were propagated.) And in *The Secret Doctrine,* Blavatsky drew from the work of Sir William Crookes, himself a Theosophist—and she always quoted Crookes at his most speculative.[5] While Blavatsky claimed that "Modern Science is every day drawn more into the maelstrom of Occultism" (*Secret* 1:149), her facile invocations of modern science did not offer much to convince the skeptic.

Yet after Blavatsky's death, and beginning with the wave of discoveries about radiation in the mid-1890s and beyond, the Theosophical journals augmented the work of sanitizing Blavatsky's doctrines. They acted as clearinghouses for information about the latest scientific discoveries gleaned from newspapers, scientific journals, and current science books. Notably, the Theosophical journals frequently engaged scientific writing that did not make any argument for a spiritualized science. The details of such "neutral" scientific articles and books—the mathematical formulae, statistics, references to articles in scholarly science journals—were all presented in an effort to "harden" the "facts" of Theosophical science. The scientific subjects that most caught the attention of Theosophical publications were the "new astronomy" fueled by Norman Lockyer's spectroscopic analyses, work on the nature of life (especially from a vitalist point of view), and, emphatically, the new atomic physics and chemistry. This extended from Victorian challenges to the irreducible multiplicity of Dalton's elements—Kelvin's vortex atom and Crookes's version of Prout's protyle enjoyed much discussion—to the latest work by J. J. Thomson, Rutherford, Ramsay, Soddy, and others on radioactivity. Moreover, the level of Theosophical engagement with physics and chemistry, as well as with the legacy of alchemy, increased dramatically in the late 1890s and into the early twentieth century. The frequent articles on the new physics and chemistry in the major Theosophical journals—*Lucifer, The Theosophical Review, The Theosophist,* and the *Theosophical Quarterly*—and book and pamphlet publications by the Theosophical Society Press adopted a strategy of sanitization similar to that employed by the Hermetic journals edited by A. E. Waite and Aleister Crowley, as discussed in chapter 1.

Lucifer had been founded and edited by Blavatsky in 1887, with Besant joining as coeditor in 1890. (She remained after Blavatsky's death in 1891, and with her coeditor G. R. S. Mead, she changed the name of the journal to *The Theosophical Review* in 1897.) Besant greatly intensified the journal's engagement with science after 1891. Her "On the Watch-Tower" column, which commenced in the March 1892 issue, served as a forum on news and articles from current newspapers and journals and emphatically engaged the latest discoveries of laboratory work in chemistry and physics. Beyond the regular scientific coverage in "On the Watch-Tower," Besant and Mead frequently wrote articles or published reviews of essays with titles such as "Confirmation of Theosophy by Science," "Theosophy, the Religion of Science," "Science on the Borderland," and the like. Olcott's *Theosophist* and the American journal *Theosophical Quarterly* also followed much of the science of the day, though they were less thorough in their coverage of science. In addition, books such as A. Marques's *Scientific Corroborations of Theosophy* and A. P. Sinnett's *Nature's Mysteries, And How Theosophy Illuminates Them* were published by the Theosophical Publishing House in Los Angeles and the Theosophical Publishing Society in London. Even if their interpretations of contemporary science might have surprised the scientists whose work they were citing, the authors of these works greatly intensified Theosophy's investment in the laboratory work of the scientific establishment. They did not simply proclaim gems of occult wisdom gleaned from ancient sources, as Blavatsky had primarily done.

Annie Besant intended her "Occult Chemistry" article in the November 15, 1895, issue of *Lucifer* to stake a Theosophical claim on precisely this kind of laboratory work: "It seems worth while to lay before the public a few observations made through these [astral] senses, partly because it is possible that they may suggest hypotheses useful as elucidating some scientific problems; and partly because science is advancing rapidly and will ere long be investigating some of these matters for itself, and it will then perhaps be well for the Theosophical Society if the first statement of facts that will then be accepted should have come from members of its body" (211). Without even identifying herself and Leadbeater as the "members of its body" who had conducted the experiments, or crediting Leadbeater as a coauthor, Besant—clearly understanding the scientific convention of publication establishing precedence for an experimental result—meant this first publication of preliminary results to establish precedent over scientific discoveries about subatomic physics that might occur after its publication.

Direct Perception versus Instrumentation

While electronic counting detectors played a role in early-twentieth-century atomic physics, the image tradition that Galison identifies was crucial to many of the major discoveries and interpretations of the field. To cite one particularly famous example—one that the press widely cited as modern alchemy's first successful artificial transmutation—in 1919 Rutherford bombarded nitrogen with fast alpha particles, producing a heavy isotope of oxygen. As Galison explains, Rutherford used a scintillation detector to detect the protons emitted during the experiment, but because the flashes of light produced could not tell him any of the details of the actual process, he interpreted it as one of disintegration. But when Rutherford and P. M. S. Blackett conducted the experiment using a cloud chamber to allow them to *see* the tracks of the particles, they not only discovered evidence of nitrogen's transmutation but also found that Rutherford had misinterpreted the process:

> Blackett discovered that the process was not one of disintegration, but one of "integration"; only two tracks were seen after the interaction occurred, meaning that the alpha particle was absorbed as the proton was ejected. The resulting nucleus was a heavy isotope of oxygen. Since all Rutherford could know from his scintillation experiments was that alpha particles infrequently caused nitrogen nuclei to emit protons—he could not "see" the actual interaction—he had assumed it was a disintegration process. Only the cloud chamber could provide a *visual* representation of the transmutation process itself and give physicists the chance to discover the intricacies of the exchange. (Galison 1997, 119)

But if new instruments such as the spectroscope, cloud chamber, ionization chamber, and the Dolezalek electrometer allowed Thomson, Rutherford, and others to infer the existence of subatomic particles, the limitations of those instruments were obvious. Of course, they could never allow scientists to perceive an atom, much less an electron, directly; the relationship between the body and mind of the observer and the object of observation was always essentially secondhand. Moreover, the relatively primitive nature of the instruments only allowed theories to progress so far. The advent of the cyclotron, the bubble chamber, and other instruments of high-energy physics were still years away.

Leadbeater and Besant's occult chemistry clearly participated in the privileging of visual data emerging in the physics and chemistry of the day, but they frequently claimed that their clairvoyant extension of physical sight was more accurate than scientific instruments could allow. They wrote, "we put [our observations] forward in the hope of stimulating work along this line, and of thus bringing to science, when its instruments fail it, the old, old instrument of enlarged human vision" (1908, 2).[6] And, beyond the issue of mere accuracy, the very nature of the relationship between the perceiving body and the object of perception was the central focus of their pursuit of the ultimate physical atom.

When Leadbeater wrote about "magnifying clairvoyance," the tensions between competing conceptions of the body—as instrument or as organic perceiver—were evident. He grasped for ways of articulating the experience of this magnifying clairvoyance (what nuclear physicist/New Age author Stephen Phillips has called "micro-psi vision"). In Leadbeater's book *The Chakras*, he writes as if the body were both an organic sensor and an inorganic instrument:

> The centre between the eyebrows is connected with sight in yet another way. It is through it that the power of magnification of minute physical objects is exercised. A tiny flexible tube of etheric matter is projected from the centre of it, resembling a microscopic snake with something like an eye at the end of it. This is the special organ used in that form of clairvoyance and the eye at the end of it can be extended or contracted, the effect being to change the power of magnification according to the size of the object which is being examined. (quoted in Phillips 1999, 5–6)

The faculty is described in organic terms—it is a kind of sight and is locatable on the body in a specific place adjacent to the normal physical eyes, and it is described as resembling a "snake with something like an eye at the end of it." Yet in the same paragraph, Leadbeater describes it in nonorganic terms, as if it were an instrument in a laboratory—a "flexible tube" made of ether with an "eye" whose power to magnify can be adjusted by mechanical extension or contraction. (Note even here that the "lens" one might expect on a tube has been figured as an organ.)

The human micro-psi perceiver is here a hybrid object. The site of interchange between the human and the porous material universe is itself a hybrid, one that was emerging in the cultural imagination of late-nineteenth-century modernity. That period's technological innovations, particularly the telegraph and telephone, weakened the boundaries between human minds and suggested to some the viability of occult concepts such as telepathy and communication with the dead. As Pamela Thurschwell notes,

> Teletechnologies such as the telegraph and the telephone suggested that science could help annihilate distances that separate bodies and minds from each other. When these new technologies begin suffusing the public imagination from the mid-nineteenth century on they appear to support the claims of the spiritualist mediums; talking to the dead and talking on the phone both hold out the promise of previously unimaginable contact between people. Intimacy begins to take on new, distinctively modern forms. (Thurschwell 2001, 3)

Moreover, as Laura Otis notes, some felt that wireless telegraphy validated occult claims for telepathy. Examining the relationship between explorations of organic communications systems, such as the nervous system, and telegraphy, Otis argues that

> The tendency to see a communications device as a continuation of one's own nervous system developed in the nineteenth century, not in the twentieth. As early as the 1870s, self-conscious telegraphers felt themselves merging with their networks, describing the transmission of signals from their brains, through their fingers, onto their keyboards, and then on down the line. Then, as now, sending electronic messages challenged the traditional notion of a bounded, delimited individual. (Otis 2001, 10)

Theosophical conceptions of clairvoyance were always vexed by a tension between naturalizing clairvoyance as simply a use of sense faculties that all humans possess (and can develop) versus perceiving the act as the construction of a hybrid human/nonhuman instrument, or cyborg, if you will. This uneasiness fundamentally derived from the position of the observer in relationship to the observed. In his 1899 book *Clairvoyance*, Leadbeater relentlessly searches for instruments by which to describe the act of clairvoyance. He describes, in three pages, one method of clairvoyance by astral current in terms of four different instruments: "the erection of a kind of temporary telephone though [astral matter]" (55); "polarization, by an effort of the human will, of a number of parallel lines of astral atoms reaching from the operator to the scene which he wishes to observe" (56); making "a telegraph line" (56); and "manufactur[ing] for himself a temporary astral telescope" (57). Each instrument bears its limitations, as is the case with physical instruments. An astral telegraph line is susceptible to "disarrangement or even destruction by any sufficiently strong astral current which happens to cross its path" (56), and the telescope's shortcomings "resemble the limitations of the man using a telescope on the physical plane. The experimenter, for example, has no power to shift his point of view; his telescope, so to speak, has a particular field of view which cannot be enlarged or altered; he is looking at his scene from a certain direction, and he cannot suddenly turn it all round and see how it looks from the other side" (57). The opposite faculty, "magnifying at will the minutest physical or astral particle to any desired size" (42), was described again in terms of an instrument: "as though by a microscope—though no microscope ever made or ever likely to be made possesses even a thousandth part of this psychic magnifying power" (42).[7]

Yet this astral or ethereal hybrid—the human with an ethereal microscope tube growing from his forehead, or with an astral telescope tube or telegraph wire extending from his body across space—was also given a more organic explanation. The clairvoyant was simply practicing a yogic *siddhi*, a special power attained through advanced training (in this case, "the power of making oneself large or small at will") (42). This allowed the Yogi to become enormous, to fill the whole universe and essentially be everywhere, or to become microscopically small, to perceive atoms or even subatomic particles directly by being inside or among them at the microlevel. But, as Leadbeater explains, "the alteration in size is really in the vehicle of the student's consciousness"—it is the "breadth of one's view" that changes (43). Leadbeater's Singhalese pupil Curupumullage Jinarajadasa, who would later become President of the Theosophical Society, was with Leadbeater and Besant as they astrally traveled across space to other planets (even claiming to have found four unknown planets in the solar system) and as they conducted their clairvoyant chemistry. He described the experimenters as if they were scientists in a laboratory, but scientists without the need of instruments:

> When using this method the investigator is awake and not in any form of trance. He employs his usual faculties for recording what he observes; he maps out on a piece of paper a sketch of what he sees and may describe his impressions so that a stenographer can take down his remarks. Just as a microscopist, looking into the microscope and without removing his eyes from the slide, can describe what he observes so that it can be recorded, so the clairvoyant investigator watching an atom or molecule can describe what he sees in front of him. What he sees is not subjective, in the sense that it is a creation of the imagination; it is as objective as is the paper on which I am writing this and the pen which I use. (Besant and Leadbeater 1951, 1)

The direct experience account, that of the clairvoyant investigator changing his or her perspective to the micro-size of the atom and experiencing it as if simply watching with physical eyes, ultimately won out, becoming the oft-repeated explanation used later by supporters of occult chemistry. Significantly, this interpretation emphasized the organic nature of the expanded human, conscious perceiver and ultimately strengthened the vitalist nature of Theosophical cosmology.

Theosophical Atoms and Victorian Ether Mechanics

Theosophical Atoms

But in spite of Theosophical vitalism (to which I shall return below) and the Theosophical attack on mechanistic science and philosophy, the atomic theory Besant and Leadbeater developed in *Occult Chemistry* and elsewhere was in many ways a mechanical theory involving interactions of ever-more-rarified particles and their vibrations. It adapted many assumptions of Victorian ether mechanics.

The model of the atom that Besant and Leadbeater constructed in *Occult Chemistry* claimed the existence not just of four states of physical matter—solid, liquid, gaseous, and an etheric state that some Victorian physicists were willing to see as another form or state of matter—but, in fact, of seven. They accepted solid, liquid, gaseous, and four etheric states, which they tied to the Theosophical subplanes of $Ether_1$–$Ether_4$.[8] Matter in each of these states is composed of aggregates of particles in geometrical configurations. (The chemical elements, according to Besant and Leadbeater, can be arranged into periodic groups according to the forms they share: "spike," "dumb-bell," "tetradhedron," "cube," "octahedron," "crossed bars," and "star.") As the clairvoyant chemist breaks down the walls holding the geometrical configurations of particles together, each atom dissociates into yet more basic particles specific to the etheric subplane. Finally, the ultimate physical atom (or UPA, as I shall abbreviate it), was the only particle on the E1 etheric subplane, and it existed in two forms, male and female. In Besant and Leadbeater's system, the UPA cannot be further dissociated and remain physical matter; the more rarified particles into which it would dissociate would be astral particles. The UPAs are formed of ten "whorls," each twisted as a spiral containing 1,680 turns. Each, in turn, contains seven finer whorls called "spirillae." The distinction between male and female forms of the UPA consists of the way force flows through each. Besant and Leadbeater defined the difference this way:

> In this ultimate state of physical matter two types of atoms have been observed; they are alike in everything save the direction of their

> whorls and of the force which pours through them. In the one case force pours in from the "outside," from fourth-dimensional space [the astral plane] and passing through the atom, pours into the physical world. In the second, it pours in from the physical world, and out through the atom into the "outside" again, *i.e.*, vanishes from the physical world. The one is like a spring, from which water bubbles out; the other is like a hole, into which water disappears. (Besant and Leadbeater 1908, 5)

More on this force and the gendering of UPAs in a moment.

Besant and Leadbeater based much of this understanding of physics on the ether hypothesis that was commonly accepted until Einstein and others rejected it in the early twentieth century. As Leadbeater wrote in *Clairvoyance*, "We are living all the while surrounded by a vast sea of mingled air and ether, the latter interpenetrating the former, as it does all physical matter; and it is chiefly by means of vibrations in that vast sea of matter that impressions reach us from the outside" (1899, 8). But this sense of a rarified ether pervading the physical world and vibrating at different frequencies was only the tip of the iceberg. In a 1907 essay included in the first edition of *Occult Chemistry* and in all subsequent editions, Leadbeater had argued that a universal medium called "koilon" contained bubbles, and that, indeed, matter consisted of this absence of koilon. (Koilon was very much like the ether of ether physics—but, as we have seen, Besant and Leadbeater required the ether to be particles.) In 1899, physics professor John Poynting of Birmingham argued before the British Association that "we dislike discontinuity and we think of an underlying identity." He suggested that matter was "mere loci of particular types of motion in this frictionless fluid.... As we watch the weaving of the garment of Nature, we resolve it in our imagination into threads of ether spangled over with beads of matter. We look still closer, and the beads of matter vanish; they are mere knots and loops in the threads of ether" (quoted in Keller 1983, 20–21). In a passage remarkably similar to the necklace imagery and conception of the etheric nature of matter Poynting proposed, Leadbeater observed of the spirillae of the UPA that they can be unwound "till the seven sets of spirillae are all unwound, and we have a huge circle of the tiniest imaginable dots, like pearls threaded on an invisible string. These dots are so inconceivably small that many millions of them are needed to make one ultimate physical atom" (Besant and Leadbeater 1908, ii).

But Besant and Leadbeater created an even more complex system of atoms. The schema extended to all seven planes posited by Theosophy. Leadbeater, in his *Textbook of Theosophy*, had schematized the seven planes of existence laid out in Theosophical teaching as:

> the first world, a "divine world" with which humans had as yet no direct contact;
> a second "monadic" world containing the "Sparks of divine Life," also beyond the reach of the clairvoyant;
> a third "spiritual world";
> a fourth "intuitional world," or "buddhic plane," from which "come the highest intuitions";
> a fifth "mental world," from whose matter "is built the mind of man";
> a sixth "emotional or astral world," thus named "because the emotions of man cause undulations in its matter"—and called "astral," they wrote, by "medieval alchemists, because its matter is starry or shining as compared to that of the denser world";
> and, finally, the seventh or "physical" world, "composed of the type of matter which we see all around us" (1912, 23).

Leadbeater and Besant both emphasized in their writings that these worlds were co-extensive with one another, that they were merely composed of different, increasingly rarified, forms of matter. And as Besant emphasized in *The Ancient Wisdom* (1897), her major contribution to making a working system from the vast sprawl of Blavatsky's tomes, humans have existences in these other planes. Each person possesses, for instance, an astral body that coexists with the physical one. The senses appropriate to these other states of matter, however, were largely underdeveloped.

Victorian Ether Physics

Ether theories had been prominent since Newton posited ether to explain the effects of gravity, but ether physics came into its own in the early nineteenth century when Thomas Young demonstrated the wave properties of light.[9] Across the century, an invisible continuous substance called ether was used to explain how waves could be transmitted through space, and by the 1870s, as James Clerk Maxwell unified electricity and magnetism into a single field theory and developed an electromagnetic theory of light, the varieties of ether postulated to carry waves of various energies had been reduced to a single ether.[10] Yet such a substance remained undetectable, even if, in theory, experiments should have been possible to detect its presence.[11]

The nature of the ether was a source of wide conjecture. As Young himself had put it, "the luminiferous ether pervades the substance of all material bodies with little or no resistance, as freely perhaps as the wind passes through a grove of trees" (quoted in Clarke 1996, 166). The ether must be an extremely rarified and completely continuous, virtually frictionless, substance pervading all matter, yet it must also have a density exceeding that of steel. Indeed, as the eminent scientist Sir Oliver Lodge pointed out in his classic exposition, *The Ether of Space* (1909), "Undoubtedly, the ether belongs to the material or physical universe, but it is not ordinary matter. I should prefer to say it is not 'matter' at all. It must be the substance or substratum or material of which matter is composed, but it would be confusing and inconvenient not to be able to discriminate between matter on the one hand and ether on the other" (117).

Kelvin's Vortex Atom

The relationship of ether to "normal" matter was a common line of inquiry in Victorian and early twentieth-century physics. As Alex Keller has shown, some Victorian physicists attempted to break down the matter/ether duality (20–22). As far back as 1867, Kelvin had introduced an atomic theory based not upon "regular" atoms swimming in the ether but upon the assumption that the atoms themselves were simply vortex rings in the ether. After reading Hermann von Helmholtz's theories of vortex motion in a frictionless liquid and witnessing Edinburgh professor Peter Tait's demonstrations of kinetic interactions between two smoke rings, Kelvin argued for "a theory of elastic solids and liquids [based] on the dynamics of... closely-packed vortex atoms" (Thomson 1867, 2–3). Kelvin theorized that "the vortex atom has perfectly definite fundamental modes of vibration, depending solely on that motion the existence of which constitutes it" (4), and went on to give a mathematical elaboration of the mechanics of such motions. As Keller relates it, "While watching Tait's demonstration in 1867, his friend Kelvin was suddenly struck with the thought that if such rings exist in the ether, they 'might well be called atoms.' They would be indivisible and eternal, ever of the same shape and volume; they would move forward in a straight line; and they could well vibrate like the oval smoke rings, as theory suggested. If tied or looped, they could account for all the connections and combinations of matter, whereby different elements come together to form stable molecules" (Keller 21). Kelvin even argued that the definite vibrations of linked vortices could explain the exact results of spectral analysis (Russell 1912, 61).

Such a hydrodynamic explanation of matter—which dispensed with the assumption, going back at least as far as Leucippus and Democritus, that atoms were impenetrable hard particles of matter—was tantalizing for Victorian energy physicists. Even when the vortex theory of the atom became increasingly untenable (Larmor, for instance, argued that it could not account for electric charge), Kelvin went on to elaborate other ether theories of atoms.[12] Bringing ether theory in line with the recent discovery of the electron, Lodge opined that an electron was simply a "strain centre" or perhaps a "singularity" in the ether (Lodge 1909, 111). And to support his argument that "ether is being found to constitute matter," Lodge quoted J. J. Thomson, who discovered the electron: "all mass is mass of the ether; all momentum, momentum of the ether; and all kinetic energy, kinetic energy of the ether" (116).

Mechanical ether theories of the atom, and Kelvin's vortex theory in particular, likewise influenced Theosophists like Besant and Leadbeater. The latter wrote, "As we study these complex arrangements, we realise the truth of the old Platonic idea that the Logos geometrises: and we recall H. P. Blavatsky's statement that nature ever builds by form and numbers" (1908, 2). As we have seen, their atomic theory was based upon the geometrical shapes assumed by vibrating strands of particles. But the mechanical properties of the vortex atom, from Kelvin's scheme, were clearly paramount in their understanding. Besant noted that each plane's atom, "in its turn, sets up a vortex in the coarsest aggregations of its own plane, and, with these coarsest aggregations as a limiting wall, becomes the finest unit of spirit-matter, or atom, of the [next] plane" (1906, 43).

But these ether theories often spurred even leading scientists into religious speculation. Like Tait and Stewart in 1875 and many Theosophists after 1877, Lodge was quick to ascribe spiritual properties to the ether. Like Crookes, Lodge had been President of the Society for Psychical Research, and he used his professional reputation to argue for the reality of telepathy, spirit mediums, and other such phenomena. Indeed, his melding of the worlds of physics and psychics was based on the ever-mysterious ether, and he clung to the ether hypothesis well into the 1930s, years after it had been abandoned by most physicists. Lodge conceived of life and consciousness in terms of ethereal condensation. Moreover, as he put it in *The Ether of Space*, "If any one thinks that the ether, with all its massiveness and energy, has probably no psychical significance, I find myself unable to agree with him" (123).

Crookes's Protyle

Crookes, Lodge's fellow scientist and psychic investigator, contributed an alchemically inflected ether/matter theory that gained wide acceptance amongst Theosophists and helped lay the groundwork for Besant and Leadbeater's occult chemistry. On February 18, 1887, some twenty years after Kelvin's vortex atom address to the Royal Society of Edinburgh, Crookes delivered a Friday evening lecture to the Royal Institution in which he propounded what he proclaimed to be "heretical" views on the nature of the elements, arguing against the idea that the chemical elements were "absolutely simple, incapable of transmutation or decomposition, each a kind of barrier behind which we could not penetrate" (Crookes 1887, 1).[13] Using spectroscopic analysis and Kelvin's cosmological theories, and appropriating the discourse of Darwinian evolutionary theory, Crookes argued, "The analogy of these elements with the organic radicles [sic], and still more with living organisms, constrains us to suspect that they are compound bodies, springing from a process of evolution" (27). Crookes hoped "that chemistry, like biology, may find its Darwin" (27). His basic idea appealed greatly to Hermetic alchemists and Theosophists alike. Though Prout had coined the term "protyle" in 1816 and laid the seeds for Crookes's theory, Crookes invoked alchemist Roger Bacon's *De Arte Chymiæ* for the term. He posited a "primal matter" (like the alchemist's *prima materia*) he called the "protyle," which "existed anterior to our elements, before matter as we now have it" (17). Crookes argued that the protyle condensed and cooled, forming vortex rings (clearly based on Kelvin's speculations) and evidencing "that universal formative principle in nature which I suggest first made itself manifest in the condensation of protyle into atomic matter" (17). Crookes suggested that the period of vortex formation, condensation, and cooling created the chemical atoms, which were the results of two forms of vibrating energy—one acting vertically, and the other horizontally, to create a pendulum effect (22). Crookes drew a periodic table, based on a pendulum motion, that Leadbeater and Besant adopted in *Occult Chemistry*. Such a scheme, Crookes concluded, could explain the elements, even positing some substances as "missing links" in the evolutionary scheme, and he argued that his pendulum diagram could predict the possibility of elements of negative atomic weight. Noting that Helmholtz viewed electricity as "probably as atomic as matter," Crookes then asked, "is electricity one of the negative elements? And the luminiferous ether another? Matter, as we now know it, does not here exist; and the forms of energy which are apparent in the motions of matter are as yet only latent possibilities" (27). Crookes's theory of the protyle not only appeared in much Theosophical and Hermetic writing to support the alchemical conception of the "prima materia," but it also seemed to give scientific validity directly to the Theosophical conceptions of extremely rarified, highly vibratory particles forming increasingly less subtle compounds. Crookes's ether, as in Besant and Leadbeater's cosmology, is a form of matter. It is more subtle than the chemical elements, but like the elements, it derives from more primal particles.

I want to emphasize, above all, that these theories of matter as stresses, strains, singularities, or vortices of ether, were mechanical (and even hydrodynamic) theories. When scientists such as Crookes and Lodge, and Theosophists such as Besant and Leadbeater, melded physics with spiritual and psychic forces via theories of the ether (and the additional particles that Theosophy added to the equation), they were lending scientific credibility to spiritual ideas. Paradoxically, in their critique of scientific materialism, they asserted a mechanical theory of spirituality. Theosophy thus required a form of vitalism to counterbalance the mechanistic tendencies of its physics.

Theosophical Vitalism and the Sexed Subatomic World

While Theosophical science, following Besant and Leadbeater's purported direct perceptions of the mechanical interactions among subatomic particles, built up a particle theory of their entire occult system, they nevertheless situated the dynamics of UPAs squarely in the evolutionary vitalist traditions that Blavatsky had appropriated as far back as *Isis Unveiled*. Vitalism, in all its permutations, was prevalent from the eighteenth century through the early twentieth century. As Bruce Clarke puts it, "The doctrine of vitalism states that in the world at large the forces that move matter about and the forces that produce and maintain living beings are completely different" (1996, 28). Moreover, just as Besant and Leadbeater's spiritual system drew heavily from Victorian ether mechanics, the doctrine of vitalism arose as a reaction against Newtonian mechanics, but depended upon Newtonian paradigms for its vocabulary and its positing of another power, the "life force," to explain the nature of living things. Vitalism itself emerged as an effort to explain life in terms of chemistry. As Clarke explains:

> Vitalism occupied the epistemological gap in life science that began to close definitively only with the emergence in molecular genetics of a theory that finally clarified the mechanisms that sorted and ordered material elements into living organisms, that produced the invariant replication of species, and that enabled the retention of evolutionary variations as they randomly arose. The doctrine of the life force began with the reasonable idea that the new chemistry of its day could fill the gap in biological knowledge.... So vitalism emerged as a scientific alternative to mechanistic reductionism, drawing its initial sustenance from early modern chemistry at a time when chemistry rather than physics was the main field in which the phenomena of electricity and magnetism were being investigated. (30)

Vitalism and evolutionary thinking became linked in a major late-nineteenth- and early twentieth-century current, influencing modernists such as Dora Marsden and D. H. Lawrence. While the French philosopher Henri Bergson (especially with the publication of *Creative Evolution* in 1907) became perhaps the most significant proponent of evolutionary vitalism at the turn of the century, Clarke has shown that the linkage between vitalism and evolution had already begun in the 1870s, and that Blavatsky directly based much of her Theosophical critique of Darwin upon a kind of theological evolutionary vitalism.

Blavatsky's main polemical purpose in *Isis Unveiled* was to undermine the materialist nature of Darwinian evolution and to build a *spiritual* system based upon an evolutionary theory revamped to include the life force and spiritual goals. She defined the terms of her argument by articulating an "emanationist" perspective against an orthodox "evolutionist" interpretation:

> EVOLUTION.—The development of higher orders of animals from the lower. Modern, or so-called *exact* science, holds but to a one-sided physical evolution, prudently avoiding and ignoring the higher or spiritual evolution, which would force our contemporaries to confess the superiority of the ancient philosophers and psychologists over themselves. The ancient sages, ascending to the UNKNOWABLE, made their starting-point from the first manifestation of the unseen, the unavoidable, and from a strict logical reasoning, the absolute necessary creative Being, the Demiurgos of the universe. Evolution began with them from pure spirit, which descending lower and lower down, assumed at last a visible and comprehensible form, and became matter. Arrived at this point, they speculated in the Darwinian method, but on a far more large and comprehensive basis.... In Evolution, as it is now beginning to be understood, there is supposed to be in all matter an impulse to take on a higher form.... The controversy between the followers of this school and the Emanationists may be briefly stated thus: The Evolutionist stops all inquiry at the borders of "the Unknowable"; the Emanationist believes that nothing can be evolved—or, as the word means, unwombed or born—except it has first been involved, thus indicating that life is from a spiritual potency above the whole. (1884, 1:xxx–xxxii)

Across her work from *Isis Unveiled* through *The Secret Doctrine,* Blavatsky posited a scheme of spiritual evolution not only of mankind but also of the inanimate world and the animal and vegetable kingdoms, all of which are pervaded by a life force. She chose a Tibetan word, "Fohat," to name this life force. Fohat was deeply indebted to the idea that electricity and magnetism must bear some relationship to the life force—assumptions Clarke and others have traced in eighteenth- and nineteenth-century vitalist chemistry.[14] In *The Secret Doctrine* Blavatsky had argued that the Fohat is "the 'bridge' by which the Ideas existing in the Divine Thought are impressed on Cosmic Substance as the Laws of Nature. Fohat is thus the dynamic energy of Cosmic Ideation; or, regarded from the other side, it is the intelligent medium, the guiding power of all manifestation, the Thought Divine transmitted and made manifest ... Fohat ... is the mysterious link between Mind and Matter, the animating principle electrifying every atom into life" (1:44).

Leadbeater drew Blavatsky's concept of Fohat into the atomic theory he and Besant were elaborating, and he clarified the origin of the life force that is instilled in all matter, animate and inanimate—and, in fact, composes all matter. The Deity pours his spirit into the universe, like "the blowing of mighty breath," and this breath "has formed within this aether an incalculable number of tiny bubbles, and these bubbles are the ultimate atoms of which what we call matter is composed. They are not the atoms of the chemist, nor even the ultimate atoms of the physical world" (1912, 18–19). These are the "dots" that make up the spirillae discussed above. Then the Solar Deity (a lesser being than the Deity) makes the solar system by exerting upon it a force, "gathering together the bubbles into ever more and more complex aggregations, and producing in this way seven gigantic interpenetrating worlds of matter of different degrees of density, all concentric and all occupying the same space" (19). The evolution of life is then a product of this Solar Deity's infusion of life force.

Each of the beings existing in the different planes has a fully developed set of sense faculties by which they apprehend only the forms of matter on that plane,[15] but, as Besant and Leadbeater argued, beings can develop the sense faculties appropriate to other planes. These leading Theosophists tended to emphasize the voluptuousness of these other senses. As Besant noted in her discussion of the development of sense organs in *The Ancient Wisdom*, "Even now there are myriads of vibrations pulsing around us in physical nature from the knowledge of which we are shut out because of the inability of our physical vehicle to receive and vibrate in accord with them. Unimaginable beauties, exquisite sounds, delicate subtleties, touch the walls of our prison house and pass on unheeded" (1897, 53). Leadbeater gushed that "one curious and very beautiful novelty brought to his notice by the development of this [astral] vision would be the existence of other and entirely different colors beyond the limits of the ordinarily visible spectrum, the ultra-red and ultra-violet rays which science has discovered by other means being plainly perceptible to astral sight"

(1918, 23–24). The experience of the subatomic world of UPAs is one of almost sensory overload: "In the three whorls flow currents of different electricities; the seven vibrate in response to etheric waves of all kinds—to sound, light, heat, etc.; they show the seven colors of the spectrum; give out the seven sounds of the natural scale; respond in a variety of ways to physical vibration—flashing, singing, pulsing bodies, they move incessantly, inconceivably beautiful and brilliant" (1908, 7).

The UPA itself is shaped like the Western symbol for the heart (a "heart-like form" [Besant and Leadbeater 1908, 5]), and in the schematic drawings of the different configurations of UPAs, they are drawn explicitly in a heart shape and are described as having "a regular pulsation, a contraction and expansion, like the pulsation of the heart" (1908, 7). Moreover, the movements and vibrations of UPAs are frequently described in anthropomorphic terms: The UPA "sings" and it "dances up and down, flings itself wildly from side to side, performs the most astonishing and rapid gyrations" (7). The molecules composed of UPAs "turn head over heels and gyrate in endless ways" (9) and are contained in their shapes by "cell-walls" (9).

The sexing of UPAs as male and female, with the traditional positive/negative characterization of the genders, makes the essence of matter a kind of subatomic sexual intercourse. Opposites attract and infuse each other with lines of life force pulsing in and out of them. Indeed, "contraception" at the subatomic level would have catastrophic consequences: The UPA

> is formed by the flow of the life-force and vanishes with its ebb. When this force arises in "space"—the apparent void which must be filled with substance of some kind, of inconceivable tenuity—atoms appear; if this be artificially stopped for a single atom, the atom disappears; there is nothing left. Presumably were that flow checked but for an instant, the whole physical world would vanish, as a cloud melts away in the empyrean. It is only the persistence of that flow which maintains the physical basis of the universe. (Besant and Leadbeater 1908, 5–6)

Such a positive/negative flow of life force, stemming from electro-vitalism, became increasingly gendered during this period as it moved into medical discussions of gender difference (see Clarke 31).

Such a gendering and polarization of the subatomic world confirmed major Theosophical tenets about the physical and spiritual nature of man. As Joy Dixon has shown, Blavatsky envisioned the "highest Deity" as without sex or form, but it did embrace polarities: "As this Absolute Spirit manifested itself in the universe, it created itself as a series of oppositions: positive versus negative, spirit versus matter, masculinity versus femininity. This complex cosmic sexual order was at once symbolic and actual.... Thus, the generation of the cosmos could be seen as both a reflection and a figuration of more mundane forms of (hetero)sexual generation" (Dixon 1997, 417). The Theosophical scheme, as Blavatsky drew it together, involved humans' only gradually becoming sexed (having developed from asexuality to androgyny or bisexuality, and then to heterosexuality) as the spirit manifested itself in the world of matter. Dixon notes, "Physical, sexual, intellectual, and spiritual development were here conflated: in order for humanity to come to true self-consciousness, it was necessary that it descend from the spiritual into the physical and material world. Entangled in its 'garment of flesh,' or 'coat of skin,' the Spirit—itself sexless and unconditioned—was increasingly identified with its physical form" (Dixon 418).

While Theosophy has often been seen as preoccupied with spiritualizing the body, and Blavatksy herself had exclaimed that "The absolutely spiritual Man is... entirely disconnected from sex" (quoted in Dixon 418), a generative and sexed universe was key to much Theosophical writing. Besant herself gave up her strong advocacy of birth control when she entered the Theosophical Society, because of its emphasis on procreative sex (Dixon 432). Moreover, as Dixon has persuasively argued, Besant and Leadbeater's version of Theosophy (referred to as "neo-Theosophy" by some critics), which insisted on tracing past lives in the Theosophical system of reincarnation, involved members in a complicated lattice of past lives of different genders. It even came to participate in sexological discussions of gender and sexual orientation, exploring "intermediate genders" and offering an alternative to Freud's account of psychosexual dynamics. As Dixon puts it, "By locating these relationships [from a long series of past lives] not only in distant times but also in distant places, these writers created an imaginary space in which the boundaries imposed by bourgeois norms could be transgressed with apparent impunity" (427). She adds, "Where sexologists tended to conflate gender identity and sexual identity, the experiences of their theosophical readers pointed to the inadequacies of such an analysis" (428). Yet Dixon observes the gender essentialism of Theosophical reincarnation accounts:

> Stories of past lives actually strengthened, even as they subverted, the power of the binary oppositions of man and woman, masculine and feminine. These binary oppositions were central to the theosophical cosmogony. As Blavatsky had argued in *The Secret Doctrine*, all manifestation involved duality, and the opposition between masculine and feminine was among the most basic of dualities. Theos-

ophists recuperated separate spheres ideology on many levels: by viewing the sexed physical body as a discipline, by detailing the specifically masculine and feminine lessons to be gained through many lives, by emphasizing—as Annie Besant did—that sexual difference functioned as a "device for the better development of complementary qualities, difficulty." (Dixon 431)

The sexing of the subatomic world, and Besant and Leadbeater's frequent descriptions of it in bodily metaphors, served to reinforce the vitalism that undergirded what was otherwise a mechanical system of particle interactions. As Hermeticists might argue, the interactions of the physical world mirrored the workings of the spiritual world. Besant and Leadbeater's efforts to create an experimental science of particle interactions required these biological, vital metaphors in order to strengthen the role of the human mind and soul and the life force of a deity in a world of particle configurations—in many ways the very task that spiritual alchemy had set for itself in the Hermetic imagination, as we saw in chapter 1.

Spiritual Alchemy and Radioactivity

Leadbeater and Besant claimed that their clairvoyant chemistry was based upon the practice of a yogic *siddhi* and that this power was a form of astral vision.[16] But their powers extended beyond passive viewing of minute particles. Like the spiritual alchemy that Theosophists and Hermeticist followers of Atwood's *Suggestive Enquiry* espoused, in which the purified alchemist could transmute simply with the mind rather than with retorts and furnaces, Besant and Leadbeater's occult chemistry also consisted of an active breaking down and purifying/simplifying of matter. As they put it, "The method by which these four etheric substates were studied consisted in taking what is called by chemists an atom of an element and breaking it up, time after time, until what proved to be the ultimate physical unit was reached" (Besant and Leadbeater 1951, 10). Each breaking up of a complex configuration lead to rearrangements and new groupings of ever more rarified particles until, like the alchemist finally reaching the *prima materia*, Besant and Leadbeater had reached the UPA.[17]

There were a few disagreeable facts to sidestep. Leadbeater had developed his clairvoyance in only forty-two days (Phillips 1999, 5) rather than in a lifetime of study and discipline, and, as Washington puts it, Besant's "hitherto limited psychic gifts had expanded overnight as a result of meeting Leadbeater"

(Washington 120). Moreover, Besant and Leadbeater, who had initially worked individually on their clairvoyant explorations of the elements, had to work together because they kept seeing the elements differently. (They explained these discrepancies by asserting that Besant had been viewing the elements sideways, while Leadbeater had viewed them from the top [Tillett 1982, 94].) Still, Besant and Leadbeater's clairvoyant powers and spiritual alchemy—and the vitalist particle cosmology that undergirded them—were given increasing scientific justification in the Theosophical journals as Theosophists could augment the mysterious powers of the ether from Victorian physics with the new atomic physics of radioactivity.

Indeed, the Theosophical infusion of matter with life, and the ability of life force and will to effect the changes in matter demanded by spiritual alchemy and occult chemistry, seemed to find some support from the newly discovered phenomenon of radiation. Besant's "On the Watch-Tower" column, for instance, noted with excitement an article on the origin of life by Butler Burke published in the *Daily Chronicle* in 1905. There, Burke noted that radium may be "that state of matter that separates, or perhaps unites, the organic and the inorganic worlds," and that radioactivity "endows matter with some of the properties of organic matter" (quoted in [Besant] 1905a, 481).

The combination of the ether and the newly discovered radioactivity seemed to virtually every Theosophist writing on chemistry and physics a confirmation of all of the occult "sciences" espoused by Theosophy. As one Theosophist, Fio Hara, put it in an article on "The Advance of Science Towards Occult Teachings" in the February 1906 *Theosophical Review*,

> To take radio-activity alone ... perhaps there is no discovery of modern times which has so disorganized the fertile but by no means plastic brain and imagination of the workers in physical science as this bomb which overthrew with a mighty force all current and reputable theories of the constitution of Matter and its inherent quality. It was the assumption that Matter existed alone in the dense ponderable condition, which we have been told by generations of scientists is its main characteristic, that caused them to fabricate the Mechanical Theory of Nature. (550)

Hara argued, "To radium we owe much, for it paved the way for patient investigations which absolutely revolutionized the world's ideas as regards the working of subtle forces, hitherto postulated but by a few brave pioneers in Nature's workshop and unacceptable to the rest" (551). In a move that by now should be familiar, Hara praised J. J. Thomson's and Larmor's research into radium for suggesting that radioactive emissions (which they saw as electrons) did not behave like normal matter. Hara saw the new ambiguous state of seemingly massless or fluctuating mass matter as evidence of Theosophical claims about subtle occult particles and energies. He then saw further scientific confirmation of Besant and Leadbeater's observations into atomic structure in a current science book by W. C. D. Whetham, FRS, called *Recent Development of Physical Science*. In it, the author (no doubt following in the footsteps of Kelvin and others) espoused a theory of matter as "a persistent strain-form flitting through a universal sea of ether" and questioned whether there might be even more subtle forms of matter (552–53).

The Theosophical journals were absolutely jubilant, in fact, over the details emerging about radium in the early twentieth century. Dedicating many columns to the "miracle of radium" and "revolutionary radium," Theosophists saw radium as a key to occult powers. Just as the Hermetic alchemists and scientists involved in the Alchemical Society had seen radioactive decay as confirming the possibility of alchemical transmutation, S. R. in "The Progress of Radium" followed Rutherford's work in *The Philosophical Magazine* on radium and uranium transformations—and argued the connection to alchemy (S. R. 1906).[18] The Theosophical magazines assiduously followed mainstream scientists, such as Ramsay and others, who claimed that the new theories of matter based upon radioactivity lent credence to alchemical visions of matter.[19]

The recently discovered powerful energies of radioactivity, gleaned from the writings of Rutherford and others, even suggested to some Theosophists the source of all yogic powers: "Is it possible that by turning his thoughts inward the Yogî obtains some control of these forces? If so, his powers may become of the same order as that said to be possessed by 'Faith,' which we are told is able to remove mountains and cast them into the sea? It is well, perhaps, that the secret of these forces is so carefully kept" (G. E. S. 1905, 519). Such an explanation of yogic powers was espoused by Besant and Leadbeater as they explained clairvoyance, the matter-manipulating powers of spiritual alchemy, and the mind/particle interactions of astral faculties.

Instrumentation and the Rhetorical Quandary of Occult Chemistry

In *Science in Action*, Bruno Latour defines an instrument or inscription device as "any set-up, no matter what its size, nature and cost, that provides a visual display of any sort in a scientific text" (1987, 68). Instruments, he argues, provide an "other world just beneath the text"—a world that is "invisible as long as there is no controversy" (69). Both the instruments and the visual displays they produce are rhetorical tools to persuade, to strengthen a fact, in Latour's analysis: "Going from the paper to the laboratory is going from an array of rhetorical resources to a set of new resources devised in such a way as to provide the literature with its most powerful tool: the visual display" (67). What would it take to challenge a scientist's findings, to undermine the persuasiveness of the visual image—the chart or graph or photo that encapsulates his interpretation of his experiment? Going to a library and looking at other books or articles will not suffice, Latour notes. One would need to be able to acquire the laboratory space and all the requisite instruments, and the technicians to use them, even to begin to refute a claim. Instruments and visual displays thus serve very powerful rhetorical ends. They are integral parts of the networks of actors scientists enlist to create and strengthen a "fact."

So what did Besant and Leadbeater accomplish by becoming the instruments of their own experiments? In many ways they played the game of scientific knowledge production astutely. They produced compelling and clear visuals: they drew the particle configurations they observed *as* they observed them, and they enlisted colleagues and artists to produce them in the most legible and impressive fashion. They cited scientific work on the subject by the well-respected Sir William Crookes and showed how their work related to his conception of the table of periodic elements. They clearly worked within the frameworks of ether physics that the Victorian period had provided for them. They obtained most of the requisite materials for their work, samples of the elements and compounds, either from Crookes or from the mineralogical museum in Dresden. They were precise in their mathematical calculations (of atomic weights, for instance). And they frequently called, in their writings, for the very thing that science required: reproducibility of results.

They also carefully grafted their concepts onto scientifically popular notions of their era. The basic ideas of the Theosophical conception of the atom, as we have seen, had already been propounded by Victorian scientists of great standing (understandings of atoms as vibratory were common, and Kelvin's vortex atom and Prout's and Crookes's theories of the protyle were obvious influences on the findings of Besant and Leadbeater). The Theosophical vision of interpenetrating realms of matter ultimately was still grounded in the ether physics that had emerged with Newton and did not fully dissipate (even with Einstein's 1905 assault upon it) until discoveries of the 1920s made the ether hypothesis unnecessary. Those concepts were in no need of sanitization.

Moreover, the larger vision of further states of increasingly rarified matter beyond even the ether—the nature of the other planes in Theosophy—and, above all, the *mode* of perceiving them, *if* accepted from the experimental data, rhetorically strengthened the persuasiveness of the spiritual system based upon them, including the Theosophical conceptions of reincarnation, astral states, and the nature of the soul and body. By taking the seemingly small step of modifying a current strand of fundamental particle theory, therefore, Besant and Leadbeater helped generate the "scientific" basis for the entire Theosophical system. Indeed, the move to posit the mind and body as the perceiving instrument, a radical intervention into sensory issues of instrumentation, was even more important than the claims about the nature of fundamental particles: If the body *can* perceive in this way, Theosophical physics *must* be scientifically correct. While scientific methods had been used to test the legitimacy of occult phenomena—the Society for Psychical Research, for example, used them to probe séances and other-worldly manifestations—occult chemistry represents a major shift. In it, the occult body was used to conduct scientific research on non-occult topics.

Yet it is on the issues of reproducibility and instrumentation that *Occult Chemistry* failed to persuade, at least outside of Theosophical circles and the small group of scientists in recent years who have been willing to work entirely at the level of theory. Besant and Leadbeater could move beyond older models of science, which based themselves upon deductions from revealed principles (alchemical or scientific deductions from the writings of the Hermetic tradition, for instance, or from the revelations of H. P. Blavatsky), by turning to experimentation. Not surprisingly, their form of experimentation did not admit of reproducibility. In spite of efforts by Stephen Phillips to conduct blind trials using a Buddhist clairvoyant to confirm Besant and Leadbeater's micro-psi visions (1996, 48), direct experience is neither convincingly verifiable nor falsifiable.

Yet the lure of a sensorially accessible subatomic world has far outlived the ether physics upon which it was based, and the advent of quark theory in the 1960s and string and super-string theory in the 1980s led occult-minded scientists to reassert the accuracy of Besant and Leadbeater's clairvoyant chemistry. Two academically trained scientists published books in 1980 and 1982 defending Besant and Leadbeater's *Occult Chemistry* research. E. Lester Smith, Fellow of the Royal Society, discoverer of Vitamin B12 in 1948, and Head of the Biochemistry Department at Glaxo Labs until 1967, and Stephen Phillips, who graduated with a degree in theoretical physics from Cambridge and a PhD from the University of California, believe that Besant and Leadbeater's insights correlated with later knowledge about the elements the Theosophists claimed to find and agreed in some measure with quark theory. As recently as 1999, Phillips published work attempting to align *Occult Chemistry*'s findings with more recent super-string theory. All of these books, and

Phillips's detailed and scientifically sophisticated defenses of Besant and Leadbeater's UPAs—which Phillips renames "micro-psi atoms"—attempt to fit the findings of *Occult Chemistry* into frameworks of quantum physics.[20] Phillips's work in the late 1970s and early 1980s on micro-psi atoms as subquark groupings gave way in the 1990s to his arguments that *Occult Chemistry* accurately predicted features of super-string theory.[21] Neither Smith nor Phillips addresses the fact that most of *Occult Chemistry*'s conceptual framework was based upon ether physics, which was virtually universally discounted by the 1920s. Smith still speaks in terms of the ether, invoking the Theosophical conception of it, and Phillips largely ignores the issue and simply works with modern scientific concepts such as the Higgs field, quarks, strings, and the like.

Phillips's entire argument, across the more than twenty years during which he has worked on *Occult Chemistry*, is that Besant and Leadbeater must have been right—not hallucinating, not fabricating their findings—because their research correlates with that of sciences that did not yet exist when they wrote *Occult Chemistry*. This correlation, for Phillips, seems to offer unprecedented, unassailable proof of paranormal powers:

> A problem facing general acceptance of paranormal phenomena by scientists is that, as many of them believe psychic abilities to violate well-established laws of nature or to contradict presuppositions of science, those who are more skeptical will always find it easier to doubt the honesty of the researcher reporting such controversial phenomena than to accept what seems incontestable evidence for their occurrence. What, however, if a psychic had claimed to see objects so small that science then neither knew anything about them nor possessed the technological capability to study these things? ... Demonstrating knowledge of some supersensory aspect of the world that is confirmed by advances in science many years later is, arguably, the most convincing type of ESP because this circumstance permits the skeptic no room for doubt or rational explanation if the correlations between scientific facts and the psychic's observations are so numerous and precise as to make the possibility of lucky guessing improbable in the extreme. (1996, xi–xii)

Phillips believed he had found such an instance in *Occult Chemistry*—and that it even provided evidence that quarks were not fundamental particles. Yet in this boundary skirmish between physics and parapsychology over the subatomic world, Phillips, Smith, and Besant and Leadbeater ultimately will not persuade the scientific world. The boundaries between occultism and parapsychology are partially drawn around issues of instrumentation and experimental protocols, and, unlike in the meetings of the Alchemical Society, there was not much border crossing happening from the scientists' direction. Phillips complains:

> some scientists will prefer to... simply [ignore] the challenge to materialistic science posed by the observations of Besant & Leadbeater. Such an example was Professor F. W. Aston, inventor of the mass spectrograph. When told in 1943 by their colleague Jinarajadasa that they had published in 1908 their discovery by psychic means of the neon-22 isotope six years before Frederick Soddy invented the name of "isotopes" and twelve years before he himself separated atoms of neon-20 and neon-22 with his mass spectrograph, Aston replied that he was not interested in Theosophy! One might have expected more curiosity to be displayed by the scientist, even though he no doubt did not accept Jinarajadasa's claim that Besant & Leadbeater had priority in discovering the neon-22 isotope. (1999, 240)

Of course Phillips is correct to point out, as he does here, that even decorated scientists can unscientifically foreclose areas of investigation simply because of their own prejudices. Yet what explains the reluctance of scientists to affirm clairvoyant chemistry? What Phillips fails to take into account is the rhetorical persuasiveness of the mass spectroscope. Science persuades on the basis of instruments and the visual displays they help create and on the reproducibility of experimental data from one similarly equipped laboratory to another. Individualized direct perception simply cannot match the rhetorical power of the modern laboratory.

The Science Group of the Theosophical Society had an Occult Chemistry Subgroup that published further work in 1934 in *The Field of Occult Chemistry*, and Geoffrey Hodson, a clairvoyant who had been part of that Science Group in the 1920s, worked with D. D. Lyness in Australia in 1958–59 to further the experiments (Hodson even picked up on the original language of *Occult Chemistry* during his observations, noting that the particle he was viewing was "pulsing" "like a heart beat" (quoted in Smith 1982, 70). Phillips himself has worked with a Buddhist clairvoyant in blind trials to try to provide experimental rigor to occult observations. Despite all this, occult chemistry can never persuade the scientific world, because its defense relies entirely upon resemblance and correlation, not upon the kind of rhetorical persuasion that Latour notes in actual reproducible laboratory work. Smith seemed to recognize this. After spending more than one hundred pages defending *Occult Chemistry* as science, he notes that:

There *is* an alternative to the notions of materialistic physicists, which may have more appeal for theosophists, and which should eventually prove reconcilable with the physicist's point of view. It is that the atoms seen by occultists are *Archetypes*. Can it be that they arose from "thoughts in the Logoic Mind," densified in stages down to the etheric level, so that they are more fundamental than the chemical atoms we know in the dense physical world? This notion would accord with the "Story of Creation" as told in theosophical literature. (100)

After falling back on Blavatsky's creation story, he also speaks to the aesthetic and spiritual power of the UPA as Besant and Leadbeater experienced it:

Not very much has been said about the U.P.A. itself, that incredibly complex, vital and beautiful heart-shaped object which indeed represents the heart of the entire physical world. It is the unit from which the whole of physical creation is built, with its glory of crystals and mountains, plants and animals in enormous variety, and man himself. Its strangely convoluted structure must have deep significance. As Geoffrey Hodson was moved to remark, when he caught sight of one unexpectedly, "It gives me the impression of a heart-shaped Divine Presence in space. It is a highly significant Logoic manifestation. It's God at the physical level, or whatever names you may use, but it is the Creator's Self in manifestation, I suggest." Phillips has been inspired to discover and reveal some part at least, of this mystery. (103)

Besant and Leadbeater's Theosophical cosmology, and its affirmation in their clairvoyant chemistry, finally offered believers a vision of a spiritual experience that was also a sensory experience of a material world—in essence, a scientific experience subject to rules of the functioning of particles and the evolution of matter. Besant and Leadbeater explained the different planes and their constituents in terms of ever more rarified particles, each of which had a sensory apparatus appropriate to it and was endowed with a life principle. Through *Occult Chemistry*, these Theosophists attempted to bridge a divide, one expressed so urgently at the turn of the century, between religion and material science. They did so by synthesizing sensuous apprehension and the language of instrumentation—and in so doing, they worked to re-enchant scientific experiment itself.

While Theosophists' claims to ownership of scientifically valid knowledge of the subatomic world ultimately foundered, as their insights lacked the scientific persuasiveness gained from instrumentation and reproducible results, a similar ownership battle over the new atomic science was being waged between the academic disciplines of chemistry and physics. As we shall see in the next chapter, chemists attempted to define their research programs—and indeed the very identity of their field—around alchemical transmutation and to garner the scientific prestige of the first artificial transmutation. In the end, this effort pitted the instrumentation of chemistry (the spectroscope and the glassware of microanalyses of gasses) against that of physics (the scintillation detector and the cloud chamber). Yet while occultists were drawing heavily upon the new atomic science to rethink and validate alchemy, alchemy, as we shall see, also became a crucially important paradigm for highly decorated academic chemists.

3

Chemistry in the Borderland

Ramsay, Soddy, and the Transmutation Gold Rush

In chapters 1 and 2, we have seen that the alchemical revival among occult groups was transformed, around the turn of the century, by occultists' direct engagement with the emerging scientific texts of atomic physics and radiochemistry. But as the second part of the book will relate, alchemy also served as a dominant trope describing the research programs of major scientists, including Nobel Prize winners. Moreover, it played a crucial role in negotiating and even blurring boundaries among the (quite non-occult) scientific disciplines of chemistry, physics, and economics.

Ernest Rutherford, Frederick Soddy, and then Sir William Ramsay documented natural transformations of one element into another in 1902 and 1903. The *artificial* transmutation of one element into another, however, was first accomplished in 1919 by Rutherford, a physicist. Indeed, the field of nuclear physics has contributed the most to our understanding of the subatomic world since the 1920s. But the scientists who most advocated transmutation as a goal of research and a heuristic principle for understanding the nature of matter—the Nobel Prize winners Ramsay and Soddy, and, in a less prominent way, Sir William Crookes—were chemists, not physicists.[1]

Newly emerging histories of chemistry in Britain and the United States included discussions of alchemy. The occult alchemical revival, too, influenced the writing and teaching of the history of chemistry in the last two decades of the nineteenth century. Both contributed to styling a significant goal for early-twentieth-century atomic science as alchemical transmutation. Let me be clear, though, that I am not arguing that occultists set the agenda for modern atomic science, or that Ramsay or Soddy were involved in occult groups. (Crookes was, but he was only a minor player in the development of theories of radioactivity.) Rather, I will show that the revival of interest in alchemy beginning in the late nineteenth century provided a trope that contributed to the early portrayal and reception of the science of radioactivity. Moreover, alchemy was strongly identified with chemistry as a discipline—so much so that chemists themselves as well as the broader public often associated the new science of radioactive elements specifically with chemistry. (Peter Oldfeld's 1929 crime thriller, *The Alchemy Murder*, simply used the word "alchemy" to stand in for the chemical industry.)

The emerging science of radioactivity necessitated negotiations between the domains of chemistry and physics. Physical chemistry, the relatively young subfield within which Ramsay and Soddy worked, was the disciplinary location of much of the chemists' work on radioactivity. Ramsay and Soddy's writings about it used metaphors of the borderland to describe its status on the boundary between chemistry and physics. The trope of alchemy also helped negotiate the borders between the even newer disciplines of radiochemistry and atomic physics during the early twentieth century. Whichever discipline could effect artificial transmutation first would be able to lay claim to the ownership of atomic science. But in spite of chemistry's having set transmutation as the agenda for the new science—and in spite of a growing number of chemists' active efforts to effect transmutation after Soddy and Ramsay identified helium as a disintegration product of radium—the instruments and methods of physics at Cambridge's Cavendish Laboratory won the prize, carrying off what by the 1920s had become "nuclear physics."

Alchemy in Chemistry Education

By the 1880s, alchemy was emerging in Britain and America as an integral part of the history, or prehistory, of chemistry; Ramsay's generation was the first in nineteenth-century Britain to emphasize alchemy's significance to the field. German historians of chemistry had begun to examine alchemy as an ancestor of chemistry in the late eighteenth and early nineteenth centuries, but they had predominantly viewed it simply as an intellectual aberration, one riddled by superstition. In short, as Jost Weyer (1976) explains, histories of chemistry such as Johann Friedrich Gmelin's *Geschichte der Chemie* (1797–99), or, in the rare English example, Thomas Thomson's *History of Chemistry* (1830–31), demonstrated Enlightenment tendencies and failed to interpret the Middle Ages on its own terms. They simply portrayed the history of science as a story of progress, leading from the darkness of the alchemist's false science (Weyer 66). Later influential histories of chemistry—such as Hermann Kopp's *Geschichte der Chemie* (1843–47) and Ernst von Meyer's *Geschichte der Chemie* (1889, with English editions in 1891, 1898, and 1906)—acknowledged alchemy's contribution of technical methods to the science of chemistry. But, like earlier historians, they took alchemical hypotheses and methods of reasoning to be examples of intellectual error (Weyer 68–69). German historians began to take more of an interest in understanding the particulars of alchemical thinking only in the last two decades of the nineteenth century, as the French chemist Marcellin Berthelot published research on original alchemical texts (Weyer 70). According to Weyer, not until Eduard Färber's 1944 *Geschichtliche Entwicklung der Chemie* was there a German effort "to find a correlation between the scientific and philosophical-religious aspects of alchemy, i.e., to consider alchemy in its totality" (72).

Still, despite the German influence on many nineteenth-century English chemists, the written accounts of alchemy in Britain are significantly different from those by German historians. In the twenty years leading up to the discovery of atomic transmutation, the occult alchemical revival in Britain sparked numerous translations of primary alchemical sources, and historians of alchemy—along with chemists themselves—could look sympathetically at the aims and accomplishments of alchemy as both a scientific and religious field, as we have seen in chapter 1.[2]

Weyer notes that during the seventeenth century and some of the eighteenth, alchemical transmutation still lingered as a current scientific problem. Hence, rather than providing histories of chemistry that included alchemy, writings from the period addressing alchemy were "polemics for or against the doctrines of alchemy," and writers espousing the new scientific ideals felt compelled to attack alchemy vehemently (65). I would argue that the late nineteenth century's resurgence of alchemical interest reignited the polemical tone characteristic of the seventeenth- and eighteenth-century debates over alchemy. Take, for example, the writings of Ramsay's boyhood friend M.M. Pattison Muir, a chemist at Cambridge who became a major historian of alchemy and chemistry. Muir published popular educational texts on chemistry, and his works exemplify alchemy's move into chemistry education. Yet, because the broader public was beginning to suspect that alchemy might be legitimate modern science, he also had to take on the position of seventeenth-century writers, launching invective against the "modern alchemist."

Muir began to write about alchemy in the late 1880s, during the revival of Hermetic societies in Britain. Among other works on the history of chemistry, he published the widely read *Story of Alchemy and the Beginnings of Chemistry* in 1902 in Britain and 1903 in the United States (as part of Appleton's "Library of Useful Stories"). One of his first major works on alchemy, *The Alchemical Essence and the Chemical Element: An Episode in the Quest for the Unchanging*, was published in 1894 in London and New York by the major publishing house Longmans, Green at the height of the pre-radioactivity alchemical revival. At the same time, Waite was completing publication of five translations of major alchemical works and of his monthly magazine, *Unknown World*, with the firm James Elliott, an effort bankrolled by Lord Stafford (Gilbert 80–81). (Waite's most significant translation, *The Hermetic and Alchemical Writings of... Paracelsus*, appeared in 1894.) Muir built upon the public interest in alchemy sparked by Waite and others, quoting extensively in his book, for instance, from Waite's new translation of Basil Valentine's *Triumphal Chariot of Antimony* (Muir 19–20). Unlike his German counterparts such as von Meyer, Muir explored alchemy extensively on its own terms, taking its mystical theology seriously: "In its grosser aspects alchemy was a futile attempt to transmute all things into gold; in its more refined aspects it was a mystical system of occult theology, and it used a language like that used by theologians in every age. And there was a third aspect of alchemy in which it appeared as an art or handicraft" (27).

Muir regarded alchemy as both religious expression and as legitimate science of its day—not simply crediting it with some technical achievements, as earlier historians had done. He further noted that alchemy was unable to achieve the insights of modern chemistry (for instance, that change is only brought about in compounds rather than in the elements themselves—remember that this was before Rutherford and Soddy's 1901–02 discoveries). Alchemy, Muir argued, lacked sufficiently accurate instruments for rigorous quantitative analysis (28–34). Indeed, in this period immediately before the discovery of radioactivity, Muir—like Crookes and Lockyer and others following spectroscopic research and developments in the periodic table—had begun to wonder if there might in fact be some kind of unity of matter that resembled the alchemical hypothesis. Exploring the periodicity of the elements, and implicitly echoing William Prout's (1785–1850) 1815 hypothesis that all the elements were somehow compounds of hydrogen,[3] Muir notes, "Chemical inquiry brings us face to face with the question of the unity of matter. Are the elements fundamentally different?... Chemistry raises a question which is very like *the* question of alchemy. Is there in nature one primary kind of matter of which, and of which only, all those things we are accustomed to call different kinds of matter are composed?" (89).

Yet, having come close to accepting the occultists' claim that the alchemical conception of matter offers insights relevant to the most modern chemistry, Muir charitably adds, "This question is like the fundamental question of alchemy, but the two are separated by a wide and deep gulf. The alchemical question was put in words that had, and could have, no exact meaning; the terms that express the chemical question are definite, because they represent the results of accurate investigation. The question must be answered, if answered at all, by chemical, not by alchemical, methods of inquiry" (89). And Muir departs from the temperate, objective tone of most of his work when he resorts to rhetorically charged attacks upon what he calls "modern alchemists"—by which he clearly means the occult devotees of the alchemical revival. Evoking the imprecision of alchemy, Muir contends that "it is worse than foolish to talk, as some people talk, of the old uncertain, uncritical, and unstable methods as higher, and nobler, and more inspiring than the accurate and penetrating methods of science" (71–73). He identifies the "modern alchemist" as a "theosophist or theologian." Those "who prefer to give what they call an explanation of natural facts by an unwieldy, creaking, rusty machinery of supernatural imaginings, rather than take the trouble to understand even the fringe of the facts that they profess to explain" (60), who look for "an explanation of material things on . . . a 'higher spiritual plane,'" are intellectually akin to "the alchemist of the middle ages." Muir argues, "It is the duty of every man who desires to advance towards the goal of tried and abiding knowledge to put aside the methods and the results of the modern alchemist, by whatever title he call himself, or however he may seek to dignify his vanities by giving them the name of science" (61). Muir stridently recapitulates the common strategy of defining what science is *not* and rhetorically differentiating "hard science" from "nebulous" occultism (see Appendix A).

Going further even than Muir, some eminent chemists stridently opposed modern alchemy and the transmutation hypotheses emerging to explain radioactivity. Toward the end of his life, Mendeleev, for example, became quite concerned about the implications of radioactivity for his scientific and chemical world view. As Michael Gordin explains, "Mendeleev's most salient exposure to radioactivity, and the genesis of most of his hostile views of the phenomenon, was his visit to the Curies' laboratory in Paris in 1902. What he saw evoked similar worries as the Spiritualists had. He wrote in his Paris notebook: '. . . [M]ust one admit whether there is spirit in matter and forces? Radio-active substances, spiritualism?'" (Gordin 2004, 213). Mendeleev insistently dismissed for scientific reasons all claims of transmutation, launching attacks on the "new alchemy" offered by Stephen Emmens (whose silver to gold transmutation claims we shall explore in chapter 4), but also on scientific theories of the transformation of matter during radioactive decay and even on advocates of Prout's hypothesis that the chemical elements were not fundamental, but were instead composed of combinations of hydrogen atoms. As Gordin explains, his opposition to Prout's hypothesis and to radioactive transformation theories was based upon his metaphysics of chemistry, his unshakeable belief in the immutability of the chemical elements (215–16). He even attempted unsuccessfully to explain radiation in terms of ether theory.[4]

Yet Muir's friend Sir William Ramsay—a far more accomplished scientist than Muir, and one of the most proficient laboratory researchers of his era—was much more engaged by the possibility that alchemy might offer insight into the goals and consequences of modern science. As we have seen, Ramsay was a member of the Society for Psychical Research, and he was deeply steeped in alchemical and Hermetic texts. His own chemistry pedagogy made room for alchemical history in his university classrooms in a way that had not been the case in the classes he had taken as a young man.

The notes Ramsay would have taken on chemistry courses taught by John Ferguson (later the honorary president of the Alchemical Society) during Ramsay's undergraduate days in the early 1870s at the University of Glasgow do not survive, but his extant notes from the period, including those on a course taught by Kelvin, do not suggest that he was given any formal instruction in alchemical history. His own course lectures, however, beginning at least as far back as the lectures on "Junior Chemistry" he gave at the University of Bristol in 1885, included copious information about alchemical thinking and contributions to chemistry. They involved quotations, for instance, from a key Hermetic text, "The Emerald Tablet of Hermes" (which Blavatsky had included in *Isis Unveiled* [1877]). Moreover, Ramsay almost certainly used as his text for "The Emerald Tablet" the Rosicrucian Publishing Company's *Hermes Mercurius Trismegistus: His Divine Pymander; Also The Asiatic Mystery, The Smaragdine Table, and the Song of Brahm* (1871) edited by the occultist Paschal Beverly Randolph.[5] While Ramsay was no practicing occultist, the texts that the alchemical revival had made available certainly augmented mainstream chemists' exposure to alchemical concepts and texts. In an 1896 chemistry course at the University of London, Ramsay devoted two entire lectures to alchemical history. He even read in its entirety a fourteen-page discourse by the fifteenth-century Benedictine alchemist Basil Valentine. He asked his class to imagine themselves medieval students. He himself would personify Valentine, lecturing to them.

Alchemy's movement into the chemistry classroom—as part of chemistry's prehistory—was also evident in the education of Frederick Soddy, who was twenty-five years Ramsay's junior. The evidence is slight at first. His notebooks from his few years at the University of Aberystwyth do not show any trace of alchemical history. At Oxford, he was exposed to Kopp's *Geschichte der Chemie* and to the work of Ernst von Meyer, whose own *Geschichte der Chemie*, like Kopp's, acknowledged alchemy as part of the history of chemistry, if embarrassingly irrational and pre-scientific, "an insult to the human understanding" (Meyer 1891, 43), and "the summit of... mental aberration" (44). But Soddy was also exposed to the work of Berthelot—a friend of Ramsay's. Berthelot's *L'Origine d'Alchemie* (1885), upon which Soddy heavily relied in his own lectures, was read widely by occultists as well as by chemists in France, Britain, and Germany, and references to it turn up in numerous occult periodicals well into the twentieth century. Moreover, Soddy read Carl Schorlemmer's *Rise and Development of Organic Chemistry*, which, while describing organic chemistry as a science that "has been developed almost entirely during the present [nineteenth] century" (1), presented alchemical history fairly dispassionately in its relationship to discoveries relevant to organic chemistry. Schorlemmer drew upon the work not only of Kopp but also of Berthelot.[6]

But even some of the introductory chemistry lectures Soddy attended in his fairly conservative undergraduate education at Merton College, Oxford, were offering a brief history of the discipline, usually following Kopp's periodization into ancient chemistry, the alchemical period, the Iatro-chemical period, and then early modern chemistry, with Boyle and Lavoisier often seen as turning points.[7] Both J. E. Marsh's lecture on "The History of Chemical Theory" in Soddy's Fall 1896 term[8] and A. F. Walden's lectures on "Historical Chemistry," held between October 1897 and March 1898, discussed Kopp's history of alchemy and chemistry, adopting his periodization. Walden also referred to Berthelot's historical work on alchemy, rather than simply to his primary chemistry papers (which Soddy was reading for other courses).[9]

Moreover, not just occultists but chemistry professors, too, were beginning to give high-profile public lectures on alchemy. Professor H. Carrington Bolton of Trinity College, Hartford, lectured at the New York Academy of Sciences in November 1880 and before the New York section of the American Chemical Society in October 1897, for instance. Across the Atlantic, Professor James Dewar, FRS, delivered a course of six lectures at the Royal Institution in London on "Alchemy in Its Relation to Modern Science" beginning in late December 1883. Comparing Bolton's 1880 lecture with that of 1897 demonstrates the new place alchemy occupied in modern chemistry's identity. In the 1880 lecture, Bolton brought to an English-speaking audience something like the German line on the history of chemistry. He described alchemy as "the father of chemistry," worthy of some detailed explication and "confer[ring] lasting obligation upon posterity" for the knowledge its experiments produced, but also unscientifically based on "superstition and unaccountable phenomena" (*New York Times* 1880, 2). In his 1897 address, "The Revival of Alchemy," Bolton still chastised some modern alchemists as "educated charlatans." But he also discussed the Hermetic alchemical societies in France, quoting the Alchemical Association of France's proposal "to assist in reviving the unitary doctrines of chemistry" (856). He admitted that "Recent discoveries in physics, chemistry and psychology have given the disciples of Hermes renewed hopes, and the present position of chemical philosophy has given the fundamental doctrine of alchemy a substantial impetus" (854). Other than Sir Norman Lockyer's spectroscopic work on elements in stars, the scientific work invoked as helping modern alchemists revive "the unitary doctrines of chemistry" referred, notably, to research conducted in chemistry and mineralogical chemistry—including work by professor of chemistry Henry Le Châtelier (1850–1936) and professor of mineralogy François Ernest Mallard (1833–94) on gaseous bodies at high temperatures, Carey Lea's 1889–91 publications in the *American Journal of Science* on allotropic forms of silver (papers that would influence alchemists attempting to convert silver into gold), and Crookes's work on "meta-elements." Bolton himself saw that the Periodic Law required chemists to explore the possibility of "the mutual convertability of elements having similar chemical properties," and he cited the work of chemist Daniel Berthelot as an example (854–55).[10]

By the 1890s, then, before Soddy and Rutherford's discovery of radioactive transmutation, the history of chemistry had already absorbed alchemy—initially as a significant, if embarrassing, ancestor of no contemporary scientific value, but finally as a science. That science's primary contentions—that the elements are transmutable and that underlying them all is a *prima materia*—increasingly suggested the alchemical coloring of late-nineteenth-century chemical debates about the Periodic Law and the nature of the elements. Again, this reappraisal of alchemical hypotheses was based on the field of chemistry, not of physics. It was but a short leap from this already established position to chemists themselves adopting alchemical transmutation as a research program for modern chemistry. Soddy, Rutherford, and Ramsay's discoveries of natural transmutation encouraged just such a jump. Indeed, alchemy was so specifically tied to chemistry that it shaped the public perception and self-representation of chemists well before Rutherford and physics achieved the "Great Work" in 1919, when he transmuted nitrogen into an isotope of oxygen by bombarding it with alpha particles.

Physical Chemistry as Borderland

Soddy and Ramsay may have taken the final step of launching chemistry on a modern alchemical research program, but this paradigm shift in chemistry was only made possible within the borderland between chemistry, physics, and occult alchemy inhabited by these scientists. The identification of "modern alchemy" as belonging to chemistry was ultimately meant to shore up chemistry's disciplinary borders against physics. Chemistry, though, had rebuilt its walls to include a great deal of territory to which physics also laid claim—and eventually retook.

Soddy complained bitterly in later life about the encroachment of physics upon what he saw as the domain of chemistry—the hegemony of the Cavendish Lab group at Cambridge, the Fullerian Professorships in Chemistry at the Royal Institution given to physicists, Rutherford's Nobel prize in chemistry, even the eventual naming of the field "nuclear physics."[11] Soddy and Ramsay's major work was done in physical chemistry, a subfield coming into its own in the late nineteenth century and propelled by three of Ramsay's friends: Jacobus Henricus van't Hoff (1852–1911) from the Netherlands; the German Wilhelm Ostwald (born in Riga, Latvia, 1853–1932), who served as chair of physical chemistry at Leipzig beginning in 1887; and Svante Arrhenius (1859–1927) from Sweden. Indeed, the connection between physical chemists and alchemical historians goes back to Hermann Kopp himself, who had become the first professor of physical chemistry at Heidelberg, where "he aimed to show that all physical properties were determined by chemical composition" (Levere 2001, 153). Some nineteenth-century chemists fought Kant's contention that chemistry was not a real science because it simply classified without explaining. Mid-nineteenth-century work—such as Faraday's research on electrolysis and Mendeleev's effort to explore the relationship of the physical properties of elements to his periodic table—led to what would become, later in the century, the subdiscipline of physical chemistry (Levere 152–53). As Levere explains, physical chemistry may be defined as "the application of the techniques and theories of physics to the study of chemical reactions, and the study of the interrelations of chemical and physical properties" (153).

Mary Jo Nye has traced the beginnings of physical chemistry back into the 1860s with Kopp's chair in physical chemistry at Heidelberg created in 1863 and a section for physical chemistry created at the University of Kharkow in 1864. But the field was clearly established by 1887, when the *Zeitschrift für physikalische Chemie* was founded. (Another key outlet, the *Journal of Physical*

Chemistry, was created in 1896.) Nye emphasizes that "the disciplinary boundary between physics and chemistry became less well defined after 1900 than in the middle decades of the nineteenth century and that physical chemistry played an important role in this development" (Nye 1993, 110). Moreover, she notes the importance of Britain to physical chemistry, as the convention of British chemists getting their education in Germany waned by the end of the nineteenth century. Not only were British chemists more disposed toward the "pragmatism and practical applications" that often drove physical chemistry than the French were, but they also benefited from a particularly fluid sense of boundaries between chemistry and physics that helped facilitate what Nye calls the "London-Manchester School" of physical chemistry: "At the turn of the century, there was slightly more permeability and flexibility still in England than in France to the boundaries between disciplines, intellectually, institutionally, and geographically.... [I]t is the very permeability... that is striking in the gradual formation of new disciplines of physical chemistry, physical organic chemistry, and a theoretical chemistry of reaction mechanisms" (195).

The boundary permeability fostered by physical chemistry made it a fertile field for the development of theories of radioactivity. Both Ramsay and Soddy had posts as physical chemists. Ramsay worked at University College, London; Soddy, after working with Ramsay on the radium-to-helium transmutation in London in 1903, went on to become the first lecturer in radioactivity as well as a lecturer in physical chemistry at the University of Glasgow under John Ferguson. Both men saw the application of physical principles as crucial to advancing the discipline of chemistry, and both spoke of the young field of physical chemistry using borderland metaphors. On March 11, 1895, when Soddy was not yet eighteen years old, he wrote his Evans Prize essay at the University of Aberystwyth on "The Relations Existing between the Manner in which the Atoms are Linked Together, and the Physical Properties of the Resulting Compounds."[12] After trotting through the work of physical chemists such as van't Hoff and Ostwald on the subject, he concluded by not only invoking the pioneer metaphors so popular in science writing of the day, but also providing a glimpse of how he envisioned his career as a physical chemist working at the boundary between chemistry and physics:

> Although much has been discovered during late years, yet it seems highly probable that only the boundaries of the subject have been skirted, and that the vast field of research on the borderland, so to speak, between chemistry and physics, is almost virgin soil, holding out a bountiful harvest to those who, not content with treading the

well beaten paths of science, are enterprising enough to attack the problems, and patient enough to overcome the difficulties, which pioneers of scientific research always have to encounter. (Soddy 1895, 24)

Boundaries for the crossing, virginity for the taking, abundant harvests, trailblazers—the very subject of physical chemistry's borderland status unleashed a profusion of stock metaphors connected with pioneering in a new world. Van't Hoff himself, as Nye notes, "described physical chemistry as a 'new world' arisen between the two 'continents' of physics and chemistry" (106).

Indeed, during the most productive and pioneering years of Soddy's life, he worked in the borderlands created by several intersecting boundaries (see Appendix A). These years saw him make groundbreaking discoveries involving the nature of matter. From 1900 to 1903, he worked at McGill with Rutherford on radioactive transformation and in London with Ramsay on the radium-to-helium transmutation, and then between 1904 and 1914 at Glasgow, he published his *Interpretation of Radium* and, above all, conducted the research on the Displacement Law and the nature of isotopes that led to his Nobel Prize in 1921. If he understood physical chemistry itself as a borderland, adding to it his first-ever lectureship in radioactivity at Glasgow certainly kept him in a liminal space between chemistry and physics. Moreover, his early position as a chemistry demonstrator working in a physics lab in the far reaches of the empire (with Montreal itself an intersection of British Canada and the legacy of French Canada) with a Cambridge-educated New Zealander must have given Soddy and Rutherford the freedom gained by working from areas on the fringes of institutions of scientific authority.[13] When Soddy returned to Britain after his work with Ramsay and a lecture tour to Australia, he went neither to Oxford nor to Cambridge but to a then more marginal chemistry department at Glasgow, where Ramsay had studied as a youth, that was now modernizing itself to include such subjects as physical chemistry and radioactivity—but under John Ferguson, a department head best known for his work on alchemical history.

Ramsay, likewise, viewed himself as a physical chemist working in a borderland, and most of his obituarists would interpret his seminal work on inert gases and his work on transmutation as belonging to physical chemistry. In an unpublished book manuscript on physical chemistry that Travers (in a note on the manuscript in the Sir William Ramsay Papers) dates to around 1893, Ramsay begins:

> The sciences of Physics and Chemistry are closely connected; there are few branches of Physics which can be studied without a fair

knowledge of Chemistry; and the Chemist, if he wishes to understand his own Science relies on Physics for the interpretation of many of the phenomena he sees; and for many of the methods which he employs. A division may be attempted, but it is in many respects an artificial one, and, especially of later years, it has been found that progress is to be made in each science by borrowing methods and ideas from its sister.

To define a borderland like this is by no means an easy task; the boundary shifts from year to year; yet a definition of the present aims of Physical chemistry may be made. We may say that the object of physical chemistry is to attempt to refer chemical changes to action between atoms and molecules and to investigate such action as regards its rate, and its extent. (Ramsay 1893?, 1)

Ramsay routinely taught physical chemistry, but he saw it as a discipline that could not be neatly cordoned off by either chemistry or physics. Its borderland status ultimately undermines the distinctions between the fields it mediates.

By 1904, when Ramsay had taken up radioactivity and transmutation as the research program that would guide the rest of his career, he became the editor of *Text-Books of Physical Chemistry,* a series published by Longmans, Green to educate the science-reading public on the emergent field. His lead-off volume, *Introduction to the Study of Physical Chemistry,* recycled some of the material from the 1893 manuscript[14] but began even more forcefully, emphasizing the difficulty of constructing a clean definitional boundary between chemistry and physics: "To define exactly the provinces of the Sciences of Physics and Chemistry is not easy. The definition that the object of Chemistry is the study of the changes which matter undergoes during the formation and decomposition of compounds, while that of Physics has reference to changes which affect matter independently of its composition, hardly meets the case" (Ramsay 1904a, 1). Ramsay argues that the physics of heat, conductivity, and the like must take into account the chemical composition of matter, and that this insight defines the new field of physical chemistry: "The birth of physical chemistry may be said to date from the recognition of this fundamental idea; where the laws or generalizations regarding properties of matter depend not merely on the masses or rates of motion of the objects considered, but also on their composition and chemical nature, their consideration falls under the heading 'Physical Chemistry' " (2).

One of Ramsay's obituaries slighted continental chemistry in favor of English by characterizing Ramsay as a quintessentially *English* chemist, one who worked without the constraint of chemical dogma. Yet the same obituary noted that this quality had gotten him into some trouble at the end of his career in his too-hasty claims for transmutation.[15] Though it would be difficult to make a case for Ramsay as an English chemist, given his education in Glasgow and Germany and his international cadre of friends and correspondents (such as Oswald, van't Hoff, Berthelot, and Mendeleev), his working from the disciplinary borderland of physical chemistry clearly gave Ramsay the freedom to rethink the nature not only of chemistry and physics but also of matter. In addition, the alchemical paradigm that Ramsay adopted as he began working with Soddy in 1903 on radium transmutation (and then pursued his own transmutation efforts for the rest of his career) permitted him to define the natural research program for a chemist as including not simply compounds of elements but also elements themselves. Indeed, the first published titles in the popular series *Text-Books of Physical Chemistry* included *Spectroscopy* by E.C.C. Baly, who was to become involved in the chemists' rush to transmutation, and *Chemical Statics and Dynamics* by J. W. Mellor, who would become a key member of the Alchemical Society within a decade. The borderland nature of the young discipline of physical chemistry seems to have helped make it possible for it to intersect with another border: this time, that delineating theories of matter that had previously prevailed only in the period's occult revival.

As we shall see in the next chapter, Soddy formulated theories that must have had roots in occult lore of his day—about ancient races, for instance, perhaps those of Atlantis who had developed atomic knowledge, created an Edenic planet, and then come to a catastrophic end or simply moved on into outer space. He posited this event as the source of the biblical story of the Fall and later began to connect atomic alchemy to the apocryphal Book of Enoch, a work of much magical authority for occultists such as Aleister Crowley. Ramsay himself mentioned telepathic communication in letters (probably facetiously), though he did receive a letter from Ostwald affirming the existence of telepathy and individuals' ability to project their life force outward onto others, and the Society for Psychical Research, to which he belonged, investigated such phenomena. Still, neither Ramsay nor Soddy, so far as I can ascertain, had direct involvement in any Hermetic order or the Theosophical Society. Soddy was teaching and researching in Scotland during the Alchemical Society's existence, and Ramsay's schedule and failing health likely would have prevented him from attending it as well. Even so, the alchemical revival had clearly informed their sense of the nature of their discipline so strongly that it may have helped guide their theorization and research agendas involving radiation and atomic transmutation along different paths from those followed by the physicists involved in turn-of-the-century atomic theory.

Back in 1900 when Soddy began his new job in McGill University's chemistry department, his first lectures on alchemy—"The History of Chemistry from the Earliest Times"—merely followed the fairly standard line he inherited from Kopp, von Meyer, and Schorlemmer, seeing alchemy as an early but mistaken manifestation of chemistry. But in a lecture entitled "Alchemy and Chemistry" later that year, Soddy made a much different claim: "The student who has traced the evolution of chemistry from its earliest beginnings and has properly interpreted the pre-Lavoisierian epoch sees that the existence of an atomic age is unquestionable. The constitution of matter is the province of chemistry, and little, indeed, can be known of this constitution until transmutation is accomplished. This is, as it has always been, the real goal of the chemist." Likewise, Ramsay's 1911 presidential address to the British Association quoted another chemist, Michael Faraday, who had claimed years before that "To decompose the metals, to reform them, and to realize the once absurd notion of transformation—these are the problems now given to the chemist for solution" (8). After his work with Rutherford had established his scientific reputation, Soddy publicly echoed Faraday's call, noting in an article on transmutation: "as Faraday remarked in his day, transmutation is the final goal towards which chemistry should aspire. The power to decompose and build up the known elements and to construct new ones at will as is now done for compounds, would elevate chemistry to an infinitely loftier plane than the rather secondary and subordinate position among the physical sciences it occupies at the moment" (Soddy 1912, 195).

Contrary to Soddy's claim that transmutation had been "the real goal of the chemist," transmutation was, in fact, still chemical heresy at the end of the nineteenth century, and had been so since the mid-eighteenth century. Despite the controversy stirred up by Prout's hypothesis, John Dalton's *A New System of Chemical Philosophy* (1808) had more or less solidified the modern conception of the chemical element as consisting of an immutable and indivisible atom that differed for each element. All atoms of lead, for example, had the same weight (this was, obviously, more than a hundred years before Soddy's discovery of isotopes) and chemical properties, and all atoms of gold had the same weight and properties, and the one could never be changed into the other nor broken down into any more elementary particles. Chemical reactions were caused by rearranging atoms. Alchemy during the 1880s had become part of the history of chemistry, and was associated specifically with chemistry in the broader culture, rather than with any other science. Before Ramsay and Soddy thrilled alchemy revivalists by reinstating transmutation as a major goal of chemistry, those histories of chemistry had portrayed alchemy as a dead end, even if a fascinating one that had shifted chemistry onto an experimental basis that it had not enjoyed in ancient times.

Chemistry's Alchemical Identity

Ramsay and Soddy, both Nobel Prize–winning chemists, transformed the role of alchemy in chemistry from that of a somewhat embarrassing ancestor to something much closer to the occultists' estimation of it: as an ancient wisdom that still offered key insights into the nature of matter and of unperceived worlds. And indeed Soddy and Ramsay faced considerable, if short-lived, opposition and skepticism from eminent elderly scientists such as Kelvin and Huggins. This tension became public at two meetings of the British Association. At the 1903 meeting in Southport, Soddy and Kelvin argued with each other about the radium-to-helium transformation, and at the 1906 meeting at York, Kelvin asserted that radium must contain helium, rather than transmute into it. Soddy and Sir Oliver Lodge, in the meanwhile, argued that the radium-to-helium transformation was truly a transmutation and not simply a decomposition of a compound.[16]

Let us return to Soddy's recollection of the key experiments from 1901 to 1903 through which Soddy and Rutherford discovered the radioactive transformation of thorium into an inert gas (a gas that Soddy and Ramsay, back in London in 1903, soon identified as helium). As we have seen in the introduction, Soddy wrote, "I remember quite well standing there transfixed as though stunned by the colossal import of the thing and blurting out—or so it seemed at the time: 'Rutherford, this is transmutation: the thorium is disintegrating and transmuting itself into an argon gas.' The words seemed to flash through me as if from some outside source. Rutherford shouted to me, in his breezy manner, 'For Mike's sake, Soddy, don't call it *transmutation*. They'll have our heads off as alchemists. You know what they are'" (Howorth 1958, 84). Rutherford, who won his Nobel Prize for these experiments, referred to the process as "transformation" rather than "transmutation," and he did not publish a book with alchemy in its title until his last book, *The Newer Alchemy*, in 1937. For Soddy, transmutation was a natural conclusion for a chemist, rather than a physicist, to draw from the experiments. (The wording of his recollection even evokes not only alchemy but also occult, "mediumistic" experience of words communicated "from some outside source.") He noted, "I was, of course, tremendously elated to have discovered transmutation—the goal of every chemist of every age" (Howorth 82), adding that his thoughts were "always occupied with transmutation. That is natural; I was a chemist" (Howorth 82). Soddy continued, "I only want to show how our brains were working, mine on transmutation and gases, Rutherford's on thorium and alpha ray emission" (Howorth 84).

Two things stand out in Soddy's words. First, he defines his field by transmutation, asserting that because he was a chemist, his thought was naturally guided by transmutation (though, of course, his sense that chemists of every age were similarly preoccupied with transmutation was completely inaccurate). Second, this way of figuring chemistry was specifically meant to delineate it from physics. It certainly irked him that Rutherford won the Nobel Prize in *chemistry* rather than in physics for this work, though in 1908 the very fact that Rutherford *did* win the prize in chemistry shows how much even the Nobel Prize committee was convinced that radioactive transmutation fell into chemistry's purview. During the rest of his career—especially beginning in 1919, when he took the Dr. Lee's Professorship of Chemistry at Oxford—Soddy railed at nuclear physics' takeover of what he saw as radiochemistry. He was particularly exercised by the physics group at the Cavendish Laboratory at Cambridge around J. J. Thomson. (This group later revolved around Rutherford, though Soddy remained good friends with Rutherford.) Indeed, for numerous reasons (many of them involving institutional issues), the program in radiochemistry Oxford had hoped to establish under Soddy, which would rival the physics program at the Cavendish, did not succeed (see Merricks 1996; Howorth). The alchemy trope and the popular conception of chemistry *as* alchemy still helped position Soddy to engage in an early boundary skirmish with physics.

For years, Soddy would write and lecture about atomic transmutation's significance to civilization and its possible uses—for ill or for good—by what he called "the modern scientific alchemist" (1912, 197) or the "real alchemist."[17] Very early on, beginning around 1903, Soddy and others writing about transmutation had realized that the energy released in the transformations was more important than the material changes themselves. As Weart has documented, writers or speakers of this era typically spoke of the jar of radium that could power an ocean liner across the seas, or of the energy in an explosion that could lift the British fleet high out of the water, or of the tons of coal that could be replaced by small quantities of radium (1988, 6–13).[18] Soddy, in particular, saw energy as the real source of wealth in civilizations, that which allowed technological progress (and, as we shall see in chapter 4, that upon which economics should focus). But he, like several other thinkers in the late nineteenth and early twentieth centuries, was concerned that civilization was rapidly depleting its old sources of energy. The dwindling coal supplies had been particularly troubling (Weart 9), and even the Second Law of Thermodynamics seemed to many to suggest that human vitality and culture, and even the Earth itself, would die from heat loss, with usable energy gradually receding into entropy (Clarke 1996, 59–81). For Soddy, transmutation was the solution to these pressing problems. Upon "the progress of physical science," as Soddy put it, "appears to hang the whole destiny of the race, spiritual, intellectual and aesthetic as well as physical and material" (1912, 201–2).

We shall focus on the energy and gold economics of transmutation in more detail in the next chapter, but for now, I want to investigate how Soddy's writings about the modern scientific alchemist became significant in his attempts to secure for chemistry the new possibilities of transmutation. While concerns about the solar system's heat death were largely those of nineteenth-century physicists and astronomers, Soddy charged chemists with work that would rescue civilization from entropy, noting that "the scientific man and particularly the chemist is under no delusions as to the nature of the problem and how completely it transcends, in order of magnitude any that have been previously solved" (1912, 200–201). At the height of the rush to transmutation between 1904 and 1914, Soddy's 1912 article "Transmutation: The Vital Problem of the Future" used alchemical allusions to position the chemist, the modern scientific alchemist, as the key to solving "the problem of transmutation." Chemistry would thus be the vital field of the future.

Even as Soddy attempted to wrest the energy issue away from physics, he also positioned the alchemist/chemist as the solver of material problems holding back progress in engineering, as he urged "the synthesis of entirely new forms of matter" (197). In the example that would become the common stock of science fiction and fantasy, Soddy argued that the chemist could overcome the material limitations of aviation science, synthesizing "a constructional material as light as wind and as strong as steel" (197). Soddy notes that "if new elements could be prepared to a definite specification by artificial synthetic processes in the same way as chemical compounds are now turned out of almost any structure required, within certain limits, this fundamental limitation of further progress could be overcome" (197). Rather than elements retaining their identities but becoming part of compounds, Soddy wished chemists to alter, fundamentally, elemental identities. By shifting attention from how elements bond and form *compounds* to how elements can be transmuted into entirely *new* elements, Soddy reversed the common view of alchemy's giving way to modern chemistry. Modern chemistry would instead give way to modern alchemy.

What I am calling the "transmutation gold rush," the efforts by Ramsay and several others to transmute an element artificially, was, in fact, a project initiated by chemists rather than physicists, and it helped shape the alchemical identity of the new science of radioactivity. Even before Ramsay and Soddy's July 16, 1903, letter and July 28, 1903, article appearing in the August 13, 1903, issue of *Nature* detailing the experiments that resulted in their identification of helium as the mystery gas produced by the radioactive transformation of radium (Ramsay and Soddy 1903), the press was already portraying Rutherford and Soddy's disintegration theory of radioactivity in alchemical terms, calling their work the first scientifically documented case of transmutation. Remarkably, though Soddy had from the beginning thought of the radium transformation in alchemical terms (see Sclove 1989), he had avoided explicitly alchemical tropes and images, such as Ouroboros, that the press was beginning to use. Even his popularizing article on the disintegration theory published in *The Contemporary Review* in June 1903, which discussed one element's transforming into another, referred only generally to alchemical terms in the theory of elemental evolution propounded by Crookes: "Chemists—that is, the more speculative of them—have often pictured a process of natural evolution of the elements from some common *protyle* (the hypothetical unit of all matter) going on under certain unattainable conditions, as for example, in the hot stars" (1903, 718). But from the moment Ramsay and Soddy's experiments proving helium transmutes from radium were publicly announced, the press insistently made the alchemical connection. *New York Times* readers had been well primed to think of alchemy as a continuing modern project by the newspaper's recent articles on Emmens (who in 1897 and 1898 claimed to have transmuted silver into gold by various chemical processes and by the exertion of extreme pressures), on other claims to transmutation (see *New York Times* 1889, 1896, 1897a, 1898, 1902, and Baskerville 1907), on Bolton's talks (1880, 1897b), as well as on the Golden Dawn (1901). While cautioning that other explanations than transmutation might exist for the phenomenon, which "[did] not prove that the dream of alchemy has become a reality," the *New York Times* article on the radium and helium experiments nevertheless no longer referred to the "disintegration theory." Rather, it adopted the language of "the theory of transmutation" (*New York Times* 1903, 8). And as the London *Times Literary Supplement* put it, "Since before the discovery of radioactivity no case of a chemical element changing had been ever observed, its internal energy defied all means of detection. But its existence has always been recognized by the chemist as a completely unknown and unknowable quantity. It is this hitherto untapped source which radium is now supposed to be drawing on throughout the centuries. Like the tail-eating serpent of the alchemist it is consuming itself, only so slowly that some has survived to tell the story" (1903, 201).

Ramsay the Modern Alchemist

Ramsay began to work in earnest to effect a transmutation. Indeed, he defined transmutation as the ability to cause a transformation, rather than simply to observe one happening naturally, as he and Soddy had done before.[19] During his September 1904 trip to the United States to give his presidential address to the Society of Chemical Industry, Ramsay was clearly already beginning early work on transmutation and imagining a process that would be the opposite of nuclear decay. As the *New York Daily Tribune*'s coverage of Ramsay's presidential address noted, "the preliminary work already done by Sir William has encouraged him to think that perhaps one kind of atom can be transformed into another by a process of building up" (1904, n.p.). Such a fusion project stood in marked contrast to watching the disintegration of a heavy element to produce a lighter element. It was so obviously inflected by alchemical thinking (the production of gold from silver or mercury, for instance) that the newspaper reporter felt compelled to compare Ramsay's interest to a relatively recent alchemical news headline:

> When the late Stephen Emmens, of this city, asserted that he had converted silver into gold scientific men laughed at him scornfully because he would not take the necessary steps to secure the judgment of competent persons upon his work. Sir William Ramsay's procedure is very different, and always has been. The guarded language which he now employs does not indicate that he has yet reached a final conclusion in regard to his latest researches. If he ever becomes fully satisfied, though, that one kind of matter can be made from another with the assistance of energy liberated by decaying radium, there is a strong probability that his belief will prove correct.

This was exactly the experiment Ramsay was beginning to undertake.

In talks between 1904 and 1907—when he first claimed to have successfully transmuted an element—Ramsay interpreted alchemy as essentially correct in imagining matter as transmutable with the appropriate addition of energy and chemical manipulations. Alchemists had failed because of the limited energy offered by their furnaces and, above all, their incorrect assumption that matter could only be changed one quality at a time. In "On Transmutation," a lecture Ramsay gave at the London Institution on January 28, 1907, and again at the Dublin Royal Society on February 15 of that year, he expounded on the alchemical understanding of matter at great length, especially that of the *prima materia* and the doctrine of transmutation. Then, turning to modern scientific views, he discussed experiments on the decay of radioactive metals (such as uranium and radium) and experiments on zinc and other common metals using ultraviolet light. The evidence, he asserted, showed that all metals may be undergoing gradual transformation and that all elements may well be compounds built up from some *prima materia* under conditions during which they are infused with large amounts of energy.

> I wish to suggest that what we term elements are, many of them, merely very stable compounds, which before they begin to change, require to absorb a very large quantity of energy. How is that energy to be applied? In all probability, the process is happening in the hotter stars. It is also possible to produce similar change on the earth, to cause a so-called transmutation. But you see how little analogy there is between ancient and modern views; the ancients thought to alter the qualities of one element that it should become identical with another; we moderns, from our conception of matter, and knowledge of the behaviour of compounds of different orders of stability, with the positive proof that radium, through its emanation, passes into helium as one of its products, and with proof, too, that metals under the influence of ultraviolet light discharge electrons can go further, and expect in the near future the change of some elements into some others. What these will be, we know not yet. (1907a, 120)

Ramsay and the other modern alchemists/chemists following his lead believed that they had found the proper energy sources for such syntheses of heavier elements in radium emanation—and eventually other sources of energy, including cathode rays and X-rays—to try to cause transmutations.[20]

Ramsay did not make all of his experimental activities public, however. The 1904 invocation by the *New York Daily Tribune* reporter of Stephen Emmens is of particular interest, because Ramsay was secretly becoming involved in a gold-making scheme by another American much like Emmens. Unbeknownst to anyone other than Mrs. Ramsay, on the 1904 United States trip Ramsay met secretly with Robert Melville Hunter of Philadelphia, to whom he referred as "the gold man" in a letter to his wife marked "Strictly Private." Ramsay wrote: "The other sheets can be shown: but...I want to tell you about the gold man, too. I saw him in Philadelphia. He didn't tell me his process: but I can guess it. He is all right—no swindler. I said—'Have you any objection to my trying it?' He replied, not in the least. If you can discover it from what I have said, you are perfectly welcome to use it." Ramsay went on to write that he was going to run the secret experiment in the guest room: "It is worth a good trial anyhow, if only from the scientific point of view" (Ramsay

1904b). As he explains in a later letter to a close friend, Henry Fyfe, Ramsay had received a letter from Hunter earlier in the year or in 1903, and Hunter had written him because of his work with Soddy on the radium transformations. In the 1906 letter to Fyfe, he identifies Hunter and notes that Hunter claimed to have been "effecting transmutation of silver into gold for months; he sent me photos of his laboratory, and his letter was very well-written, and very reasonable." Ramsay, who had written Hunter "several times" and finally arranged to call on him while in Philadelphia, guarded against the possible charge of charlatanism leveled against most self-styled alchemists. He did so by portraying Hunter in much the same way as people viewed Ramsay himself: as a socially adept and attractive gentleman and a professionalized scientist. Ramsay wrote, "he is an electric engineer, and lives in a good house, and was a nice-looking fellow—a gentlemanly American, in fact. He wrote again last summer, and said that he had now succeeded in so affecting silver that a spontaneous change into gold goes on; in fact that gold grows" (Ramsay 1906). This last—the supremely alchemical idea that gold grows in the earth in a kind of genesis that parallels human gestation—seems to have caught Ramsay's interest. (He had, in fact, lectured on this very concept.) Hunter's explanation of how silver could be transmuted into gold matched Ramsay's own understanding of scientific alchemy as applying energy to reverse atomic disintegration. Ramsay wrote to Fyfe that Hunter "based his conclusions on actual experiments, and he gave a reasonable theory, viz. that radium spontaneously changes into helium, giving out heat, or some other form of energy; but that if energy were to be imported to helium, the reverse change might be expected; and by imparting energy to silver, he had converted it into gold."

So struck was Ramsay by this modern alchemist that over the next few years he did blind experiments with assayers on the silver samples Hunter sent him, checking every three to four months both at his lab in London, alongside his colleague, J. Norman Collie, and at the assayer's office. After a few years he abandoned his hopes, because the samples' gold content (there are trace amounts in most silver) remained unchanged. Hunter, who had also sent silver samples to the chemistry professor Charles Baskerville of the College of the City of New York, nevertheless went on to try to raise $500,000 to create a factory in Philadelphia for the transmutation of silver into gold—presumably without success.[21]

American and British swindlers made a number of claims about processes for transmuting silver into gold.[22] Ramsay's seeming gullibility about such claims shows the degree to which he was obsessed by alchemical transmutation as he set off on his own course of experiments. His December 1904 article in *Harper's,* "Radium and Its Products," ended with the speculation that radium, with its powerful emission of alpha and beta rays, might well be the Philosopher's Stone—a claim that many occultists had been making since radium's discovery in 1898. Ramsay wrote:

> If these hypotheses are just, then the transmutation of elements no longer appears an idle dream. The philosopher's stone will have been discovered, and it is not beyond the bounds of possibility that it may lead to that other goal of the philosophers of the dark ages—the *elixir vitae*. For the action of living cells is also dependent on the nature and direction of the energy which they contain; and who can say that it will be impossible to control their action, when the means of imparting and controlling energy shall have been investigated? (57)

Ramsay's understanding of alchemy—of both the transmutational powers of the Philosopher's Stone and the revitalizing properties of the elixir—as a process of controlling energy gelled with the new occult understanding of alchemy.

Such thinking sparked a prodigious experimental period at the end of Ramsay's illustrious career, during which he both tried to treat a number of cancer patients with radium and tried tirelessly to effect transmutations in his laboratory. (Ironically, he succumbed to cancer of the jaw himself at the age of sixty-three and eventually believed that frequent radiation exposure had damaged his health.) During the period from 1907 to 1909, when he was president of the Chemical Society of London, Ramsay announced the results of several experiments that seemed to confirm his sense—expressed as early as 1904—that radium emanation could be the energy source needed to cause artificial transmutations. And, above all, he affirmed that the reactions of the chemical environment affected the end product of radioactive transmutation. Having already proved in 1903 with Soddy that helium was an end product of radium disintegration, Ramsay stunned the scientific community by announcing in the July 18, 1907, issue of *Nature* that "When the emanation is in contact with, and dissolved in water, the inert gas which is produced by its change consists mainly of neon; only a trace of helium could be detected." He continued by explaining that the emanation, if in contact with copper sulphate, produced argon, and that "the copper, acted upon by the emanation, is 'degraded' to the first member of its group, namely lithium" (1907b, 269). Ramsay imagined that these particular "degradations" occurred because of the place the elements occupied in the periodic table—lithium being the lowest member of the group that includes copper. Neon was an inert gas in the family that included the emanation (radon) as its highest member and helium as its lowest.

Ramsay's understanding not only of elements "growing" from transmutation but also of many of the observed transmutations to lighter elements being a process of "degradation" demonstrates just how alchemical his thinking had become. (Some physicists were calling the process "disintegration" or "transformation"; chemists might have called a similar molecular process "dissociation" or "decomposition.") The greatest test, as in alchemy, would be in the building up of a "nobler" element. But even in causing the "degradation" to a lighter element, Ramsay believed that he had effected a transmutation. While he agreed with Soddy, Rutherford, and others working on radioactive decay that the rate of transmutation could not be affected by any chemical process, he felt that he had shown that chemical processes could influence the degree and nature of the emanation degradation. He assumed that the transmutation from copper to lithium occurred naturally—but that radon's energy could accelerate the process.[23]

While some of his results were challenged, Ramsay continued to work to find conclusive proof of his transmutations through 1914. Outside of his articles in chemistry journals, Ramsay had also raised the public profile of his transmutation claims in the final chapter, entitled "Transmutation," of his 1912 book *Elements and Electrons*. After explaining the alchemical conception of transmutation, and noting Faraday's earlier nineteenth-century exhortation that chemistry adopt a transmutation agenda (the very claim Soddy also highlighted in his *Scientia* article, also of 1912), Ramsay then adds: "This hope has, in the opinion of the author, been realized" (143). After running through examples of radioactive transformation (changes occurring without human intervention), he explains his own and Collie's transmutational experiments, still defending even the copper-to-lithium experiment that Madame Curie had unsuccessfully attempted to replicate.[24] He proudly claims, "The way is now clear for an exhaustive research on the transmutations of the elements; for experiment is open to all who can command the means of utilizing powerful cathode discharges" (163).

It is almost heartbreaking to read Ramsay's triumphant claims to have effected transmutation in his laboratory notebooks, in his letters to chemist friends and to his wife, and even in his public addresses and publications in major scholarly journals such as *Nature* and the *Journal of the Chemical Society*. After feeling that he had irrefutably proved his chemical transmutations, Ramsay finally inscribed—in a lab notebook on March 31, 1913—"finis coronat opus" (the end crowns the work). The notebook held details of the work he was doing from his home laboratory with A. C. G. Egerton, using cathode rays as the energy source, for a paper to be entitled "The Synthesis of Argon." Ramsay added, "Proved that with no sulphur no argon; with sulphur argon; conditions small cathode, current rectified" (1913, 31). He then dismantled the laboratory in his London house and retired to the country (see Travers 264).

The problem was that his claims were completely incorrect. The scientist who had won a Nobel Prize for his ability to make micro-analyses of gases had introduced, in his experiments, minute quantities of gases from leaky seals or even porous glass, from occluded gases in cathode ray tube anodes, and even gases from the cigarettes he chain-smoked during his experiments. Though he was absolutely convinced that radium emanation caused copper sulphate to produce lithium, for example, or that emanation in the presence of different chemical compounds produced neon rather than helium or argon, chemists and physicists including Madame Curie, J. J. Thomson, and Lord Rayleigh—and even Ramsay's fellow researcher Egerton—either achieved negative results repeating Ramsay's experiments or discovered other, correct explanations for the presence of the elements Ramsay was detecting. The lithium, for instance, turned out to have been from his cigarettes (Travers 258).

As Thaddeus Trenn has argued, Ramsay's desire to effect transmutation had colored his experimental program. Though he had the right idea in at least some of these experiments—using bombardment by a highly powerful source of energy such as alpha rays to effect a transmutation, as Rutherford himself did successfully in 1919—he was using the methods and instruments of chemistry to detect such a transformation (Trenn 1974, 61). Rutherford was compelled to use a scintillation counter, and then a cloud chamber, to find a single transmutation of one nitrogen atom into an isotope of oxygen. He estimated that only 1 in 300,000 alpha particles could get close enough to a nitrogen nucleus to have a chance of causing a transformation (Trenn 61–62; Galison 1997, 119). Ramsay's methods of microanalysis of gases could never have detected such an event.

But beyond the disciplinary boundaries caused by the material practices of chemistry and physics at the time—chemists used spectroscopy for microanalysis of gas, and the Cavendish physicists used scintillation counters and cloud chambers for their snapshots of subatomic processes—the very borderland of physical chemistry that had taken Ramsay so close to succeeding in the alchemy-inspired race for transmutation had shaped his (mis)interpretation of the processes he was observing. Ramsay's bedrock disciplinary assumption that chemical interactions would effect changes that did not, in fact, take place chemically came from his pioneering work as a physical chemist. (Those changes did not occur at the level of the electron shell, in fact, but rather occurred in the nucleus—something that no scientist understood very well, if at all, at the time.) Remember that just when he was beginning his work on transmutation, Ramsay had defined physical chemistry as applying "where the laws or generalizations regarding properties of matter depend not merely on the masses or rates of motion of the objects considered, but also on their composition and chemical nature" (1904, 2). Such a vision of a borderland field, involving both physical and chemical properties, had shaped Ramsay's sense that chemical properties must be involved in the processes of radioactive disintegration, just as his willingness to bridge the gulf between chemistry and alchemy had shaped his positing of transmutation as a goal of scientific research.

Transmutational Chemistry's Gold Rush

While some contemporary alchemists such as Hunter, Emmens, Jollivet-Castelot, and Ayton had indeed tried to make gold, Ramsay's attempted transmutations led to a rush toward a different kind of treasure: scientific immortality. Multiple chemists pursued the same kinds of experiments that Ramsay had, believing that they too had found positive results. They attempted to position themselves within the scientific world as the first to have proven artificial transmutation. Between 1907, when Ramsay announced his supposed copper transmutations in *Nature,* and 1914, when he abandoned his efforts, several significant chemists (including J. N. Collie, Hubert Patterson, E. C. C. Baly, Thomas Merton, Irvine Masson, and A. C. G. Egerton) all participated in experiments to use either radium emanation or cathode rays and X-rays to cause chemical transmutation.

Ramsay's 1907 announcement garnered much attention both within and outside the world of chemistry. Just nine days after Ramsay's letter to *Nature,* the venerable medical journal *The Lancet* emphasized the link to alchemy that Ramsay himself had firmly established in his 1904 lectures and publications. In an article entitled "Modern Alchemy: Transmutation Realized," *The Lancet* confidently pronounced that Ramsay's expected communication to the Chemical Society on his experiments "will mark a great epoch in the history of chemical science since his investigations have shown that a given element under the powerful action of the radium emanation undergoes 'degradation' into another. In short, the transmutation of the elements is actually *un fait accompli"* (*Lancet* 1907, 244). The *Lancet* picked up Ramsay's alchemical logic, referring to the "degradation" of copper to lithium, and it accepted Ramsay's experimental results without question as "facts": "We already know that helium appears as the radium emanation disappears, while when the emanation is in contact with, and dissolved in, water neon is produced but when in contact with a solution of copper salts the chief product is argon. More marvelous still is the fact that when copper salts are used lithium appears where before was no lithium. Copper is thus 'degraded' to the first member of its family—i.e. lithium" (244). The article speculated, as Ramsay had, that all the metals might be undergoing gradual changes. It concluded by affirming alchemical wisdom—and the possibility of the impossible—with a conviction that might in other circumstances have seemed misplaced in a scholarly scientific journal: "These remarkable discoveries remind us again of the extraordinary prescience of the ancients, of the presentiments of the alchemists who evidently had some sort of a conviction that, after all, there is a primary matter from which all other elements are formed by various condensations. He is a bold man who nowadays confesses scepticism about anything. The world has seen men who have said 'it is impossible.' Generations have succeeded them who have seen the 'impossible' come to pass" (244).

Other articles turned Ramsay himself into a celebrity. On the day *The Lancet* published its article, the *New York Times,* via a "Special Cablegram," ran a front-page article—"Ramsay Sure of Discovery/Tells The New York Times That Repeated Experiments Were Made"—that described its exclusive interview with Ramsay. It further emphasized the media frenzy surrounding his announcement in *Nature:* "Sir William Ramsay has been besieged all day by newspaper correspondents eager to obtain further news of his discovery of the transmutation of metals by means of radium emanations" (*New York Times* 1907, 1). The interview with "the great scientist," as the article styled Ramsay, emphasized the significance of the new experiments over the previously proven natural transmutation of radium into helium. Though it presented Kelvin's arguments against transmutation at the 1906 British Association and noted that "In some quarters there is a disposition to find fault with The Lancet for having headed its article 'Modern Alchemy: Transmutation Realized' without waiting to know more of Sir William Ramsay's recent discoveries" (1), the article presented Ramsay's own accounts of his radium emanation transmutation directly and found the copper-to-lithium transmutation of "the utmost interest" (1). The *New York Times* followed this article three weeks later with one by Charles Baskerville entitled "Finding of Radium Now Yields Precedence, in Sensational Interest, to Ramsay's Transmutation of the Elements." Baskerville gave some history of alchemy—followed by the usual disavowals of charlatans—and then provided details of Ramsay's transmutation experiments as solid science. He ended by wondering, "Can this emanation be Bacon's 'philosopher's stone' reversed? If so, is there any way of taking the fairly abundant elements of comparatively low atomic weights, like calcium ... aluminium ... or copper even, and so saturate it with energy that it acquires properties like radium or platinum or gold? Most writers on radium think such an accumulation of energy as shall be sufficient to build up that substance impossible, at least with our known agencies. The author, however, is not so sure of it from certain experiments not yet completed" (Baskerville 1907, 9).

And the popular science press, too, quickly endorsed Ramsay's transmutational efforts and linked them firmly to those of the ancient alchemists. Baskerville, in his 1908 article for *Popular Science Monthly*, detailed not only the failed work of Emmens and Hunter but also Ramsay's and Ramsay and Cameron's 1907 work with radium emanation's transmutational effects in the presence of water (supposedly producing neon rather than helium) and producing argon rather than helium in the presence of copper salts, sulphate, or nitrate: "The emanation becomes one conventional element or another, dependent upon its environment" (1908, 50). Baskerville argued that "Ramsay's facts" were incontrovertible (50). Ramsay's experiments with copper's supposed transmutation into lithium read, he said, "like a story of magic" (51), and he argued that "Up to the time of Ramsay's work no successfully undisputed experimental facts have been offered in substantiation of these philosophic considerations. Can it be that we have Bacon's 'Philosopher's Stone' in the form of a storehouse of concentrated energy, the emanation?" (51). Of course, by January 1908, Baskerville was only repeating for a broad audience the understanding of radium as the Philosopher's Stone that Ramsay had already propounded in his 1904 *Harper's* article and that occultists had already floated. Still, the certainty that Ramsay's experiments were irrefutable was helping drive public interest in the subject. The broad perception that the new science was vindicating alchemy reached fever pitch as the experiments continued before World War I. One *New York Times* article that discussed Soddy's work and quoted extensively from *The Interpretation of Radium* was entitled "Alchemy, Long Scoffed At, Turns Out to Be True / Transmutation of Metals, the Principle of the Philosopher's Stone, Accomplished in the Twentieth Century" (*New York Times* 1911).[25]

In spite of refutations by several researchers (Trenn 58–59), Ramsay reasserted the accuracy of his results in June 1908, claiming, "if a transmutation be defined as a transformation brought about at will, by change of conditions then *this is the first case of transmutation of which conclusive evidence is put forward*" (quoted in Trenn 59). Rutherford himself challenged Ramsay's emanation experiments, even at a meeting of the Chemistry Section of the British Association in September 1908 that featured both Ramsay and a paper by Professor W. H. Hartley ("Lithium in Radioactive Minerals") that accepted Ramsay's copper-to-lithium transmutation as fact and worked out its consequences. *The Times* reported that "Professor Rutherford could not think why the emanation should behave differently when in the presence of water and when alone. He also pointed out that neon could be detected in 15 cubic centimeters of air, and remarked that Sir William Ramsay admitted the presence of enough nitrogen to correspond to a brilliant neon spectrum" (*The Times* [London] 1908b, 4a).

Despite the skepticism about Ramsay's claims shown by physicists such as Rutherford, increasingly more chemists began to involve themselves in Ramsay's transmutational quest. Ramsay's transmutation experiments with radium emanation had involved other chemists as well, and some of his work—arguing that the chemical environment affected the transmutations produced by radium—was done with A. T. Cameron (Cameron and Ramsay 1907, 1908a, 1908b). Much of the expansion of the research between 1912 and 1914 involved cathode tube experiments, and these experiments, in fact, led to the transmutational euphoria at the Chemical Society meeting in February 1913. Ramsay announced his discovery of helium in used X-ray bulbs in a meeting of the Chemical Society in January 1913 (see Ramsay 1913a). (As Trenn points out, the announcement was "somewhat surprising, since Soddy and Mackenzie had shown already in 1908 that aluminium electrodes tenaciously retain helium, neon and argon, especially after the passage of the electric discharge, *i.e.*, in old X-ray bulbs" [Trenn 63].) And Ramsay's colleague at the University of London, J. N. Collie, and Hubert S. Patterson at Leeds then began to detect both helium and neon when passing a charge through hydrogen (Collie and Patterson 1913a). The chemist E. C. C. Baly of the University of Liverpool, who had written the text on *Spectroscopy* for Ramsay's series of physical chemistry books, affirmed this work and concluded that "the case in favour of these gases being due to atomic disintegration seems overwhelmingly strong, and...this work...must rank as one of the most remarkable investigations of modern times" (quoted in Trenn 63). Collie and Patterson continued to publish papers asserting the presence of neon in the tubes and attempting to rule out sources of contamination raised by Thomson and others (occluded gases, permeable glass, and neon-contaminated hydrogen and oxygen) (1913b, 426). Irvine Masson performed experiments to test Collie and Patterson's results, and he concluded that his experiments verified the "facts" established by Collie and Patterson (Masson 233).

The chemists' frenzy over transmutation perhaps reached its peak at the meeting of the Chemical Society on February 6, 1913, at which Ramsay discussed his experiments and Collie and Patterson read papers on the alleged formation of neon and helium due to electricity discharged through hydrogen at low pressure. Professor Arthur Smithells, FRS (1860–1939), of the University of Leeds left an unpublished record of that meeting and of the gathering after it (written at 11:30 p.m. February 6, 1913) that speaks to the emotion with which chemists invested their transmutation efforts. Smithells noted that several of the chemists adjourned to Ramsay's house after the meeting:

> The conversation drifted into quiet family talk as long as I could endure. But my mind was aglow, and I could not help reverting to the great events. The absence of any sign of excitement on Ramsay's part was truly remarkable, and only confirmed my invariable experience of his true personal modesty.
>
> The scene at the Chemical Society had transcended that ever experienced at a scientific meeting. Ramsay began by giving a clear and concise account of the reasons for his *faith in transmutation,* and alluded playfully to the criticisms that had been brought against his statements about the transformation of copper into lithium. He then alluded to his experiments on the evolution of helium from the glass of an aged x-ray bulb. He said that he did no more than acknowledge a fact. (Smithells 1913, emphasis mine)

Indeed, transmutation had become an article of faith for Ramsay and many chemists.

Smithells goes on to discuss Collie's paper, adding, "The room was crowded, and the applause when Collie had finished his masterly exposition was beyond anything I had ever heard at a scientific meeting. By a strange turn of fortune I was in the chair, and after a few observations, I asked for criticism, but none came; and then Ramsay said in a few fine modest words how glad he was to feel that the burden of advancing transmutation as a fact no longer rested on him." Smithells portrays Ramsay as if he were the adept alchemist who has completed the Great Work through long and solitary toil and has sought the companionship of disciples worthy of carrying on the work—a standard narrative in Hermetic lore, and one that had been brought before the British reading public in Bulwer-Lytton's popular "Rosicrucian tale" *Zanoni* in 1842. Many years later, Egerton—who had first studied with Ramsay when he was only seventeen—still referred to him as "my master" (1963, 127).

Smithells was a significant chemist of the period, having studied with Bunsen at Heidelberg, served as professor of Chemistry at Yorkshire College (which became the University of Leeds in 1904) since 1885, and enjoyed membership in the Royal Society since 1901 (he was to serve as vice president of the Royal Society in 1916). He had even served as president of the prestigious Leeds Philosophical and Literary Society from 1902 to 1904. His personal account reveals what the official records of the Chemical Society cannot—the intensity of the emotions felt by the chemists around the issue of transmutation, and the sense that the meeting had been of historic importance. For a few brief years, much of the world of chemistry (and, not surprisingly, the members of the Alchemical Society, who followed Ramsay's work carefully and commented on it at their meetings) were absolutely persuaded that Ramsay, Collie, and the other chemists had created numerous and varied transmutations.

The popular press likewise emphasized the significance of the Chemical Society meeting. C. Ainsworth Mitchell noted that "Two papers were recently read before the Chemical Society, the importance of which to physics and chemistry it is hardly possible to over-estimate." Summarizing accounts from the *Chemical News* and the *Morning Post,* the columnist explains the papers by Ramsay and by Collie and Patterson, and notes:

> It is now accepted as a proved fact that the element radium decomposes with the formation of other elements, the simplest of which is apparently helium, and the experiments of Sir William Ramsay have indicated that the energy liberated by radium can effect the transmutation of other elements into one another; but in such cases man can only watch the changes that go on, and cannot control or vary them. But in the building-up process that has apparently now been discovered, the energy for the change is artificially supplied and controlled, and the changes are thus of a different order from the radioactive decompositions of a decaying element.
>
> To quote the words of Professor Collie—"We are possibly dealing with the primordial form of matter, the primordial atom, which when produced had all the energy necessary for forming the world. By combination of these 'atoms' the atoms of elements could be formed. Possibly the electric current directed the flow of these atoms with the full force of its energy, and with the phenomena of heat and light the elements came into existence." (1913, 146)

The chemist had become the alchemist who could create the *prima materia* and rebuild the elements, transmuting one into another. Chemistry's sense of its own disciplinary progress during this early study of radioactivity and transmutation was heightened—so much so that at the annual general meeting of the Chemical Society in March 1913, the Society's president, Percy F. Frankland, noted that the chemists need not "fear for the future prestige of their Society," given the next generation's devotion to research and success "in every branch of chemical society" (*Proceedings of the Chemical Society* 1913, 99). But, with a subtle gesture to bolster the prestige and solidify the identity of chemistry in relationship to physics, he added, "the progress of chemistry did not depend solely upon the efforts of their Fellows, for whilst during the past twenty years so many chemists had become physicists, quite recently the tables had been turned, and physicists were becoming chemists." He cites three physicists who had been debunkers of the transmutational gold rush:

> That eminent physicist, Sir Joseph Thomson, had entered the field of analytical chemistry, and had invented an absolutely new system of chemical analysis. There was also Prof. Strutt with his "active nitrogen," whilst Prof. Rutherford, in his wonderful researches on radioactivity, had revealed the existence of a whole series of new elements. Those eminent physicists had discovered, what chemists had long known, that the science was the most exacting of mistresses, making more imperious demands on the time and patience of her votaries than any of her sisters. (*Proceedings of the Chemical Society*, 99)

Not only did Frankland position chemistry as the discipline to address current questions, co-opting even the debunking physicists into the fold of chemistry, but he even went on to claim that "Chemistry was also the science of which the aim, scope, and method were least understood, not only by the general public, but by that august assemblage of persons who styled themselves 'the cultivated classes'" (99). (At this same dinner, prophesying economic turmoil if chemists succeeded in synthesizing gold, was H. G. Wells—to whom we shall return in chapter 4.)

The Alchemical Society's Response

If the alchemical revival of the 1880s and 1890s had helped lay the groundwork for transmutation to move to the center of chemists' research programs, occultists and devotees of alchemy were also exhilarated by the heyday of the rush to transmutation. Indeed, as *Nature* had reported, the Chemical Society meeting of February 6, 1913, did indeed attract "great public attention" (*Nature* 1913, 653). Among those paying attention were not only Redgrove, who was a Fellow of the Chemical Society, but also Waite and other occultists in the Alchemical Society.

Waite presented his paper "The Canon of Criticism in Respect of Alchemical Literature" to the second general meeting of the Alchemical Society on February 14, 1913, just eight days after the Chemical Society meeting. He hoped, he said, that "at our next meeting some one will come forward to speak with authority on the old dream in the light of modern science," and he went on to explain:

> It is only yesterday that we heard of a discovery by Sir William Ramsay and other scientists—working, I believe, independently—which may mean the transmutation of one chemical element into another—subject, of course, to the validity of Prof. Sir J. J. Thomson's alternative contention. We must seek to know more of the trend of recent discovery in this direction, and we need to be informed by someone who has an eye to the efforts of the past, but also a complete disregard of any *a priori* reasonings which actuated those efforts. (Waite 1913, 20)

Waite had presumably seen the report in *Nature* published the day before that presented Collie and Patterson's "Origins of Helium and Neon" as well as Thomson's objections to their work.

The astrologer and Theosophist Walter Gorn Old presided over the meeting, as Redgrove was ill at home, but Redgrove's interest in Ramsay's transmutations and writings was evident throughout his work on alchemy during this period. In the May 1913 issue of the *Journal of the Alchemical Society*, Redgrove discussed Ramsay's "Presence of Helium in the Gas from the Interior of an X-Ray Bulb" (Ramsay 1913a), published in the January 1913 *Transactions of the Chemical Society*, and Collie and Patterson's "Presence of Neon in Hydrogen after the Passage of Electric Discharge through the Latter at Low Pressures," published in the March 1913 issue of the same journal. Exploring how alchemical thinking was relevant to modern science, Redgrove noted that "The experiments described in these papers, which indicate that it may be possible either to transmute hydrogen into helium and neon by means of the electric discharge at low pressures, or else actually to build up the atoms of the two latter gases from the electrons of the cathode-rays, have already attracted a good deal of attention from the public press" (1913b, 77). Either outcome would have been welcome news to both Ramsay and Redgrove. The natural transmutations witnessed in the radioactive disintegration of uranium, radium, and thorium all involved what Ramsay had called a "degradation"—a transmutation into lighter elements. But Ramsay and Redgrove saw a neo-alchemical ability to transmute lighter into heavier elements, a building up, as an important achievement for science and for alchemy. Redgrove defended the experiments against their scientific critics (the physicists), noting that "It has been suggested that the presence of helium and neon observed in the tubes may have been due to leakage, but this suggestion is rendered very doubtful in view (1) of the large quantity of air needed, and (2) the careful and cautious manner in which the experiments and blank check experiments have been carried out" (77).

As the transmutation rush continued across 1913 and 1914, the Alchemical Society continued to engage with scientific research. The engineer Herbert Chatley, in his December 12, 1913, talk to the Society entitled "Alchemy in China," discussed Ramsay's transmutations, presumably his radon-induced supposed transmutations from copper to lithium and his observed transmutations of radium to helium. Chatley opined that "a more gradual change would produce gold as one of the descending steps" (37). And the December 1913 issue of the *Journal of the Alchemical Society* also reviewed two works that engaged with Ramsay's transmutation work: Mellor's *Modern Inorganic Chemistry* and William Kearney Carr's *Matter and Some of Its Dimensions*. (Remember that Mellor was both a member of the Alchemical Society and an author in Ramsay's series of books on physical chemistry.) Moreover, Ralph Rowbottom reviewed Redgrove's 1911 *Alchemy: Ancient and Modern; Being a Brief Account of the Alchemistic Doctrines, and Their Relations, to Mysticism on the One Hand, and to recent Discoveries in Physical Science on the Other Hand; Together with some Particulars Regarding the Lives and Teachings of the most Noted Alchemists*, in which, Rowbottom mentioned, Redgrove had engaged with Ramsay and Cameron's experiments with radium emanation on copper and lead salts (Rowbottom 1914, 55). Even the advertisements in the journal made the connection between ancient alchemy and Ramsay's experiments. The ad on the November 1914 issue for reprints of Redgrove's article, "The Transmutation of the Elements," in *Knowledge* noted that it "contains portraits of Paracelsus and the two van Helmonts, and photographs of spectra illustrating Sir William Ramsay's experiments on the transmutation of the elements."

In the preface to the 1911 edition of *Alchemy: Ancient and Modern*, Redgrove had argued, "The spontaneous change of one 'element' into another has been witnessed, and the recent work of Sir William Ramsay suggests the possibility of realising the old alchemistic dream—the transmutation of the 'base' metals into gold" (1911, xi). He referred to Ramsay and Cameron as "modern alchemists," tracing the history of their work with radium emanation as well as the debunking work of Curie, Rutherford, and Royds. By the second edition of the volume, brought out in 1922, he was still persuaded by Ramsay's work: of Rutherford's 1919 successful transmutations using alpha particles, he said that, "In view of Rutherford's results a further repetition of Ramsay's experiments would certainly appear to be advisable" (1922, vii). And Redgrove continued to use Ramsay's 1904 statement in *Harper's* about radium as the Philosopher's Stone and the *elixir vitae* in the conclusion to his own volume (1922, 140–141).

The Waning of Chemistry's Gold Rush

In spite of the excitement the race to transmutation had spurred in the worlds of chemistry and occult alchemy, the crash came in 1914. The prestige and identity transmutation efforts had conferred upon chemistry were called into question—by physicists. Criticism had already come heavily from physicists such as J. J. Thomson, who debunked some of the experiments following the announcement of the Chemical Society meeting in February 1913, as well as from Rutherford, Royds, and Robert John Strutt (Lord Rayleigh). Even sympathetic chemists such as Madame Curie had been unable to reproduce Ramsay's results. Ramsay's own student and research partner, Egerton, could not successfully repeat the experiments when he went to work in a lab in Berlin.

Strutt was the fourth Baron Rayleigh, son of John William Strutt, the third Baron Rayleigh, with whom Ramsay had collaborated on the discovery of argon. He, like Thomson, ran independent experiments that undermined Ramsay, Collie, and Patterson's results:

> Very general interest has been aroused by the observations of Collie and Patterson on [the production of neon or helium by electric discharge]. It is understood that their results have been endorsed by Sir W. Ramsay from independent evidence. The present experiments were begun in the hope of confirming the work of Collie and Patterson and of sharing in the interesting field of research thus opened up. The results, however, have been negative, whether from a failure to appreciate the proper conditions for the production of neon or from some other cause. (Strutt 1914, 499)

Strutt hinted at the cause of Collie and Patterson's findings of neon: "Most rigorous precautions have to be taken to avoid getting this [neon] spectrum from atmospheric contamination" (506). By 1914, even the chemist Thomas Merton, who had wished to confirm Collie and Patterson's findings of neon transmutation, was reluctantly forced to conclude that the presence of argon and other such gases were the products of "an exceedingly small, but continuous leak" (Merton 1914, 552). In a surprisingly personal admission for a scientific article—one that underscores the importance of their transmutation efforts to the chemists, and the affect with which they invested them—Merton adds, "It is a disappointment to me to find that I have been unable to reproduce the conditions necessary for the production of neon or helium, and have obtained only negative results" (553).[26] By mid-1914, after Egerton had presented a paper yielding negative results from Ramsay, Collie, and Patterson's experiments, Collie, Patterson, and Masson's collaborative work had begun to sound defensive. Their July 1914 collaboration aimed to refute the challenges to their 1913 conclusions that neon and helium had been produced by transmutation. They attempted to show that the glass itself and aluminum anodes did not contain neon and helium. Their concluding paragraph flatly denied what many must have come to believe by then: "We have endeavoured to put the facts of the case as fully as possible, *without reference to any preconceived theory*" (Collie, Patterson, Masson 1914, 45; emphasis mine).

The debunking received less attention in the popular press than the claims of transmutation had, though Ramsay's and Curie's celebrity ensured that Curie's inability to create lithium using his copper sulphate experiment would be covered by the London *Times* (1908a). The scientific publishers were more even-handed. The correspondent from *Nature* who reported on the February 6, 1913, meeting of the Chemical Society, at which Ramsay and Collie and Patterson presented their findings of helium and neon supposedly created in vacuum tubes, reported the "great public attention" the meeting had attracted. But he also reported Soddy's statement to the *Westminster Gazette* that in 1908 he had already explained the appearance of helium in vacuum tubes as due to the aluminum electrodes absorbing these gases during previous uses (*Nature* 1913, 654). The correspondent drew attention to the publication in the same issue of *Nature* of Thomson's different interpretation of Collie and Patterson's results (*Nature* 1913, 653). A brief article by J. W. N. Sullivan in *Scientific American* covering the Chemical Society meeting mentioned J. J. Thomson's objections and Soddy and Lodge's similar alternative explanation (226). But the longer article on the meeting in the *Scientific American Supplement* presented Ramsay, Collie, and Patterson's results uncritically. It focused on the excitement of the meeting, even describing the "cheers" that met Collie's announcement of further proof of his result (154). It also reported, under the heading "A Momentous Paper," Smithells' enthusiastic recognition of the significance of the papers:

> Prof. Smithells opened the discussion by saying that he was somewhat breathless at the papers they had heard. It required a great deal of courage for scientific workers to bring forward such results, and they must admire it. Their courage, he thought, was justified, for their experimental record was such as to justify what in others would have been extremely rash. He paid a generous tribute to the care and patience with which Mr. Patterson had conducted the experiments in his laboratory at Leeds. Of the work of Prof. Collie and Sir

William Ramsay it was unnecessary to say anything. For dramatic interest, he thought, the paper had never been surpassed.... Prof. Smithells moved that the thanks of the Society be given to the authors, to whom they felt a great obligation, for their momentous communication. (*Scientific American Supplement* 1913, 155)

Thomson's correct explanation—like Soddy's, that the gases were occluded in the metal of the anodes (1913, 645–46)—did not dampen the chemists' enthusiasm for their efforts. Smithells, though, had sounded a small and, as it turns out, entirely correct note of caution, saying that "The obvious criticism was that in the work enormous weight had necessarily been laid on spectroscopic evidence, and his limited experience in this connection had taught him caution, but he felt sure that the authors were too experienced to fall into such pitfalls" (*Scientific American Supplement* 1913, 155).

It was Egerton who finally convinced Ramsay that he had been wrong. Egerton was, again, not only a sympathetic chemist but also Ramsay's research partner, and even he failed to reproduce Ramsay's results. Ramsay's findings—that had prompted the claim "finis coronat opus"—were never published. In spite of continuing efforts into the mid-1920s to use his chemical methods to cause transmutation, the field was essentially left to Rutherford and the physicists. Rutherford's 1919 transmutation was verifiable with the proper instrumentation, and Cockcroft and Walton's cyclotron at Cavendish in the early 1930s set the course for the high-energy particle physics of the rest of the twentieth century.

The press eagerly portrayed Rutherford's 1919 transmutations (as it had with Ramsay's 1907 "transmutations") to be the first successful work of alchemy, claiming that Rutherford had "solved the riddle of the transmutation of matter, the secret sought by the ancient alchemists" (*New York Times* 1919, 2) and invoking the failure of Ramsay's experiments.[27] Still, the chemists tried one last time in the 1920s to revive the experimental program of Ramsay, Collie, Patterson and others. In an unpublished "Note on Transmutation Experiments" from 1927, Egerton revisits Merton's, Strutt's, and others' inability to confirm the positive results of Ramsay, Collie, and Patterson, writing that "since those days experiments have been made in America on the explosion of tungsten wires, and which, though at first promising . . . led to negative results, followed by the supposed transmutations of mercury into gold, of lead into thallium made by [Adolf] Miethe, by [Arthur] Smits and others. These have all been definitely negatives, and are of rather different character from the type of work which was engaging Ramsay's immediate attention" (1927a, 1). Berlin chemist Adolf Miethe and Hans Stammreich claimed in 1924 to have synthesized gold from mercury using ultraviolet rays from mercury vapor lamps. (*Scientific American* in December 1924 tried to replicate Miethe's experiments, with negative results.) University of Amsterdam professor Arthur Smits and A. Karssen, inspired by Miethe's methods, claimed to have transmuted lead into mercury and thallium.[28] Even Soddy's research student Fritz Paneth (who had worked with Soddy in his Glasgow lab from 1911–13 and whose work with George de Hevesy at the Vienna Institute of Radium Research on radioactive tracers helped earn de Hevesy the 1943 Nobel Prize in chemistry) became involved in the resurgence of transmutation efforts by chemists. Collie, Patterson, and Masson's pre-War claims to the transmutation of helium and neon were briefly revived, too, this time by R. W. Riding and E. C. C. Baly, who explained the production of helium as having "its origin in the disintegration of the nitrogen atom" (Riding and Baly 1925, 193).

The press again picked up on the enthusiasm for alchemical transmutation and, once more, placed it squarely within the field of chemistry. Reporting on Paneth and Peters's results, *Current History* proclaimed, "Throughout the ages the alchemist has held out the hope of changing the undesirable into the desirable. As the successor to the mystic of the Middle Ages there is the modern chemist working in new fields where physics and chemistry meet" (Watson 1926, 393). Though the article gave Rutherford credit for the only transmutation broadly accepted by scientists, it (perhaps not surprisingly) incorrectly identified Rutherford as a *chemist* and misleadingly made Rutherford's transmutation sound like a chemical process of removing an element from a compound: "Already transmutation has been claimed by a number of investigators, and in one case at least the scientific world generally accepts the fact that transmutation has been accomplished. Sir Ernest Rutherford, the British chemist, a decade ago knocked H (standing for the chemical element hydrogen) out of many of the lighter elements, including nitrogen, boron, fluorine, sodium, aluminum and phosphorus" (Watson 393).

But, as Egerton reveals, Paneth's attempts to transmute hydrogen into helium by using palladium turned out to have been in error: "Since these experiments, Paneth has found that transmutation does not account for the helium formed, but that leakage through the glass (which is supposed porous) accounts for his results" (1927a, 2). He laments that Baly's work on transmutations requiring the presence of nitrogen also had failed. Egerton concludes that leakage through heated glass or at stopcocks accounts for the rare gases supposedly produced by transmutation in these experiments (3).

Egerton had become involved with Ramsay just as Ramsay began his serious thinking about transmutation. After having had an interview with Ramsay at Ramsay's house at the end of 1903 in which the two discussed the radium transmutations into helium (Egerton 1963, 127), Egerton had commenced his studies at University College in October 1904. He attended Ramsay's lectures just as Ramsay returned from his 1904 trip to America during which he had lectured on the transmutational possibilities of the new science and visited R. M. Hunter's alchemical laboratory to view his silver-to-gold transmutation experiments.[29] Egerton had even been part of Ramsay's last transmutation experiments in his London home, and, after leaving for Germany in 1914, he reluctantly published a paper with results that negated his own work with Ramsay. In many ways, Egerton in the 1920s had given further life to the alchemical program of his teacher, Ramsay, thinking of the stripping down and building up of atoms in much the way Ramsay had. Even though the experiments of Ramsay and the ensuing rush of transmuting chemists had been flawed, Egerton still held out hopes for the project and for chemistry's stake. Egerton clearly wanted Ramsay's experiments to have succeeded, admitting that "all the same, there remain points which are still difficult to explain" (1927a, 3). And he concluded, "There is little doubt that atoms will be stripped and rebuilt sometime in the future, and the first to go forth into that untracked territory was Sir William Ramsay. The proof of the spontaneous conversion of emanation into helium was a discovery which first blasted the way. It cannot be said that the last attempts at transmutation were a false trail, for they will form ground from which by careful experiment, renewed efforts will be made" (1927a, 3). There is no mention in this account of Rutherford's successful and persuasive 1919 nitrogen transmutations at the Cavendish, or of the kind of thinking about instrumentation that would lead Cockroft and Walton at the Cavendish or Ernest Lawrence in California to create proton accelerators and cyclotrons to disintegrate nuclei more effectively. Egerton himself—like the chemists reviving transmutation experiments—was sidestepping and even ignoring the physicists' successes.

Chemistry would lose the ownership of atomic theory to nuclear physics in a boundary struggle that had begun at the turn of the century. But the very borderland created by bringing alchemical notions into contact with the already liminal subfield of physical chemistry had set the transmutational agenda of the new atomic science. Ultimately, it helped create a paradigm shift—one that moved the understanding of atoms and elements away from Daltonian concepts of the preceding century. Yet, the resurgence of claims by chemists in the 1920s to have synthesized gold from mercury, following Miethe's work in Berlin, led to an unexpected public anxiety during shaky post-War economic times—concerns about the repercussions of modern alchemy for the gold standard. It is to the realm of economics and monetary theory that our chronicle of modern alchemy and its consequences must now turn.

4

Atomic Alchemy and the Gold Standard

After some three millennia of alchemical efforts to transmute a base metal into gold and after the widespread scientific and popular press frenzy over atomic transmutation in the early twentieth century, a modern alchemist finally succeeded in producing gold. The climactic moment occurred, however, not in 1907, or even in 1919, but in 1980. By then, the scientists at the University of California at Berkeley who used a particle accelerator to change a small amount of bismuth into one-billionth of a cent's worth of gold (at the cost of $10,000 [Levere 2001, 1]) had embarked on research that was more a sideline curiosity than a world-changing event or even a profound scientific achievement. Yet in the 1920s, public fascination with the alchemical nature of the new atomic sciences had reached such a pitch that the consequences of transmutation began to seem relevant to fields other than religion and science. The possibility that an alchemist, radiochemist, or nuclear physicist might actually harness the mysterious alpha and beta rays to synthesize gold seemed to many to entail fantastic and alarming consequences—especially for the world economy.

The preceding chapters have portrayed the consequences for science and for occult alchemy of their mutual interest in material transmutation. This chapter explores different cultural consequences of modern alchemy in relationship to monetary anxieties during the Depression Era. In particular, it narrates how the idea of modern alchemy intensified questioning of the gold standard and of the moral foundation of scientific aspiration. By the late 1920s and early 1930s, as the West slid into the Depression, modern alchemy began to migrate into discussions of monetary theory and portrayals of economic concerns in the press. Atomic alchemy broke down barriers not only between occultism and science but also between those subjects and economics or monetary theory. Nowhere was this more evident than in fears about the gold standard's stability in postwar Britain and America.

This period witnessed a number of calls for abandoning a metallic monetary standard. Such calls frequently came from so-called money cranks who fought against the monetary establishment. An insistent, though not always coordinated, movement pushing for monetary and economic reforms briefly attained some visibility in the 1920s and '30s. Schemes included Guild Socialism, Social Credit, and stamped money, and among the key figures in Britain and America were A. R. Orage, Clifford Hugh Douglas, and Arthur Kitson.[1] Bridging the fields of monetary theory and modern alchemy was none other than Frederick Soddy. Soddy had just won the 1921 Nobel Prize in chemistry (as the Nobel committee put it, for his "important contribution to our knowledge of the radioactive bodies, and [his] pioneer works on the existence and nature of isotopes" [quoted in Howorth 1958, 224]). But his move from chemistry into economics in the 1920s damaged Soddy's professional standing as a scientist far more than any public statements about alchemy ever could have.

It has been commonly understood that the carnage and tragedy of the First World War and the economic crises that followed it steered Soddy into economics (Merricks 1996, 108). Other notable public figures, such as Ezra Pound, followed a similar path for like reasons—though Pound's political sympathies moved him into fascism, while Soddy remained on the Left. As we shall see, however, Soddy's alchemical interests helped him connect chemistry to monetary theory. He would eventually cast that relationship as both moral *and* scientific.

In one sense, the gold standard already was a moral notion for economists. It was the prime manifestation of what Nicholas Mayhew has called a "moral idea of money" (2000, xi)—the idea that a gold-backed currency is "a constant and unchanging currency unit with which to measure personal or public obligations" (xi). The gold standard was meant to ensure stability in both the domestic economy and international trade, and it was almost an article of faith for most economists. As Mayhew notes, "So irrevocable did it all seem that when the [British] National government of 1931 did eventually devalue and abandon gold, its Labour Cabinet predecessors complained that no one had told them you could do that" (214–15).

But a different moral conception of value was employed by occultists, who rescripted the nature of a "gold standard." In 1907, the year of Ramsay's high-profile transmutation claims—and a time of economic crisis, during which an alarming quantity of British gold drained across the Atlantic to America—Isabelle de Steiger published *On a Gold Basis: A Treatise on Mysticism*. De Steiger, whom we have encountered as a vice president of the Alchemical Society, a member of the Golden Dawn, and a prominent proponent of spiritual alchemy, chose occult publisher and future Alchemical Society member Philip Wellby to bring out the book. She dedicated it to Mary Atwood, "my best teacher, the author of 'A Suggestive Enquiry into the Hermetic Mystery,'" and a major initiator of the Victorian spiritual alchemy concept. De Steiger advocated a mystical gold standard, distinguishing between a false modern sense of value rooted in material gold and a permanent, spiritual basis for value: "though the false basis of material gold may be the goal of a debased modern humanity, yet the true religion that would bless mankind is never destroyed, but is an eternal place built on the perfect gold Basis of Immortal Truth" (1907, 333). De Steiger appropriates the logic of the gold standard and the terms by which economists valued gold—i.e., its intrinsic and permanent value—to undergird spiritual and moral concerns. Indeed, she situates the moral imperatives of her mystical spirituality in economic terms that, after the War, would become central to the critiques launched by the money cranks at a system that, they argued, encouraged hoarding, stifled the healthy circulation of money, and prevented the laborer from a just share of society's overall wealth. De Steiger admonishes:

> But if a man, having the gold of truth, lazily hoards it, too idle to seek to put it out to interest, or from any other motive misuses it, then is that man rich in knowledge but poor in love to his fellowman; and thus intellectually despising him, he will find it *hard* to enter into the kingdom, and regeneration will not come near him.
>
> Regeneration is for both rich and poor in this world's coin if they are rich in generous interest, sympathy, and respect, and full of kindness to their fellowman. (330–31)

De Steiger concludes her 349-page treatise by folding together into a mystical framework concepts of permanence that evoke the material world of economics—the gold standard—and notions of stability, such as the "Stable Atom" derived from mysticism but echoing the science of radioactivity. Beneath the world of material transmutation asserted by atomic scientists and by alchemists lies a substratum of immutable spiritual value:

> But with the fear there is also the twin feeling, hope—hope which blossoms into the eventual knowledge that man can have a certainty

that there is behind all a *permanence* in the Infinite and Eternal God, the Divinity symbolized to us in Revelation as our Father waiting for us, his children, to come back willingly, and with all the added knowledge of experience, to our birthplace; no longer a temporary inn, but the gold Basis of eternity; hope that the Stable Atom will, in the end of man's dwelling in this Kingdom of Time, bring him by the royal road home to a royal palace—wherefrom stretches the illimitable future of Divinity. (349, emphasis in original)

As we shall see, the problems that frequently occurred with the gold standard were understood by most during the late nineteenth and early twentieth centuries to concern the supply of available gold. Rarely did anyone question the intrinsic value of gold, or that such a material was required to stabilize the world of commerce. By the 1920s, modern alchemy began to suggest to many that no material had unalterable intrinsic value.[2] If one metal could be changed into another, if the natural abundance of an element could be changed, or if gold could simply be manufactured by an atomic scientist or an alchemist, how could any metal serve to buttress a monetary system? Such questions led to alarming scenarios about the collapse of the world economy, but they also caused many to begin to rethink the nature of money and to emphasize its basis in human work and need. The ethics of human action, rather than the permanent value of a material, took precedence in these visions. Even the engine that drives human work—energy—came to the forefront of many new conceptions of money. Just as the spiritual alchemy notion gave Victorian and early-twentieth-century occultists a nonmaterial ethical and spiritual goal for alchemical research (even as it gave way to a spiritualized vision of real, material laboratory transmutations), the energy created by atomic transmutation gave modern alchemists a nonmaterial justification for pursuing transmutation. Energy for the benefit of man came to be seen, as Soddy would put it, as the "real alchemy," as opposed to the "false alchemy" of mere gold transmutation.

During the 1920s and the Depression Era, the fears of economic collapse and hopes for monetary restructuring caused by modern alchemy registered most vividly in American science fiction. Alchemy and, in particular, the new scientifically validated understanding that matter might be transmuted through various processes of energy bombardment did not spur Britain, America, and Western Europe to abandon the gold standard. Numerous market crises, the First World War, and changing governmental responses to depressions helped lead the West away from the classic gold standard and toward the Bretton Woods system and beyond. But the transmutational possibilities that modern alchemy raised did draw attention to the problems of a metallic standard for money—whether the bimetallism of silver and gold or a pure gold standard—and to the nature of money itself.

The occultists and many scientists helped feed the popular press's appetite for alchemy. Alchemical transmutations that had been a topic for occult or gothic literature now became a key theme for science fiction as well. This new generation of science fiction was written during the years of monetary crisis and eventual abandonment of the gold standard, between the turn of the century and the early 1930s. Perhaps the fullest elaboration of modern alchemy's threat to the gold standard appeared in the emerging sci-fi pulps of Hugo Gernsback between 1926 and the mid-1930s. These sci-fi stories particularly thematized the effects of modern alchemy—of metallic transmutations caused by the instruments and science of nuclear physics and radiochemistry—on the world economy and used the theme to interrogate the nature and perils of a metallic currency. Their authors imagined, in a way that would look familiar to Soddy, how science might move society beyond the crises and limitations that a metallic system of exchange imposed on twentieth-century economies. Indeed, the arc from an occult alchemical classic like Edward Bulwer-Lytton's *Zanoni,* in the mid-nineteenth century, through the atomic alchemy stories of the turn of the twentieth century to Depression-era narratives traces a blurring of lines between occult or gothic and science fiction, and even between those genres and the monetary reform pamphlet.[3] The occult alchemy that had helped shape the discourse of atomic science and the modern alchemy portrayed in science fiction shared an important feature that resonated with British and American society during the period. They registered alchemical transmutation as a moral issue—at a moment in Western economic history that saw unprecedented anxieties about the monetary system.

The Gold Standard: Confidence and Crisis

The modern gold standard in Britain began with the Bank Charter Act of 1844 that established Bank of England notes fully backed by gold. In the United States, its origins were in the Coinage Act of 1873 (the so-called Crime of 1873) when the United States abandoned a bimetallic gold and silver path for a monometallic gold standard. With the Gold Standard Act of 1900, the United States government set the gold quantity that backed each United States dollar. British sterling financed a large portion of world trade and provided a seemingly stable, convertible currency that was interconnected with the American economy (as well as with those of several other countries). It is clear in retrospect that, even through the classic gold-standard period of the late nineteenth century to 1914, the gold standard could not always guarantee stability. It could even damage the economy. But the conception of gold as a real and unchanging bearer of value, rather than a mutable token of exchange—in other words, an inherently valued commodity—was tenacious during the period. As Mayhew explains, "A precious-metal currency is not necessarily an unchanging one, and the value of precious metal also fluctuates. Scholars, economists, and government ministers have for centuries sought a stable currency, and many have put their faith in metal without really grasping that the value of silver and gold will vary in accordance with supply and demand just like any other commodity" (xi).

Adherence to a gold standard flew in the face of nineteenth-century bimetallic theory and significant regional economic interests. Indeed, the very thing that made precious metals seem enduringly valuable—their rarity—also led to problems. In what Glyn Davies calls "bimetallism's final fling," the gold and silver bimetallism of the United States and France in the 1860s was designed to create more stability than a monometallic standard. Theoretically the money supply would be less restricted with two metals, avoiding inflation (Davies 2002, 494). The Coinage Act of 1873 briefly ended the coining of silver dollars, and large silver deposits were discovered in Nevada in the 1870s; both drove the price of silver down. Banking and economic interests in the cities of the Northeast opposed any return to free silver (that is, the unlimited coinage of silver) for fear of inflation. The silver mining interests in the West and rural communities of the West and South, however, called for a return to bimetallism in order to prop up both silver and farming goods prices. The free silver movement reached its apex in William Jennings Bryan's run for the presidency on the Democratic ticket in 1896 (and his famous "cross of gold" speech, delivered at the Democratic Convention). Bryan was decisively defeated. The gold standard seemed to have triumphed (Davies 494–99; Galbraith 1975, 97–100).

In Britain, the security of the British pound had proved key to London's position as the financial capital of the world before World War I. As Sir William Harcourt, Gladstone's chancellor, wrote in 1892: "London...is the Metropolis of the Commerce of the World to which all nations resort to settle their business. This I believe...to be owing to the soundness of our monetary system, London being the only place where you can always get gold. It is for that reason that all the exchange business of the world is done in London" (quoted in Mayhew 176). But such optimism about the availability of gold was not always justified.

The problem with silver had been its increasing abundance; demand problems nagged the gold standard. While the value of gold, which resulted more from its scarcity than from any of its intrinsic properties, seemed to ensure monetary stability, both Britain and the United States during the classical gold-standard period suffered from problems of gold supply and reserves. A number of financial panics culminated in a run on gold reserves in the United States Treasury and on gold stocks in 1893 (Galbraith 99). Moreover, in 1907, when Ramsay first declared that he had caused transmutations in his laboratory, a financial catastrophe in America led to a run on British gold. The Knickerbocker Trust and the Trust Company of America (the third- and second-largest trusts in the United States) collapsed in late 1907, and some 246 banks failed in 1907 and 1908.[4] This climate led to the creation of the Federal Reserve in 1913. But the panic of 1907 reached well beyond American shores, causing serious gold supply problems in Britain as gold drained across the Atlantic to nervous American investors.

Even in the nineteenth century, the gold supply was subject to unstable periods of shortage and abundance. A spike in gold production caused by the Californian and Australian strikes of the 1850s was followed by a decline in production in the 1870s, just as France, Germany, Switzerland, Belgium, and Holland went onto the gold standard. In the 1880s, Britain had begun to discuss a return to bimetallism to ease gold shortages, but gold discoveries in South Africa again raised gold production dramatically. Britain's emergence from a lengthy depression (1873–96) coupled with the new supplies from South African mines finally put an end to bimetallist schemes (Mayhew 176–77, 190). The international gold standard between 1890 and 1914 required an accumulation of £1,000,000,000—and only the supplies of gold generated by new discoveries in South Africa, the United States, the Yukon, Russia, and Australia made the widespread adoption of the gold standard possible (Drummond 1987, 17).

In sum, the period from 1902—when Rutherford and Soddy's work on radioactive transmutation was published—until the early 1930s saw crippling problems in the gold standard. Britain abandoned the gold standard during the crisis brought on by the War in 1914. It and other Western nations that had discarded the gold standard returned to it briefly in the later 1920s: Britain in 1925, France in 1926, Italy in 1927, Norway in 1928, and Portugal in 1929. In 1931, Britain again abandoned the gold standard until the Bretton Woods Agreement in 1944 created a limited variant of the gold standard and the International Monetary Fund (Mayhew 214–15). And in the United States, due to Depression-era banking and monetary crises, Franklin D. Roosevelt's first act as president was to declare a bank holiday to buy time to begin banking reform. In an executive order of April 5, 1933, he confiscated most privately held gold, and in January 1934 the Gold Reserve Act replaced the Gold Standard Act of 1900, bringing gold out of private hands and banks and into the Treasury. This ended the internal circulation of gold in the United States (Davies 516).

Modern Alchemy and Monetary Anxiety

The challenges facing Western powers' banking systems and governments during the gold-standard years were frequently those of shortages due to runs on gold during financial crises. But the alchemical dream of creating gold, long seen as a vain delusion or as the territory of charlatans hoping to bilk the greedy and the gullible, began to provoke serious thoughts about two issues: first, the catastrophic financial repercussions of synthetic gold on gold-standard economies, and second, the very nature of money.

Concerns about the impact that a modern alchemist's transmuted gold might have on the economy had been periodically expressed in the United States since Stephen Emmens's 1897 claims to have created gold from silver. As one article entitled "The Revival of Alchemy" published in *Science* put it: "In the United States two notable events have occurred within twelve months, one of which seems to threaten financial revolution" (Bolton 1897, 862). Edward C. Brice's claims to have manufactured gold from antimony were dismissed by the United States Patent Office, but Emmens's claims, and his sale of six ingots of an alloy of silver and gold to the United States Assay Office, were harder to dismiss (862). But before the First World War and the rising concern about the gold standard in America and Britain, many newspaper articles were more interested in issues of alchemical fraud than they were about threats to the national economies of the West.[5] Moreover, there were no credible and verifiable scientific transmutations until after the War.

Doubts about the viability of the gold standard increased during the economically fragile postwar period. At the same time, legitimate scientists initiated a second phase of efforts to transmute a base metal to gold in the wake of Rutherford's successful 1919 transmutation of nitrogen. Consequently, concerns began to surface about alchemical gold's effect on the economy. Even the federal government of the United States felt compelled to issue a statement to calm public fears. During the postwar depression—before the economy began to recover during the "Coolidge prosperity" in late 1923 or 1924—some officials in the Harding administration commented publicly about the repercussions of synthesized gold. In January 1922, a front-page article in the *New*

York Times reported one such official statement: "The recent revival of interest in alchemy and published suggestions that artificial gold might become so abundant the natural metal would lose its value as a basis for currency brought from the United States Geological Survey today a statement that no occasion exists for chemists to hope for, nor economists to fear, the prospect of the precious metal being produced in the laboratory" (*New York Times* 1922, 1). The spokesman for the United States Geological Survey stressed, "No one has yet succeeded ... in making gold or in obtaining it from any other chemical element. The feat cannot be safely called impossible, but it is fairly certain that if any chemist should succeed in transforming into gold some substance that has hitherto been regarded as a simple element the process would be so difficult and costly as to make the gold far more expensive than the natural metal" (1).

The next year, however, a government scientist was willing to speculate publicly that alchemical gold's potential effect on the economy entailed the need for real exploration of monetary reform. The *Times* reported, "The alchemist's problem of transmutation of elements has been solved by modern science, according to Paul D. Foote, a 'modern alchemist' from the United States Bureau of Standards, who lectured yesterday to the Department of Physics of the Summer school at Columbia University on 'The Alchemist'" (*New York Times* 1923, 16). Like Soddy, Foote argued that energy was the payoff to transmutation: "the older alchemists desired to create gold; the modern alchemist would destroy it. For the energy from the destruction of gold is immensely valuable" (16). But the *Times* article quickly turned to what at the time was probably the more engaging subject, the economic consequences of synthesized gold: "The economic consequences of a commercial application of the scientific principles of alchemy would be tremendous, according to Foote. Gold could be produced in such floods that the Governments of the world could save themselves only by demonetizing the metal and making a new standard" (16). Without specifically naming Yale professor Irving Fisher, a key proponent of a goods-based dollar, Foote argued that alchemical gold would "involve the replacement of the gold dollar by the 'goods' or 'market basket' dollar." The *Times* added that Foote "saw no permanent harm in such a financial revolution—in fact, he rather hoped that it would come. If alchemy could rationalize our monetary system it would not by any means be the least of its triumphs" (16).

But even as the economy improved during the Coolidge administration, new gold transmutation reports from legitimate scientists could immediately raise public concern. In 1924, the German photochemist and photography pioneer Adolf Miethe (1862–1927)[6] of the Charlottenburg Technical College in Berlin was thought to have transmuted mercury vapors into gold. Rather than emphasizing Miethe's supposed scientific achievement, the *New York Times* headlines blared: "SYNTHETIC GOLD MIGHT DISRUPT WORLD / Commercial Use Would Mean Chaos in Finance / Without Regulation, Economist Says" (Bent 1924, xx3). The article featured three side-by-side illustrations that ominously interposed a depiction of medieval alchemists at work (entitled "The Alchemists Search for the Secret of Making Gold") between a photo of "Gold Mining at Nome, Alaska" and one of "Moving Gold in New York Streets." The photos portrayed the willingness of men to endure the harsh conditions of Alaska in search of fortunes in gold and the heavy security such an important monetary instrument demanded in the heart of American capitalism. Yet it is precisely that order—an order based on the stable value of gold—that the alchemists, with their potentially sinister secrets, ultimately seemed to threaten.

Silas Bent opened his eight-column *Times* article with the by-now-familiar paeans to the medieval alchemists in light of the discoveries of the modern alchemist: "At last, the philosopher's stone! A German chemist, idling with a quartz lamp and electric rays and quicksilver vapor, has blundered upon the secret which gave color to medieval mysticism and alchemy, the formula which charlatans pretended to have, which kings and Popes sought, and which Governments made an excuse for debasing their currencies. Mercury has been made over into gold." Similarly, he ended his article singing the praises of the medieval alchemists as "the great men of that day." Paracelsus was "the true pioneer of the modern chemist and the prophet of a revolution in general science." "Their methods," Bent concluded, "were mostly absurd, but their faith [in transmutation] was well founded."

As we have seen, such comparisons between medieval alchemy and atomic science were common by 1924, but the article highlighted the growing concern with monetary issues. It was dominated by an interview with Benjamin M. Anderson Jr., "economist of the Chase National Bank of New York," on the subject of the impact that inexpensive alchemical transmutation might have on the national and world economy. Anderson reassured readers that such a scenario was only hypothetical. Bent had pointed out that it cost Miethe about $2,000 for the electric current to manufacture the $300 worth of gold he thought he had produced. But Bent then provocatively reported that "a battery of chemists in New York is making a series of tests to see whether the thing can be commercialized." As we have seen in the previous chapter, such commercial gold-making schemes had been proposed since the turn of the century by men such as Emmens and Hunter, and they were at least momentarily taken seriously by scientists and journalists alike. As Bent reported, B. E. Free, editor of *Scientific American,* had brought over an apparatus like Miethe's for passing electrical current and ultraviolet rays through mercury vapor, and planned to have NYU's Professor H. H. Sheldon try to replicate the experiments. In the two years following Bent's article, Miethe's experiments sparked arguments within the German Chemical Society and transmutation efforts by other German chemists (including those by his own pupil Alois Gaschler, who claimed to have transmuted gold into mercury). Chemists from Britain to Japan made new transmutation claims. In 1928, the *New York Times* even devoted an article to a new publication by French alchemist François Jollivet-Castelot, *La Fabrication Chimique de l'Or,* in which Jollivet-Castelot offered a process for manufacturing gold on an industrial basis. The *Times* reporter immediately made the connection to France's efforts to return to its gold standard, noting, with perhaps a gentle sarcasm, "For months France waited anxiously for the franc to be given a settled, official value in gold. She had seen England bring the pound up to its pre-war mark, Italy stabilize the lira. The Bank of France was putting up a gold reserve, but many doubted whether there would be enough. But what an amount of thought and planning might have been spared had it been known that it was possible to step into the laboratory of a patriotic alchemist and see him whisk gold out of a crucible of base metals!" (*New York Times* 1928, 46). The reporter, though, noted that the two chemists who had tried to replicate Jollivet-Castelot's transmutations had not found the method tenable as an industrial process, because once again, the gold cost more to manufacture than it was worth: "Here is the only flaw. The wave of the magician's wand transmuting base metal into gold costs more than the precious stuff itself" (46).

The gold found in Miethe's experiments was ultimately shown to have been an impurity in his mercury. But at the time of Bent's 1924 article, Miethe's initial results were sufficiently alarming to merit the interview with an economist of Anderson's stature to discuss its implications. In the article, Anderson vividly portrayed the truly shocking effects of inexpensively synthesized gold. Prices, he asserted, "would rise with startling and disastrous suddenness." Gold's value "would collapse.... Such a tremendous drop in the value of gold as compared with goods and of dollars as compared with goods, would ruin creditors... There would be an era in which the technologist, the industrialist, and the business man who thinks in terms of orderly industrial and commercial processes had no chance. The speculator and the gambler would win. If turned loose haphazard, such a discovery would be perhaps the greatest menace mankind has known." Like Soddy in *The Interpretation of Radium* and Foote in his lecture, Anderson saw atomic transmutation's real value to human society as liberated energy. And like H. G. Wells, whose 1914 novel *The World Set Free* not only predicted nuclear bombs but also portrayed the collapse of the world economy, Anderson hypothesized that human society and markets could only be salvaged by international cooperation. Anderson saw that the topic of alchemical transmutation entailed questions about the nature of money that would be important to gold-standard debates over the next decade. For example, he raised, though dismissed, Irving Fisher's suggestion of basing the dollar on a composite of commodity prices, while still allowing dollars to be redeemed in gold held by the Treasury.

Early Alchemical Forebodings

Even as early as 1900, the year the Gold Standard Act set the quantity of gold backing the United States dollar, boundaries between gothic or occult literature and science fiction were beginning to blur, articulating fears about what a successful alchemist might do to the world economy. But the discovery of a natural abundance of gold at that time was still seen as a more likely threat to the economy. One such text that intimated a threat from scientific alchemy was Garrett P. Serviss's *The Moon Metal* (1900). Serviss (1851–1929) was an American author, editor, lecturer, and writer of science journalism and science fiction, as well as a cofounder of the American Astronomical Society. He was also one of the foremost science fiction novelists and popular science journalists in America before World War I (Bleiler 1999, 667). Like other science fiction writers, he used his five novels and one novella (*Edison's Conquest of Mars, The Moon Metal, A Columbus of Space, The Sky Pirate, The Second Deluge,* and *The Moon Maiden*) to explore the not-yet-realized possibilities and ramifications of current scientific knowledge.

The Moon Metal was published in 1900 after the discoveries of radiation, X-rays, and cathode rays. Then, perhaps due to its increasing relevance after the discovery of atomic transmutation by Rutherford and Soddy at McGill in 1901–1902, it was republished in a magazine in 1905. Serviss explores the implications of the mysterious science of cathode rays for the world economy by using conventions from gothic fiction—including the sinister and mysterious villain who seems to use occult powers, and alchemy in particular, to further his nefarious schemes.

In order to make his concerns about a precious-metal-based economy all the more devastating, Serviss's novel posits a perfectly functioning gold standard that achieves all the aims that the classic gold standard never entirely achieved in reality. The narrator explains that after the abundance of silver "rendered it unsuitable for money," it was entirely removed from coins (something that did not actually happen in the United States until the Coinage Act of 1965). The gold standard, then:

> had become universal, and business all over the earth had adjusted itself to that condition. The wheels of industry ran smoothly, and there seemed to be no possibility of any disturbance or interruption. The common monetary system prevailing in every land fostered trade and facilitated the exchange of products. Travelers never had to bother their heads about the currency of money; any coin that passed in New York would pass for its face value in London, Paris, Berlin, Rome, Madrid, St. Petersburg, Constantinople, Cairo, Khartoum, Jerusalem, Peking, or Yeddo. It was indeed the "Golden Age," and the world had never been so free from financial storms. (1900, 4–5)

But in the near future (the novel is set in 1949), gold is discovered in great supply in Antarctica. Serviss had already witnessed the Western mining booms that devalued silver too much for it to serve as a basis for the monetary supply; the novel was published just four years after William Jennings Bryan's failed 1896 run for the presidency on a bimetallic platform. Serviss would have recently seen abundant gold discoveries in South Africa, too, which had rescued the British gold standard in the 1880s and 1890s. *The Moon Metal* was one of the first novels of the era to portray economic vulnerability caused by an *excess* of gold.

As a result of this excessive supply, "The price of gold dropped like a falling stone, with accelerated velocity, and within a year every money centre in the world had been swept by a panic. Gold was more common than iron. Every government was compelled to demonetize it, for when once gold had fallen into contempt it was less valuable in the eyes of the public than stamped paper" (7). Ironically, after a process for hardening gold is discovered, the once precious substance becomes useful as a noncorrosive building material, replacing steel (7). Platinum cannot serve as a monetary replacement for gold, as new discoveries devalue it as well. Serviss thus points out that a metallic monetary standard is based on something humans cannot control or even predict, the natural abundance of resources in the earth. Notably, Serviss even turns to possible chemical solutions to the problem, explaining that "The chemists sought [a substitute] in their laboratories and the mineralogists in the mountains and deserts" (8). Even a financial congress gathering in New York to represent the financiers of Europe and America cannot solve the monetary crisis, and various systems of paper money based on "agriculture or mining or manufacture" cannot bring the needed stability (8–9). Serviss's novel thus sets up a quandary that tests not only turn-of-the-century reliance on the gold standard but also theoretical index replacements for it, such as those soon to be proposed by Fisher and by Soddy.

In steps a mysterious scientist, Max Syx, who brings a new metal, artemisium, forward to stabilize the world's monetary supplies—giving himself, of course, a huge cut of the economy and making himself a billionaire. Syx claims to be mining the artemisium at the Grand Teton mountain in Wyoming, but the protagonist of the story, an engineer named Andrew Hall, believes that the villain is in fact fabricating the artemisium through transmutation. Hall asks the narrator, "Do you believe in alchemy?" (75). It turns out that Syx has been mining it from the moon with a (truly scientifically impossible) process of cathode ray transfer. In this monetary parable/science fiction novel, Serviss may well even have had in mind a common saying in the financial markets. Mayhew explains how the Bank of England could change interest rates to restore gold reserves depleted in economic crises. He notes that a Bank of England interest rate of "seven percent, they used to say in the City, would bring gold from the moon" (Mayhew 194).

Serviss's novel suggests that metallic monetary standards, and the greed that drives the production of the metallic medium, inevitably lead to economic disaster. After Hall discovers Syx's process of mining the "moon metal" and sets up his *own* production company, Syx gets his revenge by spreading the secret broadly across the world, starting a rush on artemisium—and an attendant economic collapse, as it is over-mined. The only solution Serviss can imagine involves tightly restricting the metal's supply through international governmental cooperation.

Had the novel been written two years later, when Soddy and Rutherford published their theory of radioactive transmutation, it might have explicitly based artemisium on radioactive transmutation. But cathode rays held out the greatest imaginative potential to challenge the nature of matter in 1900. ("Better Than Alchemy" is the title of the chapter in which Syx's cathode ray process is discovered.) Serviss's novel serves as an early example of the alchemy trope used to guide thinking about cutting-edge science and monetary policy.

Within only two years of Soddy and Rutherford's papers on atomic transformation as the mechanism for radioactivity, writers of popular fiction did indeed make the shift from cathode rays pulling an unknown element from the moon to radium emissions and other such atomic technologies causing alchemical transmutation—and similarly fretted about the consequences to the gold-standard economy of the West. Rider Haggard's *Ayesha: The Return of She* (1904–05) was noteworthy, as we have mentioned, because of its vision of an ancient queen with Hermetic knowledge using radium to transmute iron ore into gold. But *Ayesha* also raises the specter of economic collapse in the face of alchemical gold. Leo, Ayesha's beloved, objects that the world "has set up gold as the standard of wealth. On it all civilisations are founded. Make it as common as it seems thou canst, and these must fall to pieces. Credit will fail and, like their savage forefathers, men must once more take to barter to supply their needs." They would inevitably return to a state like the past, in which people "smashed in each other's heads with stone axes" (165). Ayesha argues in favor of a return to a more primitive, precapitalist society: "What if I prove your sagest chapmen fools, and gorge your greedy money-changers with the gold that they desire until they loathe its very sight and touch? What if I uphold the cause of the poor and the oppressed against the ravening lusts of Mammon? Why, will not this world of yours be happier then?" (165). Leo fears the uncertainty of such a re-created world, and Ayesha gives up her scheme, saving the world from it only for a personal whim, because of her love for Leo: "Since thou dost desire it, that old evil, the love of lucre, shall still hold its mastery upon the earth. Let the peoples keep their yellow king" (165). Yet, as Ayesha had reminded Leo and Holly, the power of transmutation is within reach of *science* and is something she had discovered centuries ago. Fiction aside, the implied threat to the gold standard and the world economy from a capricious scientist must have seemed very real in 1904.[7]

Soddy and Pre-War Monetary Concerns

As early as 1903, Soddy began to speculate publicly about the importance of energy to human history—and the stunning new possibilities that radioactivity offered for mankind's future. As with Serviss and Haggard, alchemy began to connect the new science to issues of monetary supply well before such connections provoked appreciable public anxiety in the 1920s. At the annual meeting of the British Association for the Advancement of Science in York in 1906, the address by BAAS president E. Ray Lankester set the iconoclastic, even revolutionary, tone of the meeting. Lankester pointed out how many areas of received scientific opinion were being upended by the new work on radium. But for Lankester, scientific revolution had to remain firmly rooted in accepted mainstream understandings of the boundaries of scientific knowledge. As a professor of zoology at University College, London, Lankester had led attacks on spiritualism and the Society for Psychical Research, famously revealing in a September 1876 letter to the *Times* the deceptions used in séances by the American medium and spirit writer Henry Slade (Oppenheim

1985, 23). Given Lankester's presidential remarks at the BAAS, Soddy seemed the perfect choice to open the discussions in the physics section of the meeting. His lecture, "The Evolution of the Elements," was said to have "made a profound impression" (*The Eastbournian* ca. 1910, 41). Soddy began his talk by noting the great changes in scientists' understanding of the elements in the last few years. While he gave credit to the preceding generation for helping reveal how the chemical elements functioned, he argued that the new science might well necessitate a philosophical change in chemistry. As he would do routinely on the lecture circuit, Soddy emphasized that the new discoveries in radioactivity offered radical solutions to "the practical problems of life and the future welfare of the race" (Soddy n.d. [ca. 1906], 1). Yet he might have made Lankester wince when, to help reconceptualize the philosophical principles entailed by the new discoveries, he turned back 1500 years to alchemy. Using Berthelot as his source, he argued for the alchemical emphasis on the evolution of the elements:

> More than fifteen hundred years ago, as M. Berthelot has pointed out, the symbol by which matter was everywhere expressed was a serpent, the body coiled into a circle and the head devouring the tail, bearing the central motto, "εν το παν." This was derived from the Greeks, who, in imagination, untrammeled by knowledge, far surpassed even the most advanced theory of to-day, supposing that material evolution proceeded in a cycle, and thus were able to arrive intuitively at a system at once continuous, consistent, and eternal, avoiding the inherent difficulties connected with the beginning and end of the process which troubles us to-day. From that time till quite recently, although the idea of continuous evolution of matter was never absent, experimental knowledge advanced steadily along lines which seemed almost to disprove the possibility of any such process. (Soddy, n.d. [ca. 1906], 2)

Soddy admitted that the current knowledge disproved alchemical claims to transmutation, because scientists now understood that enormous quantities of energy would have been necessary to effect such a change.

Yet alchemy nevertheless helped channel the talk toward issues of gold and monetary supply—and Soddy offered one of his earliest public statements on the subject.

> So far as the economic evidence goes, the scarcity of gold is a matter of concentration, like that of radium, for in small quantities it is,

like radium, very widely distributed. Seeing that 500 tons of gold were produced last year, the element can hardly be considered scarce in any other sense of the word. It has the remarkable property of being found just whenever the demand for it increases, and the providential character of this behaviour makes me suspect that a law similar to that regulating the scarcity of radium is in question. If this turns out to be well founded, the theory of currency will be reduced to a branch of physics. We may anticipate a more scientific system of currency being devised than the present, which in 1904 cost the world from fifty to a hundred million pounds value thrown away in the unproductive labour of maintaining the gold and silver currency. (9–10)

A few years later, in 1908, Soddy held six popular lectures at the University of Glasgow to introduce the public to the new scientific understanding of the radio-elements, and he speculated freely on what they might entail. As we shall see, Soddy had provocative ideas about energy's importance to the development of human history. He imagined that with atomic science, man might reshape life on Earth. (He even suggested that humans might have done so in some distant past before meeting with disaster—which gave rise to legends of the Fall of Man and the Garden of Eden.) These lectures went on to become the basis of Soddy's popular science tour-de-force, *The Interpretation of Radium* (1909). In them, though, Soddy also briefly linked the elemental composition of the Earth and the relative abundance (or scarcity) of certain elements to socioeconomic questions. Returning to his speculations about the scarcity of gold and radium from his 1906 BAAS lecture, Soddy wrote: "It is . . . natural to inquire whether the scarcity of elements like gold is fixed by the operation of similar physical laws to those which regulate the rarity of radium. The race has grown used from the earliest times to the idea that gold is a metal possessing a certain fixed degree of value, enabling it to be used safely for the purposes of currency and exchange. It is no exaggeration to say that the whole social machinery of the Western world would be dislocated if gold altered violently in its degree of rarity—if, for example, in some hitherto unpenetrated fastness of the globe a mountain of gold came to be discovered" (1909, 211).

While Soddy wrote his major economic and monetary pamphlets and books after the First World War, his alchemical musings on the nature of the elements invariably led him to consider the role of gold in the world economy *before* the War and *before* his involvement with the monetary reformers. In 1912, long before he had struck up a friendship with Arthur Kitson, Soddy penned an article entitled "Transmutation: The Vital Problem of the Future." There, Soddy referred to gold as "not wealth, but merely its conventional symbol, adopted for convenience as a medium of exchange." He challenged economic orthodoxy, arguing that real wealth was a function of energy: "[A]n economist might not at once be prepared to accept the doctrine, to which physical science of the last half-century plainly leads, that so far as human affairs go, wealth and available energy are synonyms, and that the poverty or affluence of this planet are primarily measured only by the dearth or abundance of the supply of energy available for its life and work" (1912, 187). Medieval alchemists had aspired to create gold because of its perceived intrinsic value; modern alchemists, who had a very real possibility of transmuting an element into gold, emphasized the much greater value of the *energy* such a transmutation would release. At this point in Soddy's thinking, modern alchemy had already underscored the arbitrary nature of gold as a medium of exchange and the basis of the pre-War monetary system: "The world has advanced in thought.... The special value of gold is, of course, merely conventional and could and would be changed by a stroke of the legislator's pen" (195). Soddy thus argued that "Energy, not gold, will be the quest of the modern scientific alchemist." Indeed, because of the energy released, the "modern scientific alchemist would probably be more eager to succeed first in turning gold into silver than the opposite" (196–97).

H. G. Wells's *The World Set Free:* Modern Alchemy Destroys the Economy

For Soddy, before the war, alchemy linked atomic transmutation to gold and thus to the nature of monetary systems, to some degree. Writers such as Serviss and Soddy had imagined massive gold strikes' damage to the economy. And in 1914, Soddy's 1908 lectures—collected in *The Interpretation of Radium*—inspired H. G. Wells to write *The World Set Free*. Wells's novel, dedicated to *The Interpretation of Radium*, more fully portrayed modern alchemy's implications for the world than anyone, including Soddy, had yet done. The book's claim to fame today is that it was the first novel to depict a nuclear war. John Canaday has neatly summed up the connections among Manhattan Project physicist Leo Szilard's work on the bomb, Wells's *The World Set Free* (which the Manhattan Project physicists read as they worked on the bomb), and Soddy's *The Interpretation of Radium:* "The first nuclear weapons were in an important sense...a scientific interpretation of a fictional interpretation of a scientific interpretation of radioactive substances" (Canaday 228).

Less noted today is the fact that *The World Set Free* also posited the collapse of world economies as a direct result of atomic transmutation. In Wells's novel, gold was one of the by-products of the newly harnessed atomic energy that powered cars and houses. It thus became worthless. Wells begins his novel in a Soddyian vein, with a chapter entitled "The Sun Snarers" that recounts the history of mankind's use of energy. When he reaches the late medieval period in his story, Wells notes:

> Hitherto Power had come to men by chance, but now there were these seekers, seeking, seeking among rare and curious and perplexing objects, sometimes finding some odd utilisable thing, sometimes deceiving themselves with fancied discovery, sometimes pretending to find. The world of every day laughed at these eccentric beings, or found them annoying and ill-treated them, or was seized with fear and made saints and sorcerers and warlocks of them, or with covetousness and entertained them hopefully; but for the greater part heeded them not at all. Yet they were of the blood of him who had first dreamt of attacking the mammoth; every one of them was of his blood and descent; and the thing they sought, all unwittingly, was the snare that will some day catch the sun. (179)

Of course, for Wells, these men became the modern scientists—da Vinci, Galvani, and others. But they also included Roger Bacon, "and half the alchemists were of their tribe" (180). And the alchemists, with their enquiries into the nature of matter, lead the novel to a boy named Holsten, who attends the lectures of a Professor Rufus in Edinburgh on "Radium and Radio-Activity" (185). Wells's depiction of Professor Rufus at his compelling talks about radioactivity and its potential uses is a thinly veiled portrait of Soddy delivering his 1908 "Interpretation of Radium" lectures in Glasgow. In the novel, these talks inspire Holsten to search for the secret to artificial transmutation and hence nuclear energy, to overcome "the problem which was already being mooted by such scientific men as Ramsay, Rutherford, and Soddy in the very beginning of the twentieth century" (189). Holsten finally succeeds in 1933 when he transmutes bismuth into gold.

Of course, alchemy dictates the response to Holsten's discovery: "What chiefly impressed the journalists of 1933 was the production of gold from bismuth and the realisation albeit upon unprofitable lines of the alchemist's dreams" (194). But by 1953, Holsten and scientists and engineers develop atomic engines, and the world is rapidly changed. The alchemical dream becomes a nightmare. The engines, now used for individual flying machines, create gold as a waste product: "gold was undergoing headlong depreciation, all the securities upon which the credit of the world rested were slipping and sliding, banks were tottering, the stock exchanges were scenes of feverish panic.... [T]hese were the black and monstrous under-consequences of the Leap into the Air" (196). Wells continues: "In the year 1955 the suicide rate for the United States of America quadrupled any previous record. There was an enormous increase also in violent crime throughout the world. The thing had come upon an unprepared humanity; it seemed as though human society was to be smashed by its own magnificent gains" (196). This insight into the unexpectedly disastrous consequence of sudden scientific advances dominates most of the rest of the novel.

Wells uses the atomic transmutation of bismuth to gold and its devastating economic effects only as the initial demonstration of an assault on the sense of intrinsic value and immutability of virtually all of the social conventions of 1914. Such conventions are shown to be the product of human choice, not intrinsic worth. Gold, and hence a gold-standard monetary system, is worthless when it becomes merely a waste product. Land values plummet when personal flying machines free humans from the system of land value based upon proximity to desired areas. The value of human labor and the industrial wage system are undermined, as machines do the labor of thousands of men. The distribution of wealth becomes a meaningless concept when the material comforts of the world are made available to all. And last in Wells's series of such challenges to social norms: war. Warfare becomes an even more ghastly, unwinnable, unsustainable human endeavor when atomic bombs can obliterate all of the world's major cities and destroy millions of lives. In short, war becomes untenable. As Wells neatly sums it up, "By the spring of 1959 from nearly two hundred centres, and every week added to their number, roared the unquenchable crimson conflagrations of the atomic bombs; the flimsy fabric of the world's credit had vanished, industry was completely disorganised and every city, every thickly populated area, was starving or trembled on the verge of starvation" (240).

Ultimately, the far-sighted and level-headed leaders remaining in the world agree to a single world government that will use science to solve human problems, completely restructure society, and control all the nuclear bomb-making materials. (The novel remains relevant to contemporary geopolitics. It predicts states with illicit weapons programs and portrays the need for a united world to destroy such rogue actors, as well as for all the individual countries to give up their own claims to nuclear weapons.)

Soddy and the Money Cranks

Whether Wells's novel affected Soddy as much as Soddy's *Interpretation of Radium* influenced Wells is impossible to determine, but Soddy's move into monetary theory in the postwar period was, in some ways, already implicit in his alchemical vision of the new science.[8] Modern alchemy—the atomic science of transmutation, with all its alchemical connections to spiritual systems, gold, and even greed—that Soddy had been exploring in his pre-War writings may have helped turn this Nobel Prize–winning chemist into what was commonly called a "money crank."

The so-called money cranks, or currency cranks, were theorists working against the grain of accepted economic theory to ascribe the faults of the modern economy to its monetary and banking practices. Soddy began to engage with economics after the First World War, beginning in the Labour Party and moving on to more radical currents of economic thought (Merricks 108–32). By 1920, Soddy was clearly showing the influence of the controversial economics that Victorian sage John Ruskin elaborated in *Fors Clavigera* and *Unto This Last*. Merricks notes that Soddy especially affirmed Ruskin's sense of economics as a science and his understanding of wealth as a product of circulation. Soddy's assault on monetary and economic policies that seemed to stifle the flow or circulation of money was much in line with Ruskin's thinking. This form of economic analysis has been characterized as "under-consumptionist" because it emphasizes the problems caused not by under-production, but rather by under-consumption. The monetary theories that engaged Soddy were all of this variety. Positing economics and wealth in terms of available energy, Soddy applied principles from the physical sciences to create a thermodynamic explanation for the flow of money (Merricks 112–13). His economic explorations led him briefly into contact with the National Guilds League, which followed Ruskinian ideals and advocated abolition of the wage system and institution of self-governing guilds to structure industry. He quickly took up more radical and specifically monetary theories. As Merricks puts it, he "mov[ed] on to the monetary reformers Silvio Gesell and Arthur Kitson, with whom he agreed, at least to a limited extent, and J. M. Keynes, Major Douglas and A. R. Orage, with whom he disagreed. It is probable that he was influenced, initially at least, by reading *New Age*" (115), Orage's radical cultural and political weekly. Gesell and Kitson both squarely blamed monetary and banking practices for economic problems, and they advocated solutions based on monetary theory. The German-born Silvio Gesell (1862–1930) founded the Free Economy League in Switzerland and garnered followers in Germany, Switzerland, and Austria as well as in Australia, Canada, Argentina, England, and the United States (Myers 1940, 26). He sought to remedy business crises and damaging price fluctuations by instituting a scheme to increase the amount of money in circulation. He advocated a system of stamped money that would gradually lose its value if it were not spent, just as goods deteriorate if not sold (Myers 54).

In England, the most prominent of the "new economic" movements was Social Credit. Though Soddy did not agree with some of his ideas, Major C. H. Douglas (1879–1952), who founded the Social Credit movement, was an important sparring partner for Soddy. Social Credit gained considerable strength in the 1920s as Guild Socialism waned. It called for a socialization of credit wherein every individual, regardless of his or her efforts or skills, would receive a "national dividend," which Douglas saw as the "logical successor to the wage" (quoted in Merricks 116).

Much more to Soddy's liking, though, was Arthur Kitson (1860–1937), who had been publishing in the *New Age* since 1912 and became Soddy's friend and ally in the 1920s. Kitson had advocated wresting control of credit away from the banking system. (He saw that system as a usurious conspiracy, with all the anti-Semitic overtones that carries; he even espoused the fraudulent anti-Semitic *Protocols of the Learned Elders of Zion* that was held out as "evidence" for a Jewish conspiracy aimed at world domination.) Kitson had argued for expanding the money supply since his 1895 book, *A Scientific Solution to the Money Question*. His books, including *The Money Problem* (1903) and *A Fraudulent Standard* (1917), greatly influenced Soddy. Soddy and Kitson both attended the second annual conference on Social Credit in 1925 and were involved in a split within the organization over how its aims should be achieved (Merricks 119).

It is beyond this book's scope to rehearse the complicated history of these economic proposals and the left- and right-wing movements they spawned in the 1920s and 1930s—or Soddy's full relationship to them. Anyone familiar with Ezra Pound's search for the causes of World War I and his descent into fascism will recognize Douglas, Gesell, Kitson, and the Social Credit movement as stops on Pound's road to the far Right and to anti-Semitism. While remaining predominantly on the Left politically, Soddy's economic writings in the 1920s, especially beginning with his 1924 pamphlet *The Inversion of Science* and his 1926 book *Wealth, Virtual Wealth and Debt*, contributed to a critique of the monetary and banking systems in line with that of the above theorists. He called for nationalizing banks, prohibiting banks from making profits, and replacing the gold standard with an index number. The number might be based on the budget of a working-class family's household and could be set by statisticians. The index number would control the amount of money in circulation, rather than allowing supplies of gold or bank decisions to control such an important issue. The banking and monetary system as it had existed, Soddy argued, would inevitably lead to world war.

Soddy's ideas influenced Yale professor Irving Fisher, whose work on index numbers we have already seen cited in the *New York Times* in discussions about the gold standard and modern alchemy. They also influenced the Technocracy movement in the United States, which would play a role in some of the science fiction pulp magazines I will examine momentarily. Indeed, Soddy's theories of economics as a science of energy even left a mark on economics in the later twentieth century. Juan Martinez-Alier, in his noted *Ecological Economics: Energy, Environment and Society* (1987), attempts to rehabilitate Soddy's economic writings, particularly his critique of the economic theory of growth. Martinez-Alier is especially interested in Soddy's definition of "real wealth" as something that comes from the energy of the sun, something that must be consumed and cannot be saved. Summarizing Soddy, he explains:

> Part of this wealth took the form of so-called capital goods and was carefully measured as financial capital, that is, as credits against the community. Real wealth, in the form of a wheat crop, for instance, would rot if stored for any length of time, whereas the wealth which took the form of so-called capital goods, and was registered as financial capital, was supposed not to rot but, on the contrary, to grow independently at compound interest, *ad infinitum*. This was a convention of human society... but could not run permanently counter to the principles of thermodynamics.... The economists were victims of this delusion. Keynes seemed to believe that wealth—and not debt—increased according to the rules of compound interest. (128)

Soddy worked to promulgate an economics that could increase wealth, in the form of available energy, rather than debt.

But Soddy was not always his own best advocate, in the world of economics at least. Not only did he alienate his scientific colleagues at Oxford but he also failed to garner widespread support for his ideas. One writer in 1940 argued that "if Frederick Soddy had given to his monetary scheme some simple and easily understood title like 'Stamped Money' or 'Social Credit' he might have become the leader of a movement with its own newspapers, its followers pouring out votive offerings, and even its shirts of a special hue. Instead, he endowed his plan with such names as 'Social Energetics' and 'Ergosophy'" (Myers 71). I would like to emphasize, though, that the general direction of his thinking—to imagine value in energy and in functional systems that allowed an increase of human happiness and a wider distribution of wealth—were being cast in terms that the discussions of modern alchemy had set for critiques of the gold standard. If all matter was mutable, then the particular configuration of matter was not itself inviolably valuable. A metal-backed currency limited the flow of money—the flow of energy, basically—in the name of something that had no real value in and of itself, a precious metal. The gold standard was merely a convention, and a flawed one at that, just as the modern alchemists saw the medieval alchemists' pursuit of gold as a mistake, given the far greater value they could have gained from the energy liberated in transmutation. These issues were moral issues for Soddy—just as some Hermeticists argued that alchemy was not truly about the transmutation of gold but rather about the spiritual transmutation of the alchemist, even if the practice involved real laboratory work.

Late in his life, as a result of the atomic bombs dropped on Japan during the War and the atomic energy programs developing in the United States and the United Kingdom (one component of which was located on the Berkshire Downs at Harwell, just twelve miles south of Oxford), Soddy regained his interest in atomic science, even writing a final book on the subject: *The Story of Atomic Energy* (1949). Even at this late date, Soddy still used alchemy to describe relationships between science, moral issues, and money. Just a few days after the August 6, 1945, atomic bomb explosion over Hiroshima and the August 9 bombing of Nagasaki, Soddy penned a magazine article in which he raised concerns about the misuses of science: "To anyone at all aware of the nature of the new power science has so light-heartedly and irresponsibly put into the hands of men drunken with conflict and still thinking relatively in terms of stone-axes, flint arrows, and boomerangs, the last item is *not* news... scientific men can probably control the Titan they have unleashed, but as the ancient tag has it, who controls scientific men?" (1945b, 8). The article raised Soddy's decades-long concerns about the control of scientific knowledge by governments and people uninterested in the public good. It went on to cast the moral dimensions of the problem in terms of alchemy: "When it is real alchemy that is wanted, and it is a question of national life and death to get it, a race against time to get it before it is destroyed by it—real experts were forthcoming, and by a stupendous scientific achievement they won in what has been described as the most tremendous gamble in history, in which even the most optimistic would have rated the chances of success as very small" (8).

Soddy shifts from a distinction in his economic writings of the 1920s and 1930s between "real wealth" and "virtual wealth" (in which "virtual wealth" was not necessarily a morally negative term, but an aspect of any society that possessed a monetary system) to one between "real alchemy" and "false alchemy." "Real alchemy" becomes synonymous with legitimate scientific achievement—in this case, the race to master atomic energy. In the very next line, the other term, "false alchemy," immediately connects Soddy's chain of thought not to bad uses of science, but again to money, to bad banking and economic policies and greed: "Why then are the nations *already* so prematurely, and without the slightest democratic sanction, to be committed to the ruinous overlordship of the false alchemists, of the Bretton Woods kidney, the bankers who can bring money into existence like rabbits out of a hat and make it vanish again, spreading social contagion through the whole body politic?" (1945, 8–9). While the article more broadly articulates Soddy's concerns about the impressive science behind the bomb being misused to ensure American global hegemony, alchemy once again immediately connected atomic transmutation to the moral issues of the gold standard and monetary policies. The Bretton Woods agreement that brought the International Monetary Fund and a kind of limited gold standard into existence had been signed in July 1944, more than a year earlier. Yet "false alchemy" immediately entailed Bretton Woods in Soddy's mind. As Merricks puts it, "By this time, his disillusionment with any kind of government or controlling authority was so complete that, even though the reforms he had been advocating for the past twenty years were at last to be enacted, they would be ineffective" (Merricks 166).

The real alchemy/false alchemy trope became so important to Soddy that he originally intended to entitle his final popular scientific publication on radioactivity *Real Alchemy* (meant to replace *The Interpretation of Radium* and its 1932 successor, *The Interpretation of the Atom*). In 1940, as Soddy began to revise *The Interpretation of the Atom*, he considered calling it *The Interpretation of the Atom, Modern Alchemy* (ca. 1932–1940)—a name multiple textbooks on radioactivity had already adopted. But after the War and as late as 1946, as he revised it into its final form, he began simply calling it *Real Alchemy*. It was serialized in *Engineering* from 1947 through 1948, and it finally came out in book form in 1949 as a New Atlantis Publication titled *The Story of Atomic Energy*.

The Story of Atomic Energy begins with "Alchemy to Chemistry," a chapter that lays out the origins of chemistry in alchemy and traces alchemical practices in Egypt, Greece, China, Arabia, and medieval Europe until they finally transform into modern experimental science in the seventeenth century. He briefly notes, "As alchemy neared its close as an openly studied and reputable subject its doctrines became ever more and more fantastic. There are numerous circumstantial accounts of actual transmutations being performed by scientific people of high repute and unquestioned integrity, but all the articles examined which are reputed to have been made of artificial gold are imitations. There can be little doubt that those deceived were the victims of the kind of ingenuity that now goes to salt gold-mines" (1949, 7). It is unclear why Soddy changed the title of his volume from *Real Alchemy* to *The Story of Atomic Energy*, but this initial section condensed into six pages what in manuscript had been a twenty-seven-page section on alchemy, concluding with a section entitled "The Late Phase of False Alchemy" that focused on the financial chicanery of late medieval alchemy.

Occult Intersections: Atomic Alchemy in Atlantis
and the Book of Enoch

But if Soddy's concerns about monetary theory originated in his musing on alchemy and modern science, and then followed his migration into the ranks of the so-called money cranks, just what debt, if any, did his thinking owe to the *occult* alchemical revival? Soddy's enthusiasm for alchemy as a science that could inform modern chemistry aligned him more directly with occultists than with most chemists at the turn of the century, before the discovery of radioactive transmutation caused scientists to rethink the relationship of alchemy to chemistry. In a 1901 class lecture at McGill that seems to have preceded his discovery with Rutherford of atomic transmutation, he argued against historians of chemistry who "have almost severed the connection between alchemy and chemistry" and who portrayed it "as a curious and harmful aberration of the human intellect during the dark ages." He even challenged the most significant historian of alchemy, the French chemist Marcellin Berthelot, rejecting Berthelot's opening sentence in his widely influential *Les Origines de l'Alchimie*, "La Chimie est née d'hier"——"Chemistry was born yesterday."[9]

But it is difficult to assess Soddy's exposure to occult writings during any period of his life. He destroyed most of his personal correspondence that did not directly relate to science and economics, and he did not keep a diary or leave documents that might suggest what kinds of nonscientific reading he did or even much of what he did in his spare time.[10] His scientific outlook and the surviving historical records of the occult revival make it all but impossible to believe that Soddy was ever involved in a secret Hermetic society like the Golden Dawn or its successors, or even in something like the Theosophical Society. However secular his worldview was, though, Soddy's writings betray the influence of some major strands of the occult revival: He privileged alchemy, of course, but more specifically, some of his work contains speculations that locate him directly in a current of late-nineteenth-century occult thinking that posited a lost Atlantean civilization as the origin of much alchemical and other occult knowledge. Soddy incorporated elements of the occult narrative of Atlantis into his thinking—in particular, the positioning of Atlantis as a source of a secret tradition of advanced magical or scientific knowledge and the notion that the Atlanteans had brought about their own destruction through this knowledge. But Soddy then rescripted Atlantis as an atomic scientific superpower that met its end in an atomic accident.

The last quarter of the nineteenth century saw a resurgence of interest in the myth of Atlantis. Ignatius Loyola Donnelly (1831–1901), who had been lieutenant governor of Minnesota and a member of Congress, published his most popular book, *Atlantis: The Antediluvian World* in 1882, and it has since gone through more than fifty editions in several languages (Ellis 1998, 38–39). Based on a fanciful synthesis of geography, history, mythology, and oceanography, Donnelly asserted that Plato's accounts in the *Critias* and the *Timaeus* of Atlantis and its sinking into the ocean were historically true and pertained to a large island in the Atlantic off the entrance to the Mediterranean. Moreover, he argued, it was the world's first civilization, and its citizens brought their knowledge to colonies along the Gulf of Mexico and the Mississippi in North America, the Amazon and Pacific coast of South America, as well as Egypt, Western Europe, Africa, the Baltic, the Black Sea, and the Caspian Sea. Above all, Donnelly argued that virtually all myths and gods, from the Garden of Eden and the Elysian Fields to the Greek, Phoenician, Hindu, and Scandinavian gods, had their origin in Atlantis, as did the Phoenician alphabet. (The Scandinavian gods were merely the royal families of Atlantis.) The Egyptian and Peruvian sun religions derived from the original religion of Atlantis. Donnelly contended that Atlantis sank in a natural catastrophe with only a small number of people escaping, and that the story of its sinking survived as the Flood myths (Ellis 39–40).

Occultists, however, advocated Atlantis chronicles of their own. Most famously, H. P. Blavatsky, who argued that the oceanographic studies of the *Challenger* expedition (1873–1876) proved that Atlantis had existed (Ellis 65), offered Atlantis as a source of ancient wisdom in India, Babylon, Egypt, and Greece in *Isis Unveiled* (1877).[11] Blavatsky provided extensive commentary on Atlantis in numerous articles and in *The Secret Doctrine*, arguing that it had existed almost a million years ago but had come to its end not just through a natural disaster, as Donnelly's account had it, but through its own misapplied magical and scientific powers. As historian Philip Jenkins argues:

> Donnelly's ideas were taken up enthusiastically by Theosophists and others, who claimed that the remnants of Atlantean wisdom could

> be traced in various parts of the world, including Egypt and Tibet: once again, we see how Western and Asian mystery traditions were integrated into a new synthesis. Theosophists offered a detailed history of Atlantis over hundreds of thousands of years, describing how it was destroyed after its rulers turned to black magic and claiming that its fall was the historical basis of most mythologies worldwide. The Hebrew myth of the Fall, for instance, reflected human memories of this lost golden age.... Like Theosophy and pyramidology, the Atlantis myth implied that great spiritual wisdom was to be found in alien cultures and that these secrets had been passed on through the traditions of occult movements or secret societies, perhaps in coded form. (Jenkins 2000, 73–74)

Moreover, some Hermetic alchemical societies also claimed the sages of Atlantis and Lemuria as a source of their alchemical knowledge.[12]

Though Soddy was clearly not a card-carrying Theosophist or in any way a follower of Madame Blavatsky, the Atlantis vogue of the late nineteenth century and especially the occultists' vision of Atlantis—both as the source of secret wisdom and as a civilization that had destroyed itself through its own knowledge—are unmistakably present in Soddy's thinking about alchemy's relationship to the emerging science of radioactivity. Soddy's writings elaborated his own synthesis of contemporary scientific thinking and the imaginative possibilities of occult themes, of what Atlantis historian Richard Ellis terms "Atlantean fantasy."[13] The occult influence on Soddy's Atlantean fantasy helped give shape to his concerns about the dangers of misused scientific knowledge.

In Soddy's 1908 *Interpretation of Radium* lectures, he laid out the current state of knowledge about radiation and radium, discussing with scientific specificity (but in relatively accessible terms) the history of the last decade of discoveries in radioactivity and current interpretations of them. But the lectures and book concluded with more imaginative, less strictly scientific speculations about the uses of such knowledge and the powers of the energy released by atomic transmutation. Returning to the subject of alchemy, Soddy noted:

> One is tempted to inquire how far the unsuspected aptness of some of these beliefs and sayings to the point of view so recently disclosed [on radioactive transmutation] is the result of mere chance or coincidence, and how far it may be the evidence of a wholly unknown and unsuspected ancient civilization of which all other relic has disappeared. It was curious to reflect, for example, upon the

remarkable legend of the philosopher's stone, one of the oldest and most universal beliefs, the origin of which, however far back we penetrate into the records of the past, we do not seem to be able to trace to its source. (242)

Like Ramsay in his 1904 *Harper's* article, Soddy remarks:

> The philosopher's stone was accredited the power not only of transmuting the metals, but of acting *as the elixir of life*. Now, whatever the origin of this apparently meaningless jumble of ideas may have been, it is really a perfect and but very slightly allegorical expression of the actual present views we hold to-day. It does not require much effort of the imagination to see in energy the life of the physical universe, and the key to the primary fountains of the physical life of the universe to-day is known to be transmutation. (1908, 242–43)

Soddy does little more here than restate his early contention that the new atomic chemistry is fundamentally a kind of modern alchemy.

Yet in his 1908 lecture Soddy also pushed the connection further, asking, "Was then this old association of the power of transmutation with the elixir of life merely a coincidence?" (243). In a remarkable flight of imagination that bears quoting at some length, he answers this question with an idea based on a common occult understanding of the origins of occult knowledge, but he gives it a scientific twist:

> I prefer to believe it may be an echo from one of many previous epochs in the unrecorded history of the world, of an age of men which have trod before the road we are treading to-day, in a past possibly so remote that even the very atoms of its civilization literally have had time to disintegrate.... Can we not read into [alchemical traditions] some justification for the belief that some former forgotten race of men attained not only to the knowledge we have so recently won, but also to the power that is not yet ours? Science has reconstructed the story of the past as one of a continuous Ascent of Man to the present-day level of his powers. In face of the circumstantial evidence existing of this steady upward progress of the race, the traditional view of the Fall of Man from a higher former state has come to be more and more difficult to understand. From our new standpoint the two points of view are by no means so irreconcilable as they appeared. A race which could transmute matter would have little need to earn its bread by the sweat of its brow. If we can judge from what our engineers accomplish with their comparatively

restricted supplies of energy, such a race could transform a desert continent, thaw the frozen poles, and make the whole world one smiling Garden of Eden. Possibly they could explore the outer realms of space, emigrating to more favourable worlds as the superfluous to-day emigrate to more favourable continents. One can see also that such dominance may well have been short-lived. By a single mistake, the relative positions of Nature and man as servant and master would, as now, become reversed, but with infinitely more disastrous consequences, so that even the whole world might be plunged back again under the undisputed sway of nature, to begin once more its upward toilsome journey through the ages. The legend of the Fall of Man possibly may indeed be the story of such a past calamity. (243–45)[14]

As Spencer Weart has shown, fears that an atomic experiment might result in the destruction of the earth were arising around this time—and Soddy himself had helped ignite these fears. He noted in May 1903 that the Earth is "a storehouse stuffed with explosives, inconceivably more powerful than any we know of, and possibly only awaiting a suitable detonator to cause the earth to revert to chaos" (quoted in Weart 17).[15] But in 1908 Soddy drew upon the occult Atlantis of the late nineteenth century to posit a *past* civilization that had already destroyed itself. In Soddy's account, the Atlanteans destroyed themselves with science rather than with magic. In his 1917 Aberdeen lecture, "The Evolution of Matter," Soddy challenges the notion of science as a slow, steady progress, noting that "there is [no] valid ground for the belief that the startling advance civilisation had made in the past hundred years or so is in any way the climax or natural culmination of the slow and by no means even continuous progress previously" (3). He explicitly identifies Atlantis as the source of his conceptions of a scientifically advanced race that had disappeared from the face of the Earth—and the alchemical tradition as the incomplete remnant of its knowledge, "the distorted parrot-like repetitions of the wisdom of a lost Atlantis."

Moreover, Soddy turned to the apocryphal Book of Enoch, a source much used by Blavatsky, Crowley, and other occultists as an origin story for occult knowledge. The Book of Enoch parallels the details and the moral vision of the Fall and the Deluge in Atlantean chronicles. While the Book of Enoch, a Jewish text of at least the second or third century B.C.E., had been a significant force in early Christianity, it had later been disavowed by the church and was believed lost. It came into occult lore in the sixteenth century when John Dee and Edward Kelly purported to have recovered the secret writings and Enochian language and to have learned its great magical powers. Dee and Kelly's

Enochian magic influenced the Golden Dawn—via Mathers—and Crowley, who adapted it to his own magical systems. In 1773 the explorer James Bruce brought back three manuscripts of the entire book from Abyssinia (Aramaic fragments were discovered much later among the Dead Sea Scrolls), and an English translation was published in 1821. But the then definitive English translation, upon which Soddy took many notes, was R. H. Charles's 1912 edition—an edition still in print and listed among best-sellers at many occult online booksellers, who find that the Golden Dawn and the Crowleyian adaptations of Enochian magic still reach a large readership.

As early as 1901, while preparing for his lecture on "Alchemy and Chemistry" at McGill, Soddy took notes on Berthelot's *Les Origines de l'Alchimie* that focused on Berthelot's account of the Book of Enoch as an influence on alchemical lore and on the writings of Zosimus and other early alchemists: "An apocryphal work attributed to Enoch which played an important role in the first centuries of Christianity, relates how the fallen angels lived with mortals and revealed to them sorcery, enchantments, the properties of roots and trees, magic signs and the art of observing the stars, the use of bracelets and armaments, of painting, and of painting the eyebrows and all sorts of dyes, by which the world was corrupted. This is frequently quoted by authors of the 2nd and 3rd century" (Soddy, 1900b, 2–3). Soddy took notes from Berthelot's writing about the cursed nature of the angels who had fallen in love with mortal women, and about later writers who even considered their knowledge itself cursed. Soddy was captivated by the dangers of such powerful knowledge: "Science can corrupt as well as serve, do evil as well as good" (3). But at this early date, he does not seem to have done any independent readings in the Book of Enoch. Nor did he note that the Book is a deluge story, tied to Genesis and the survival of Enoch's great-grandson, Noah—one of the Flood myths that Donnelly and occultists claimed as a veiled Atlantis narrative.

But by 1908, during his lectures on *The Interpretation of Radium,* Soddy had clearly come to a sense of the possible devastation that advanced knowledge—indeed, that the ability to transmute matter—might wreak upon mankind. Soddy's revision of the occult understanding of Atlantis—for him, destroyed not by black magic but by its own forays into atomic energy—would be elaborated more fully by one of the most famous of twentieth-century Atlantis proponents, the American "sleeping prophet," Edgar Cayce (1877–1945). Cayce, whose influence on contemporary New Age lore can still be felt today, was cured of a speech problem by hypnosis. He went on to help other patients with hypnosis and with osteopathic and homeopathic cures. But more significantly, during his own self-induced hypnotic "sleeps" over a forty-three-year period, he would give past-life readings of other people. His accounts of what he "saw" in the past were dictated to stenographers, who wrote down some 14,000 of his visions (Ellis 71–72). Of the 2,500 life readings of individuals, 700 of them explored individual incarnations in Atlantis (Cayce, Schwartzer, and Richards 1988, 25).

In the picture of Atlantis that Cayce disseminated, the Atlantean civilization flourished on an Atlantic continent between around 50,000 B.C.E. and 10,000 B.C.E., when the last remnants of Atlantis sank beneath the sea. The account involves three major periods, and three destructions that ended them: Around 50,000 B.C.E., part of the continent was destroyed; in 28,000 B.C.E., the rest of the land was separated into islands; and in 10,000 B.C.E., the remaining islands sank (Cayce, Schwartzer, and Richards 26). The Atlanteans, whose life span was 500–700 years, were so technologically advanced that they flew about in flying machines, employed advanced communications devices, and had nuclear regenerative medical technologies. They also possessed lasers and could control nuclear energy for both peaceful and destructive purposes (see Cayce 1968; Cayce, Schwartzer, and Richards 1988). Yet in spite of their sophistication, they also were divided into two warring factions: the followers of the Law of One and the sons of Belial. As Cayce said on February 11, 1939:

> [I]n the Atlantean land during those periods when there were those determining as to whether there would be application of the laws of the children of One or of the sons of Belial in turning into destructive channels those influences of infinite power as were being gained from the elements as well as from what is termed spiritual or supernatural powers in the present. Entity wavered between choices and when the destruction came about by the use of those rays as were applied for beneficial forces, entity misapplied ability—*hence the influence of atomic energies or electrical forces of any nature becomes a channel for good or bad today.* (Cayce, Schwartzer, and Richards 44)

The Atlanteans had materialized from thought projections and used "the activities of the creative forces of the Law of One" for mutual benefit (Cayce 64). The first destruction, in around 50,722 B.C.E., seems to have resulted from an effort to destroy the animal life that was overrunning the earth and involved death rays and airships (77). Echoing the Book of Enoch, the sons of Belial became selfish in their exploitation of the earth, their materiality, and their sexual pursuits (65–66). They used nuclear devices to trigger volcanoes and earthquakes to destroy part of Atlantis during the second disaster, dividing the continent into three large islands and some smaller ones (Cayce

74). Finally, the Atlanteans realized that their remaining islands were sinking, and most left to join others who had fled earlier strife and gone to Egypt, the Yucatan, the Pyrenees, Peru, and parts of Nevada and Colorado (Cayce, Schwarter, and Richards 42). Such a vision of an Atlantis destroyed by its misuse of atomic powers and occult abilities follows directly in the line of thinking that Soddy had initiated in his 1908 *Interpretation of Radium* lectures and had directly linked to Atlantis in his 1917 Aberdeen address. The nuclear dynamic that led to the destruction of Atlantis is the very dynamic that the world barely averted in Wells's novel by forming a world government to turn nuclear science to benevolent uses.

Later in Soddy's life, Atlantis had been replaced more explicitly by the Enochian vision. As he took notes in 1945 for his *Real Alchemy* book (which became *The Story of Atomic Energy*), he turned explicitly to Charles's 1912 *Book of Enoch* translation. Whether he had owned the book since 1912, or even owned the book at all, is impossible to determine. Soddy's extensive notes on Charles's translation in one of his notebooks of 1945 gave detailed accounts of two aspects of Enoch. He focused on the story of the angels bringing the ennobling of metals and other sciences and arts to mankind. But he seemed equally interested in the Deluge precipitated by the corrupting power of forbidden knowledge. As he noted, the angels "defiled themselves with women and revealed to them all kinds of sins and the women had born giants and the *whole earth* had been filled with blood and unrighteousness." Soddy concluded, "This I think is all there is of interest" (1945a).

During his lengthy explications of the history of alchemy in *The Story of Atomic Energy*, Soddy discusses the Book of Enoch to ascribe the destruction of mankind to the forbidden alchemical knowledge: "there is an ancient legend that, before, and as the reason for, the Flood, the art of ennobling metals was brought down to earth by demons. Traces of this legend are to be found in the Bible, as in Genesis, VI, 1–4, but, in a greatly expanded form, the story is told in the Apocrypha, Book of Enoch, VI–IX" (1949, 2). Soddy has reduced the complicated moral vision of the Book of Enoch to a simple combination of Fall and Deluge attributable to one knowledge, that of alchemical transmutation. Self-destruction through the misuse of science and cupidity as a motive for obtaining scientific knowledge (the latter a common charge against the medieval alchemist, even in Soddy's writings) concerned Soddy for the last fifty years of his life and led him down paths to economics and monetary policy. His rescripting of the popular occult narratives of Atlantis and Enoch as issues of the abuse of scientific knowledge found fertile ground in twentieth-century culture.

Modern Alchemy and the Gold Standard in the Sci-Fi Pulps

If modern alchemy was born at the nexus of science and occultism, by the 1920s it had thoroughly entered science fiction literature. This science fiction grafted to itself occult alchemy and even the concerns of monetary reform pamphlets. Nowhere was this overlap more evident than in the pioneering science fiction pulp magazines published by Hugo Gernsback in the 1920s and 1930s. Gernsback (1884–1967) was born in Luxembourg, but he immigrated to the United States in 1905. Though he founded a radio station and was a pioneer in early television broadcasts, he is best known for having in 1926 created the first periodical entirely devoted to science fiction: *Amazing Stories*. Gernsback intended the science fiction in his journals to entertain but also to include "scientific fact and prophetic vision" (Westfahl 1990, 27). *Amazing Stories* was intended to serve a didactic function, teaching nonscientists, but it also was aimed at scientists, whose visions of the consequences and future of scientific invention it attempted to engage. *Amazing Stories* was even designed to resemble the scientific journals in appearance and format, and Gernsback added something like peer review of the science in his pulp magazines when he included, at the beginning of each issue of the later *Wonder Stories*, a list of scientific experts. "These nationally-known educators," he pointed out, "pass upon the scientific principles of all stories" (quoted in Westfahl 40).

When Gernsback launched his publications, the gold standard was much in the news. As noted above, Britain and much of Western Europe returned to the gold standard between 1925 and 1929. Britain left it again in 1931, and America faced the economic repercussions of its gold standard during the Great Depression. Roosevelt signed his executive order taking gold out of private circulation in 1933. During these years, the Gernsback pulps *Amazing Stories* (and spin-offs *Amazing Stories Quarterly* and *Amazing Studies Annual*), *Astounding Stories*, and *Wonder Stories* (as well as *Science Wonder Stories* and *Thrilling Wonder Stories*) helped frame how the atomic alchemist's possible ability to synthesize gold would affect a gold-standard economy. Collectively, the modern alchemy stories in the Gernsback pulps provide a remarkable view of developing anxieties about the gold standard.

As we have seen, though the radiochemists' efforts had not led to documentable transmutations in the pre-War era, Rutherford had been able to effect the first atomic transmutation in 1919. Miethe's supposed mercury-to-gold transmutations in 1924 had set off a wave of new efforts by chemists, and in the late 1920s and early 1930s—when Gernsback's pulps were revolutionizing science fiction publishing—John Cockcroft and Ernest Walton's particle accelerator and Ernest Lawrence's cyclotron were opening up new possibilities for intervening in the subatomic world. After centuries of fantastic and scarcely credible claims by alchemists to have performed transmutation, by the 1920s and 1930s, the ability to synthesize gold seemed so plausible that the science fiction stories taking up this theme did not even bother to set them in a distant future or call upon the intervention of alien technologies. Rather, these stories were set in the present (or near future), and they featured the daring, sometimes slightly crazy nuclear scientist as a modern alchemist synthesizing gold using augmented versions of recognizable technologies—e.g., cathode rays, particle accelerators, and alpha-particle bombardment from radioactive elements. But more than simply exploring the fact of such a transmutation, these stories were often concerned with its repercussions for modern banking and finance. They explicitly linked their portrayal to current developments in the United States government's emerging stance toward the circulation of gold during the Depression.

Between 1927 and 1936, sixteen stories appeared in the Gernsback sci-fi pulps that portrayed the transmutation of various substances into gold via atomic technologies. (Or, in a few cases, they featured the transmutation of gold into less valuable metals.) In 1927, as Miethe's experiments "transmuting" mercury vapor to gold were raising alchemical hopes, Gernsback published two transmutation stories: a reprinting of an Edgar Allan Poe story, "Von Kempelen and His Discovery," in *Amazing Stories* and a long tale, Abraham Merritt's "Face in the Abyss," in *Amazing Stories Annual*. The gold transmutations effected by the German scientist von Kempelen in Poe's 1849 story were not, of course, portrayed in terms of the radioactive transmutations that would only be discovered more than fifty years later, but the editorial note to the story explicitly did make such a connection.

> Recently, we were reading in the daily papers and in the scientific journals, about the transmutation of mercury into gold. With our present theories of chemistry, this appears to us to be not only a possibility, but even a probability. In this story Edgar Allan Poe once more appears in the role of scientific prophet—a role which he so often filled. What he describes in this story, written nearly a century ago, is just such a transmutation as the German chemist [presumably Miethe] claims to have done—namely, the transmutation of mercury into gold. (Poe 1849, 364)

The story and the new illustrations accompanying it in *Amazing Stories* describe the transmutation apparatus in essentially alchemical terms (the brick furnace, the crucibles, the changing lead mixed with antimony "and some *unknown substance*") (Poe 365). The narrator asserts, "That he had actually realized, in spirit and in effect, if not to the letter, the old chimera of the philosopher's stone, no sane person is at liberty to doubt" (366). But the story was consonant with many of the other modern alchemy stories that would be published in the late 1920s and early 1930s, as it addressed the economic effects of synthetic gold. The narrator concludes his story by speculating about whether the gold rush to California and California's immediate social transformation therefrom would have happened if the world had known of von Kempelen's discovery. He notes a decline in the value of gold, adding, "In Europe, the most noticeable results have been a rise of two hundred per cent in the price of lead, and nearly twenty-five percent in that of silver" (Poe 366). Merritt's "Face in the Abyss" added the other ingredients to what would become a familiar recipe: It involved transmutation from radiation and the moral consequences of money-lust. It portrayed the disintegration and transmutation into gold of three greedy adventurers who invade the hidden realm of a post-Atlantean race with seemingly magical powers, endless wealth, and a radiation-filled cavern from which "jewels grow like fruit in a garden and the living gold flows forth" (Merritt 78). The narrator of "The Face in the Abyss" notes, "The cavern of the Face . . . I think was a laboratory of Nature, a gigantic crucible where under certain rays of light a natural transmutation of one element into another took place" (Merritt 81).[16]

The next year's modern alchemy publication in *Amazing Stories*, David M. Speaker's "The Disintegrating Ray," explicitly featured human-controlled transmutation of mercury into gold and also raised the specter of its ill consequences for society. In Speaker's story, a college professor develops a "high frequency . . . disintegrating ray" that would change the number of electrons in atoms—thereby, in Speaker's conception, transmuting one element into another and liberating vast energies for mankind's use. As an experiment, the narrator, a student, asks him to make gold from mercury—which he does. The narrator then points out what seems obvious to him: "It is certainly the most wonderful creation of the age, but don't you see that if you put this invention out on a large scale, you will destroy the exchange system of the world? . . . Don't you understand that if these machines are distributed, gold, silver, and other precious metals will be manufactured galore?" (1928, 1091). The story ends with an explosion in the lab that destroys the professor and his machine before anyone else has learned of it.

While these early *Amazing Stories* pieces raise the possibility that transmutation might affect economic or monetary issues, they do not grapple with the possible consequences in any sustained way. Yet the stock market crash in

October 1929, the beginning of the Great Depression, the abandonment by Britain and other countries of the gold standard in the early 1930s, FDR's bank holiday at the beginning of his first term, and his banning of private trading and ownership of gold in 1933 caused a shift in the modern alchemy stories in Gernsback's journals. They quickly began to engage transmutation's ramification for the gold standard, but they also addressed the nature of money and even of political power during the Depression Era. Anxieties about the moral consequences of a metallic currency—not just about *which* metal, gold or silver, should support currency and bank notes—crystallized around the figure of the modern alchemist and expanded the arena of monetary debate well beyond the circles of Social Credit and so-called money cranks.

The pulp sci-fi stories published in the Gernsback periodicals during the Depression track how economic and monetary anxieties dovetailed with the stunning rethinking of the nature of matter that the previous three decades had styled as modern alchemy. Indeed, the stories affirm that:

1. The monetary theory of at least the thousand years preceding the twentieth century had, as a bedrock assumption, that matter is absolutely fixed and unchangeable in its elemental forms.
2. Modern alchemy's claims that atoms were not indivisible and immutable and that humans could effect elemental transmutation entailed a rethinking of the nature of money during a moment of economic and monetary crisis.
3. This destabilization of earlier conceptions of the basis of currency caused great anxiety, but also some hopes for establishing a new, more scientific basis for currency (Soddy's goal).
4. Scientists themselves had come to be seen as the new magicians, possessed of secret and almost miraculous powers to destroy or save an economy, and, thereby, an entire society.
5. The nature and use of scientists' secret powers was thus of the greatest moral significance.

Even in stories in which a mad or criminal scientist uses atomic technologies to transmute gold into a virtually worthless metal, it is ultimately another scientist who, working with the federal government (or more specifically, with the Federal Reserve), saves the day for the United States.

The modern alchemy stories published during the Hoover years demonstrated a real anxiety about the economy's destruction via transmutational attacks on the Federal Reserve and on banks' gold reserves. The Federal Reserve had, of course, been created to avoid monetary crises like those in the bank panics of 1893 and 1907. But in the early 1930s, as the gold standard again slipped into crisis, the Gernsback pulps imagined that the government might not be able to defend itself against the seemingly magical power of transmutation. Only scientists could create havoc by transmuting gold reserves into worthless metals, and only scientists could save society from such a menace. The atomic alchemy trope thus became a vehicle for asserting that scientists, even more than the state, would safeguard the well-being of the world.

Two modern alchemy stories published by Gernsback in 1930 involved sinister plots by mad scientists to threaten the gold reserves of the banking system. The editor's note before Gernsback regular Captain S. P. Meek's "Radio Robbery," published in *Amazing Stories* in February 1930, calls transmutation "a pet theme for writers of science fiction." It merely noted: "It has long been a dream of metallurgists to conquer the science of transmutation of metals.... We are well on the road to synthetic foods, why not synthetic metals?" (1047). But the story itself is a piece of science fiction detective work: A sinister scientist synthesizes gold from polymerized copper and hydrogen, sells it to the Federal Reserve Bank in Philadelphia, and then breaks it back down into copper using powerful radio waves. The forces of government authority—the Chief of Detectives from City Hall, the police sergeant investigating the case, the District Attorney, the President of the Bank, and the Chief of the Federal Secret Service, Carnes, are unable to fathom how such a transmutation could take place until Carnes calls in a scientist, Bird of the Bureau of Standards, to solve the mystery. (Recall that the *New York Times* described a real Bureau of Standards scientist as a "modern alchemist" in 1923.) In the modern alchemy stories, the good scientist is often carefully described as virile and manly—a fitting heroic character for the tough work of solving crimes and fighting villains. Even if hints at the effeminate and retiring scholarly figure might remain, the scientist hero is a man of action, and his contemplative faculties are at the service of a man of action. Bird, for instance, is comfortably married and "stood well over six feet in height and was broad and burly in proportion. His prognathous jaw and unruly shock of curly hair gave him the air of a prizefighter, and it was not until an observer noticed his hands that the scientist stood revealed. Long slender delicate hands they were; the hands of a musician or a sleight-of-hand performer, with long tapering sensitive fingers stained in splotches by acid. 'Hello, Carnes,' he roared in a bull-like voice" (1051). The evil scientist, in turn, is described as either mentally cracked, or physically deformed, or both. In "The Radio Robbery," the bad scientist, Wallace, is a four-foot-tall hunchback with bandy legs and arms "that hung nearly to his knees" but with "the face of a Grecian God" (1054).

As with Meek's "Radio Robbery," H. and Maurice James's "Mystery Metal" in *Science Wonder Stories* (1930) and another by Meek, "Vanishing Gold," in *Wonder Stories* (1932) feature the tough scientist who solves the crime and defeats the twisted scientist. But both clarify the consequences of an atomic attack on gold. The editor introduced "The Mystery Metal" by arguing that "Sooner or later, some scientist will find the key to transmute one metal into another, and when that time comes, mankind will burst its age-old fetters and become a super-race. The tremendous amounts of energy let loose during the transmutation, science hopes, can be used to run all of our machinery. The present story deals with transmutation, but for a strange purpose. It illustrates the power wielded by the scientific mind" (899). Indeed, the story hardly lives up to the editor's remarks about the benevolent uses of atomic energy. The insane evil scientist turns the gold in the Interstate Bank and Trust Company into a mysterious metal by a super cathode ray. He thus precipitates a credit crisis much like those of 1893 and 1907 and the 1929 market crash: "The city was in a panic. The masses are strangely apathetic to scientific problems, except when they touch that which is so dear to them, their pocketbook; but this new menace struck them as forcibly as anything could. A financial panic was threatened. People rushed to the banks to withdraw their funds; riots occurred which needed the police to prevent street bloodshed. Great excitement prevailed in Wall Street" (900). Lester, the good scientist, discovers the secret and tracks down Kay, the insane scientist who is killed by his own ray in a room like that of the alchemist in the literary imagination—"a shabby living room, poorly furnished. On a table were a few dusty books, a pair of chemist's balances, and a few vials" (900).

Meek's 1932 offering, "Vanishing Gold," again featured Carnes and Bird, this time solving the crime as gold in the Federal Reserve vaults is disappearing and slowly changing into copper. This time, the editor explicitly linked the story to the gold-standard crises around the world: "With the world in chaos over the gold standard, and half the nations on the verge of financial bankruptcy, the value of the gold in a nation's treasury may determine the prosperity or poverty of its citizens. But suppose that gold were slowly, imperceptibly, but surely to vanish, to evaporate into the thin air? What would happen if no known cause were found, and no remedy could be provided?" (1320). Indeed, as Carnes and the muscular scientist Bird leave the bank, "a strident-voiced newsboy greeted them. '*Extra! England Abandons Gold Standard! Big Gold Shortage! Extra!*'" (1324). The fear of gold shortage and its stifling effect on a Depression economy was articulated in this story as the evil scientist uses radium rays to disintegrate gold. The good scientist defeats him—and reverses the process (1329).

In virtually all of these stories, it is not simply gold's commodity status that comes into question but indeed the stability of any monetary system based upon elements that modern alchemy has proved to be mutable. The anxiety about the gold economy could reach epic proportions. In a two-part story in late 1933 set a few years in the future, Sidney Patzer envisioned a mysterious ruthless dictator, the "Lunar Consul," taking over the world, partially by creating financial chaos: "On Feburary 1, 1947, all the gold in the world is turned to lead by some invisible, penetrating ray. This causes a world financial panic, and the value of silver soars to unprecedented heights" (2:493). In these tales, the fear that gold could be destroyed or transformed into a worthless substance seemed to point to the West's economic insecurities as it began to drop its brief reinstatement of the classic gold standard.

As the first Roosevelt administration began in 1933, however, the evil modern alchemist who transmutes gold into a base metal to cause economic panic could himself transmute into a heroic modern alchemist—one who transmutes gold into base metals in order to rescue the world from a corrupt and unscientific monetary system. Drastic measures taken to clean up corruption in industry and the financial sector emerged from the ethos of the early months of FDR's first term, and, in a work like Nathan Schachner's three-part "The Revolt of the Scientists," published in *Wonder Stories* between April and June 1933, the issue of elemental mutability was used specifically to interrogate any metal-based currency system and, in fact, the whole industrial/financial/political complex. Science fiction became a testing ground for real social and political change and for a specifically scientific populist autocracy—styled a "technocracy."[17]

After FDR was sworn in on March 4, 1933, his first official act (on March 5) was to call a special session of Congress to address the financial panic causing a run on banks. The banks did not have enough cash in their vaults to meet depositor demands and thus failed, leading to more runs by panicking depositors on yet more banks. Roosevelt proclaimed a four-day national bank holiday, beginning on March 6, to stop the collapse of the banking system. He gradually allowed solvent banks to reopen, and most had reopened by the beginning of April, but under heavier regulation. On April 19, FDR officially took America off the gold standard, which prevented much of the gold from flowing to Europe, fixed the price of gold, and prohibited Americans from privately owning or hoarding gold.

But on March 3, 1933—the day before FDR took office—a think tank calling itself Technocracy Incorporated formed to spread its ideas through the Depression-riddled country. The editor of *Wonder Stories* prefaced the first part of Schachner's "Revolt" by noting:

> Albert Einstein recently called upon the world's twenty-five best minds to organize to settle some of the world's problems. Technocracy hints that technicians should take over the operation of all industries. Do these significant statements mean that science is now emancipating itself from the domination of business men and militarists? At the moment we do not know. But we do know that men of science are becoming increasingly dissatisfied with the use made of their intellectual output.
>
> Certainly therefore a time may come when scientists will be forced to break away entirely from law and order and try, as Mr. Schachner shows in this marvelous story, to create by illegal means a new world, "nearer to their heart's desire." (821)

Schachner's story created a fictionalized group of scientist vigilantes who take on an illegal liquor racket in Part 1 and the oil industry under a thinly veiled Rockefeller and Standard Oil (named Harry D. Stoneman, of Standard Petroleum) in Part 2. Finally, they address the rest of the major industries and the underlying power of the banking industry—run by J. L. Claremont, standing in for J. P. Morgan—and the gold and credit note basis of the economy in June's "Final Triumph" installment. These "technocrats" were based on the real Technocracy Incorporated, a group led by industrial engineer Howard Scott that had formed in 1919 as the Technical Alliance of North America and worked for fourteen years on plans, loosely based on Thorstein Veblen's work, that encouraged the abolition of ownership of industries and the price system. Technocracy Incorporated called for power to be given over each industry and the energies and resources it needs to a group of technological elites—technocrats—rather than politicians. The movement never amounted to much as a political force in America. Its few thousand members espoused vague aims of dominating Mexico and the Caribbean, and, as Martinez-Alier notes, they "organized cavalcades of grey cars, predicted the apocalyptic collapse of the system, and had an obsession with the Vatican. By the 1950s, what remained of the movement was so out of touch with reality that one of its periodicals claimed in 1959 that Fidel Castro was 'a Vaticanist fascist'" (145).

Yet in its heyday in the 1930s, Technocracy Incorporated was also based partially on Soddy's economic writings and his interest in energy. Indeed, because the Technocrats bought so many copies of Soddy's *Wealth, Virtual Wealth and Debt* (1926), the publisher brought out a new American edition in 1933 (Myers 71). They did, however, critique Soddy for holding on to the need for a basis for money and not endorsing their energy certificate concept (Martinez-Alier 147).

Schachner's three-part story propagandizes for the Technocracy movement, if it could be called a movement at that point. It explores Technocracy ideals such as "continental control" of energy sources and key industries. It uses modern alchemy, however, to articulate Technocracy's position against a currency based on a fluctuating commodity and on hoarding and lending. After the scientist hero Adam Roode and his Technocrats use cutting-edge scientific gadgetry and theories (taken a bit beyond the state of the art for 1933) to dispatch the liquor mob bosses and to wrest control of oil reserves from private companies, reorganizing the oil industry and finally other major industries, the final episode in June 1933 pitted them against the financial sector. The editor specifically linked the story to the bank crisis, noting

> The national bank holiday stirred the American people as few things have. It brought them face to face with those mystical things called money, bank credits, deposits and other things the man on the street has always taken for granted.... Mr. Schachner had written the final installment of his masterful "Revolt of the Scientists" around this theme. Scientists take a hand in this tremendous game of dealing with billions of dollars; with the lives of millions. Bankers for once find themselves confronted with forces that they are not trained to deal with. And the results... we shall see.... Mr. Schachner has pictured very forcefully in this series what would happen should scientists decide to use their gifts in the creation instead of the destruction of lives and properties. (3:27)

In this last installment of "The Revolt of the Scientists," J. L. Claremont claims, as Morgan had done in 1893 and 1907, to be working night and day to reorganize credit structures and save the country from financial collapse, but instead is merely working to bankrupt technocracy-controlled industries and to get a stranglehold on the food supply by foreclosing on farms across the country (an amplification of anxieties many displaced farmers must have felt about the nature of the banking system during the Depression). But Roode threatens: "You are quite smug and secure about your power. But what is it based on? Money and credit! Money—that means gold in the last analysis; credit—mere scraps of paper; mortgages, notes, stocks, bonds, contracts; that is all. Without that, what are you? Nothing, nothing at all!" (3:33). And, of course, Roode makes good on the implied threat and uses a powerful electrical ray to knock electrons off gold atoms, somehow turning it into tin, and thereby rendering completely worthless all of Claremont's gold reserves. After $150,000,000 worth of gold is destroyed in this way, a massive run on the banks by depositors in spite of the Federal Reserve and the United States

Treasury's efforts to rush gold to them ("There wasn't enough money in the world to stem [the rush]!" [36]) nearly ruins Claremont and his banking cronies. The President orders the banks closed, as Roosevelt had done in reality, places an embargo on gold shipments—"The nation to be considered off the gold standard" (36)—and orders the technocrats arrested. Finally, the technocrats, having rid the nation of gold as a medium of exchange, finish their plan by chemically destroying all the ink signatures on all the paper notes in Claremont's banks, erasing half a billion dollars in debt in a single day. After that, with the financial industries in ruin, the "new deal" president (obviously meant to be FDR) joins with the technocrats and the nation, reorganizing the federal government as a President and a lower house. He replaces the Senate with elected members of industry and puts scientists, engineers, and other technocrats in charge of all industries: "No man, woman or child was henceforth to lack the necessities of life.... The new day had dawned!" (3:87).

In Schachner's moral vision of a new technocratic America, the heroic scientist/modern alchemist highlighted the inefficiency and corruption of a metallic currency and a credit-based financial structure by transmuting the gold to tin. By the mid-1930s other stories used the modern alchemist similarly to articulate anxieties about the nature of money, but through the opposite process—by synthesizing gold. Roosevelt's first term saw works in *Amazing Stories* that explicitly invoked the occult alchemical tradition and hinted at vast economic consequences if the modern alchemist, using atomic techniques, could transmute base substances into gold freely.

Gernsback's editor's note before Peter Schuyler Miller's "Jeremiah Jones, Alchemist," in *Amazing Stories* from May 1933 claims that "this story depicts what we may call modern alchemy, and indicates that the modern professors of the art are going in the footsteps of the old votaries. It is interesting to follow out the curious ramifications which the author has introduced into this narration" (142). The "curious ramifications" are the plots by local town leaders to enrich themselves in a gold-making scheme that is then hijacked by a sinister chemist, who has experience in "under-cover coining" (148). The evil chemist plans to flood the world with synthetic gold, drive down the prices to "where they make radiator caps out of it" (149), then buy up investments at rock-bottom prices in a depression and buy up the gold to make it scarce again, thus driving up the prices. The Depression was obviously on everyone's mind in 1933, and the underworld thug, Baum, claims, "In six weeks you'd be in a depression that would make 1932 look sick! An' like innocent little lambs you'd be wiped out" (149).

But the story begins with the disinterested and voraciously curious scientist Jeremiah Jones arguing that "the alchemists of medieval times were undoubtedly the greatest scientists the world has known" (142). Miller injects into Jones's arguments a portrait of alchemists consonant with many of the recent histories of chemistry and alchemy. These ancestors of modern chemists hid their wisdom in coded manuscripts, had no scientific concept of universal law, and worked by "chance and by instinct... Their minds were enormous catalogues of facts and formulas, cluttered together without the slightest regard for system or relation" (143) and were based on religion. Yet Jones goes beyond most mainstream histories of chemistry to argue that some did indeed transmute gold, create the elixir of life, and perform other marvelous feats. To prove his point, he orders a book of an ancient Indian alchemist who wrote in Sanskrit. (This figure lived to be 350 before being stepped on by an elephant [144].) Jones decides to translate his formulae into modern scientific terms. He creates a love potion from the ancient text that works on his cat, and then he goes on to synthesize gold. But a friend asks him for the formula and then sets up a company with locals to synthesize gold. After a few pages of colorful encounters with underworld thugs who propose to destabilize the world economy, it turns out that the synthetic gold, while having most of the attributes of true gold, gives off the green plume of copper in a flame. The schemes all fall apart.

But the narrator goes back to Jones's house and learns that he had quickly discovered that the alchemist knew how to make an alloy out of copper, lead, and other metals that approximated gold (the very notion of Egyptian alchemy as early metallurgy making gold-like alloys that histories of chemistry put forth). The twist at the end of the story is that Jones really *had* transmuted and produced real gold as well: "I did that too. Quite simple, but costly. I used the obvious method—bombardment of mercury with alpha particles to break down the structure of the nucleus. The new G.E. tube made it quite simple, but it is not a cheap process. It has no commercial possibilities..." (151). A tiny amount, Jones explains, "cost as much as five pounds of the natural stuff. But it gives all the tests—spectrum and all. It's real gold. Those alchemists were wonderful men, and great scientists, but they hadn't our technique" (151). After raising the specter of ancient alchemy leading those of sinister purpose and no scientific or moral sense to plunge the world back into depression, Miller portrayed his true scientist as interested only in knowledge—a true modern alchemist using what he probably imagined to be Miethe's techniques with bombardment of mercury vapor. (He seems to be confusing cathode rays—electrons—with alpha rays.) As with most of the other modern alchemy stories in the Gernsback periodicals, even though they evoke and even praise medieval alchemy, these are science fiction rather than occult stories. Medieval alchemy is redeemed *as science* rather than as spiritual practice, and then, in the case of "Jeremiah Jones, Alchemist," modern atomic science trumps alchemy and produces the real gold.

Yet the production of real gold, the modern alchemy scenario that had been vividly portrayed by Wells in 1914, also began to appear as a problem in the pulps after the stock market crash of 1929. In these stories, the modern alchemical creation of synthetic gold has especially alarming consequences: It floods the economy and causes its collapse. In the month after the crash, Gernsback published Walter Kateley's "The Gold Triumvirate" in *Science Wonder Stories,* claiming in a prefatory note: "Sooner or later, gold, as well as all other metals, will be made synthetically. Alchemy is no longer a dream, for already our physicists have succeeded in changing one element into another. Of course, we are still at the threshold of 'alchemistry,' and it may be centuries before precious metals can be produced" (515). The editor added: "Our author shows that having too much gold may become a curse rather than a blessing. Too much of any precious metals will be just as bad as an acute shortage of them—at least, under our present monetary system. And when such a situation occurs, some other standard must be evolved. But this should not be very difficult" (515). Kateley's story proceeded with the now increasingly common scenario of a scientist using some version of the new radio-chemistry/atomic physics (in this case X-ray bombardment under high pressure of elements whose atomic numbers—iron 26 and iodine 53—add up to gold's 79). With the by now obligatory reference to the aspirations of the ancient alchemists, a group of three chemistry-educated friends launches a "gold triumvirate," not to destroy the market by flooding it with gold but to introduce their synthetic gold slowly and under the disguise of legitimate mining and smelting businesses, to prop up gold-standard economies and make themselves rich. But the story affords Kateley the opportunity, mostly through the scientist/banker of the story, Myron Kingsbury, to raise the issue of the nature of money in a metal-based currency. Unlike some other metals useful to industry, gold's value is not in its use, Kingsbury explains, nor does it truly back the money of any country:

"We say that the paper is just as good as the gold, because gold is in the treasury behind it.

"Yet we all know that there is four or five times as much money in circulation as there is gold in existence; and if one would count checks, stocks, bonds and other forms of collateral as money, there is some 27 times as much money in this country as there is gold, and even more in some foreign countries.

"But the people think the Government is back of all this money, with its taxing power. And for purposes of revenue, all property belongs to the government. So, you see, it is for the most part not the value of the gold, but the faith of the people in the stability of the government, that is the foundation of all monetary values." (Kateley 518)

Kingsbury mentions other possible ways of valuing money, including Irving Fisher's "Fisher dollar"—"that is, the average value of a stated amount of a hundred or more stable articles of merchandise" (520). Yet he also observes that flooding the market with gold would cause economic collapse and social calamity. Finally, after the triumvirate has made itself fantastically wealthy and bought up every asset it can find, even successfully propagandizing to convince other countries and even states and cities to adopt a gold standard, money begins to depreciate and widespread monetary free-fall ensues when a disgruntled employee reveals the secret production of gold. The problem for the economy is not the increased gold supply but rather the public's perception of the nature of its money when it learns that gold can be synthesized. The new understanding of matter is more unsettling to the gold standard than a big new gold strike in the Yukon would be. After worldwide economic collapse, Kateley writes that "in the last report [in the newspapers] there was an announcement that the governments of the United States, and Great Britain had appointed a joint commission to decide upon a new medium of exchange, and establish a new standard of values; and, if necessary, an entirely new system of currency" (557). The conclusion bears out Gernsback's didactic prefatory note, in which he asserts that a more scientific and less self-contradictory and susceptible monetary system than the gold standard would "not be very difficult" to establish. In the spirit of Wells's *World Set Free*, a scientifically precipitated world crisis must lead to international cooperation and a scientific solution. Such a story about financial panic must have had special resonance in the month after the stock market crash of October 1929.

Other stories in the Gernsback periodicals continued to explore the theme of atomic science's enabling a modern alchemy.[18] Isaac R. Nathanson's "Gold" appeared as direct interventions into national policy issues in the early FDR years. The editor made the connection explicit in his prefatory note, referring directly to the gold confiscation of 1933: "In the national finances of the United States the subject of gold has played a very prominent part, and has even led to very radical measures, far too radical in the opinion of some, to get all gold coins and bullion, so called, into the Treasury, and here we have a story about gold which seems to fit in very well with the government operations of today" (Nathanson 1934, 95). In Nathanson's story, the young scientist, Lewis

Walling, has discovered processes for releasing atomic energy, bombarding beryllium with alpha rays, and imagines an array of idealistic and even spiritual results of atomic energy that were much the same as those elaborated by Soddy in the *Interpretation of Radium* twenty-five years earlier:

> Homes and public buildings heated or cooled for a few pennies. Automobiles and railroads and airplanes that will run smoothly and noiselessly without refueling months on end. Metallurgy revolutionized. Industries operated at a negligible cost of power, bringing costs of all commodities down..... Inexhaustible power always on hand, leading mankind on to the conquest of the whole universe. Why, even interplanetary travel, long the dream of dreamers, could, with the aid of atomic power, at last be seriously attempted; thus enabling mankind to exploit the illimitable resources of the whole Solar System and beyond, to the glorification and material as well as spiritual enrichment of all humanity. (99)

The young idealist is thwarted by investors' general lack of interest in his schemes, but he then discovers the alchemical implications of his work. In his process, mercury transmutes into gold: "In his search for the secret of the internal energy of the atom, he had stumbled onto a most valuable by-product—the synthesis of pure gold; had succeeded in accomplishing the dream of the ages—transmutation of one of the baser elements into real gold!" (100). Yet he is ignored even by the gold magnate, Wilbur Morris. In a fit of pique he declares, "No time for foolishness, eh? I'll show him. I'll make his precious gold mines about as useful as a load of coal in hell" (104), and he proceeds to "let loose a flood of gold that will make old gold-grubbing Morris look like a piker" (104). He sells vast quantities of gold to the United States Treasury officials, who, by law, must buy any new gold he offers them, and he begins to cause fears about the gold standard:

> If continued at the rate the shipper was pouring it in, the high government officials as well as high financial circles doubted not that the gold standard of the world might topple of its own weight. Worse still, and aside from the possible threat to the established standards of money and exchange, with the concomitant dislocation of trade and industry, the great influx of this new gold, unless properly controlled, was bound to bring about a tremendous rise in the price of all commodities to an extent which might result in a great upheaval of the entire economic and social order throughout the wide world. (106)

Walling is eventually dragged before the Senate Committee on Currency and Finance. A senator asks Walling to "visualize the incalculable damage which may result from an uncontrolled supply of gold coming in such unlimited quantities" (108), but Walling refuses to admit that his gold is causing such damage, and he argues that the process is under his control. Moreover, he says, "the world is badly in need of more gold right now, and lots of it. So far there has not been enough to go around" (108). He goes on to argue, as many of the money cranks had, that the scarce gold supply limits the economy:

> With an ample supply of gold as the basis of real money, which everybody will accept with confidence, money and credit will become plentiful, bringing about a healthful expansion in all lines, ushering in new life and hope. Prices of long depressed commodities will raise, farm product and land values will go up, labor will receive higher wages. Consumption will then increase by leaps and bounds, causing a demand for the world's goods that will put a sudden end to the unspeakable horrors of unemployment. (109)

After attempts to steal his gold-making secret by Morris and his thug engineers, who almost take Walling's life, he ultimately announces that he has been synthesizing the gold: "The public was amazed. 'Greatest Discovery of All Time,' 'Synthetic Gold,' 'Dream of the Ages,' were some of the flaming headlines" (114). Nathanson chooses a nationalistic and ultimately conservative resolution to the crisis that Walling precipitates. The story never returns to Walling's earlier schemes of ending human suffering and raising the spiritual level of humanity through atomic energy. The idealism of Soddy and the tempered hopes of Wells are completely abandoned in favor of essentially a synthetic gold-standard solution: "A few months later, to the relief of the entire world, the now famous scientist turned over to his great Government the entire secret science of his gold-making art" (114). Nathanson seems to envision something like the pump-priming Keynesian economics that will undergird a new deal, but imagines a solution entirely based on the expansion of a gold-standard money supply.

The stories Gernsback published in his journals during the crisis years of the late 1920s and the 1930s clearly did not all agree in their diagnosis of the monetary and economic troubles. Kateley's story, for instance, explicitly rejects the kind of enhanced gold-standard solution Nathanson advocated a few years later; instead, he used atomic alchemy to argue against any precious-metal-backed currency in favor of other solutions, such as, perhaps, the Fisher dollar. But these stories all used the scenario of a modern alchemist using the new atomic science to synthesize or destroy gold to foreground the moral implications of the nature of money. The ranks of crooks, mad scientists, and unscrupulous business leaders who parade through these stories emphasize that individual desires and greed perpetuate monetary policies that deepen misery. "Real money," whether a new scientifically backed gold standard or a scientifically and benevolently created nonmetallic system, is money that furthers humanity's aspirations, not the power of the few. And in these stories, scientists, whether organized Technocrats or individuals like Walling or Bird, are the hope for a moral money system and just society.

The startling scenarios elaborated in the fiction, from Serviss's turn-of-the-century novel through the mid-1930s sci-fi pulps, remained just that—fictionalized possibilities that never came to pass in reality. Though the classic gold standard was supplanted by the mid-1930s, it was not a modern alchemist but rather a global depression and a new governmental willingness to challenge monetary orthodoxy that sealed its fate. But the alchemical trope pervading the new atomic science even into the 1930s retained the vitality, like a rhizome, to send out shoots in a number of different areas of early twentieth-century culture.

Epilogue

Until the United States ended the convertibility of dollars to gold in 1971 and thus signaled the end of the limited gold-standard system of Bretton Woods, the science fiction plot of an atomic attack on the gold standard emerged from time to time. But real atomic bombs dropped on Japan in 1945, and the cultural and political realities of the Cold War then altered the plot, essentially leaving the alchemical references behind. One well-known example of such a Cold War refiguring was the 1964 James Bond film, *Goldfinger*. The villain in the movie, Auric Goldfinger, is a gold bullion dealer who is hoarding gold and plans to invade Fort Knox, where the U.S. gold reserves are housed. As in the science fiction of the 1920s and '30s, Goldfinger plans to use atomic technology to destabilize the gold standard and plunge Western economies into chaos. Yet rather than transmute the gold into a worthless metal or flood the market with gold using modern atomic alchemy, Goldfinger intends to detonate a nuclear bomb inside the vaults of Fort Knox in order to destroy or irradiate (and thus contaminate) the U.S. gold supply. Beyond attempting to make himself unimaginably wealthy and powerful, Goldfinger works at the behest of the communist Chinese government, which hopes to destroy the West. While the nature of money, the stability of the gold standard, the mutability of matter in general, and rogue scientists gave rise to anxieties expressed in the modern alchemy stories earlier in the century, the fears that clearly animated Cold War culture included nuclear bombs, radioactive contamination, and communist plots against the West. A few writers attempted to reinvoke the alchemical understanding of nuclear physics in the postwar era, as Edith Sitwell did in her 1947 "Three Poems of the Atomic Age" (consisting of "Dirge for the New Sunrise," "The Shadow of Cain," and "The Canticle of the Rose").[1] The atomic bomb, though, had clearly supplanted alchemy as the major focus of public attention after 1945.[2] Scientists working in atomic physics and radio-chemistry no longer needed alchemical tropes to formulate research programs or even to present their research publicly.

All the same, alchemy remained a significant presence in twentieth-century occultism. And in occult circles, the connection between alchemy and nuclear physics continued beyond World War II. Ithell Colquhoun (1906–1988), the British surrealist painter, served as a link between the Golden Dawn generation and post-World War II occultism. She was a cousin of the British Hermeticist and alchemical devotee E. J. Langford Garstin (1893–1955). Garstin, an initiate of the Alpha et Omega Lodge of the Golden Dawn in the early 1920s (an offshoot of the original Golden Dawn), wrote *The Secret Fire: An Alchemical Study* (1932) and *Theurgy or the Hermetic Practice: A Treatise on Spiritual Alchemy* (1930). He shared the original Golden Dawn's enthusiasm for Atwood's *Suggestive Inquiry into the Hermetic Mystery* and its emphasis on spiritual alchemy. Garstin became an eloquent spokesman for spiritual alchemy and was able to place himself into a mesmeric trance state similar to that advocated by Atwood. Colquhoun herself was involved in several Hermetic and Druidic occult orders, and she furthered her interest in alchemy and in the Golden Dawn through her access to Garstin's library.[3] Yet like so many other occultists in the post-radiation period, Colquhoun emphasized that alchemy, in spite of its spiritual dimensions, was, in fact, a kind of nuclear physics. As we have seen in chapter 1, in her 1975 biography of Mathers (*Sword of Wisdom*), she asserted that alchemy "is not chemistry of any kind, not even so-called Hyperchemistry; it is rather an aspect of nuclear physics, and its well-attested transmutations result from nuclear reaction brought about by a still-unknown process" (270).

The vastly influential French post–World War II occult classic, *Le Matin des Magiciens* (1960) by Louis Pauwels and Jacques Bergier, similarly asserted the connections between alchemy and nuclear physics. Published in England as *The Dawn of Magic* (1963) and in America as *The Morning of the Magicians* (1964), the book's American dust jacket claimed that Pauwels and Bergier had "shaken the convictions of hundreds of thousands of educated people in France, Italy, Germany, Portugal, Holland, and England" and had "been supported by such eminent scientists as J. Robert Oppenheimer, Julian Huxley, Bertrand Russell" and "by such writers as Robert Graves, Henry Miller, Jean Cocteau,

Aldous Huxley." Following a line of thinking espoused by Soddy as far back as 1908, Pauwels and Bergier viewed alchemy as "one of the most important relics of a science, a technology and a philosophy belonging to a civilization that has disappeared" (65). While Pauwels and Bergier acknowledged that the alchemists had caused a spiritual self-transmutation with their work, they were adamant that alchemy be redeemed—not just by mystics uninterested in the material practice but, above all, by scientists. As the authors saw it, "alchemy is the only para-religious activity that has made a real contribution to our knowledge of reality" (67). So important was the scientific knowledge hidden in alchemical manuscripts and books, they asserted, that nuclear scientists ought to be searching through them for directions in their own research: "In the alchemist literature of our own century we often find the latest discoveries in nuclear physics before they have appeared in university publications; and it is probable that the treatises of tomorrow will be dealing with the most advanced and abstract theories in physics and mathematics" (68).

More recently, Robert A. Nelson's collection, *Adept Alchemy* (1998), continues to assert alchemy's scientific validity and its relationship to modern atomic science. Nelson's anthology intends to help alchemists working in the so-called "dry path" to transmutation. It includes extracts and summaries of work from the Middle Ages through the late twentieth century by Hermetic alchemists, chemists, and physicists, including the 1980 transmutation of bismuth into gold by scientists at the Lawrence Berkeley lab. (Nelson also includes the more controversial methods of Joe Champion in the 1990s. Champion was convicted of fraud in Arizona because he had not produced the results he claimed for investors.) Across the century, then, followers of occult alchemy have clearly continued to make connections to modern atomic science.

Indeed, occult alchemy's turn to material science after the discovery of radioactive transmutation has left a twentieth-century legacy of alchemical laboratory research. In France, Jollivet-Castelot's work through the 1930s had aimed at material transmutations. The mysterious alchemist Fulcanelli's 1926 publication of *Le Mystère des cathédrals* (The Mystery of the Cathedrals), which argued that the Gothic cathedrals of Paris and other towns preserved Hermetic information about actual processes for transmutation, inspired the practicing alchemist Eugène Canseliet (1899–1982) to pursue transmutation for decades. Similarly, in England, Archibald Cockren—who wrote *Alchemy Rediscovered and Restored*—was a practicing laboratory alchemist. Baron Alexander von Bernus (1880–1965) and others in Germany set up laboratory programs for alchemical work. In America, beginning in the 1940s, Orval Graves, of the Ancient and Mystical Order of the Rose Cross and the Rose + Cross University, ran experiments with a small circle. Albert Richard Riedel (1911–1984), under the name Frater Albertus, founded the Paracelsus Research Society and published *The Alchemist's Handbook* (1960).[4]

Very recent historians of alchemy, in fact, now see the spiritual alchemy hypothesis of the occult revival as historically inaccurate. They support the position held by early twentieth-century occult alchemists and historians that alchemy, in addition to its spiritual dimensions, was truly a material practice (see, for example, Principe and Newman 2001, and Newman and Principe 2002). Moreover, they deny that the chemical and physical processes in alchemical writings were simply code for entirely spiritual processes and reject the notion that alchemists had been able to transmute matter by an act of will.

Yet the spiritual alchemy that was a legacy of the mid-Victorian occult revival—of Atwood's *Suggestive Enquiry* and the American Ethan Allen Hitchcock's *Remarks upon Alchemy and the Alchemists* (1857)—and of the early Golden Dawn years *has* also survived, if in a slightly different form. Across the twentieth century it became grafted to the discourse of psychotherapy (and, in particular, to psychoanalysis). One of the most significant figures to promote the Golden Dawn–style Hermeticism after the 1920s, Israel Regardie, wrote a key interpretation of alchemy that drove home the growing interrelationship between spiritual and psychological interpretations of alchemy. His 1936–37 volume, *The Philosopher's Stone: A Modern Comparative Approach to Alchemy from the Psychological and Magical Points of View*, begins by noting that "Modern scholarship still leaves unsolved the question as to whether alchemical treatises should be classified as mystical, magical, or simply primitively chemical. The most reasonable view is, in my opinion, not to place them exclusively in any one category, but to assume that all these objects at one time formed in varying proportions the preoccupation of the alchemists. Or, better still, that different alchemists became attracted to different interpretations or levels of the art" (13). While Regardie is said to have become convinced in the 1970s of the merits of alchemy as a chemical process—and even sustained significant injury to his lungs during a laboratory experiment—in 1936 and 1937, the psychological and spiritual perspectives on alchemy were clearly foremost in his mind.[5]

Regardie lamented the psychological pathologies of modern life in very specific pseudopsychoanalytic terms:

> Existence and the ordinary turmoil of life, the struggle and the confusion which sooner or later binds consciousness by manifold links to an unevolved infantile and emotional attitude towards life, create anxiety and deep-seated fears.... Fear and anxiety give rise in early life to automatisms and compulsive behaviour, to what might be

called a shrinkage of the sphere of consciousness. It sets up an involuntary habitual contraction of the ego.... Continued sufficiently long, this attitude develops into mental rigidity, into a closed and crystallized conscious outlook, complacent and narrow, in which all further growth is impossible. (17)

Regardie explains that alchemy promises relief: "Now, it is with this rigidity of consciousness, with this inflexible crystallized condition of mind, that Alchemy, like modern Psychotherapy, proposes to deal, and moreover, to eradicate.... The crystallization of the field of consciousness, with its consequent narrowing of the possibilities of experience, produces a species of living death. The alchemists proposed to kill death. Their object, by the psychological method of interpretation, was to disintegrate this inflexible rigidity of mind" (17–18). Moreover, alchemy not only operates as psychotherapy but also offers a way to enhance the practitioner's spiritual life:

Not only does Alchemy envisage an individual whose several constituents of consciousness are united, but with the characteristic thoroughness of all occult or magical methods it proceeds a stage further. It aspires towards the development of an integrated and free man who is illumined. It is here that Alchemy parts company with orthodox Psychology. Its technique envisages a religious or spiritual goal. In much the same terms as Eastern philosophy, Alchemy propounds the question, "What is it, by knowing which, we have all knowledge?" (18–19)

Like many of the fin-de-siècle occultists studied in Alex Owen's *The Place of Enchantment*, Regardie wholeheartedly endorsed the conviction that ritual magic was an experiment upon the modern self. Regardie's thinking continued a line already espoused before World War I by Alchemical Society member Elizabeth Severn, whom we met in chapter 1. Severn combined training in early psychoanalysis with an interest in occult alchemy, and she saw alchemy as a practice of both spiritual and psychological self-transmutation. Freud himself had interests in occultism, though he erected scientific boundaries between his work and that of most occultists. Another early psychoanalytic pioneer inspired by the spiritual alchemy hypothesis, the Austrian Herbert Silberer, published an alchemical interpretation of psychoanalysis entitled *Probleme der Mystik und Ihrer Symbolik* (1914), which was criticized by Freud. (Some felt that this rejection contributed to Silberer's suicide.) It influenced a number of figures greatly, including the artist Max Ernst (Warlick 2001, 18–60).

Looming large over the second half of the twentieth century is another figure, though, whom Silberer's book on alchemy and psychoanalysis affected and who in turn influenced Regardie: the Swiss psychoanalyst Carl Jung. Jung ultimately set the terms of a psychological interpretation of alchemy for much of the rest of the century. As a boy and young man, Jung was deeply steeped in occultism and in a Swiss countryside still rife with beliefs in spirits, demons, and the like. The most important occult phenomenon of Jung's early life was, without a doubt, spiritualism. Jung's maternal grandfather believed that he was constantly surrounded by the ghosts of the dead, and he asked his daughter Emilie Preiswerk (who became Jung's mother) to keep the spirits from passing behind his back and disturbing him while he wrote sermons. His grandfather's second wife, Augusta Faber, also claimed to have "second sight" and the ability to communicate with spirits after falling into a thirty-six-hour cataleptic state. Emilie, who was born in 1848—the same year that the Hydesville knockings gave birth to spiritualism—also claimed the ability to communicate with the dead (Charet 1993, 67–69). Jung's experiences as a young man doing psychic research and attending séances during which his cousin, the medium Helene Preiswerk, assumed other personalities led him to develop a psychological practice of teaching patients to communicate with subpersonalities within their own psyches (Hayman 1999, 192).

But Silberer's work on alchemy and psychology inspired him, and Jung even took the term "imago," a key to his theories of psychological types, from Silberer (Hayman 192). Jung pursued research into alchemy for much of the rest of his life, publishing over a thousand pages of writings on the subject. His studies escalated in 1926, when he had a dream in which he was a seventeenth-century alchemist performing the Great Work, and again after 1928, when the German Sinologist Richard Wilhelm sent Jung a manuscript and translation of the Taoist Chinese alchemical manuscript *The Secret of the Golden Flower*. (Regardie had been reading Jung's 1929 commentary on *The Secret of the Golden Flower* while writing *The Philosopher's Stone*.) In one of his most important works, *Psychology and Alchemy* (1944), Jung presented a psychological theory by which alchemy provided keen insight into his crucial concepts of transference and integration. The integration of the psyche at the level of the personal unconscious was a self-transmutation, and the stages of alchemical transmutation each corresponded to stages of therapy. The Philosopher's Stone was essentially the psychological individuation process (see McLynn 1996, 428–32). Jung continued this work over the next decade, collaborating with the Nobel Prize–winning physicist and important theorist of quantum mechanics Wolfgang Pauli. Jung and Pauli explored Pauli's dreams. They also examined relationships between modern depth psychology and the challenges to our perceptions of reality in quantum mechanics, relationships between matter and spirit, and unity and duality.[6] This period culminated in another work on alchemy and psychology, Jung's 1954 *Mysterium Coniunctionis*.

Yet Jung still did not have Regardie's depth of knowledge about ritual magic. It took Regardie, who was uniquely positioned within the worlds of Golden Dawn and Enochian magic traditions and Jungian psychoanalysis, to make the major breakthrough. In 1938, he followed his *Philosopher's Stone* with a major volume entitled *The Middle Pillar*. In the new book, he not only insisted on the link between ritual magic and psychology but even suggested that psychotherapists should help their patients by using the Lesser Banishing Ritual and the Middle Pillar exercise from the Golden Dawn in therapeutic sessions. He provided step-by-step instructions for performing the rituals (invaluable to aspiring Hermeticists). The two paradigms—clinical psychoanalysis and occult ritual magic—had finally completely merged. Regardie noted that the Philosopher's Stone was "a symbol for spiritual illumination and expanded consciousness" (1939, 186).

At the beginning of the twenty-first century, the century of psychoanalysis may be giving way to that of brain chemistry and neuroscience. Psychotherapy is now supplemented and sometimes even replaced by antidepressants, antipsychotics, and other pharmaceutical responses to the chemistry of the brain. Neuroscience is beginning to provide physical explanations for cognition, emotion—even subjectivity. At this border of science and our deepest sense of our mental and even spiritual selves, alchemy is again demonstrating its relevance and durability. One final realm in which alchemical tropes became (and remain) common is that of psychedelic drugs.[7]

The nineteenth- and early twentieth-century occult revival was certainly rife with drug experimentation. Hashish, mescaline, opium, nitrous oxide, soma, cocaine, and heroin were used by some in occult circles to achieve appropriate ecstatic or trance states for magical ritual, increase clairvoyance, facilitate communication with the gods, and even produce visions in magic mirrors. Blavatsky was a frequent hashish user. She said of it, "hasheesh [sic] multiplies one's life a thousand fold. My experiences are as real as if they were ordinary events of actual life. Ah! I have the explanation. It is a recollection of my former existences, my previous incarnations. It is a wonderful drug, and clears up a profound mystery" (quoted in Deveney, *Randolph* 1997, 539). Paschal Beverly Randolph used hashish mixed with opium and other drugs in elixirs that he produced and sold for the last few decades of his life to heighten experiences of sexual magic.

The connection of spiritual alchemy and alchemical self-transmutation tropes to psychic states produced by drugs may even have had its origins in fin-de-siècle occultism. Golden Dawn member Arthur Machen's (1863–1947) classic novel, *The Hill of Dreams,* narrates the transformation of Lucian Taylor, a young writer, through an erotic experience of contact with a pagan world in the Welsh countryside. His experience and its sexual, spiritual, and aesthetic effects upon his psyche are often described in psychedelic terms—"like that of a drug, giving a certain peculiar color and outline to his thoughts" (1907, 120)—and in alchemical terms as well. His aesthetic transformation of his impressions is explicitly described as "the powder of projection, the philosopher's stone transmuting all it touched to fine gold; the gold of exquisite impressions" (100). Machen seems to confirm the spiritual alchemy interpretation that was so prevalent in the Golden Dawn for a time, but he gives an aesthete's interpretation to it: "[H]e became more than ever convinced that man could, if he pleased, become lord of his own sensations. This, surely, was the true meaning concealed under the beautiful symbolism of alchemy. Some years before he had read many of the wonderful alchemical books of the later Middle Ages, and had suspected that something other than the turning of lead into gold was intended" (99–100). Even Lucian's "interminable labor" of expressing his transformation in the book he is writing is described as a hopeless alchemical exercise (188). At the end of the novel, Lucian's spiritual/sexual/aesthetic self-transmutation is directly linked to a drug. The landlady holds up an empty bottle and says, "he would take it, and I always knew he would take a drop too much one of these days" (199). His seeming insanity and incomprehensible babbling and scribbling, and eventually his death, are attributed to taking the drug. Yet the novel ends: "The man took up the blazing paraffin lamp, and set it on the desk, beside the scattered heap of that terrible manuscript. The flaring light shone through the dead eyes into the dying brain, and there was a glow within, as if great furnace doors were opened" (200). The internal transmutation is complete, and the alchemical furnace glows on.

Alan Watts (1915–1973), who was widely known as an interpreter of Buddhism, Taoism, and other Eastern religions and philosophies to the West, first tried LSD for a psychiatric research group. His seminal essay, "The New Alchemy" (1960), links alchemical self-transmutation to a mystical experience of LSD and is widely quoted and cited on Web sites dedicated to psychedelic alchemy. As Watts notes, the effects of LSD on the brain, leading to a mystical experience, might well seem to suggest a material, chemical basis for spirituality—revealing again the tangle of spirituality and material science that we have seen going all the way back to Theosophy's multi-planar particles and the Alchemical Society.[8] Indeed, a multitude of books in recent years—discussed widely on alchemy Web sites and listservs—argue that many religious practices from ancient rites (or even religion itself) to the self-transmutations of alchemy were based upon various entheogenic substances, from ergots such as *Clavicepts purpurea* to the mushroom *Amanita muscaria* (for example, see Shelley 1995; Ruck 2006; Wasson, Kramrisch, Ott, and Ruck 1986; Wasson, Hofmann, and Ruck 1998; and Heinrich 2002). Alchemy is no longer the central trope for discussing and understanding nuclear physics and radiochemistry that it was through the 1930s, but its connection to atomic science persisted across the twentieth century and into the twenty-first in occult alchemy circles. Its move into the realms of psychoanalysis and brain chemistry suggests that its ability to destabilize boundaries between religion and science—and even between the sciences—remains alive and well.

Appendix A

Boundary-Work, Border Crossings, and Trading Zones

Modern Alchemy raises questions about boundaries among disciplines or fields of knowledge and how those boundaries are redrawn, transgressed, or productively blurred. Issues such as these have been theorized for some time by sociologists, anthropologists, and historians of science. I have deliberately avoided much of these disciplines' vocabulary in this monograph in order to make its story as broadly accessible as possible, but I would like to give a brief account of the conceptual work to which this project owes an immense debt.

One strategy that sociologists or anthropologists of science might detect in the relationship between occultism and science is what Roy Wallis has named "sanitization." Wallis argues that practitioners of "pseudo-sciences" who espouse scientifically rejected theories can engage in sanitization—the strategic imitation of the institutions, forms of citation and reference, and methods of mainstream science—in order to win broader public validation. As we have seen in chapter 2, sanitization clearly occurs in *some* occult engagements with science and can be seen in much of the referencing of mainstream and even cutting-edge science in Theosophical writings. Indeed, the clairvoyant Theosophical research of "occult chemistry" pushes sanitization to its extreme by directly offering itself as a legitimate and fully scientific research program engaged with the latest in atomic theory.

But sanitization alone is not a sufficient concept for describing the two-way exchanges between occultism and science that sometimes occurred. The rich relationship between occultism and mainstream science we have seen in chapter 1 on the Alchemical Society, for example, complicates interpretive schema by which one might theorize the boundaries of occultism and science. Interpreting the Alchemical Society's exploration of the possible room for alchemical doctrine *within* modern science requires additional theoretical tools. Theories of "boundary-work" by sociologist Thomas F. Gieryn and anthropologist David Hess, of "border crossing" and "borderlands" in the work of cultural anthropologist Sharon Traweek, of "boundary objects" in the studies of sociologist Susan Leigh Star, philosopher James R. Griesemer, and historian Geoffrey Bowker, and of "trading zones" in the work of historian Peter Galison, help suggest frameworks by which we can grasp the significance—for twentieth-century alchemy and atomic science—of the move out of the secret vaults of the Golden Dawn and into the Alchemical Society. Moreover, they help illuminate the other complex instances of cross-disciplinary collaboration, boundary blurrings, and mutual interactions among different domains of science, occultism, and even monetary theory that *Modern Alchemy* seeks to describe.

In examining the mainstream scientific side of the divide that occultists attempt to bridge with sanitization, Gieryn introduces the concept of "boundary-work." Scientists capitalize on the immense cognitive authority of science by identifying, in a public arena, what is *not science*, rhetorically mapping their domain of knowledge. Noting the increasing failure of efforts from Comte through Popper to demarcate science from other kinds of knowledge by looking for properties internal to science, Gieryn attempts to "restate the problem of demarcation" by arguing that demarcation is a practical and ideological effort by scientists (Gieryn 1983, 781–82). He argues that boundary-work is "a rhetorical style common in 'public science' . . . in which scientists describe science for the public and its political authorities, sometimes hoping to enlarge the material and symbolic resources of scientists or to defend professional autonomy" (782).[1] Both Wallis and Gieryn correctly emphasize that the cultural prestige and authority is on the scientific side of the boundary. In Wallis, practitioners of "pseudo-sciences" try to cross that boundary to appropriate scientific authority. In Gieryn's formulation, scientists try to strengthen that boundary in order to reject the pseudoscientific, or, in the case at hand, the occult.

Hess extends Gieryn's conception of boundary-work to both sides of the boundary. For Hess, not only scientists but also groups that have been dismissed as nonscientific or pseudoscientific participate in boundary-work, constantly attempting to redraw lines of demarcation. Of his work exploring New Agers, parapsychologists, and self-professed skeptics in postwar American culture,

Hess argues that such boundary-work "can operate in complex and multiple ways":

> My analysis shows not only how scientists engage in boundary-work to distinguish science from nonscience, but also how a variety of other groups construct boundaries (and consequently themselves as groups) not only with respect to more orthodox scientists and skeptics but with respect to each other. In short, scientific boundaries are recursive, nested, and multiple; there are layers of scientificity that become clearer as one unfolds levels of skepticism and "pseudo-scientificity" both within and across discursive boundaries. Boundary-work therefore is going on in all directions, not just in the direction of orthodox science toward religion and "pseudoscience."
> (Hess 1993, 145–46)

Occult engagements with atomic physics and chemistry exemplify the kind of boundary work that Hess elaborates, in which groups strategically attempt to manipulate "layers of scientificity." Such a dynamic was at play in many late-nineteenth-century occult writings, including those of many Golden Dawn members.

The history of the Alchemical Society and the movement of occultists from the secret reaches of the Golden Dawn to the public arena of the Society can be understood as a case of boundary-work. But to what end, and for whose benefit? The participation of established scientists with successful careers—including the Honorary President, John Ferguson, the Regius Chair of Chemistry at the University of Glasgow, who remapped the chemistry department to include more modern subdisciplines—would seem to preclude the common scenario that Gieryn explores, in which scientists must demarcate science from nonscience to protect scientific "turf."

Hess's articulation of fluid and ever-changing boundaries for two or more sides simultaneously provides a supple method for charting the boundary-work of a group like the Alchemical Society and for seriously exploring alchemy's implications for modern science at a time when many had relegated alchemy to the superstitions of the Middle Ages. The unusual kind of boundary-work occurring in the Alchemical Society suggests the extraordinary permeability of traditional boundaries between science and occultism at the moment when the new scientific paradigm of radioactivity and particle physics was being born. In order to explain and convince not just the broader public but also each other of the nature of the strange new phenomena under observation, and to explore the spiritual implications of the new science, mainstream scientists in the Society willingly looked to previously dismissed occult imagery and ideals. Likewise, occultists, as in the case of the Golden Dawn members who joined the Alchemical Society, were increasingly drawn out of the networks of secret societies and small private publications into a much more visible public arena to negotiate the boundaries of their beliefs.

Yet the example of the Alchemical Society might trouble even the complexity of a model that explores both sides of a boundary. To carry the cartography metaphor a little further, we might see the Alchemical Society as a kind of border town—neither entirely on the side of mainstream science nor in the occult hinterland. In such a space, the boundary between occultism and science could be renegotiated to the mutual benefit of both sides by a group not collectively identifying itself definitively with either. Such a radical positioning occurred at a moment in history during which a seemingly pseudoscientific occult concept—alchemy—was beginning simultaneously to serve the popular press, the broader public, and the scientific community in its understanding of the ramifications of the new atomic science.

The work of Sharon Traweek helps identify the kinds of negotiations that a border town like the Alchemical Society might permit. In her study of particle physics at the other end of the twentieth century, Traweek explores the strategic utility of what she calls "borderlands," places "where different standards clash, where one train gauge encounters another, where left- and right-driving cars meet head on, where nationalities fester and hyphenate" (1992, 458). Traweek's understanding of borderlands emerged from her field work at KEK, the National Laboratory for High Energy Physics, in Tsukuba Science City in Japan. She notes that "the Japanese word for people, actions, situations, and things out of place is *bachigai*" (450), and virtually every aspect of KEK and Tsukuba Science City appears *bachigai*.

Traweek explores the many ways in which borderlands such as Tsukuba Science City allow a strategic manipulation of the conventions and structures of scientific work. KEK is a highly sophisticated science laboratory located in a province that is seen by many Japanese to be a "hick" province, not the "real" Japan, and it falls outside the usual structures of university and national politics in Japan (456). Yet the institution's position outside the normal circuits of power and scientific culture allows it to appeal to international science communities and to reshape scientific culture in Japan. It is largely free from the control of the established universities and their models of resource allocation (in which powerful professors control access to resources [456]).

Not only is Tsukuba Science City in a liminal institutional position in Japan, but it also brings together Japanese and foreign scientists and even Japanese scientists who have found themselves shunned by broader Japanese society for having been abroad working in foreign universities for many years.

Scientists coming from such different positions are able to make strategic use of each other in a borderland, a place where even the choice of what language to use in any given situation allows different types of negotiations for resources, position, and ownership of scientific knowledge.[2]

While Traweek's study points out the difficulties of doing physics from a marginal position within the international scientific community, it also highlights how borderland status allows strategic actions and interactions that would have been virtually impossible elsewhere. I suggest that the Alchemical Society functioned in precisely this way. It allowed marginalized pseudoscience and its occult advocates to interact with legitimate scientists; moreover, it permitted scientists to rethink the purposes and goals of their own research through interaction with occultists. Left- and right-driving cars were meeting head-on—but not crashing.

But we must expand our conceptual tool kit a bit more to understand how such a borderland could exist so productively, even if only briefly, in the Alchemical Society. The tool we need is the notion of a "boundary object" employed by Star and Griesemer, and Bowker. Star and Griesemer offer a refinement of actor-network theory and its attendant concept of translation in the production of scientific knowledge that speaks directly to the complexity of the occult/science interactions in the Alchemical Society. Noting the centrality of actor-network theory to their work, Star and Griesemer summarize it thus: "In order to create scientific authority, entrepreneurs gradually enlist participants (or in Latour's word, 'allies') from a range of locations, re-interpret their concerns to fit their own programmatic goals and then establish themselves as gatekeepers.... Latour and Callon have called this process *interessement,* to indicate the translation of the concerns of the non-scientist into those of the scientist" (1989, 389). As Star and Griesemer's study of the Museum of Vertebrate Zoology at Berkeley in the early twentieth century shows, however,

> a central feature of [the Museum's] situation is that entrepreneurs from more than one social world are trying to conduct such translations simultaneously. It is not just a case of *interessement* from non-scientist to scientist. Unless they use coercion, each translator must maintain the integrity of the interests of the other audiences in order to retain them as allies. Yet this must be done in such a way as to increase the centrality and importance of that entrepreneur's work. (389)

Star and Griesemer suggest that the successful cooperation in science of actors from sometimes radically different social worlds depends upon "methods standardization" and "boundary objects." They define boundary objects as "those scientific objects which both inhabit several intersecting social worlds... *and* satisfy the informational requirements of each of them" (393). Boundary objects, they continue, "are objects which are both plastic enough to adapt to local needs and the constraints of the several parties employing them, yet robust enough to maintain a common identity across sites.... These objects may be abstract or concrete. They have different meanings in different social worlds but their structure is common enough to more than one world to make them recognizable" (393). An example of such a boundary object in Star and Griesemer's case study would be the dead birds preserved in the museum. The birds meant different things to amateur bird watchers, philanthropists, professional scientists, university administrators, and others, yet each group used the birds for its own purposes. As Bowker and Star put it in a more recent work, "The creation and management of boundary objects is a key process in developing and maintaining coherence across intersecting communities.... [Boundary objects] are working arrangements that resolve anomalies of naturalization without imposing a naturalization of categories from one community or from an outside source of standardization" (1999, 297).

Hermetic and Rosicrucian circles such as the Golden Dawn began to engage more publicly with science after the discoveries of radiation, radioactive transformation, and radium, and in the case of the Alchemical Society, at least two boundary objects allowed the mutual interaction of occultists and atomic scientists: (1) alchemy as a classification and a set of ideals, and (2) radiation itself. Both these boundary objects were abstract and largely text-based (the interpretation of alchemical texts, and the frequently secondhand interpretation and accounts of radiation). As we have seen in chapter 1, the Golden Dawn had officially disseminated alchemical knowledge privately through specific manuscripts. But the existence of alchemy and accounts of research on radiation as boundary objects was enabled by a completely different interaction structure in the Alchemical Society, which employed a framework by which a paper was read aloud at a meeting, was then discussed, and finally was published (along with a synopsis of the discussion) in a monthly journal for further dissemination to the membership and to the press. Such a structure and the boundary objects upon which it was predicated enabled a mutually functional interaction between groups from sharply different social worlds, permitting a synthesis of the seemingly conflicting goals of occultism and modern science. They also helped shape the popular press's understanding of the newly emerging discourse of atomic physics.

As Traweek has argued, borderlands are not powerless margins but sometimes can generate surprising advantages. The strategic value that members of the Alchemical Society found in the Society's strange meeting of scientists and occultists was its ability to serve as a debating forum in which occultists interested in science and scientists interested in alchemy could hammer out an understanding of the uses of alchemical thinking in a modern atomic age. No other such forum existed at the nascence of modern atomic theory. The debates fostered by the borderland status of the Society self-consciously raised issues of the spiritual implications of science, the unity of nature, and the uses of analogy in the production of scientific understanding (they were never as simple as a straightforward use of alchemy as an analogy for atomic science). They reveal, too, a complex sense of scientific discourse as permeable.

Alchemy and radioactivity served as boundary objects that allowed groups from such different social worlds to work together. But unlike the examples discussed by Star, Griesemer, and Bowker, these boundary objects also served a disruptive function, as, I would argue, boundary objects in a borderland necessarily must. They helped to break down discourse boundaries as much as they enabled the productive coexistence of different discourses and purposes.

However, it is also possible in a situation that Traweek would label a borderland for highly productive disciplinary or subfield interactions to result in real breakthroughs but nevertheless not negate disciplinary boundaries. Peter Galison turns to anthropology and linguistics to suggest the "trading zone" as a model for examining collaboration between different disciplines or subcultures within a field. "What is crucial," he explains,

> is that in the local context of the trading zone, *despite* the differences in classification, significance, and standards of demonstration, the two groups can collaborate. They can come to a consensus about the procedure of exchange, about the mechanisms to determine when goods are "equal" to one another. They can even both understand that the continuation of exchange is a prerequisite to the survival of the larger culture of which they are part.
>
> I intend the term "trading zone" to be taken seriously, as a social, material, and intellectual mortar binding together the disunified traditions of experimenting, theorizing, and instrument building. Anthropologists are familiar with different cultures encountering one another through trade, even when the significance of the objects traded—and of the trade itself—may be utterly different for the two sides. And with the anthropologists, it is crucial to note that nothing in the notion of trade presupposes some universal notion of a neutral currency. Quite the opposite, much of the interest of the category of trade is that things can be coordinated (what goes with what) without reference to some external gauge. (Galison 1997, 803)

Galison emphasizes that groups collaborating in a trading zone need not, and, in fact, often do not, lose their distinctness:

> Indeed, far from melting into a homogeneous entity, the different groups often maintain their distinctness, whether they are electrical engineers and mechanical engineers, or theorists and engineers, or theorists and experimenters. The point is that these distinct groups, with their different approaches to instruments and their characteristic forms of argumentation, can nonetheless coordinate their approaches around specific practices.... Note that here, as in any exchange, the two subcultures may altogether disagree about the implications of the equivalencies established, the nature of the information exchanged, or the epistemic status of the coordination. (Galison 1997, 806)

Indeed, Galison explains that "In the trading zone both sides impose constraints on the nature of the exchange" (806), and the collaboration itself can even reinforce the various subcultures involved (829).

An example in Galison's work of such a trading zone is the "Rad Lab" established in 1940 at MIT to develop radar systems for the U.S. military but reorganized after Pearl Harbor to emphasize the production of completed projects. This laboratory brought together physicists, engineers, and administrators, and, as Galison puts it, "the war forced theoretical physicists... to spend day after day calculating things about devices and, through these material objects, linking their own prior language of field theory to the language and algebra of electrical engineering" (Galison 1997, 824). The theoretical physicists in this collaboration learned from the engineers to "concentrate on what you actually *want to measure,* and design your theory so that it does not say more than it must to account for these particular quantities" (827). Yet none of the engineers or scientists gave up their disciplinary identity during these collaborations. The radar technology they developed surely was a boundary object in Bowker, Star, and Griesemer's sense, in that the physicists, engineers, military advisers, and ultimately military users of the technology used it and benefited from it in different ways. Yet Galison's trading zone concept captures well the mechanism that enabled such productive collaborative exchanges.

Though the Alchemical Society included academic chemists in its ranks, and productively worked out spiritual implications of modern science for them, none of the scientists in the Alchemical Society directly contributed to the major discoveries and theoretical innovations of modern atomic theory. But Ernest Rutherford and Frederick Soddy's laboratory at McGill was the site of a collaboration that contributed one of the most important breakthroughs in the early theorization of radioactivity. Rutherford and Soddy enjoyed the productive freedom from institutional constraints that exemplifies a borderland in Traweek's sense, but it could also be described as a trading zone in Galison's sense. As we have seen in chapter 3, Soddy very much highlighted the distinct disciplinary contributions that Rutherford brought to their collaboration as a physicist and Soddy as a chemist. Remember that Soddy had emphasized his immediate recognition of the significance of transmutation in their experiment, because, as he put it, he was "always occupied with transmutation. That is natural; I was a chemist" (Howorth 1958, 82). Soddy continued, "I only want to show how our brains were working, mine on transmutation and gases, Rutherford's on thorium and alpha ray emission" (Howorth 84). Each scientist maintained his sense of the concerns and experimental techniques of his own field, yet was able to collaborate and produce conclusions that either field individually might have missed. Rutherford then left the trading zone of his McGill laboratory to run physics laboratories at Manchester and then Cambridge, whereas Soddy left to join chemistry departments at Glasgow, Aberdeen, and finally Oxford.

However, Ramsay, Collie, and the other chemists we have seen in chapter 3 attempting to document artificial transmutation were not, in fact, working in a trading zone. They were chemists working with other chemists in chemistry labs and discussing their results at meetings of the Chemical Society and elsewhere—albeit with physicists such as J. J. Thomson and others attending and commenting on their work. Attempting the boundary work of positioning transmutation as a distinguishing feature of chemistry as a field, and upholding their chemists' methods in the face of objections from physicists, the chemists reached the limitations of their current laboratory methods and spectroscopic analysis. The research performed by the chemists in London, then, primarily remained an unsuccessful collaboration among chemists. Though operating within the confines of a single discipline was not what doomed their efforts (Rutherford at the Cavendish worked primarily with other physicists and succeeded), a fertile collaboration merging the concerns, techniques and instruments of physics and chemistry, such as the one that had contributed to the success of Rutherford and Soddy's trading zone at McGill, might have increased the chances that Ramsay and his colleagues could have succeeded in documenting their transmutations (indeed, some, though not all, of their suppositions proved correct, even if they were unable to detect the successes of their efforts with the instruments they used).

But the institutional borderland (though not an actual laboratory, meeting place, or physical collaboration) at which virtually all of these chemists worked was the intersection of physics and chemistry known as physical chemistry. As we have seen in chapter 3, this field—that Nye has shown emerged by the 1860s and came into its own in the mid-1880s—thrived in England at the turn of the century when radioactivity research became a field, partially because of the looser disciplinary boundaries in British academic institutions. Physical chemists understood their field as flourishing in a liminal space between chemistry and physics, and often spoke of it using tropes of adventure, exploration, and border-crossing. It is perhaps no surprise, then, that the chemists most actively interested in the new field of radioactivity that was engaging physicists would be the physical chemists. The alchemical interests of two of the most significant British physical chemists of the period, Soddy and Ramsay, emerging as they did from the alchemical revival of the late nineteenth century, then helped pave the way for the marvelously fertile and boundary-blurring alchemical tropes of the early twentieth century in the British and American reception of the new research, and in the occult adaptations of it.

Yet it might be a mistake to think of the field of physical chemistry itself as a border crossing in Traweek's sense or a trading zone in Galison's, in spite of its drawing upon the concerns of both chemistry and physics. The fact that it had been fairly securely established as a field already in the decades leading up to the discovery of radiation, and, indeed, as a field of *chemistry*, gave it a solid institutional identity. While the collaboration of a physical chemist with a physicist, as in the case of Soddy and Rutherford at McGill, could create a trading zone or border crossing, the efforts by physical chemists in London to transmute an element might more accurately be seen as an instance of boundary-work, or perhaps "boundary maintenance." Physical chemists attempted to lay claim to the study of radioactivity for their field. The claims that the element seemingly created through transmutation differed when the target was in the presence of different elements (as in Ramsay's experiments) as well as the chemists' efforts to document their transmutations with spectroscopes ultimately failed. This represents a boundary skirmish won by physics.

Appendix B

Occult Interest Books by Alchemical Society Members

An incomplete list of books of occult interest published by Alchemical Society figures (other than Waite) includes:

Emile Boirac: *Our Hidden Forces ('La Psychologie Inconnue') An Experimental Study of the Psychic Sciences*, trans. W. De Kerlor (New York: Frederick A. Stokes, 1917).
J. B. Craven: *Doctor Robert Fludd (Robertus De Fluctibus) the English Rosicrucian: Life and Writings* (Kirkwall, Orkney: W. Peace, 1902).
Isabelle De Steiger: *On a Gold Basis: A Treatise on Mysticism* (London: Philip Wellby, 1907; Rider, 1909).
John Ferguson: *Bibliotheca Chemica: A Catalogue of the Alchemical and Pharmaceutical Books in the Collection of the Late James Young* (Glasgow: Maclehose, 1906, and several later editions through the 1950s).
J. W. Frings: *Occult Arts: An Examination of the Claims Made for the Existence and Practice of Supernormal Powers, and an Attempted Justification* (London: Rider, 1913).
Walter Gorn Old (Sepharial): *The New Manual of Astrology* (London: Nichols, 1909); *Prognostic Astronomy* (London: L. N. Fowler, 1901); *Eclipses* (London: L. N. Fowler, 1915); *The Book of the Simple Way of Laotze* (London: Philip Wellby, 1904; Rider, 1913; Philadelphia: David McKay, 1915); *Shu Link or the Chinese Historical Classic*, trans. Old (London: Theosophical Publishing

House, 1904; and New York: John Lane, 1904); *The Manual of Astrology in Four Books, Treating of the Language of the Heavens, the Reading of a Horoscope, etc.* (London: W. Foulsham, 1962; Sterling Publishing Co., 1972).

H. Stanley Redgrove: *Matter, Spirit and the Cosmos* (London: Rider 1910, 1916), *Alchemy: Ancient and Modern* (London: Rider, and Philadelphia: David McKay, 1911, 1922); *Bygone Beliefs* (London: Rider, 1920); *Joseph Glanvill and Psychical Research in the Seventeenth Century* (London: Rider, 1921); with I. M. L. Redgrove, *Roger Bacon: The Father of Experimental Science and Medieval Occultism* (London: Rider, 1920); *Purpose and Transcendentalism: An Exposition of Swedenborg's Philosophical Doctrines in Relation to Modern Thought* (London: Kegan Paul, Trench, Trubner, 1920); *Joannes Baptista van Helmont: Alchemist, Physician, and Philosopher* (London: Rider, 1922), with I.M.L. Redgrove.

Elizabeth Severn: *Psycho-Therapy: Its Doctrine and Practice* (London: Rider and Co., 1913, and through a fourth edition in 1935; Philadelphia: David McKay, 1913 in multiple impressions; New York: David McKay, 1916).

Ralph Shirley: *Occultists and Mystics of All Ages: The Mystery of the Human Double: The Case for Astral Projection* (New Hyde Park, N.Y.: University Books, 1965).

Waite's occult publications are too numerous even to begin to list. See R. A. Gilbert, *A. E. Waite: A Bibliography* (Wellingborough, Northamptonshire: Aquarian Press, 1983).

Appendix C

A Partial List of Alchemical Society Members

A complete list of those members mentioned in the minutes of the meetings of the Alchemical Society (though by no means a complete list of its members), along with their position within the Society and the date at which they joined the Society or were first mentioned:

Abdul-Ali, Mr. Sijil. (Auditor, 1913–May 1913; Hon. Sec., May 1913–)
Chatley, Prof. Herbert. BSc (Lond.), MICEI, of Tangshan Engineering College, North China (1913–)
Collins, Col. J. LLB (1913)
Craven, The Venerable J. B. DD, Archdeacon of Orkney (Hon. Vice-President, 1913–)
Decker, Johnson. (1914)
Dunlop, Mr. D. N. (1913–, Editor of *The Path*)
Ferguson, Prof. John. MA (Glas.), LLD (St. Andrews), FIC, FCS, of Glasgow University (Hon. Pres., 1913–)
French, Miss A. K. (1914)
French, Miss Mary. (1915)
Frings, J. W. (1913)
Gibson, Lt. Col. Jasper. VD, LLB (Lond.) (1913)
Higgs, Mr. Fred.
Hinton, Mrs. (1914)
Hopgood, Dr. (1914)
Horton, Mr. William. (Ordinary Member of Council, 1913–)

Hylton, Mr. F. (1913)
Jollivet-Castelot, François. (President of the French *La Société Alchimique de France;* elected an Honorary Member of the Alchemical Society, March 1914)
Jutsum, J. Arthur. (Ordinary Member of Council, 1913–)
de Kerlor, Mons. W. (1913; Ordinary Member of Council, May 1913–)
L'Amy, Mr. Ramsay. (1915)
Locke, Miss A. A. (1913)
Loring, Mr. F. H. (1915)
Marson, Mr. Thomas. (1914)
Mellor, Dr. Joseph William. DSc (1913–)
De Mengel, Mr. Gaston. (Ordinary Member of Council, 1913–)
De Mengel, Mrs. Gaston. (1914)
Miles, Miss Clarissa. (Ordinary Member of Council, 1913–)
Old, Mr. Walter Gorn. (Hon. Vice President, 1913–; Hon. Secretary, 1913–May 1913)
Parsons, Mr. Nigel M. (1913–)
Payne, Miss D. Marion. (1915)
Pembroke, Mr. Leonard F. (Auditor, 1913–)
Pool, Rev. John J. PhD, BSc, FZS, FRGS (1913–)
Prag, Mr. Jacob. (1914)
Redgrove, Mr. Cyril W. (1914)
Redgrove, H. Stanley. BSc (London), FCS (Editor, Acting Pres., 1913–)
Rowbottom, Mr. B. Ralph. (Auditor, May 1913–)
Severn, Dr. Elizabeth. PhD (Chicago) (Hon. Vice-President, 1913–)
Shirley, Mr. Ralph. (Editor of *The Occult Review*, Honorary Vice-President, 1913–)
Stapley, Sir Richard. (Hon. Vice-President, 1913–)
de Steiger, Mme. Isabelle. (Hon. Vice President, 1913–)
Waite, Arthur Edward. (Hon. Vice President, 1913–)
Wellby, Philip Sinclair. MA (Cantab.) (Hon. Treas. 1913–)

Visitors to Meetings:
Cox, Mr. Donald W. (1915)
Gardiner, Mr. F. A. FLS, Hon. Treas. of The Swedenborg Society (1915)
Creswell, Mr. K. A. C. (1915)

Notes

INTRODUCTION

1. E.g., Shah ca. 1929, Noyes and Noyes 1932, and Fisk 1936. Interestingly, in more recent years, the title has been resurrected by Glenn T. Seaborg (1994), the Nobel laureate nuclear chemist who discovered plutonium and other transuranium elements, worked on the Manhattan Project, and served on John F. Kennedy's Atomic Energy Commission.

2. See the seminal work of Sclove 1989 and Trenn 1974 on this issue in relationship to Soddy and to Ramsay.

3. Alex Keller's *The Infancy of Atomic Physics: Hercules in His Cradle* (1983) is one of the finest such studies. Emilio Segrè's *From X-Rays to Quarks: Modern Physicists and Their Discoveries* (1980) is another excellent history, one that also focuses on the personalities of the physicists.

4. I am deliberately using the term "spiritual" to describe a broad range of understandings by scientists and occultists of ways in which new conceptions of matter and energy related to religion or to the sacred more generally. As we shall see, these understandings were quite varied. Some individuals were convinced that alchemy and the new science could transform the soul of the participant; others believed that the science of radioactivity granted access to an intangible world of the spirit, or to otherworldly powers. Still others felt that gaining insight into the mysterious workings of matter and energy revealed something about the divine nature of the physical laws of the universe.

5. Much recent work in the sociology and anthropology of science has examined boundary issues in science. See Appendix A for the insight such work provides into the subject of this book.

6. See Henderson 1998, 22–28, on the importance of this phenomenon to French culture.

7. See Winter 1998 for a detailed discussion of these aspects of mesmerism in Britain and beyond.

8. Winter notes that "Animal magnetism extended the conventions that represented the invalid as sensitive and authoritative, both in extraordinary stories of exemplary invalids such as these and in many individual experiences, some recorded in the press and some not, across Victorian Britain" (Winter 216).

9. See Francis King for a brief account of the Hydesville knockings. King emphasizes the importance of American spiritualists to the British occult revival, and sees them as "in many ways merely the old cult of necromancy in a nineteenth-century guise" (King 1970, 31).

10. For the American reaction against spiritualism, culminating in 1887 and 1888, see Jenkins 2000, 39–41.

11. Home can only loosely be considered an American medium. He was born in Scotland, immigrated to America at the age of nine to be with his parents, and then spent most of his adult life in Europe.

12. In her groundbreaking work, *Giordano Bruno and the Hermetic Tradition* (1964) highlighting the influence of Hermeticism on Renaissance thought, and indeed on early modern science, Frances Yates made clear not only that the Hermetic corpus was in fact a product of Neoplatonic and gnostic writers of the second and third centuries C.E., but that, as she puts it, "this huge historical error was to have amazing results" (6). She argues,

> So we can understand how the content of the Hermetic writings fostered the illusion of the Renaissance Magus that he had in them a mysterious and precious account of most ancient Egyptian wisdom, philosophy, and magic. Hermes Trismegistus, a mythical name associated with a certain class of Gnostic philosophical revelations or with magical treatises and recipes, was, for the Renaissance, a real person, an Egyptian priest who had lived in times of remote antiquity and who had himself written all these works. The scraps of Greek philosophy which he found in these writings, derived from the somewhat debased philosophical teaching current in the early centuries A.D., confirmed the Renaissance reader in his belief that he had here the fount of pristine wisdom whence Plato and the Greeks had derived the best that they knew. (6)

13. For a brief but useful summary of the Rosicrucian legend, see King 9–14.

14. See Goodrick-Clarke 2005 for the nuances and history of these terms in the eighteenth and nineteenth centuries.

15. Deveney 2005, 977–78. For a full treatment of Randolph's life and influence, see Deveney 1997.

16. Rifts quickly occurred within the Rosicrucian community. Péladan, like Lévi, saw his occultism as consonant with Roman Catholicism, and felt that de Guaita's influence on the Order was too pagan. He broke with the order in 1890 to create the

Catholic Order of the Rosy Cross of Temple and Grail. And in 1892, he even established a series of annual Rosicrucian salons to promote art, music, and theater, arguing in his 1894 *L'Art idéaliste et mystique* that "From year to year the Rosicrucian idea wins over both artists and the public" (quoted in McIntosh 1972, 174). The Theosophical Society opened a branch headed by Lady Caithness, Duchesse de Pomar, who felt that she was the reincarnation of Mary Queen of Scots (McIntosh 157).

17. See the Web site of the Rosicrucian Order of Alpha+Omega at: http://www.golden-dawn.com/temple/index.jsp.

18. See, for example, Hutchison, who sought "to re-evaluate current conceptions of the role of occult qualities in the Scientific Revolution" by showing shifts in understanding of occult qualities from "insensible," as opposed to "manifest" qualities, to one in which occult qualities were considered to be "unintelligible" to science. Hutchison notes that "many leaders of the Scientific Revolution can be seen to be explicitly urging the acceptability of occult entities" (1982, 233). Indeed, as Hanegraaff argues in Faivre and Hanegraaff's *Western Esotericism and the Science of Religion* (1998), Frances Yates in her 1964 *Giordano Bruno and the Hermetic Tradition* helped revise the historiography on Western esotericism: "To demonstrate that a well known figure such as Bruno (traditionally pictured as a hero and martyr of scientific progress) had been a hermetic magician of a rather extreme kind, and that generations of scholars had been all but blind to the fact, amounted to a bombshell under an entire tradition of mainstream academic historiography" (Hanegraaff 1998, ix).

19. As Winter notes, "In the later phase of mesmerism's Victorian history, important changes took place in the authoritative status of the sciences and medicine. By 1870 new disciplinary divisions in science and medicine, brought on by reforms in university education and the new laboratories, left less space for the lines of inquiry that mesmerism required" (Winter 6).

20. However, as Oppenheim has pointed out, "Ironically, some psychical researchers were as eager as the spiritualists to force the methods of science into the service of an unseen, immaterial world. Their work, instead of building on scientific discoveries, misunderstood, misapplied, and distorted them" (Oppenheim 1985, 3).

21. As Owen has argued, this "new occultism" of the late nineteenth century contributed to "a newly conceptualized subjectivity, that innovative sense of self that so often characterized those self-identified 'we moderns' of the fin de siècle" (Owen 2004, 7).

22. Joscelyn Godwin argues that claims that Bulwer-Lytton was an initiate or belonged to any Hermetic or Masonic Order are mere rumors with no real evidence to substantiate them. His contacts with the occult world were real. He had even attended two séances with the most famous medium of his day, Daniel Dunglas Home, and had been one of only three people attending Lévi's famous 1861 evocation of Apollonius of Tyana. But Godwin argues that Bulwer-Lytton was a skeptic who distanced himself from many of the spiritualists and occultists whose activities he explored. His election as "Grand Patron" of the Societas Rosicruciana in Anglia in 1872 was without his consent (Godwin 2005, 215).

23. Holly, the narrator, writes in a note, "Ayesha was a great chemist; indeed, chemistry appears to have been her only amusement and occupation. One of the caves was fitted up as a laboratory, and, although her appliances were necessarily rude, the results that she attained, as will become clear in the course of this narrative, were sufficiently surprising" (Haggard 1887, 235).

24. Haggard writes in an explanatory footnote to Holly's narrative:

Recent discoveries would appear to suggest that this mysterious "Fire of Life," which, whatever else it may have been, was evidently a force and no true fire, since it did not burn, owed its origin to the emanations from radium, or some kindred substance. Although in the year 1885, Mr. Holly would have known nothing of the properties of these marvelous rays or emanations, doubtless Ayesha was familiar with them and their enormous possibilities, of which our chemists and scientific men have, at present, but explored the fringe. (1905, 167)

25. For a valuable discussion of Weber in relationship to the new occultism, see Owen 2004, 10–12.

26. See Gieryn 1983, 784. Gieryn, a sociologist of science, has called such rhetorical efforts to solidify a superior intellectual position for science by demarcating it from the non or pseudoscientific "boundary-work."

27. As Harrington explains: "The new 'holistic' science of life and mind that was to replace the old Machine science was really more a family of approaches than a single coherent perspective. The need to do justice to organismic purposiveness or teleological functioning—to questions of 'what for?' and not merely 'how?'—was central in all cases" (1996, xvii).

CHAPTER 1

1. See, for example, the accounts of Howe 1972, Torrens 1972, King 1970, and Colquhoun 1975.

2. Several accounts of the rituals and history of the Golden Dawn have been published, and few of them have been able to avoid the partisanship that tore the original group apart. Ithell Colquhoun's *Sword of Wisdom: MacGregor Mathers and "The Golden Dawn"* is little more than a hagiography of MacGregor Mathers, while accounts by Crowley and Israel Regardie (see, for example, Regardie's *What You Should Know about the Golden Dawn* [1936]), both of whom published large sections of the Golden Dawn rituals in spite of their pledge of secrecy, are, not surprisingly, tilted in favor of Crowley. Histories of the Golden Dawn exploring Yeats's role in it tend to be written by Yeatsian literary historians and are sympathetic to Yeats's perspective. R. A. Gilbert's account of Waite's involvement in the Golden Dawn and in his own successor to it retains historical balance: R. A. Gilbert, *A. E. Waite: Magician of Many Parts* (1987). Among the most useful accounts of the broader field of magical societies in England that included the Golden Dawn are King 1973 and Howe 1972.

3. For a brief account of Old's life, see Lewis 1994, 401. Lewis notes that unlike some other Theosophical astrologers, "Sepharial was interested in astrology as a practical science rather than as some esoteric art produced by marrying it to theosophy" (401).

4. Science studies scholars would say that alchemy and radiation functioned as "boundary objects" that facilitated the interaction between occultists and scientists. Alchemy and radiation were both abstract and largely text-based, as they involved the interpretation of alchemical texts and the frequently secondhand accounts of radiation. See Appendix A.

5. The Golden Dawn spawned both subordinate societies within it—such as Florence Farr's Sphere Group for ritual meditation and astral vision—and a number of successor groups as it splintered around 1901. These included Dr. R. W. Felkin's Stella Matutina, Aleister Crowley's A.A., and the Ordo Templi Orientis (Order of the Temple of the East, over whose British initiates Crowley assumed control in 1912 [Carter 1999, 40–42]).

6. According to Gilbert, Mme. and Mr. Horos "had tricked Mathers out of parting with G. D. rituals and had set up in London a spurious temple of their own that was a cover for sexual debauchery.... and in September 1901, Mr. Horos was charged with rape, found guilty—after a trial at which the Golden Dawn was held up to ridicule—and gaoled for fifteen years; his wife was sentenced to seven years imprisonment for aiding and abetting him" (Gilbert 113).

7. A typical example of Atwood's vague efforts to appropriate modern science to support a Hermetic world view can be found in the following tortured prose:

> Yet, notwithstanding so much scepticism and the slur which ignorance has cast now for centuries upon every early creed and philosophy, modern discoveries tend evermore to reprove the same; identifying light, as the common vital sustenant, to be in motive accord throughout the human circulatory system with the planetary spheres and harmonious dispositions of the occult medium in space; and as human physiology advances with the other sciences in unison, the notion of our natural correspondency enlarges, proving things more and more minutely congruous, until at length, the conscious relationship would seem to be almost only wanting to confirm the ancient tradition and lead into its full faith. (163)

8. As Waite put it in his opening leader, "In the Beginning," *Unknown World* 1 (August 15, 1894): 1–7, "The departments of Occult Science and history particularly embraced by the present editorial scheme are:—White and Black Magic, Necromancy, Divination, Astrology, Alchemy, Witchcraft, Crystallomancy, Elementals and Elementaries, the Rosicrucians, the Illuminati, Esoteric Freemasonry, the Mysteries, the Mystics, Hermetic Philosophy, the Archaeology of the Secret Sciences" (1894, 2). *Unknown World* included work by Theosophists and Golden Dawn members alike. It exhibited a particular fondness for various schools of mysticism, including several articles and reviews on what Philip Jenkins has termed the "sexual mysticism" of Thomas Lake Harris's Brotherhood of the New Life (Jenkins 2000, 39).

9. References abound to both Thorpe and *Watts Dictionary* in Soddy's course notebooks, for example, in his notes for his year of general chemistry studies at University College of Wales, Aberystwyth (Soddy 1894).

10. Ayton's correspondence mentions Thomas W. Wilson (a founding member of the Horus Temple of the Golden Dawn at Bradford, and a chemist in York), and often involves discussions of homeopathic cures. Howe notes that "during the 1890s the membership of the Golden Dawn included at least half a dozen qualified physicians who were homeopaths" (Howe in Ayton 1985, 35).

11. Colquhoun writes that Mathers prevented lower level adepts from studying the more powerful secrets of alchemy (273).

12. King notes: "In the original Golden Dawn there had been a small group that had practiced alchemy under the guidance of the Rev. W. A. Ayton, but this type of work seems to have fallen into abeyance shortly after 1900" (135). He explains that the Hermanubis Temple in Bristol in the 1940s "was also responsible for a revival of the study of the western alchemical tradition" and worked using only the grades of the original Golden Dawn (134).

13. Working with University College London, I have not been able to determine whether either Jones or Baker studied with Ramsay or took degrees there.

14. As Francis King puts it, "the magical teachings and practices used in the A.A. during its early period were those of the Golden Dawn...with a certain amount of Yoga and other oriental practices grafted on to them" (91).

15. Turning to contemporary atomic theory, the narrator argues that there are

> beings whose senses are on a different range to ours.... We also have reason to believe that this total range is almost inconceivably great. It is not merely a question of the worlds of the microscope and the telescope; these are mere extensions of our gamut. But we now think that a molecule of matter is a universe in most rapid whirl, a cosmos comparable to that of the heavens, its electrons as widely separated from each other, in proportion to their size, as the stars in space. Our universe, then, in its unmeasured vastness, is precisely similar in constitution to one molecule of hydrogen; and we may suppose that it is itself only a molecule of some larger body; also that what we call an electron may itself be a universe—and so on forever. This suggestion is supported by the singular fact, that the proportion in size of electron to molecule is about the same as that of sun to cosmos, the ratio in each being as 1 to 10,000,000,000,000,000,000,000. (Crowley 1929, 217)

While arguing what is essentially the understanding of Heisenberg or virtually any other contemporary atomic physicist or chemist, the narrator rhetorically dresses up atomic science in occult guises for occult ends: "Electrons are quite as elusive as ghosts; we are only aware of them as the conclusion to a colossal sorites. The evidence for ghosts is as strong as that for any other phenomenon in nature" (217).

16. In her 1975 study of Mathers and the Golden Dawn, she notes that there are many twentieth-century practicing alchemists in France and elsewhere (Colquhoun 269).

17. On the covers of the *Journal,* Lewis advertised works "Covering the widest range of subjects, including Anthropology, Chemistry (Technical, Theoretical and Applied), Electricity, Engineering, Geography, Geology, Microscopy, Mining, Physics, Physiology, Travels, Zoology, etc.," with subscriptions from one guinea per year.

18. In May 1914, for financial reasons, it transferred its meetings to M. de Kerlor's lecture room in the Occult Club at 1 Piccadilly Place, W. (Abdul-Ali 1914, 109).

19. In the 1914 "Report of Honorary Secretary," Abdul-Ali boasted that the journal was circulating in China, India, Australia, and America, as well as in Britain, but he exhorted members to increase membership by publicizing the Society (109). As the Society came under strain during the War, in his secretarial report to the Third Annual Meeting, Abdul-Ali noted that membership was holding steady, but that attendance at meetings had declined (87). In that same meeting, Thomas Marson went as far as to offer a resolution "That every endeavour be made to increase the membership of the Society, and that present members be requested to undertake as far as possible to introduce new members, and make known the aims of the Society" (Abdul-Ali 1915, 85).

20. These reviews were probably based upon materials supplied to them by someone in the Society, perhaps Redgrove, since some of the language in these reviews repeats language appearing elsewhere, such as in *Nature.*

21. The *Athenæum* occasionally included mild and balanced articles on subjects like Theosophy and occultism, and some of Sir Oliver Lodge's more extreme notions. It even reviewed in its "Science" column Alchemy Society member J. W. Frings's *The Occult Arts,* which, it noted, "examines their status from the point of view of modern science" (Anon. 1913, 320).

22. The reviewer quoted Rutherford's assertion that "there is so far no good evidence that the ordinary inactive chemical elements can be transformed by the radiations from active matter" (Anon. 1912, 732).

23. The anonymous *Nature* review of Redgrove's 1911 book, *Alchemy, Ancient and Modern,* was negative and dismissive, even patronizing at times, suggesting that Redgrove should stick to chemistry. Summarizing Redgrove's book, the reviewer notes:

> The author of this book thinks he perceives in the trend of modern chemical doctrine an approximation of the fundamental dogmas of philosophical alchemy, as these were understood and taught by its greatest exponents. The application of the principles of evolution to the genesis of chemical elements has, in his opinion, brought us back to the "basic idea" permeating all alchemistic theory, and that, in his judgment, the time is gone when it may be regarded as legitimate to point to alchemy as an instance of the aberrations of the human mind. (Anon. 1911, 375)

However, the reviewer viewed most alchemy as sure fraud, and argued that "theories in chemistry stand or fall by facts. The ancient alchemists certainly never proved their theories. Have the modern alchemists done any better?" (375), and went on to note that "There is really no evidence that modern science is permeated by the spirit of alchemy, and, therefore, strictly speaking, there is no meaning in the phrase 'modern alchemy'" (375). Yet, as we shall see in later chapters, numerous scientists and science writers had already employed such language and would do so with increasing regularity over the next few decades. Moreover, the next review during the Alchemical Society years of a Redgrove book in *Nature* was more respectful and less defensive. The reviewer, φ, praised Redgrove's "emphasis on the validity of the laws of nature" and lined up his exploration of the subjectivity of experience with both eighteenth- and nineteenth-century thinkers like Berkeley and Mill, as well with "the mysticism of John Smith the 'Cambridge Platonist,' Boehme, and Swedenborg" (φ 1915, 4).

24. Good sources of summary information about Redgrove's career are: *Literary Yearbook, 1922*, 1079; and *Who Was Who Among English and European Authors, 1931–1949* (1978), vol. 3 N–Z, 1178.

25. In fact, Mellor's *Modern Inorganic Chemistry* (Mellor 1912) and Redgrove's *Experimental Mensuration* (Redgrove 1913c) were reviewed in the same column, "Notices of Books," *Chemical News* 107 (February 28, 1913): 106–108.

26. Moore grapples with the vortex theory of atoms elaborated by Helmholtz and Kelvin, and the more recent electronic theory of atoms propounded by J. J. Thomson (Moore 1912, 72). But he pushed the new physics in distinctly occult directions that those physicists would have rejected: "Science is beginning to regard matter as a form of energy and our observations of the human mind, thought impulses, show evidence in favour of energy being a form of mind. Thus it would appear that matter originated indirectly from mind" (75).

27. As Redgrove put it in the "Preface" to the 1911 edition of *Alchemy: Ancient and Modern:*

> All metals (and, indeed, all forms of matter) are one in origin, and are produced by an evolutionary process. The Soul of them all is one and the same; it is only the Soul that is permanent; the body or outward form, *i.e.*, the mode of manifestation of the Soul, is transitory, and one form may be transmuted into another.... The old alchemists reached the above conclusion by a theoretical method, and attempted to demonstrate the validity of their theory by means of experiment; in which, it appears, they failed. Modern science, adopting the reverse process, for a time lost hold of the idea of the unity of the physical universe, to gain it once again by the experimental method. It was in the elaboration of this grand fundamental idea that Alchemy failed. If I were asked to contrast Alchemy with the chemical and physical science of the nineteenth century I would say that, whereas the latter abounded in a wealth of much accurate detail and much relative truth, it lacked philosophical depth and insight; whilst Alchemy, deficient in such accurate detail, was characterised by a greater philosophical depth and insight; for the alchemists did grasp the fundamental truth of the Cosmos, although they distorted it and made it appear grotesque... hence their views cannot be accepted in these days of modern science. But if we cannot approve of their theories *in toto*, we can nevertheless appreciate the fundamental ideas at the root of them. And it is primarily with the object of pointing

out this similarity between these ancient ideas regarding the physical universe and the latest products of scientific thought, that this book has been written. (xii–xiii)

Redgrove further honed this thesis in his 1920 volume, *Magic and Mysticism*.

28. De Steiger's talk about the Atwood thesis and the idea of alchemical writing as a secret code led to a significant debate over the purpose of the Alchemical Society. In the discussions following De Steiger's talk, D. N. Dunlop, the editor of *The Path*, suggested that the talk "had made plain an opportunity for the Society to undertake a great work for humanity, namely the practical work of Alchemy, mystically understood." Waite argued that ancient alchemists "were concerned with the same work as the mystics within the Church living the life of contemplation; but they had carried the experiment a stage further, and embodied the results of their experiences in symbolic texts. It was, he considered, the chief aim of the Society firstly to decode these texts, and thus gain the secret knowledge, which could then be practically applied." Redgrove

> agreed with Mr. Waite that the chief work of the Society must consist in decoding the alchemical text. It was the business of the Society to get at the root of the matter and produce a complete explanation of the origin and significance of Alchemy. Mr. Dunlop's suggestions were also of much interest, but such practical work was the business of individuals, rather than of a Society as a whole; though were it possible to reveal it, the Society would be profited by an account of any such experiment. (*Journal of the Alchemical Society* 1913c, 31–32)

29. For instance, Waite corrected Redgrove's argument that the alchemical mystical perspective derived from their contemporaries' theology. He countered that in the twelfth through the fourteenth centuries, theology was "scholastic and not mystical" (1913, 21). So Flamel, Lully, and others were not deriving their mysticism from "current theology, mystical or otherwise: they belonged to another school" (21). He also noted that purely mystical alchemy was a latecomer, in the sixteenth century, so the metallurgic interpretation predated the purely mystical one (29).

30. Severn nods to one of Atwood's premises, noting that "we have reason to believe that the Chemical symbolism used was for the purpose of veiling something of a spiritual nature, and this position is the one held in the book entitled *A Suggestive Enquiry*, written some sixty-five years ago" (Severn 1914, 111). But she adapts Atwood's thesis to a psychoanalytic paradigm and a psychological emphasis:

> Just what it is that was hidden is not so clear, but under the great law of analogies, the transmutation of the baser metals into nobler ones clearly may indicate a process of spiritual growth through which each soul some time passes.... The changes are in ourselves; and the evolution of a human soul from a state of self-*un*consciousness to a Supreme Realization is the greatest expression we know of that law of growth which we observe in the material world, where the single cell finally evolves into a highly complex and intelligent being. (111)

31. Abdul-Ali summarizes the correspondences of alchemical thinking to modern science thus:

> Let us summarize the conceptions which may now be formed concerning the constitution of the physical universe. There is first energy, which, since it is conserved, should be considered a fundamental physical entity. Indeed, we may go so far as to say that it is the only fundamental physical entity of which we know, since it is the only thing of whose conservation we have good assurance. It may therefore be called "substance," *the* substance of the physical universe, that which underlies all natural phenomena. It is more fundamental than the ether, for the ether is the medium in which it operates. It is more fundamental than matter, which is said to be measured by "mass"; for "mass" is the derived factor in kinetic energy, just as "self-inductance" is the derived factor in the energy of electricity in motion. Moreover, according to the electrical theory of matter, the "mass" or "inertia" of the atom is a function of the number and velocity of electrically charged particles constituting it.
>
> Secondly, there is ether, the sole vehicle in space for the transmission of energy, and the medium which, so to speak, unites energy with matter. Thirdly, there are the ultimate atoms which, prior to their condensation into matter, we have called "the protyles," and which within the elementary atom become electrons and positive electricity.
>
> It seems to me that these three concepts bear considerable resemblance to the three alchemical concepts defined earlier in this paper, and called respectively "The Soul of the World," "The Spirit of the World," and "The First Matter." "The Soul of the World" is the ubiquitous, immanent and creative essence in things. Evidently the phrase describes something very much like energy in the sense I have suggested. The principal difference is that to us the term "energy" denotes a concept which has a definite mathematical expression, although, of course, we do not know the nature of energy considered as "substance"; while to the alchemists such names as "The Soul of the World" had a quite general and undefined meaning. Then "The Spirit of the World" or "Fifth Essence," considered as the medium by which the Soul held intercourse with its Body (*i.e.*, matter) is analogous to the ether, the medium of energy transmission, as already explained. The connection between "First Matter" and the protyles is obvious. It remains for me to deal with the concept of the Four Elements. These are often thought to denote the hot, cold, moist and dry principles or qualities of bodies; but we may also suppose that the "elements," earth, water, air, and fire, represent respectively the solid, liquid, gaseous, and what may be called incandescent-gaseous states of matter, although this is by no means a satisfactory or complete interpretation. It must be confessed that the subject of the elements is a difficult one, and I have not yet found explanations for it in the language of modern science. (1913, 43–44)

32. Rowbottom was an advocate of scientific precision. Judging by his knowledge of scientific journals, he may have had some scientific training. He was an auditor of the Society and gave a paper on the alchemist Roger Bacon at the March 1914 meeting. In it, he quoted Ernst von Meyer's claim in the 1906 English translation, *A History of Chemistry*, that Bacon "is to be regarded as the intellectual originator of experimental research, if the departure in this direction is to be coupled with any one name" (Rowbottom 1914a, 76).

CHAPTER 2

1. Historians of science and science studies theorists have in the past few decades begun to examine the relationships among instrumentation, experimentation, and conceptual models, and have provided increasingly nuanced accounts of the role of instrumentation in the emergence of and shifts in scientific theory (e.g., Franklin 1986, Galison 1997, Latour 1987, Le Grand 1990, and Lenoir 1986).

2. In the United States, two publishers have recently brought the 1951 third edition of *Occult Chemistry* back into print: Kessinger Publishing in March 1997 and the Theosophical Publishing House in November 2000. In the U.K., Paperbackshop's Echo Library just brought out an edition of it in January 2005.

3. There are numerous histories of the Theosophical Society. Ryan 1975 is an affirmative history of the Society and hagiography of Blavatsky published by the Theosophical University Press, whereas Washington 1995 is more skeptical and detailed. Johnson 1994 is one of the few studies to walk a middle path, arguing that Blavatsky's "Masters," while not necessarily endowed with superhuman powers, did indeed exist, and the book provides historical details of the Europeans, the Egyptian and Indian religious and political reformers, and the British government agents in India who served as Blavatsky's masters.

4. As Peter Washington puts it:

> Olcott compared Blavatsky with Darwin, and [*Isis Unveiled*] is a deliberate challenge to that master, whose evolutionary theory she trumps by asserting that the evolution of monkeys into men is merely one stage in a long chain which allows men to evolve into higher beings. Blavatsky thereby transforms evolution from a limited socio-biological theory into an explanation of everything from atoms to angels. Instead of opposing religion with the facts as presented by Victorian science, she attempts to subsume those facts into a grand synthesis that makes religious wisdom not the enemy of scientific knowledge but its final goal. (52)

5. For example, she quotes Crookes's assertions of vitalism at the chemical level as an antidote to the heat-death of the universe that seemed to be entailed by the Second Law of Thermodynamics (1888, 1:603), or second-hand accounts of his lectures on the protyle, with assertions of its similarity to thinking in the Bhagavad Gita (1:681).

6. Oliver Lodge had argued that the ether could indeed be perceived by the human eye, "truly an ethereal sense-organ" (Lodge 1909, 114). But Theosophists might argue that what untrained humans are perceiving with their physical eyes is not the ether itself, but rather the effects of its vibrations and oscillations.

7. Using almost verbatim the description of the powers of the astral microscope in his manual, *The Astral Plane,* Leadbeater went on to argue that

> The hypothetical molecule and atom postulated by science are visible realities to the occult student, though the latter recognizes them as much more complex in their nature than the scientific man has yet discovered them to be.... and a scientific investigator who should acquire this astral sight in perfection, would not only find his experiments with ordinary and known phenomena immensely facilitated, but would also see stretching before him entirely new vistas of knowledge needing more than a lifetime for their thorough examination. (1918, 23)

8. More ponderously, adapting scientific conventions, they created Greek names for each: "Three states of matter exist between the atomic state and the gaseous.... For the sake of clearness and brevity in description, we have been obliged to name these states; we call the atomic state of the chemist *elemental;* the state which results from breaking up chemical elements, *proto-elemental;* the next higher, *meta-proto-elemental;* the next higher, *hyper-meta-proto-elemental;* then comes the atomic state. These are briefly marked as El., Proto., Meta., and Hyper" (1908, 8).

9. For thoughtful accounts of the history of ether physics, see Schaffner 1972 and Clarke 2001. Larmor 1900 and Lodge 1909 provide two classic treatises on the history of ether and its significance. Though Lodge's appeared four years after Einstein had shown that the ether hypothesis could be dispensed with entirely, it was not until the early 1920s that most physicists relinquished the concept. Kostro 2000 has even argued that Einstein, while abolishing the material ether of Victorian physics, introduced a relativistic ether in 1916 and in his later work.

10. As Bruce Clarke notes of "the luminiferous/electromagnetic medium of late-classical wave theory": "Instead of several ethers conveying particular forms of energy, now a single ether conveyed multiple energies" (Clarke 2001, 166).

11. Indeed, the failure of the Michelson-Morely experiments of the 1880s to detect the ether helped lead to the abandonment of the ether hypothesis in the twentieth century (see Clarke 2001, 167).

12. Kelvin argued, as Russell summarizes it, that

> a positive electron is an atom which, by attraction, condenses aether into the space occupied by its volume. Similarly, a negative electron rarefies, by repulsion, the aether remaining in the space occupied by its volume. The stress produced in the aether outside two such atoms by the attractions and repulsions which they exert on the aether within them would cause apparent attraction between a positive and a negative electron and apparent repulsion between two electrons, both positive or both negative. (Russell 1912, 62–63)

13. This address recapitulated material Crookes had presented in 1886 in a talk to the Chemical Section of the British Association for the Advancement of Science, of which Crookes was president (see Keller 1983, 12–13).

14. As Blavatksy defined it in her *Theosophical Glossary*, Fohat represents "the active (male) potency of the Sakti (female reproductive power) in nature. The essence of cosmic electricity. An occult Tibetan term for *Daiviprakriti*, primordial light: and in the universe of manifestation the ever-present electrical energy and ceaseless destructive and formative power. Esoterically, it is the same, Fohat being the universal propelling Vital Force, at once the propeller and the resultant" (1892, 121).

15. In his *Textbook of Theosophy*, Leadbeater explains that

> Each of these worlds has its inhabitants, whose senses are normally capable of responding to the undulations of their own world only. A man living (as we are all doing) in the physical world sees, hears, feels, by vibrations connected with the physical matter around him. He is equally surrounded by the astral and mental and other worlds which are interpenetrating his own denser world, but of them he is normally unconscious, because his sense cannot respond to the oscillations of their matter, just as our physical eyes cannot see by the vibrations of ultra-violet light, although scientific experiments show that they exist, and there are other consciousnesses with differently-formed organs who *can* see by them. A being living in the astral world might be occupying the very same space as a being living in the physical world, yet each would be entirely unconscious of the other and would in no way impede the free movement of the other. The same is true of all other worlds. (1912, 25–26)

16. Jinarajadasa explains that "one who has trained himself 'can make himself infinitesimally small at will.' This does not mean that he undergoes a diminution in bodily size, but only that, *relatively*, his conception of himself can be so minimized that objects which normally are small appear to him as large. The two investigators had been trained by their Eastern Gurus or Teachers to exercise this unique faculty of Yoga, so that when they observed a chemical atom it appeared to their vision as highly magnified" (Besant and Leadbeater 1951, 1).

17. While Leadbeater often participated in separating out the constituent chemical elements of compounds, it was Besant who routinely did "the work of breaking up each element through the various subplanes, resolving them finally into separate Anu" (1951, 381).

18. S. R. noted that "The nature of the ultimate product will be interesting from the point of view of alchemy. Professor Rutherford says it may be similar to lead" (1906, 560).

19. For instance, Besant commented on Sir William Ramsay's November 26, 1903 lecture to the London Institution on the properties of radium, where he argued that "it seemed that the dreams of the alchemists were not such folly as the wiseacres had thought, even though their methods did amount, as someone has said, to little more than 'a sort of cookery.' It might happen that in time the changing of tin

into gold would be no more difficult than the manufacture in the laboratory of an indigo which has practically displaced the natural product" (quoted in [Besant] 1904, 488). Besant also highlighted, for instance, Professor Darwin's claim to the British Association at Cape Town that "Although even the dissociative stage of the alchemistic problem still lay beyond the power of the chemist, yet, modern researches seemed to furnish a sufficiently clear idea of the structure of atoms to enable them to see what would have to be done to effect a transformation of the elements" ([Besant] 1905, 2).

20. For instance, Phillips knows, as Besant and Leadbeater did not in 1895 when they began their experiments (though they never addressed quantum mechanics, even in the 1930s when it was well established), that the intervention of an observer would affect the quantum state of the particles observed. So Phillips argues that what Besant and Leadbeater were seeing, as they exerted their psychokinetic powers upon sub-atomic particles to slow them down and steady them, were not in fact atoms, but instead "an object-observer interaction" (the micro-psi atom), which is "a multi-omegon bound system formed from *two* nuclei of the element as a result of the ground state of the superconducting Higgs vacuum being perturbed over an atomic-sized region of space by the act of micro-psi observation" (1980, 101). Omegons were subquark particles that Phillips had theorized in his non-occult physics experiments. He makes the eighteen UPAs that Besant and Leadbeater saw as making up the hydrogen nucleus (which physicists saw as being made up of a single proton) correlate with his subquark theory by suggesting that the three quarks of a proton are each made up of three omegons, hence nine particles. Besant and Leadbeater, he says, were looking at two hydrogen nuclei together—hence eighteen omegons (or UPAs).

21. Phillips notes in the preface to *ESP of Quarks and Superstrings* (1999) that

> In 1984 (the *annus mirabilis* of superstring theory, which conceives of subatomic particles as like bits of string) I realized for reasons too technical to discuss here that, if superstrings exist, they could not be omegons. On account of this—as well as to forestall false criticism that the case for ESP of subatomic particles presented in my earlier book rests upon the validity of an as yet untested theory of particle physics—I have used neither my omegon model nor any other published subquark model as the theoretical framework for my analysis. Similarly, (and also to avoid technical discussion comprehendible only to particle physicists), I have intentionally avoided making in terms of superstring theory *specific, model-dependent* interpretations of Leadbeater's clairvoyant description of subquarks. I am content to point out its remarkable similarity to the superstring picture. (x)

CHAPTER 3

1. Crookes's spectroscopic researches led to his discovery of thallium and to his elaborating the theory of the protyle, from which all other elements evolved (discussed

in Chapter 2). These, his explorations of radiant matter, and his invention of the spinthariscope—a device for registering radioactive emissions—were of some significance to the early study of radioactivity. But Crookes was of less importance to nascent theories of radioactivity than Ramsay and Soddy were, so I shall focus here on Ramsay and Soddy and the chemists whose transmutational research programs they inspired.

2. It is possible that the differences between German and English education in chemistry in the nineteenth century—indeed the very source of the weakness of English science education in comparison to that in Germany, and the cause of Soddy's condemnation of his chemistry education at Merton College, Oxford—may have given English chemistry educators more rein to explore the heuristic value of alchemy. As Merricks explains, Germany emphasized laboratory training and rigorous education in scientific technology. In England,

> practical, experimental science was seen to be the province of the gentleman amateur, making his own discoveries and providing spectacular effects to amuse his visitors. As an increasing emphasis on practical, experimental skills grew, laboratory-based research institutions developed within universities. However, the source of funding—private individuals and not the state—points to a continuing tension between the aristocratic ideal of the amateur scientist and the newer notion of the scientist as a professional. This tension was especially marked at the Clarendon, where the amateur ideal lingered into the twentieth century with disastrous effects on teaching and the building of research departments. (1996, 19)

3. In two papers in 1815 and 1816, Prout argued that, because the known atomic weights of the elements seemed to be integer multiples of the weight of hydrogen, the other elements must be arrangements of hydrogen elements. This thesis remained actively debated during the 1820s until careful measurements of atomic weights of elements in the early 1830s disproved it (see Brock 82–108).

4. As Gordin puts it, "Interpreting the situation in fin-de-siecle physical sciences as chemistry under attack by superstition and sloppy reasoning, and exasperated by people letting their irrational preferences dissuade them from proper scientific method, Mendeleev undertook a chemical interpretation of the ether that would harness the inert gases to stave off the twin dangers of radioactivity and Prout" (Gordin 2004, 217).

5. The wording of translations of "The Emerald Tablet" from various Latin and Arabic sources varies widely, but Ramsay was clearly using the text Randolph used in his volume. Randolph attributes his translation to John Everard, but its wording differs significantly from Everard's 1640 translation of "The Emerald Tablet"—and occult publisher George Redway's 1884 edition of Everard's translation of *The Divine Pymander of Hermes Mercurius Trismegistus* does not include a translation of "The Emerald Tablet" other than that in the preliminary essay by Hargrave Jennings, which also differs significantly in wording (Hermes Trismegistus 1884).

6. In his typescript lecture notes for "Lectures on the History of Chemistry from earliest times," which he gave at McGill from 1899–1900, Soddy observes in his introductory lecture that Kopp's *Geschichte der Chemie* is "a standard work on Alchemy," but that von Meyer's *A History of Chemistry from Earliest Times to the Present Day*, trans. McGowan 1888, is "very complete but a little uninteresting" (Soddy [1899–1900]). He heaps praise on Schorlemmer's *Rise and Development of Organic Chemistry*, calling it "one of the most fascinating books on the subject" (1). By the next year's McGill lectures, "Alchemy and Chemistry" (1900a), Soddy had come to rely primarily on Berthelot, rather than Kopp or von Meyer, as his authoritative source on alchemical history.

7. Early twenty-first-century historians of alchemy and chemistry now have demonstrated how much alchemical ideas were involved in the early modern experimental science of the seventeenth century, including that of Boyle himself, as well as Newton and George Starkey. Starkey was an experimental chemist who was the author of the important alchemical text *The Marrow of Alchemy* (1654–55), published under the name Eirenaeus Philoponus Philalethes, and held to be of great alchemical importance by Waite and Golden Dawn alchemists. See Newman and Principe 2004, and Principe 1998.

8. Soddy 1896.

9. Soddy 1897–1898.

10. While Bolton's lecture gave examples of modern alchemical charlatans and seemed less than serious about some of the French Hermetic groups he discussed, the *New York Times* coverage of the speech focused primarily on the positive issue of modern science's relationship to alchemy. Its headline "The Revival of Alchemy" was followed by the subheadlines "Dr. H. Carrington Bolton Lectures on the Modern Aspect of Chemistry's Forerunner" and "Many Still Believe in It" (*New York Times* 1897, 6).

Even as early as January 1884, Dewar's course of six public lectures at the Royal Institution not only introduced the concerns and history of alchemy in great detail, but also concluded that modern chemistry is concerned with the alchemical question of the nature of elements.

> He had now, he said, reached the epoch of the modern alchemists. The old visions of sudden riches and fadeless years to be found in torturing nature into yielding up her secrets had vanished never to return, but the great question on which the light of modern science was being poured at this hour was whether those bodies passing as elements, including the metals old and new, might not after all, at least some if not every one, turn out to be compounds. Such a result which many deemed quite likely, would strangely resemble a recurrence of the dreams of the infancy of chemistry in this ripe age. (*Times* 1884, 3c)

Indeed, this last supposition would become increasingly significant to chemistry, but Dewar was premature in pronouncing the end of alchemical goals of transmutation of metals and the prolongation of life through an *elixir vitae*.

11. Much of Howorth's (occasionally intemperate) biography of Soddy was dedicated to fighting the war against the hegemony of physics on Soddy's behalf. Soddy felt, with some justice, that his role in the Soddy-Rutherford collaboration was being left out of histories of the field by the 1950s. Howorth documents Soddy's complaints in great detail, noting that "Soddy once exclaimed: 'One often hears that physics and chemistry are now one subject. God forbid! But even if it were so, it does not give physicists any right to steal the work of chemists, or for that matter the Fullerian Professorship in Chemistry at the Royal Institution, which has happened more than once'" (1958, 75).

12. Soddy lost out to John Russell, who won the Evans Prize (Howorth 36).

13. See Traweek's concept of the borderland and the strategic issues facing those working in laboratories away from the centers of scientific authority (Traweek 1992; also, see Appendix A). Howorth, rather than emphasizing Soddy and Rutherford's position on the margins of the British scientific establishment, prefers to read the collaboration as the fruits of empire: "It seems to have been curiously hidden or ignored, that this realization, of such immense importance to the future of the world, was a peculiar triumph of the wide-flung Dominions of the British Empire—Canada, New Zealand, and Australia, at the antipodes of the earth! While Rutherford and Soddy began their pioneering work in Montreal, W. H. Bragg, in Adelaide, added his quota with his meticulous work on the ranges of the alpha rays" (54).

14. I am assuming that Travers is correct that the manuscript dates to the earlier period and is not simply a first draft of what became the 1904 *Introduction*.

15. In the obituary in *Nature*, A. M. Worthington noted:

> It has been well remarked of Ramsay that he stood to the outside world for an essentially British school of chemistry. To describe him as original would be like saying water is wet. He was of the essence of originality, and, during the time the writer knew him, entirely without any apparent sheet-anchor of fixed conviction or established belief in scientific doctrine, which at all times, in a science somewhat prone to let go sheet-anchors, made him a unique and almost incomprehensible personality. It is true that in his later years he suffered from the defects of these qualities, and he failed to criticize sufficiently his own ideas and experimental results before making them public. (Worthington 1916)

16. As Kelvin put it in a 1903 letter to Ramsay, "The hypothesis of evolution in the atom or transformation in its substance, coupled with the supposition that the energy emitted by the radium is taken out of store in the atom, seems to me utterly improbable." And Travers notes that in June 1903, at a private dinner for Madame Curie and Kelvin, "Madame Curie did her best to convert her dinner partner to the disintegration theory, without success" (252).

Huggins had written to Ramsay on July 19, 1903: "What is the explanation of He in Ra? I am very loth to take the alchymistic view that there is true transmutation of Ra into He" (Huggins 1903a). The next day, Huggins wrote Ramsay again, advocating his own view that Radium must be a compound of helium and something else—not an element disintegrating—but the level of commitment of chemists to the new transmutation theory seems to have been great enough that Huggins would doubt that Ramsay would accept such a theory: "I am so glad to read that you consider the idea that the so-called element, radium, may possibly be a compound of He and X, not inadmissible. I had thrown out the idea, but with much hesitation, as I did not know how it would be regarded by chemists" (Huggins 1903b). For Soddy's argument with Kelvin at the British Association meeting of 1903, see Howorth 91.

17. As we shall see in the next chapter, Soddy attempted to strip away the false alchemist of the middle ages who either was a charlatan or was only concerned about pecuniary gain through transmutation, from the scientific alchemist, and later applied the "false alchemist" designation to those who would engage in science for material motives (as in making atomic weapons instead of advocating sharing atomic energy with all), or those who endorsed the monetary and economic policies he opposed.

18. Soddy was fond of this rhetorical flourish and frequently advanced his own figures about radium/coal equivalents. Weart notes that Crookes claimed in 1903: "the energy locked within one gram of radium, he calculated, could hoist the entire [British Navy] fleet several thousand feet into the air" (Weart 1988, 25).

19. As Ramsay put it in his 1912 popular volume, *Elements and Electrons:* "A distinction must be drawn between 'transmutation' and 'transformation'; the former may be understood to refer to a change accomplished by human agency; the latter, to a change over which no control may be exercised" (143).

20. As Ramsay had explained to the Society of Chemical Industry in September 1904,

> There is a general disposition now to explain the strange phenomena which characterize the behavior of radium—among them the evolution of a gas that slowly turns into helium—by assuming that some of the atoms of the first mentioned element disintegrate, and in so doing liberate stored energy. Sir William asked himself if it were not practicable to reverse the process and build up an element, by a proper combination of material and energy. The latter would be required in a concentrated form, but a supply could apparently be secured by the breaking down of a radio-active substance. (*New York Daily Tribune* 1904, n.p.)

And, later that month in an address at the International Congress of Arts and Science in St. Louis, he explained that

> It would appear that if energy can be poured into a definite chemical matter, such as glass, it undergoes some change, and gives rise to bodies capable of being tested, for I imagine that radio-active forms of matter are produced, either identical with or allied to those at present known. And just as radium and other radio-active elements suffer degradation spontaneously, evolving energy, so I venture to think that if energy be concentrated in the molecules

of ordinary forms of matter, a sort of polymerization is the result, and radioactive elements, probably elements with high atomic weight, and themselves unstable, are formed. (Ramsay 1905, 219)

21. Baskerville noted in an address to the New York Section of the American Chemical Society on October 11, 1907, that:

> Mr. R. M. Hunter, of Philadelphia, has written concerning "synthetic gold" as follows:
>
> I have so perfected the process that in my judgment, based upon my actual experience, gold may be manufactured at enormous profit, and to this end I have designed a plant to be erected in Philadelphia and am at this moment negotiating for the $500,000 capital for its erection. I realize that the public and most scientific men are adverse to belief in the possibility of such an enterprise, but I know what I am doing and can afford to allow public sentiment to follow its own course.
>
> ...On request, Mr. Hunter promptly forwarded me samples of silver in which the gold is "growing" and some "grown-up" gold, said to have been produced by his secret process. I have not made analyses of the samples, which are here exhibited. (Baskerville 1908, 48)

By sending legitimate chemists such as Ramsay and Baskerville samples to test, Hunter was following in the footsteps of Emmens, who in 1897 had sent samples and instructions for repeating his process to Sir William Crookes, who was unable to reproduce Emmens's results. In 1898, Emmens launched his Argentaurum Company, which advertised that for each ounce of silver submitted by investors it would return 3/5 of an ounce of gold. Emmens's efforts to start the company failed, though, when his patent application for the process was turned down (Nelson 2000, 58).

22. A. S. Russell noted that "'Transmutation' was associated with bogus chemistry at the start of the century—there were several public announcements (and in Glasgow a company was floated) that gold or mercury had been made by transmuting lead" (Howorth 90).

23. For general discussions of Ramsay's transmutation efforts, see Trenn 1974, 57–63; Travers 1956, 251–64; and Egerton 1927a and 1927b.

24. He noted that "It is only right to add that Madame Curie carried out a similar experiment, using a platinum vessel, instead of one of glass or silica, and obtained no lithium." But, he confidently adds, "It requires considerable practice ... to detect very small quantities of matter" (1912, 157).

25. The article mentions previous scientists' scoffing at the Philosopher's Stone and all the recent attempts to deceive scientists and businessmen with claims of transmutation to silver or gold, but then notes that "the odd thing is that after solemn men of weight in the world of learning have been for generations showing us what fools or knaves the alchemists were, modern science takes a sharp turn and shows that they were in their fundamental contention probably quite right" (*New York Times* 1911, SM12).

26. Collie borrowed Merton's apparatus and conducted many experiments with it, concluding that "the presence of neon and helium in vacuum tubes, after the electric discharge has been passed, is due to an air leak seems most improbable" (1914, 556).

27. The *New York Times* article, "Alchemists' Goal Reached by Briton," had as subheadings "Ramsay Made Like Claim / But British Chemist Died Without Making Full Reports of His Experiments." The headline seems to imply that Ramsay might have succeeded but died before he could divulge his methods—an assertion as inaccurate as the article's description of Ramsay as "the distinguished chemist of Cambridge University" (1919, 2).

28. For a good general summary and bibliography of the Miethe and Smits experiments and other experiments attempting to synthesize gold from mercury, see Nelson 91–94 and 103–110.

29. Egerton 1963, 128. Egerton was fond of Ramsay, and notes, in defense of Ramsay's "optimism" (by which he means his quickness to forge ahead with a premise that turned out to be incorrect),

> His optimism led him often to the desired goal. Any criticism laid against him on the score of his optimism must be laid aside, without it we should have had no Sir William and no helium! I remember three occasions on which new gases were announced to have been discovered (not published); once at a laboratory dinner when Coates had got what was thought to be coronium, once when an element was apparently changed by radium, and once when together we got a minute trace of residual gas from the bombardment of sulphur with cathode rays. The spectrum of the latter turned out to be an unusual mercury spectrum; what the others became I never learnt. There is no wonder that his enthusiasm was unbounded considering the chain of successful and epoch making discoveries that he had made. (129)

CHAPTER 4

1. Silvio Gesell was an important monetary reform figure in Germany, Switzerland, and Austria who also attracted some interest in the Anglophone countries. For an early and wide-ranging summary and critique of these positions, see Myers 1940, and for a more thorough exploration of the history and progeny of the Social Credit movement, see Finlay 1972.

2. Ironically, a version of this quandary had already been explored in alchemical debates about art versus nature in the late thirteenth century. As William R. Newman has explained, the alchemist Roger Bacon (1214–1294) had argued in the 1260s that alchemical gold could be created that would be more pure than the twenty-four carats of natural gold (Newman 2004, 88), but Thomas Aquinas (1225–1274) had raised concerns about whether alchemical gold was legal for purposes of minting (Newman 95). Following Aquinas's concerns, the Thomist Giles of Rome wondered in the late thirteenth century, "given that man can make gold, whether it is

permissible to sell such gold." As Newman explains, Giles "is unequivocally convinced that artificial gold cannot be made. At this point he reveals the true nature of his argument, saying that even if gold that would withstand the assayer's test of cupellation could be made, it would still not be legal tender, since it would not have all the medical properties of natural gold" (Newman 1989, 438).

3. Indeed, as Michael Gordin has helpfully reminded me, there is an important precedent for such a blurring of science fiction and occultism around alchemy: Mary Wollstonecraft Shelley's seminal science fiction gothic novel, *Frankenstein or, The Modern Prometheus* (1818). As a youth, Victor Frankenstein steeps himself in the oeuvre of the alchemists, reading Cornelius Agrippa, Paracelsus, Albertus Magnus, and others who had been rejected by the modern science of the late eighteenth century. Having not been formally schooled in modern science at that age, Victor writes, "My dreams were therefore undisturbed by reality; and I entered with the greatest diligence into the search of the philosopher's stone and the elixir of life. But the latter obtained my most undivided attention: wealth was an inferior object; but what glory would attend the discovery, if I could banish disease from the human frame, and render man invulnerable to any but a violent death!" (Shelley 1818, 34). Frankenstein soon enters a modern scientific education in chemistry, and it isn't long before Frankenstein uses the methods of modern science (adopting some vaguely alluded-to but largely undefined electrical process) in the service of his passion, derived from the alchemists, to defy death. He animates dead tissue, creating the monster.

Mary Shelley clearly derived her science-fiction vision from the scientific experiments of Luigi Galvani and others in the eighteenth century who applied electricity to animal muscles, for instance, to make a frog leg twitch. Some even attempted the reanimation of the dead by shocking corpses. But by the 1920s and 1930s, scientists had actually accomplished an alchemical feat. Artificial transmutation was a demonstrated reality after Rutherford's 1919 experiments. While Shelley's novel certainly predates their efforts by a century, the modern alchemy science fiction authors could draw in some detail upon confirmed science and on technologies that already existed. The scientific plausibility and realistic detail of these stories must have augmented the anxieties a Depression-era nation faced concerning the nature of money.

4. Even more banks had collapsed in the panic of 1893 (Davies 2002, 502).

5. The *New York Times*, for example, carried several such stories in the immediate pre-War period. One such article in 1910, "Chemist C. B. White Replies to Gleason," detailed how White had helped uncover "chicanery" at the "Alchemy Test" in Scranton, Pennsylvania, when Gleason had claimed to make silver from base metals (*New York Times* 1910a, 12). The article sparked a letter to the editor, under the title "Modern Alchemy," detailing other such claims (*New York Times* 1910b, 6). In January 1913, "Alchemic Gold Company" reported that "there exists a company for making gold by alchemy" in London, and the company, the Alchemy Gold Company, Ltd, had charged two men with stealing "alchemic gold" from it (*New York Times* 1913, 1).

6. Miethe and a friend, Johannes Gaedicke, had invented magnesium flash powder in 1887, and Miethe was involved in research in color photography and film.

7. See Weart on the figure of the "dangerous scientist," who is capable of literally destroying the world with atomic science, though Weart does not focus on the dangers such a scientist poses to the economy (1988, 21–24).

8. Wells's *The World Set Free* may have had an effect not just on the scientists of the Manhattan Project decades later, but also on Soddy himself. Wells's portrayal of the material transmutation leading to a moral re-evaluation of social and cultural certitudes (beginning with the gold standard) may well have helped nudge Soddy into monetary theory in the post-World War I period. Exploring Soddy's involvement in economics, Linda Merricks traces the influence of Ruskin and of contemporary monetary theorists on Soddy's thinking. She notes that "What is missing is any sign of a particular moment or event which led to this new specific direction for his interests" (Merricks 1996, 112).

9. See Berthelot 1855, 1. In the manuscript of Soddy's lecture "Alchemy and Chemistry," Soddy argues:

> Chemists however have come to regard alchemy as the product of an ignorant and superstitious age, and have failed to acknowledge any connection between the mental attitude which gave rise to it and that which has produced modern science. The historians of chemistry in the last century indeed—Thomas Thomsen at the commencement, Wurtz in the middle, and Berthelot towards the close—have almost severed the connection between alchemy and chemistry. Instead of regarding the former as the normal and logical beginning of the latter, Thomsen looked upon it rather as a curious and harmful aberration of the human intellect during the dark ages. Wurtz has said that chemistry was founded by Lavoisier after having been for ages a mere collection of obscure receipts. Berthelot expresses the same idea in the words "Chemistry was born yesterday." (Soddy 1900a, 2)

Richard Sclove argues, plausibly, that this talk was written *before,* not after, Soddy and Rutherford discovered atomic transmutation (1989, 168).

10. Merricks explores the reasons behind this dearth of material (9).

11. Blavatsky argues that the Atlantean sages were ancestors of modern sages, "a handful of thoughtful and solitary students, who pass their lives in obscurity, far from the rumors of the world, studying the great problems of the physical and spiritual universes. They have their secret records in which are preserved the fruits of the scholastic labors of the long line of recluses whose successors they are" (1877, 1:557).

12. H. Carrington Bolton explained in "The Revival of Alchemy" that French Hermetic societies designed "to resuscitate alchemical doctrines and practices," such as the Ordre de la Rose-Croix and L'Ordre Martiniste, "claim that their secret mysteries were bequeathed by the last sages of Atlantis and by the Lemures to their brethren in Asia and Egypt, dwellers in sanctuaries whence issued Krishna, Zoroaster, Hermes, Moses, Pythagoras and Plato" and that this knowledge was passed on by "secret alchemical societies" through the ages (1897, 856).

13. Ellis explains that "In 'Atlantean fantasy,' the writer begins with some sort of demonstrable actuality—such as the Mid-Atlantic Ridge or the ruins of the Minoan

palace at Knossos—and then speculates, often wildly, about how this particular subject might be related to Atlantis" (1998, 5).

14. This passage was repeated with little alteration in the 1912 and 1920 editions of *The Interpretation of Radium*, the change being to change the nature of the catastrophe from "a single mistake" to "some unknown reason." Sclove notes that Soddy's belief in an earlier atomic age wavered in later years (175).

15. Weart notes that Rutherford, too, had suggested that "some fool in a laboratory might blow up the universe unawares," and that, even after Rutherford had realized that this was impossible, other writers had picked up on the possibility and created anxiety about such a scenario (Weart 18–20).

16. The notion of radium-filled caverns creating precious jewels and metals by transmutation seems to have been a fixture in science fiction stories of the period. The 1929 novella *The Radium Pool*, first published in *Science Wonder Stories* by Ed Earl Repp, also features a radium pool that transmutes a cave into precious metals and jewels, acts as a fountain of youth, and provides telepathic and death ray abilities to Jovians who have come to appropriate its radium for Jupiter, the most powerful planet in the universe.

17. Indeed, Schachner derived some of the science of his story directly from Soddy, citing Soddy's *The Interpretation of the Atom* from 1932 (Schachner 1933, pt. 1, 821).

18. One of the strangest of these stories is Paul Ernst's (1899–1985) 1934 tale, "The Stolen Element." As a scientist in the story puts it, "The old alchemists bent over stews containing bats' wings, powdered horn of unicorn, lead, and gold, and attempted to change the base metal into gold. Magic, it was thought to be. But if that is magic, the modern scientist is a magician. For with this process base metal *can* be changed into gold" (108). But the scientist's real goal is not the production of gold but of a synthetic element with an atomic number of 93, one that will be unbelievably hard and useful to industrial processes. His lab assistant, however, is corrupted by the old alchemical dream, and after murdering the scientist and working out an elaborate scheme for self-enrichment by synthesizing gold, he receives his just reward in an accident: his arm turns to pure gold. He is left painfully dragging himself toward the knife he has just used to kill another assistant.

EPILOGUE

1. For an exploration of Sitwell's efforts to use alchemical tropes to reinvest atomic science with an ethical sensibility after Hiroshima, see Morrisson 2002.

2. Spencer Weart's *Nuclear Fear* (1988) explores the images that dominated Western anxieties about radiation and atomic warfare in great detail. In *War Stars: The Superweapon and the American Imagination*, H. Bruce Franklin seeks to explain the seeming "pell-mell rush toward self annihilation" (1988, 4) in the era of nuclear weapons through a history of imaginings of superweapons. He describes the developing American "fantasies about superweapons" as not simply fantasies, or "expressions of psychology and culture," but also a "material force" that "shape[d] the thinking of inventors and leaders and common people" (5).

3. Colquhoun was a member of the Ancient Order of the Phoenix, based on Israel Regardie's rituals, the Order of the Pyramid and the Sphinx, based on Enochian magic, the O.T.O., and Grant Nu's Isis Lodge, and was a member of English and French Druid Orders.

4. One of the most useful roadmaps of alchemical laboratory activity across the twentieth century, from which this information is derived, can be found in Caron 2005.

5. As Chic Cicero and Sandra Tabatha Cicero put it on the Golden Dawn's Web site in a biographical piece on Regardie, "Israel Regardie" (http://www.hermeticgoldendawn.org/Documents/Bios/regardie.htm): "At the time he didn't believe in the validity of laboratory alchemy, (but later in the 1970's while working with practical alchemists such as Frater Albertus of the Paracelsus Research Society, he changed his mind on the matter. Unfortunately one of his alchemical experiments went wrong and he seriously burned his lungs in the lab. He gave up the practice of alchemy and suffered from the effects of the accident until the end of his life)" (Cicero and Cicero 1997).

6. For a book-length study of the relationship between Jung and Pauli, see Gieser 2005.

7. It only takes a brief Web search to turn up dozens of references to "psychedelic alchemy" (sometimes linked to the term "ethno-botany"), in which psychedelic drugs initiate a self-transmutational experience linking magical to psychological discourses in the twentieth century. Even the "Emerald Tablet" of Hermes Trismegistus, so crucial to occult revival Hermeticists a century ago, has been interpreted in terms of psychedelic drugs aiding in the alchemical "fermentation" process. See Alchemy Lab n.d., http://www.experiencefestival.com/a/Alchemy/id/5870.

8. Though Watts sounds a note of caution:

> To many people such claims are deeply disturbing. For one thing, mystical experience seems altogether too easy when it simply comes out of a bottle, and is thus available to people who have done nothing to deserve it, who have neither fasted nor prayed nor practiced yoga. For another, the claim seems to imply that spiritual insight is after all only a matter of body chemistry involving a total reduction of the spiritual to the material. These are serious considerations, even though one may be convinced that in the long run the difficulty is found to rest upon semantic confusion as to the definitions of "spiritual" and "material." (Watts 1960)

APPENDIX A

1. For more on the cognitive authority of science and its role in boundary-work, see Gieryn 1995, 405. Gieryn's conception of boundary-work is one of "strategic practical action" (1999, 23), and he argues that scientists "use boundary-work to pursue or protect several different 'professional goals'" (23), varying the strategies and the rhetorical positioning of science depending upon those goals:

Among the most common cartographic tropes is this: if the stakes are autonomy over scientists' ability to define problems and select procedures for investigating them, then science gets "purified," carefully demarcated from all political and market concerns, which are said to pollute truth; but if the stakes are material resources for scientific instruments, research materials, or personnel, science gets "impurified," erasing the borders or spaces between truth and policy relevance or technological panaceas. (1999, 23)

2. Japanese physics was in a marginal position compared to that of America and Europe, and foreign physicists were brought in to help gain acceptance for the lab's search for quarks. But, as Traweek explains, "the Japanese needed the aliens in order for the laboratory to gain credibility in the international high energy physics community; the foreigners were afraid they were losing status by even being there" (1992, 451). Moreover, many of the Japanese working at Tsukuba had worked for as many as twenty years at foreign universities. They took the opportunity to move back to a place where they would still have access to "world-class equipment" and "the traditional ways of Japanese universities are not so strong" (457). Traweek discovered that "foreigners made strategic use of being at the edge of their universe" (451), especially by using Japanese when it became convenient, and Japanese scientists often made strategic use of the English language.

Works Cited

Abdul-Ali, Sijil. 1913. "An Interpretation of Alchemy in Relation to Modern Scientific Thought." *Journal of the Alchemical Society* 1:3 (March 1913): 34–45.

———. 1914. "Report of the Honorary Secretary," in "Report of Second Annual Meeting." *Journal of the Alchemical Society* 2:13 (May 1914): 107–10.

———. 1915. "Report of the Honorary Secretary," in "Report of Third Annual Meeting." *Journal of the Alchemical Society* 3:19 (May 1915): 85–87.

Alchemy Lab. N.d. "Alchemy: The Emerald Tablet and Emerald Formula." http://www.experiencefestival.com/a/Alchemy/id/5870.

Anon. 1911. "*Alchemy, Ancient and Modern.*" *Nature* 86 (May 18, 1911): 375.

Anon. 1912. "Radio-Activity." *The Athenæum* 4442 (December 14, 1912): 732.

Anon. 1913. "Notices of New Books." *The Athenæum* 4483 (September 27, 1913): 320.

Atwood, Mary Anne. 1850. *A Suggestive Inquiry into the Hermetic Mystery: With a Dissertation on the More Celebrated of the Alchemical Philosophers Being an Attempt Towards the Recovery of the Ancient Experiment of Nature.* Reprint of 1918 William Tait edition. Kila, Mont.: Kessinger Publishing, n.d.

Ayton, W. A. 1985. *The Alchemist of the Golden Dawn: The Letters of the Revd. W. A. Ayton to F. L. Gardner and Others 1886–1905.* Edited by Ellic Howe. Wellingborough, Northamptonshire: The Aquarian Press.

Baly, E. C. C. 1905. *Spectroscopy.* London, New York, Bombay: Longmans, Green.

———. "Inorganic Chemistry." *Annual Reports on the Progress of Chemistry for 1914* 11 (1914): 41–47.

Baskerville, Charles. 1907. "Finding of Radium Now Yields Precedence, in Sensational Interest, to Ramsay's Transmutation of Elements." *New York Times* (August 18, 1907): SM9.

———. 1908. "Some Recent Transmutations." *Popular Science Monthly* 72:1 (January 1908): 46–51.

Bent, Silas. 1924. "Synthetic Gold Might Disrupt World." *New York Times* (November 23, 1924): xx3.

Berthelot, Marcellin. 1855. *Les Origines de l'Alchimie*. Reprint, Bruxelles: Culture et Civilisation, 1966.

Besant, Annie. 1895. "Occult Chemistry." *Lucifer* 17, no. 99 (November 15, 1895): 211–19.

———. 1897a. *The Ancient Wisdom: An Outline of Theosophical Teachings*. Reprint, London: Theosophical Publishing Society, 1906.

———. 1897b. "Theosophical and Mystical Publications." *Theosophical Review* XXI:121 (September 1897): 92–96.

———. 1898. "Theosophical Activities." *Theosophical Review* XXII:128 (April 1898): 185.

———. 1904. "Sir William Ramsay on 'Alchemy.'" *Theosophical Review* 33:198 (February 15, 1904): 487–88.

———. 1905a. "Radio-Activity Again?" in "On the Watch-Tower." *Theosophical Review* 36:216 (August 1905): 481–88.

———. 1905b. "Science and Alchemy." *Theosophical Review* 37:217 (September 1905): 1–2.

Besant, Annie, and Charles W. Leadbeater. 1908. *Occult Chemistry: A Series of Clairvoyant Observations on the Chemical Elements*. London: Theosophical Publishing Society.

———. 1951. *Occult Chemistry: A Series of Clairvoyant Observations on the Chemical Elements*. Adyar, India: Theosophical Publishing House.

Besant, Annie, and G.R.S. Mead. 1898. "Science on the Borderland." *Theosophical Review* XXII:130 (June 1898): 294.

Blavatsky, Helena Petrovna. 1877. *Isis Unveiled: A Master-Key to the Mysteries of Ancient and Modern Science and Theology*. Vol. 1, *Science*. Reprint, New York: J. W. Bouton, 1884. Vol. 2, *Theology*. Reprint, Pasadena: Theosophical University Press, 1972.

———. 1888. *The Secret Doctrine: The Synthesis of Science, Religion and Philosophy*. 2 vols. Reprint, London: Theosophical Publishing House, 1928.

———. 1892. *The Theosophical Glossary*. London: Theosophical Publishing House.

Bleiler, Richard (ed.). 1999. *Science Fiction Writers: Critical Studies of the Major Authors from the Early Nineteenth Century to the Present Day*. 2nd edition. New York: Scribner's.

Bolton, H. Carrington. 1897. "The Revival of Alchemy." *Science* 6:154 (December 10, 1897): 853–63.

Booth, Martin. 2000. *A Magick Life: The Biography of Aleister Crowley*. London: Hodder & Stoughton.
Bowker, Geoffrey C., and Susan Leigh Star. 1999. *Sorting Things Out: Classification and Its Consequences*. Cambridge, Mass.: MIT Press.
Brock, William H. 1985. *From Protyle to Proton: William Prout and the Nature of Matter, 1785–1985*. Bristol and Boston: Adam Hilger.
Bulwer-Lytton, Edward. 1842. *Zanoni*. Caxton Edition. London: Routledge, n.d.
———. 1862. *A Strange Story*. Caxton Edition. London: Routledge, n.d.
———. 1871. *The Coming Race*. Caxton Edition. London: Routledge, n.d.
Cameron, A. T., and William Ramsay. 1907. "The Chemical Action of Radium Emanation. Part II. On Solutions Containing Copper, and Lead, and on Water." *Journal of the Chemical Society* 91 (1907): 1593–1606.
———. 1908a. "The Chemical Action of Radium Emanation. Part III. On Water and Certain Gases." *Journal of the Chemical Society* 93 (1908): 966–92.
———. 1908b. "The Chemical Action of Radium Emanation. Part IV. On Water." *Journal of the Chemical Society* 93 (1908): 992–97.
Canaday, John. 2000. *The Nuclear Muse: Literature, Physics, and the First Atomic Bombs*. Madison: University of Wisconsin Press.
Carlson, Maria. 1993. *"No Religion Higher than Truth": A History of the Theosophical Movement in Russia, 1875–1922*. Princeton: Princeton University Press.
Caron, Richard. 2005. "Alchemy V: 19th–20th Century." In Hanegraaff et al., *Dictionary* 1:50–58.
Carter, John. 1999. *Sex and Rockets: The Occult World of Jack Parsons*. Venice, Cal.: Feral House.
Cayce, Edgar Evans. 1968. *Edgar Cayce on Atlantis*. New York: Hawthorn.
Cayce, Edgar Evans, Gail Cayce Schwartzer, and Douglas G. Richards. 1988. *Mysteries of Atlantis Revisited*. San Francisco: Harper and Row.
Charet, F. X. 1993. *Spiritualism and the Foundations of C. G. Jung's Psychology*. Albany: SUNY Press.
Chatley, Herbet. 1913. "Alchemy in China." *Journal of the Alchemical Society* 2:8 (December 1913): 33–38.
Chemical News. 1913. "Notices of Books." Vol. 107 (February 28, 1913): 106–8.
Cicero, Chic, and Sandra Tabatha Cicero. 1997. "Israel Regardie." http://www.hermeticgoldendawn.org/Documents/Bios/regardie.htm.
Clarke, Bruce. 1996. *Dora Marsden and Early Modernism: Gender, Individualism, Science*. Ann Arbor: University of Michigan Press.
———. 2001. *Energy Forms: Allegory and Science in the Era of Classical Thermodynamics*. Ann Arbor: University of Michigan Press.
Collie, J. Norman. 1914. "Note on the Paper by T. R. Merton on 'Attempts to Produce the Rare Gases by Electric Discharge.'" *Proceedings of the Royal Society*, Series A, 90:A621 (August 1, 1914): 554–56.
Collie, J. N. and Hubert Patterson. 1913a. "Origins of Helium and Neon." *Nature* 90 (February 3, 1913): 653–54.

———. 1913b. "The Presence of Neon in Hydrogen after the Passage of the Electric Discharge through the latter at Low Pressures." *Journal of the Chemical Society Transactions* 103:1 (1913): 419–26. [The preliminary note of this article was in *Proceedings of the Chemical Society of London* 29:410 (February 15, 1913): 22. Part II in *Proceedings of the Chemical Society* 29:418 (June 28, 1913): 216–21.]

Collie, J. Norman, Hubert S. Patterson, and Irvine Masson. 1914. "The Production of Neon and Helium by the Electrical Discharge." *Proceedings of the Royal Society of London.* Series A. 91:A623 (November 2, 1914): 30–45 (communicated July 23, 1914).

Colquhoun, Ithell. 1975. *Sword of Wisdom: MacGregor Mathers and "The Golden Dawn."* New York: Putnam.

Crookes, William. 1887. *Genesis of the Elements.* London: Royal Institution.

Crowley, Aleister. 1909a. "Editorial." *Equinox* 1:1 (March 1909): 1–3.

———. 1909b. "An Account of the A.A." *Equinox* 1:1 (March 1909): 7–13.

———. 1909c. "LIBER: E.VEL EXERCITIORVM SVB FIGVRÂ IX." *Equinox* 1:1 (March 1909): 25–28.

———. 1929. *Moonchild.* Reprint, York Beach, Maine: Samuel Weiser, 2000.

Dalton, John. 1808. *A New System of Chemical Philosophy.* Manchester and London: Bickerstaff, 1808–27.

Davies, Glyn. 2002. *A History of Money: From Ancient Times to the Present Day.* Cardiff: University of Wales Press.

De Steiger, Isabelle. 1907. *On a Gold Basis: A Treatise on Mysticism.* London: Philip Wellby.

———. 1913. "The Hermetic Mystery." *Journal of the Alchemical Society* 2:7 (November 1913): 17–31.

Deveney, John P. 1997. *Paschal Beverly Randolph: A Nineteenth-Century Black American Spiritualist, Rosicrucian, and Sex Magician.* Albany: SUNY Press.

———. 2005. "Paschal Beverly Randolph." In Hanegraaff et al., *Dictionary* 3:976–79.

Dixon, Joy. 1997. "Sexology and the Occult: Sexuality and Subjectivity in Theosophy's New Age." *Journal of the History of Sexuality* 7 (1997): 409–33.

———. 2001. *Divine Feminine: Theosophy and Feminism in England.* Baltimore: Johns Hopkins University Press.

Drummond, Ian M. 1987. *The Gold Standard and the International Monetary System 1900–1939.* London: Macmillan Education.

The Eastbournian. ca. 1910. "Frederick Soddy, F. R. S." Box 170, Folder 9. Frederick Soddy Papers, Bodleian Library, Oxford University.

Egerton, A. C. G. 1915. "The Analysis of Gases after Passage of Electric Discharge." *Proceedings of the Royal Society.* Series A. 91:A627 (March 1, 1915): 180–89 (communicated June 10, 1914).

———. 1927a. "Notes on Transmutation Experiments." MS. 1927. Sir William Ramsay Papers, University College, London.

———. 1927b. "Critique and History of the Work." MS. August 1927. Sir William Ramsay Papers, University College, London.

———. 1963. *Sir Alfred Egerton F.R.S. 1886–1959: A Memoir with Papers*. Privately printed for Lady Egerton by the Curwen Press, Plaistow.

Ellis, Richard. 1998. *Imagining Atlantis*. New York: Knopf.

Ernst, Paul. 1934. "The Stolen Element." *Astounding Stories* (September 1934): 107–17.

Faivre, Antoine. 1994. *Access to Western Esotericism*. Albany, N.Y.: SUNY Press.

Faivre, Antoine, and Wouter J. Hanegraaff (eds.). 1998. *Western Esotericism and the Science of Religion*. Leuven, Belgium: Peeters.

Ferguson, John. 1906. *Bibliotheca Chemica: A Bibliography of Books on Alchemy, Chemistry, and Pharmaceutics*. 2 vols. London: Derek Verschoyle, 1954.

———. 1913. "Some English Alchemical Books." *Journal of the Alchemical Society* 2:6 (October 1913): 1–16.

Finlay, John L. 1972. *Social Credit: The English Origins*. Montreal: McGill-Queens University Press.

Fisk, Dorothy. *Modern Alchemy*. 1936. London: Faber and Faber; New York: Appleton-Century.

Franklin, Allan. 1986. *The Neglect of Experiment*. Cambridge: Cambridge University Press.

Franklin, H. Bruce. 1988. *War Stars: The Superweapon and the American Imagination*. New York: Oxford University Press.

Frings, J. W. 1913. *The Occult Arts: An Examination of the Claims made for the Existence and Practice of Supernormal Powers, and an Attempted Justification of Some of Them by the Conclusions of the Researches of Modern Science*. 2nd ed. Philadelphia: David McKay.

Fulcanelli. 1926. *Le Mystère des Cathédrales: Esoteric Interpretation of the Hermetic Symbols of The Great Work. A Hermetic Study of Cathedral Construction*. Trans. Mary Sworder. Las Vegas: Brotherhood of Life, 1990.

Galbraith, John Kenneth. 1975. *Money: Whence It Came, Where It Went*. Boston: Houghton Mifflin.

Galison, Peter. 1987. *How Experiments End*. Chicago: The University of Chicago Press.

———. 1997. *Image and Logic: A Material Culture of Microphysics*. Chicago: The University of Chicago Press.

Garstin, E. J. Langford. 1930. *Theurgy or The Hermetic Practice*. Berwick, Maine: Ibis, 2004.

G. E. S. 1905. "Electrons and Clairvoyance." *Theosophical Review* 35:210 (February 1905): 518–19.

Gibson, Jasper. 1914. "An Interpretation of Alchemical Symbolism with Reference to the Writings of Edward Kelly." *Journal of the Alchemical Society* 3:15 (December 1914): 17–25.

Gieryn, Thomas F. 1983. "Boundary-Work and the Demarcation of Science from Non-Science: Strains and Interests in Professional Ideologies of Scientists." *The American Sociological Review* 48:6 (December 1983): 781–95.

———. 1995. "Boundaries of Science." In *Handbook of Science and Technology Studies*, ed. Sheila Jasanoff, Gerald E. Markle, James C. Petersen, and Trevor Pinch. Thousand Oaks, Cal.: Sage Publications. 393–443.

———. 1999. *Cultural Boundaries of Science: Credibility on the Line*. Chicago: The University of Chicago Press.
Gieser, Suzanne. 2005. *The Innermost Kernel: Depth Psychology and Quantum Physics. Wolfgang Pauli's Dialogue with C. G. Jung*. Berlin: Springer.
Gilbert, R. A. 1987. *A. E. Waite: Magician of Many Parts*. Wellingborough, England: Crucible.
Glover, David. 1996. *Vampires, Mummies, and Liberals: Bram Stoker and the Politics of Popular Fiction*. Durham, N.C.: Duke University Press.
Godwin, Joscelyn. 2005. "Edward George Bulwer-Lytton." In Hanegraaff et al., *Dictionary* 1: 213–17.
Goodrick-Clarke, Nicholas. 2005. "Hermeticism and Hermetic Societies." In Hanegraaff et al., *Dictionary* 1: 550–58.
Gordin, Michael D. 2004. *A Well-Ordered Thing: Dmitrii Mendeleev and the Shadow of the Periodic Table*. New York: Basic Books.
Haggard, H. Rider. 1887. *She*. Reprint, New York: Books, Inc., n.d.
———. 1905. *Ayesha: The Return of She*. Reprint, London: Macdonald, 1972.
Hanegraaff, Wouter. 1998. "Introduction: the Birth of a Discipline." In Faivre and Hanegraaff. *Western Esotericism*, vii–xvii.
———. 2005. "Occult/Occultism." In Hanegraaff et al., *Dictionary* 2: 884–89.
Hanegraaff, Wouter J., et al. (eds.). 2005. *Dictionary of Gnosis and Western Esotericism*. 2 vols. Leiden: Brill.
Hara, Fio. 1906. "The Advance of Science Towards Occult Teachings." *Theosophical Review* 37:222 (February 1906): 548–54.
Harrington, Anne. 1996. *Reenchanted Science: Holism in German Culture from Wilhelm II to Hitler*. Princeton: Princeton University Press.
Hayman, Ronald. 1999. *A Life of Jung*. New York: Norton.
Heinrich, Clark. 2002. *Magic Mushrooms in Religion and Alchemy*. Rochester, Vt.: Park Street Press.
Henderson, Linda Dalrymple. 1998. *Duchamp in Context: Science and Technology in the Large Glass and Related Works*. Princeton: Princeton University Press.
Hermes Trismegistus. 1884. *The Divine Pymander of Hermes Mercurius Trismegistus. Translated from the Arabic by Dr. Everard. (1650) With introduction & preliminary essay by Hargrave Jennings*. London: Redway.
Hess, David J. 1993. *Science in the New Age: The Paranormal, Its Defenders and Debunkers, and American Culture*. Madison: University of Wisconsin Press.
Howe, Ellic. 1972. *The Magicians of the Golden Dawn: A Documentary History of a Magical Order, 1887–1923*. Reprint, York Beach, Maine: Samuel Weiser, 1984.
Howorth, Muriel. 1958. *Pioneer Research on the Atom: Rutherford and Soddy in a Glorious Chapter of Science: The Life Story of Frederick Soddy*. London: New World Publications.
Huggins, William. 1903a. Letter to William Ramsay. July 19, 1903. Sir William Ramsay Papers, University College London.

———. 1903b. Letter to William Ramsay. July 20, 1903. Sir William Ramsay Papers, University College London.
Hutchison, Keith. 1982. "What Happened to Occult Qualities in the Scientific Revolution?" *Isis* 73:267 (1982): 233–53.
James, H., and Maurice James. 1930. "The Mystery Metal." *Scientific Wonder Stories* (March 1930): 898–901, 932.
Jenkins, Philip. 2000. *Mystics and Messiahs: Cults and New Religions in American History*. Oxford: Oxford University Press.
Johnson, K. Paul. 1994. *The Masters Revealed: Madame Blavatsky and the Myth of the Great White Lodge*. Albany: SUNY Press.
Journal of the Alchemical Society. 1913–1915. H. Stanley Redrove, ed. London: H. K. Lewis.
———. 1913a. "Abstract of Discussion." 1:1 (January 1913): 15–16.
———. 1913b. "Abstract of Discussion." 2:2 (February 1913): 31–32.
———. 1913c. "Abstract of Discussion." 2:3 (March 1913): 46–48.
———. 1913d. "Abstract of Discussion." 2:7 (November 1913): 31–32.
———. 1914. "Abstract of Discussion." 3:14 (November 1914): 4–11.
Jung, C.G. 1954. *Mysterium Coniunctionis; An Inquiry into the Separation and Synthesis of Psychic Opposites in Alchemy*. Trans. by R. F. C. Hull. New York: Pantheon, 1963.
Kateley, Walter. 1929. "The Gold Triumvirate." *Science Wonder Stories* 1:6 (November 1929): 514–21, 557.
Keller, Alex. 1983. *The Infancy of Atomic Physics: Hercules in His Cradle*. Oxford: Oxford University Press.
Kelvin, Lord. 1903. Letter to William Ramsay. August 22, 1903. William Ramsay Papers, University College London. [Quoted in Travers 1956, 252.]
King, Francis. 1970. *Ritual Magic in England: 1887 to the Present Day*. Reprint, London: New English Library, 1973.
Kitson, Arthur. 1895. *A Scientific Solution of the Money Question*. Boston: Arena.
———. 1903. *The Money Problem*. London: Grant Richards.
———. 1917. *A Fraudulent Standard: An Exposure of the Fraudulent Character of our Monetary Standard: With Suggestions for the Establishment of an Invariable Unit of Value*. London: King.
Kopp, Hermann. 1843–47. *Geschichte der Chemie*. 4 vols. Braunschweig, Germany: Vieweg und Sohn.
Kostro, Ludwik. 2000. *Einstein and the Ether*. Montreal: Apeiron.
Lancet. 1907. "Modern Alchemy: Transmutation Realised." (July 27, 1907): 244.
Larmor, Joseph. 1900. *Aether and Matter: A Development of the Dynamical Relations of the Aether to Material Systems on the Basis of the Atomic Constitution of Matter*. Cambridge: Cambridge University Press.
Latour, Bruno. 1987. *Science in Action: How to Follow Scientists and Engineers through Society*. Cambridge, Mass.: Harvard University Press.
Leadbeater, C. W. 1899. *Clairvoyance*. London: The Theosophical Publishing Society.

———. 1912. *A Textbook of Theosophy*. 11th ed. Adyar, India: Theosophical Publishing House, 1971.

———. 1918. *The Astral Plane: Its Scenery, Inhabitants, and Phenomena*. 5th ed. Los Angeles: Theosophical Publishing House.

Le Grand, Homer (ed.). 1990. *Experimental Inquiries: Historical, Philosophical and Social Studies of Experimentation in Science*. Boston: Kluwer Academic Publishers.

Lenoir, Timothy. 1986. "Models and Instruments in the Development of Electrophysiology, 1845–1912." *Historical Studies in the Physical and Biological Sciences* 17:1 (1986): 1–54.

Levere, Trevor H. 2001. *Transforming Matter: A History of Chemistry from Alchemy to the Buckyball*. Baltimore: Johns Hopkins University Press.

Lévi, Éliphas. 1856. *Dogme et rituel de la Haute Magie*. Paris: Germer Baillière.

———. 1860. *L'Histoire de la magie*. Paris: Germer Baillière.

Lewis, James R. 1994. *The Astrology Encyclopedia*. Detroit: Gale Research.

Literary Yearbook. 1922. N.p.: Routledge.

Lodge, Oliver. 1909. *The Ether of Space*. New York: Harper.

Loring, F. H. 1913. *Studies in Valency*. London: Simpkin.

———. 1921. *Atomic Theories*. London: Methuen.

———. 1922. *Definition of the Principle of Equivalence*. London: Lloyd.

———. 1923. *The Chemical Elements*. London: Methuen.

Machen, Arthur. 1907. *The Hill of Dreams*. Reprint, Doylestown, Penn.: Wildside Press, n.d.

Marques, A. 1908. *Scientific Corroborations of Theosophy; A Vindication of the Sacred Doctrine by the Latest Discoveries*. Rev. ed. London: Theosophical Publishing Society.

Martinez-Alier, Juan, with Klaus Schlüpmann. 1987. *Ecological Economics: Energy, Environment and Society*. Oxford: Blackwell.

Masson, Irvine. 1913. "The Occurrence of Neon in Vacuum-tubes Containing Hydrogen." *Proceedings of the Chemical Society* 29:418 (June 28, 1913): 233.

Mayhew, Nicholas. 2000. *Sterling: The History of a Currency*. New York: Wiley.

McIntosh, Christopher. 1972. *Eliphas Lévi and the French Occult Revival*. London: Rider.

McLynn, Frank. 1996. *Carl Gustav Jung*. New York: St. Martin's.

Meek, Captain S. P. 1930. "The Radio Robbery." *Amazing Stories* (February 1930): 1046–55, 1065.

———. 1932. "Vanishing Gold." *Wonder Stories* (May 1932): 1320–29.

Mellor, Joseph William. 1902. *Higher Mathematics for Students of Chemistry and Physics*. London and New York: Longmans, Green.

———. 1904. *Chemical Statics and Dynamics, Including the Theories of Chemical Change, Catalysis, and Explosions*. London: Longmans.

———. 1912. *Modern Inorganic Chemistry*. London and New York: Longmans, Green.

———. 1922. *A Comprehensive Treatise on Inorganic and Theoretical Chemistry*. London and New York: Longmans, Green.

Merricks, Linda. 1996. *The World Made New: Frederick Soddy, Science, Politics, and Environment.* Oxford: Oxford University Press.

Merritt, Abraham. 1927. "The Face in the Abyss." *Amazing Stories Annual.*

Merton, Thomas R. 1914. "Attempts to Produce the Rare Gases by Electric Discharge." *Proceedings of the Royal Society.* Series A. 90:A621 (August 1, 1914): 549–53.

Meyer, Ernst von. 1891. *A History of Chemistry from Earliest Times to the Present Day.* Trans. George M'Gowan. Reprint, New York: Arno, 1975.

Miller, Peter Schuyler. 1933. "Jeremiah Jones, Alchemist." *Amazing Stories* (May 1933): 142–51.

Mitchell, C. Ainsworth. 1913. "Chemistry: The Birth of an Atom." *Knowledge* 36 (April 1913): 145–46.

Moore, William R. "Alchemy and Modern Science." *The Occult Review* 15:2 (February 1912): 71–79.

Morrisson, Mark. 2002. "Edith Sitwell's Atomic Bomb Poems: Alchemy and Scientific Reintegration." *Modernism/Modernity* 9:4 (November 2002): 605–33.

Muir, M. M. Pattison. 1894. *The Alchemical Essence and the Chemical Element: An Episode in the Quest for the Unchanging.* London: Longmans, Green.

———. 1902. *The Story of Alchemy and the Beginnings of Chemistry.* London: Newnes.

Myers, Margaret G. 1940. *Monetary Proposals for Social Reform.* New York: Columbia University Press.

Nathanson, Isaac. 1934. "Gold." *Amazing Stories* 8:9 (January 1934): 95–114.

Nature. 1913. "Origins of Helium and Neon." Vol. 90 (February 13, 1913): 653–54.

———. 1915. Obituary for John Ferguson. Vol. 96 (October 14, 1915): 192.

Nelson, Robert A. 2000. *Adept Alchemy.* Jean, Nev.: Rex Research.

Newman, William R. 1989. "Technology and Alchemical Debates in the Late Middle Ages." *Isis* 80:3 (September 1989): 423–45.

———. 2004. *Promethean Ambitions: Alchemy and the Quest to Perfect Nature.* Chicago: The University of Chicago Press.

Newman, William R., and Lawrence M. Principe. 2002. *Alchemy Tried in the Fire: Starkey, Boyle, and the Fate of Helmontian Chymistry.* Chicago: The University of Chicago Press.

——— (eds.). 2004. *George Starkey: Alchemical Laboratory Notebooks and Correspondence.* Chicago: The University of Chicago Press.

New York Daily Tribune. 1904. "Ramsay on Radium. Tells of Experiments. To Deliver Address to Society of Chemical Industry To-day." (September 11, 1904). Sir William Ramsay Papers, University College London.

New York Times. 1880. "Alchemy and Chemistry: Lecture Before the Academy of Sciences By Prof. Bolton, of Trinity." (November 16, 1880): 2.

———. 1889. "The Dream of the Alchemist." (January 17, 1889): 8.

———. 1896. "The Alchemist's Secret Out: A Delegate Discovers that Gold Can Be Manufactured Easily." (July 26, 1896): 2.

———. 1897a. "National Capital Chat . . . A Failure to Make Gold . . ." (May 30, 1897): 24.

———. 1897b. "The Revival of Alchemy: Dr. H. Carrington Bolton Lectures on the Modern Aspect of Chemistry's Forerunner." (October 17, 1897): 6.

———. 1898. "A Latter-Day Alchemist." (July 29, 1898): 12.

———. 1901. "Alchemists of To-Day." (December 29, 1901): SM16.

———. 1902. "Dr. Stephen H. Emmens's Work." (February 20, 1902): 8.

———. 1903. "Radium and Helium." (November 28, 1903): 8.

———. 1907. "Ramsay Sure of Discovery." (July 28, 1907): 1.

———. 1910a. "Chemist C. B. White Replies to Gleason." (September 25, 1910): 12.

———. 1910b. "Modern Alchemy." (May 29, 1910): 6.

———. 1911. "Alchemy, Long Scoffed At, Turns Out to Be True." (February 19, 1911): SM12.

———. 1913. "Alchemic Gold Company." (January 10, 1913): 1.

———. 1919. "Alchemists' Goal Reached by Briton." (December 9, 1919): 2.

———. 1922. "Says Synthetic Gold Cannot Compete with Natural Metal." (January 19, 1922): 1.

———. 1923. "Predicts a Utopia When Atoms Work." (July 31, 1923): 16.

———. 1928. "Transmuted Gold." (July 8, 1928): 46.

Noyes, William Albert, and W. Albert Noyes, Jr. 1932. *Modern Alchemy*. Springfield, Ill.: C. C. Thomas.

Nye, Mary Jo. 1993. *From Chemical Philosophy to Theoretical Chemistry: Dynamics of Matter and Dynamics of Disciplines 1800–1950*. Berkeley: University of California Press.

Old, Walter Gorn. 1913. "Report of the Honorary Secretary," in "Report of the First Annual Meeting." *Journal of the Alchemical Society* 1:5 (May 1913): 66–67.

Oldfeld, Peter. 1929. *The Alchemy Murder*. New York: Washburn.

Oppenheim, Janet. 1985. *The Other World: Spiritualism and Psychical Research in England, 1850–1914*. Cambridge: Cambridge University Press.

Otis, Laura. 2001. *Networking: Communicating with Bodies and Machines in the Nineteenth Century*. Ann Arbor: University of Michigan Press.

Owen, Alex. 1989. *The Darkened Room: Women, Power and Spiritualism in Late Victorian England*. London: Virago.

———. 2004. *The Place of Enchantment: British Occultism and the Culture of the Modern*. Chicago: The University of Chicago Press.

φ. 1915. "The Limitations of Science." *Nature* 96 (September 2, 1915): 3–4.

Patzer, Sidney. 1933. "The Lunar Consul." *Wonder Stories*. Part I (November 1933), Part II (December 1933): 492–531.

Pauwels, Louis, and Jacques Bergier. 1964. *The Morning of the Magicians*. Trans. Rollo Myers. New York: Stein and Day.

Phillips, Stephen M. 1980. *Extra-Sensory Perception of Quarks*. Wheaton: Theosophical Publishing House.

———. 1996. *Evidence of a Yogic Siddhi. Anima. Remote Viewing of Subatomic Particles*. Wheaton, Ill.: Theosophical Publishing House.

———. 1999. *ESP of Quarks and Superstrings*. New Dehli: New Age International.

Poe, Edgar Allan. 1849. "Von Kempelen and His Discovery." Reprint, *Amazing Stories* (July 1927): 363–66.

Principe, Lawrence. 1998. *The Aspiring Adept: Robert Boyle and His Alchemical Quest: Including Boyle's "Lost" Dialogue on the Transmutation of Metals*. Princeton: Princeton University Press.

Principe, Lawrence M., and William R. Newman. 2001. "Some Problems with the Historiography of Alchemy." In *Secrets of Nature: Astrology and Alchemy in Early Modern Europe*, ed. William R. Newman and Anthony Grafton. Cambridge: MIT Press. 385–434.

Proceedings of the Chemical Society. 1913. "Annual General Meeting." 29:413 (March 14, 1913): 96–103.

Prout, William. 1815. "On the Relations between the Specific Gravities of Bodies and the Weights of their Atoms." *Annals of Philosophy*. 6 (November 1815): 321–30, 472.

———. 1816. "Corrections of a Mistake in the Essay on the Relation between the Specific Gravities of Bodies." *Annals of Philosophy*. 7 (1816): 111–13.

Ramsay, William. 1885. Lectures on "Junior Chemistry. Begun Octr. 1885 40 Lessons." Item #36. Sir William Ramsay Papers, University College London.

———. 1893? Untitled manuscript on Physical Chemistry. Item #37. Sir William Ramsay Papers, University College London.

———. 1904a. *Introduction to the Study of Physical Chemistry*. London: Longmans, Green.

———. 1904b. Letter to Margaret Ramsay. N.d., but shortly after September 18, 1904. Sir William Ramsay Papers, University College London.

———. 1904c. "Radium and Its Products." *Harpers* (December 1904): 52–57.

———. 1905. "Present Problems of Inorganic Chemistry (an address at the International Congress of Arts and Science, St. Louis, September 1904)." *Smithsonian Report for 1904*. Washington, Government Printing Office, 1905: 207–20. Sir William Ramsay Papers, University College London.

———. 1906. Letter to Henry Fyfe. 25 January 1906. Sir William Ramsay Papers, University College London.

———. 1907a. "On Transmutation. A Lecture delivered at the London Institution, Jan. 28th 1907 . . . [and] Again at the Dublin Royal Society: Feb 15, 1907." MS. Sir William Ramsay Papers, University College London.

———. 1907b. "Radium Emanation." *Nature* 76 (July 18, 1907): 269.

———. 1911. "Presidential Address." The British Association for the Advancement of Science. Portsmouth. Sir William Ramsay Papers, University College London.

———. 1912. *Elements and Electrons*. London: Harper.

———. 1913a. "The Presence of Helium in the Gas from the Interior of an X-Ray Bulb." *Transactions of the Chemical Society* (January 1913): 103.

———. 1913b. Laboratory Notebook VII. 1913. Sir William Ramsay Papers, University College London.

Ramsay, William, and Frederick Soddy. 1903. "Experiments in Radio-Activity, and the Production of Helium from Radium." *Nature* (August 13, 1903): 354–55.

Randolph, Paschal Beverly (ed.). 1871. *Hermes Mercurius Trismegistus: His Divine Pymander. Also The Asiatic Mystery, The Smaragdine Table and the Song of Brahm.* Boston: Rosicrucian Publishing Company. Reprint, Des Plaines, Ill.: Yogi Publication Society, n.d.

Randonvilliers, Jean-Baptiste Richard de. 1842. *Dictionnaire des Mots Nouveaux.* Paris: Pilout.

Redgrove, H. Stanley. 1909. *On the Calculation of Thermo-Chemical Constants.* London: n.p.

———. 1910. *Matter, Spirit and the Cosmos. Some Suggestions towards a Better Understanding of the Whence and Why of their Existence.* London: Rider.

———. 1911. *Alchemy: Ancient and Modern.* 1st ed. London: Rider. American ed., Philadelphia: David McKay.

———. 1912. *A Mathematical Theory of Spirit; Being an Attempt to Employ Certain Mathematical Principles in the Elucidation of Some Metaphysical Problems.* London: Rider.

———. 1913a. "The Origin of Alchemy." *Journal of the Alchemical Society* I:1 (January 1913): 2–14.

———. 1913b. "Periodical Literature." *Journal of the Alchemical Society* I:5 (May 1913): 77.

———. 1913c. *Experimental Mensuration; An Elementary Test-Book of Inductive Geometry.* New York: Van Nostrand.

———. 1915a. *The Magic of Experience: A Contribution to the Theory of Knowledge.* London: Dent.

———. 1915b. "Report of Third Annual Meeting." *Journal of the Alchemical Society* III:13 (May 1915): 85–87.

———. 1920a. *Magic and Mysticism: Studies in Bygone Beliefs.* New Hyde Park, N.Y.: University Books, 1971.

———. 1920b. *Roger Bacon: The Father of Experimental Science and Mediæval Occultism.* London: Rider.

———. 1920c. *Purpose and Transcendentalism; An Exposition of Swedenborg's Philosophical Doctrines in Relation to Modern Thought.* London: Kegan Paul, Trench, Trubner.

———. 1922a. *Alchemy: Ancient and Modern.* 2nd ed. London: Rider.

———. 1922b. *Joannes Baptista Van Helmont, Alchemist, Physician and Philosopher.* London: Rider.

Redgrove, H. Stanley, and I. M. L. Redgrove. 1921. *Joseph Glanvill and Psychical Research in the Seventeenth Century.* London: Rider.

Redgrove, H. Stanley, and Geoffrey Martin, Ernest A. Dancaster, J.M. Dickson, Frank B. Gatehouse, E. Jobling. 1916. *Industrial Gases: Including the Liquefaction of Gases and the Manufacture of Hydrogen, Oxygen, Nitrogen, Carbon Dioxide, Sulphur Dioxide, Ammonia, Producer gas, Illuminating gas, Acetylene, Ozone, etc., etc.* London: Lockwood.

Regardie, Israel. 1936. *What You Should Know about the Golden Dawn.* Reprint, Phoenix: New Falcon Publications, 1993.

———. 1937. *The Philosopher's Stone: A Modern Comparative Approach to Alchemy from the Psychological and Magical Points of View.* Reprint, Kila, Mont.: Kessinger Publishing, n.d.

———. 1938. *The Middle Pillar: The Balance Between Mind and Magic.* Reprint, edited by Chic Cicero and Sandra Tabatha Cicero. St. Paul, Minn.: Llewellyn, 2004.

Repp, Ed Earl. 1929. *The Radium Pool.* Reprint, Los Angeles: Fantasy Publishing, 1949.

Riding, R. W., and E.C.C. Baly. 1925. "The Occurrence of Helium and Neon in Vacuum Tubes." *Proceedings of the Royal Society,* Series A, 109:A749 (September 1, 1925): 186–93.

Rowbottom, B. Ralph. 1914a. "Roger Bacon." *Journal of the Alchemical Society* 2:11 (March 1914): 75–83.

———. 1914b. "Reviews." *Journal of the Alchemical Society* 2:12 (April 1914): 104–6.

Ruck, Carl A. 2006. *Sacred Mushrooms of the Goddess: Secrets of Eleusis.* Berkeley: Ronin.

Ruggiu, Jean-Pascal. 1996. "Rosicrucian Alchemy and the Hermetic Order of the Golden Dawn." http://meleph.free.fr/alchemy.htm.

Ruskin, John. 1862. *"Unto this Last": Four Essays on the First Principles of Political Economy.* London: Smith, Elder.

———. 1871–1884. *Fors Clavigera: Letters to the Workmen and Labourers of Great Britain.* Sunnyside, Orpington, Kent: George Allen.

Russell, Alexander. 1912. *Lord Kelvin: His Life and Work.* London: Jack.

Rutherford, Ernest. 1913. *Radioactive Substances and Their Radiations.* Cambridge: Cambridge University Press.

———. 1937. *The Newer Alchemy; Based on the Henry Sidgwick Memorial Lecture Delivered at Newnham College, Cambridge, November, 1936.* Cambridge: Cambridge University Press.

Ryan, Charles J. 1975. *H. P. Blavatsky and the Theosophical Movement: A Brief Historical Sketch.* 2nd ed. Pasadena, Cal.: Theosophical University Press.

Sapere Aude [William Wynn Westcott]. 1893. *The Science of Alchymy: Spiritual and Material.* London: Theosophical Publishing Society.

Schachner, Nathan. 1933. "The Revolt of the Scientists." *Wonder Stories.* Pt. 1 (April 1933): 806–21; pt. 2 (May 1933): 947–61, 985; pt. 3 (June 1933): 26–57, 86–87.

Schaffner, Kenneth F. 1972. *Nineteenth-Century Aether Theories.* Oxford: Pergamon.

Schorlemmer, Carl. 1889. *The Rise and Development of Organic Chemistry.* Rev. ed., edited by Arthur Smithells. London: Macmillan, 1894.

Scientific American Supplement. 1913. "The Birth of the Atom. Has Matter Been Synthesised." 108:10 (March 8, 1913): 154–55.

Sclove, Richard. 1989. "From Alchemy to Atomic War: Frederick Soddy's 'Technology Assessment' of Atomic Energy, 1900–1915." *Science, Technology, & Human Values* 14 (Spring 1989): 163–94.

Seaborg, Glenn T. 1994. *Modern Alchemy: Selected Papers of Glenn T. Seaborg.* River Edge, N.J.: World Scientific.

Segrè, Emilio. 1980. *From X-Rays to Quarks: Modern Physicists and Their Discoveries.* Berkeley: The University of California Press.

Senf, Carol A. 2002. *Science and Social Science in Bram Stoker's Fiction.* Westport, Conn.: Greenwood.

Serviss, Garrett P. 1900. *The Moon Metal.* Reprint, Naperville, Ill.: FAX Collector's Editions.

Severn, Elizabeth. 1914. "Some Mystical Aspects of Alchemy." *Journal of the Alchemical Society* 2:13 (May 1914): 110–17.

Shah, Chandoo N. ca. 1929. *Modern Alchemy: Or, The Story of the Atom.* Los Angeles: Hartson Press.

Shelley, Mary Wollstonecraft. 1818. *Frankenstein, or The Modern Prometheus. The 1818 Text.* Edited by James Rieger. Chicago: The University of Chicago Press, 1982.

Shelley, William Scott. 1995. *The Elixir: An Alchemical Study of the Ergot Mushrooms.* Notre Dame, Ind.: Cross Cultural Publications.

Sinnett, A. P. 1901. *Nature's Mysteries, and How Theosophy Illuminates Them.* London: Theosophical Publishing Society.

Smith, E. Lester. 1982. *Occult Chemistry Re-Evaluated.* Wheaton, Ill.: Theosophical Publishing House.

Smith, Ernest Lester, and V. Wallace Slater. 1934. *The Field of Occult Chemistry.* London: Theosophical Publishing House.

Smith, Thomas. 1908. *Life of John Dee.* Translated by W. A. Ayton. London: Theosophical Publishing Society.

Smithells, Arthur. [1913.] "The researches on the transformation of elements at University College London. From a note by Professor A. Smithells." [Morris Travers writes: "Copy, original returned to Smithells"]. Sir William Ramsay Papers, University College London. Vol. XV, Part II, #274.

Soddy, Frederick. 1894. "General Chemistry Notes from various sources. UCW Aberystwyth. F. Soddy." Notebook Item #64. Frederick Soddy Papers, Bodleian Library, Oxford University.

———. 1895. Evans Prize Essay: "The Relations Existing between the Manner in which the Atoms are Linked Together, and the Physical Properties of the Resulting Compounds." Item #93. Frederick Soddy Papers, Bodleian Library, Oxford University.

———. 1896. "Chemistry Note Book. Merton College. October 1896." Lecture notes (including lectures by J. E. Marsh). Item #70. Frederick Soddy Papers, Bodleian Library, Oxford University.

———. 1897–1898. "Lectures Veley, Walden, Elford." Merton College. October 1897–March 1898. Bound typescript lecture notes. Item #73. Frederick Soddy Papers, Bodleian Library, Oxford University.

———. [1899–1900]. "Lectures on the History of Chemistry from earliest times." Typescript. Item #99. Frederick Soddy Papers, Bodleian Library, Oxford University.

———. [1900a] "Alchemy and Chemistry." Typescript. Item #100. Frederick Soddy Papers, Bodleian Library, Oxford University.

———. [1900b]. "Notes from Les Origine de l'Alchimie (Berthelot)." Manuscript notes. Box 179, Item #100. Frederick Soddy Papers, Bodleian Library, Oxford University.

———. 1903. "Recent Advances in Radioactivity." *Contemporary Review* 83 (May 1903): 708–20.

———. n.d. (ca. 1906). "The Evolution of the Elements." Pamphlet "(Ordered by the General Committee to be printed *in extenso*.)" British Association for the Advancement of Science. Box 172, in Item 44. Frederick Soddy Papers, Bodleian Library, Oxford University.

———. 1909. *The Interpretation of Radium: Being the Substance of Six Free Popular Experimental Lectures Delivered at the University of Glasgow, 1908.* London: John Murray.

———. 1912. "Transmutation: The Vital Problem of the Future." Offprint from *Scientia* 11 (1912): 186–202. Item #439, Box 172, in Item #44. Frederick Soddy Papers, Bodleian Library, Oxford University.

———. 1917. "The Evolution of Matter." Offprint from the *Aberdeen University Review*, February 1917. Box 172, in Item #44. Frederick Soddy Papers, Bodleian Library, Oxford University.

———. 1924. *The Inversion of Science and a Scheme of Scientific Reformation.* London: Henderson.

———. 1926. *Wealth, Virtual Wealth and Debt: The Solution of the Economic Paradox.* London: Allen & Unwin.

———. 1932. *The Interpretation of the Atom.* New York: Putnam.

———. ca. 1932–1940. "Interpretation of the Atom and Modern Alchemy Revision." MS Notebook. Box 185, Item #177. Frederick Soddy Papers, Bodleian Library, Oxford University.

———. 1945a. "Misc. notes on books read, mainly on Atomic Piles. 1945." Brown ex bk. Papers, Box 185, Item #174. Frederick Soddy Papers, Bodleian Library, Oxford University.

———. 1945b. "The Moving Finger Writes." *Cavalcade* (August 18, 1945): 8–9.

———. 1949. *The Story of Atomic Energy.* London: Nova Atlantis.

Speaker, David M. 1928. "The Disintegrating Ray." *Amazing Stories* (February 1928): 1088–91.

S. R. 1906. "The Progress of Radium." *Theosophical Review* 37:222 (February 1906): 559–60.

Star, Susan Leigh, and James R. Griesemer. 1989. "Institutional Ecology, Translations and Boundary Objects: Amateurs and Professionals in Berkeley's Museum of Vertebrate Zoology, 1907–39." *Social Studies of Science* 19:3 (August 1989): 387–420.

Stewart, Balfour, and P. G. Tait. 1875. *The Unseen Universe, or, Physical Speculations on a Future State.* London: Macmillan.

Stoker, Bram. 1903. *The Jewel of Seven Stars.* New York: Harpers.

Strutt, R. J. 1914. "Attempts to Observe the Production of Neon or Helium by Electric Discharge." *Proceedings of the Royal Society of London*, Ser. A., 89:A613 (February 2, 1914): 499–506.

Sullivan, J. W. N. 1913. "Has Matter Been Synthesised? An Account of Some New Experiments." *Scientific American* 108:10 (March 8, 1913): 226.

Thomson, J. J. 1913. "On the Appearance of Helium and Neon in Vacuum Tubes." *Nature* 90:2259 (February 13, 1913): 645–47.

Thomson, William [Lord Kelvin]. 1867. "On Vortex Atoms." *Proceedings of the Royal Society of Edinburgh* 6 (1867): 94–105.

Thurschwell, Pamela. 2001. *Literature, Technology and Magical Thinking, 1880–1920*. Cambridge: Cambridge University Press.

Tillett, Gregory. 1982. *The Elder Brother: A Biography of Charles Webster Leadbeater*. London: Routledge & Kegan Paul.

Times (London). 1884. "Alchemy." (10 January 1884): 3c.

———. 1908a. "The French Academy of Sciences. Mme. Curie and Sir W. Ramsay." (August 12, 1908): 5f–6f.

———. 1908b. "British Association." (September 9, 1908): 4a.

Times Literary Supplement (London). 1903. "The Disintegration Theory of Radioactivity." No. 76 (June 6, 1903): 201.

T. M. L. 1913. "Chemistry: Pure and Applied." *Nature* 90 (February 20, 1913): 668–70.

Torrens, R. G. 1972. *The Secret Rituals of the Golden Dawn*. Denington Estate, England: The Aquarian Press.

Travers, Morris W. 1956. *A Life of Sir William Ramsay K.C.B., F.R.S.* London: Edward Arnold.

Traweek, Sharon. 1988. *Beamtimes and Lifetimes: The World of High Energy Physicists*. Cambridge: Harvard University Press.

———. 1992. "Border Crossings: Narrative Strategies in Science Studies and among Physicists in Tsukuba Science City, Japan." In *Science as Practice and Culture*, ed. Andrew Pickering. Chicago: The University of Chicago Press. 429–64.

Trenn, Thaddeus J. 1974. "The Justification of Transmutation: Speculations of Ramsay and Experiments of Rutherford." *Ambix* 21 (1974): 53–77.

Waite, A. E. 1891. *Lives of the Alchemystical Philosophers*. London: George Redway.

———. 1893. *The Hermetic museum, restored and enlarged; most faithfully instructing all disciples of the sopho-spagyric art how that greatest and truest medicine of the philosopher's stone may be found and held. Now first done into English from the Latin original published at Frankfort in the year 1678; containing twenty-two most celebrated chemical tracts*. London: Elliott.

———. 1894a. *The Hermetic and Alchemical Writings of Aureolus Philippus Theophrastus Bombast, of Hohenheim, called Paracelsus the Great: Now for the first time faithfully translated into English/Edited with a biographical Preface, elucidatory Notes, a copious Hermetic Vocabulary, and Index*. London: Elliott.

———. 1894b. "In the Beginning." *Unknown World* 1:1 (August 15, 1894): 1–7.

———. 1894c. "What Is Alchemy?" *Unknown World* 1:1 (August 15, 1894): 7–11.

———. 1913. "The Canon of Criticism in Respect of Alchemical Literature." *Journal of the Alchemical Society* 1:2 (February 1913): 17–30.

Wallis, Roy. 1985. "Science and Pseudo-Science." *Social Science Information* 24:3 (1985): 585–601.

Warlick, M. E. 2001. *Max Ernst and Alchemy: A Magician in Search of a Myth*. Austin: University of Texas Press.

Washington, Peter. 1995. *Madame Blavatsky's Baboon: A History of the Mystics, Mediums, and Misfits Who Brought Spiritualism to America*. New York: Schocken.

Wasson, R. Gordon, Albert Hofmann, and Carl A. P. Ruck. 1998. *The Road to Eleusis: Unveiling the Secrets of the Mysteries*. Los Angeles: William Dailey Rare Books.

Wasson, R. Gordon, Stella Kramrisch, Jonathan Ott, and Carl A. P. Ruck. 1986. *Persephone's Quest: Entheogens and the Origins of Religion*. New Haven: Yale University Press.

Watson, Davis. 1926. "Cathode Ray a New Tool of Science." *Current History* 25:3 (December 1926): 392–96.

Watts, Alan. 1960. "The New Alchemy." Available at http://druglibrary.org/schaffer/lsd/alchemy.htm.

Weart, Spencer R. 1988. *Nuclear Fear: A History of Images*. Cambridge: Harvard University Press.

Wells, H. G. 1914. *The World Set Free*. In *The First Men in the Moon, The World Set Free, and Short Stories*. London: Odhams, n.d. 165–312.

Westcott, W. Wynn. 1893–1911. *Collectanea Hermetica*. 10 volumes. London: Theosophical Publishing Society.

——— [as "Sapere Aude"]. 1894. *Aesch Mezareph; or purifying fire. A chymico-kabalistic treatise collected from the Kabala denudata of Knorr von Rosenroth. Translated by a lover of Philalethes, 1714. Preface, notes and explanations by "Sapere Aude."* London: Theosophical Publishing Society.

Westfahl, Gary. 1990. "'An Idea of Significant Import': Hugo Gernsback's Theory of Science Fiction." *Foundation: The Review of Science Fiction* 48 (Spring 1990): 26–50.

Weyer, Jost. 1976. "The Image of Alchemy in Nineteenth and Twentieth Century Histories of Chemistry." *Ambix* 23:2 (July 1976): 64–79.

Who Was Who Among English and European Authors, 1931–1949. 1978. N.p.: Gale Research. Vol. 3, N-Z, 1178.

Williams, Charles. 1930. *War in Heaven*. Reprint, Grand Rapids, Mich.: Eerdmans, 1985.

Wilson, Robert Anton. 1999. "Introduction." In *Sex and Rockets: The Occult World of Jack Parsons*, by John Carter. Venice, Cal.: Feral House, 1999. vii–xxiii.

Winter, Alison. 1998. *Mesmerized: Powers of Mind in Victorian Britain*. Chicago: The University of Chicago Press.

Worthington, A. M. 1916. Obituary for William Ramsay. *Nature* (August 10, 1916). Offprint. William Ramsay Papers, University College London.

Yates, Frances A. 1964. *Giordano Bruno and the Hermetic Tradition*. Chicago: The University of Chicago Press.

———. 1972. *The Rosicrucian Enlightenment*. Reprint, New York: Barnes & Noble, 1996.

Yeats, William Butler. 1897. "Rosa Alchemica." In *Mythologies*. New York: Collier, 1969. 267–92.

Index

A.A., 20, 45, 50. *See also* Crowley, Aleister
   and scientific sanctioning, 46–47
Abdul-Ali, Sijil, 52, 59, 60–61, 215 n. 19
   on alchemy and modern science, 60, 218 n. 31
actor-network theory, 91, 199
Aksakov, Nikolaevich, 15, 21
Albertus, Frater (Albert Richard Riedel), 187–88
Alchemical Association of France, 104
alchemical revival, 5, 43, 99, 102, 160, 204
   and atomic science, 5, 9, 11–12, 29, 64, 97, 109, 127
Alchemical Society, 10, 29, 33, 40–64, 65, 94, 109, 192
   as borderland, 53, 59
   and boundary of science and occultism, 34, 49, 53, 56, 59, 196–202
   and chemists' transmutation claims, 126, 127–29
   founding of, 49–51
   at International Club, 51
   interpretations of alchemy by, 49, 57–59, 63
   members of, 205–6, 207–8
   public aspirations of, 50–52
   and radiation, 33, 60
   scientific credentials of, 49–50, 53
alchemy. *See also* radiation; gold standard
   in chemistry education, 98–104
   and drug use, 191–93
   Enlightenment rejection of, 3–4
   and Hermetic unity, 63
   and monetary theory, 10
   and pharmacology, 4
   and psychoanalysis, 58, 188–91
   in science fiction, 139, 168–83
   sources of, 3
   spiritual, 35–37, 57, 58, 66, 68–69, 88–90, 186, 188
Alexander II, 15
Alpine Club, 44
Amazing Stories, 168, 169, 170, 172, 177
Amazing Stories Annual, 169
American Journal of Science, 104
Ancient and Mystical Order Rosae Crucis (AMORC), 19, 187
Anderson, Benjamin M., Jr., 144–46
Anderson, Carrick, 53
Aquinas, Thomas, 228 n. 2
Arrhenius, Svante, 105
Arrowsmith, Jane, 14
Aston, F. W., 94
Athenæum, 52, 215 n. 21
Atlantis, 160–67
atomic bomb, 7, 29, 145, 151–52, 158, 185
atomic energy, 63, 112–13, 181

atomic science
  image history of, 8
  material history of, 8
  standard history of, 5–8
Atwood, Mary Anne, 36–39. See also alchemy, spiritual
  A Suggestive Inquiry into the Hermetic Mystery, 35, 36, 42, 57, 58, 88, 186, 188, 213 n. 7
Ayton, Rev. W. A., 35, 41–42, 49, 121, 214 n. 12

Bacon, Roger, 123, 153, 228 n. 2
Baker, Julian L., 42, 45
Baly, E. C. C.
  transmutation efforts of, 109, 121, 124
Bank Charter Act of 1844, 139
Baskerville, Charles, 117, 122, 123, 227 n. 21
Becquerel, Henri, 4, 6
Bent, Silas, 144–45
Bergier, Jacques, 186–87
Bergson, Henri, 84
Bernus, Alexander von, 187
Bertalanffy, Ludwig von, 29
Berthelot, Daniel, 104
Berthelot, Marcellin, 99, 109, 150
  L'Origine d'Alchemie, 103, 160, 165
Besant, Annie, 41, 64, 88. See also occult chemistry
  Ancient Wisdom, The, 79, 85
  "On the Watch-Tower" columns of, 72, 89
Blackett, P. M. S., 73
Blavatsky, H. P., 15–16, 33, 41, 67, 69–72, 72, 81, 92, 95, 164, 191
  and Atlantis, 161–62
  on "Fohat," 84–85
  Isis Unveiled, 69, 70, 83–84, 102
  The Secret Doctine, 70–71, 84–85
Bohr, Niels, 6, 7
Bolton, H. Carrington, 103–4, 114
Born, Max, 7
boundaries
  and border crossings, 50, 53, 196, 198–201, 203, 204
  and boundary objects, 196, 199–201
  and boundary-work, 196
  of chemistry and physics, 10, 96, 97, 105, 201–4 (*see also* physical chemistry)
  and new occultism, 38
  of nuclear physics and economics, 10, 97, 136
  permeability of, 55–59
  of religion and science, 5, 8, 29, 34, 50, 56, 65, 95, 193
  of science fiction and gothic, 146
  and trading zones, 196, 201–4
Bowker, Geoffrey, 196, 199, 201
Boyle, Robert, 103
Bretton Woods, 138, 141, 159, 185
Brice, Edward C., 142
British Association for the Advancement of Science (BAAS), 22, 78, 111, 121, 123–24, 149–50
Brodie-Innes, J. W., 25
Brotherhood of the New Life, 212 n. 8
Bryan, William Jennings, 140, 147
bubble chamber, 8, 66, 73
Büchner, Ludwig, 48
Builders of Adytum, 20
Bullock, Percy, 42
Bulwer-Lytton, Edward, 19, 211 n. 22
  The Coming Race, 23
  and Éliphas Lévi, 22
  "The Haunted and the Haunters," 23
  and spiritualism, 23
  A Strange Story, 23
  Zanoni, 22–24, 25, 125, 139
Bunsen, Robert, 125
Burke, Butler, 89
Butlerov, A. M., 15, 21

Cambridge Association for Spiritual Inquiry (or "Ghost Society"), 21
Cameron, A. T., 123, 124, 129
Canaday, John, 152–53
Canseliet, Eugène, 187
Carlson, Maria, 16
Case, Paul Foster, 20
cathode rays, 5, 6, 8, 22, 66
  in occult and science fiction, 26, 146, 148, 169, 173, 178
  in transmutation efforts, 116, 119–21, 124, 128, 228 n. 29
Cavendish Laboratory, 6, 7, 9, 98, 105, 111–12, 120, 132, 134, 203
Cayce, Edgar, 165–67
Chadwick, James, 7
Champion, Joe, 187
Charles, R. H., 165, 167
Chatley, Herbert, 54, 55, 129
Chemical News, The, 52, 54, 126

Chemical Society, 22
  and transmutation claims, 60, 118, 124–27, 130–32
chemistry, histories of, 10, 56
  alchemy in, 97–101, 111–14
  British vs. German, 99
Cicero, Chic, and Sandra Cicero, 232 n. 5
Clarke, Bruce, 83–84, 220 n. 10
cloud chamber, 8, 66, 67, 73, 96, 120
Cockren, Archibald, 187
Cocteau, Jean, 186
Coinage Act of 1873, 139–40, 147
Cold War, 8, 29, 185–86
Collie, John Norman, 44, 45, 50, 117, 203
  transmutation claims by, 60, 119, 121, 124, 125, 128, 130–33
Colquhoun, Ithell, 41, 43, 49, 186, 232 n. 3
Cook, Florence, 22
Coolidge, Calvin, 143
Clymer, Reuben Swinburne, 19
Craven, Venerable J. B., 55
Crookes, Sir William, 26, 54, 67, 91, 100, 222 n. 1
  and boundary of science and religion, 83
  and cathode ray experiments, 7–8
  occult involvement of, 9, 19, 39
  and protyle, 39, 59, 60, 65, 68, 81–83, 114
  and Society for Psychical Research, 22
  and spinthariscope, 66
  and Theosophical Society, 71
Crowley, Aleister, 20, 43, 44, 47, 72, 109, 164–65
  chemistry education of, 44
  introduction to Golden Dawn, 44–45
  Moonchild, 32, 42, 47
  and radioactivity and X-rays, 47–48
  and Scientific Illuminism, 22, 44–49, 50
Curie, Marie, 6, 26, 67
  and William Ramsay's transmutation claims, 119–20, 129, 130–31
  and Society for Psychical Research, 22
Curie, Pierre, 6

Dalton, John, 4, 12, 65, 110, 134
Darwin, Charles, 70
Davies, Glyn, 140
de Broglie, Louis, 7
Dee, John, 18, 164
de Guaita, Stanislas, 19, 210 n. 16

de Hevesy, George de, 133
de Kerlor, W., 62
Democritus, 80
de Sennevoy, Baron Dupotet, 19
de Steiger, Isabelle, 33
  and Atwood, Mary Anne, 58, 59, 137, 217 n. 28
  interpretation of alchemy, 58
  On a Gold Basis: A Treatise on Mysticism, 137–38
Dewar, James, 103–4, 224 n. 10
disenchantment (Max Weber), 28–29, 34
Dixon, Joy, 86–88
Dobbie, Sir J. J., 53
Donnelly, Ignatius Loyola, 161
Douglas, Major Clifford Hugh, 136, 155–56
Driesch, Hans, 29
Du Bois-Reymond, Emil, 29
Dunlop, Daniel Nicol, 33

Eckenstein, Oscar, 45
Edison, Thomas, 16
Egerton, A. C. G., 119–21, 125, 130–34, 228 n. 29
Einstein, Albert, 78, 91
electrons
  discovery of, 6
  wave and particle properties of, 7
Elixir of Life, 4, 8, 23, 41, 63, 118, 163
Elliott, James, 11, 43, 100
Ellis, Richard, 230 n. 13
"Emerald Tablet of Hermes, The," 102, 223 n. 5
Emmens, Stephen, 102, 114, 115, 116, 121, 123, 142, 144
English Mechanic, The, 52
Enoch, Book of, 109, 160–67
Equinox, The, 43, 45, 47. *See also* Crowley, Aleister
  and publication of occult rituals, 45–46
Ernst, Paul, 231 n. 18
ether, 7, 22, 37, 59, 60, 65, 71, 74, 77–83, 89–93, 102, 218 n. 31, 220 nn. 6, 9, 10, 11, 223 n. 4
  and occultism, 71, 78, 93
extrasensory perception (ESP), 93, 222 n. 21

Faber, Augusta, 190
Faivre, Antoine, 13
Faraday, Michael, 40, 105, 110, 119
Färber, Eduard, 99

Farr, Florence, 19, 213 n. 5
Federal Reserve, 141, 171–73, 176
Felkin, R. W., 20
Fellowship of the Rosy Cross, 20, 28
Ferenczi, Sándor, 58
Ferguson, John, 11, 49, 53, 54, 56, 102, 106–7, 197
    against spiritual alchemy thesis, 58
    Bibliotheca Chemica, 56
Fisher, Irving, 157, 180
Flamel, Nicholas, 34
Foote, Paul D., 143
Fox, Kate and Margaret, 14–15
Frankland, Percy F., 126–27
Fraternitas Rosae Crucis, 19
Free Economy League, 155
Freud, Sigmund, 87, 189
Frings, J. W., 61, 215 n. 21
Fulcanelli, 187
Fyfe, Henry, 117

Gaedicke, Johannes, 229 n. 6
Galison, Peter, 8
    on image vs. electronic detectors, 66, 73
    on trading zones, 196, 201–4
Gardner, Frederick Leigh, 41–42, 49
Garstin, E. J. Langford, 186
Gaschler, Alois, 145
Gernsback, Hugo, 139, 168–72, 177–80, 182
Gesell, Silvio, 155, 228 n. 1
Gibson, Lt.-Col. Jasper, 62–63
Gieryn, Thomas F., 196–97, 212 n. 26, 231–32 n. 1
Gilbert, R. A., 38, 43
Glaser, Donald. *See* bubble chamber
Gmelin, Johann Friedrich, 98
Godwin, Joscelyn, 211 n. 22
Golden Dawn, Hermetic Order of, 19–20, 50, 51, 114, 160, 186, 191, 192, 197
    and alchemy, 11, 32–33, 35–43, 214 n. 12
    and atomic physics, 48–49
    and boundary of occultism and science, 34–43, 196, 200
    chemists of, 42
    founding of, 32
    and Horos scandal, 35, 49, 213 n. 6
    and spiritual alchemy, 35–41
Goldfinger, 185
Gold Reserve Act of 1934, 142

gold standard. *See also* Roosevelt, Franklin D.
    bimetallism and, 141
    history of, 139–42
    instability of, 136
    in science fiction, 168–83
    transmutation's threat to, 135–83, 142–49
Gold Standard Act of 1900, 139, 142, 146
gold transmutation, successful, 135, 187
Gonne, Maud, 19
Gordin, Michael D., 21, 101–2, 223 n. 4, 229 n. 3
Graves, Orval, 187
Graves, Robert, 186
Great Depression. *See* gold standard
Gregory, Lady Augusta, 41
Griesemer, James R., 196, 199–201
Guild Socialism, 156

Haeckel, Ernst, 48
Haggard, H. Rider
    Ayesha: The Return of She, 27, 148–49
    She, 27
Hara, Fio, 89
Harcourt, William, 140
Harding, Warren G., 142
Harper's, 63, 117–18, 123, 129, 163
Harrington, Anne, 29, 212 n. 27
Harris, Thomas Lake, 212 n. 8
Hartley, W. H., 123–24
Hauffe, Friederike, 14
Heisenberg, Werner, 7
    and uncertainty principle, 7
Helmholtz, Hermann von, 29, 80, 82, 216 n. 26
Helmont, Jan Baptista van, 56, 129
Hermes Trismegistus, 17, 18, 210 n. 12
Hermeticism, 17–20
    Neoplatonic and gnostic origins of, 17, 210 n. 12
Hess, David J., 196–97
Hitchcock, Ethan Allen, 188
Hockley, Frederick, 19, 41
Hodson, Geoffrey, 94–95
Holy Grail, 28
Home, Daniel Dunglas, 15, 210 n. 11, 211 n. 22
Horniman, Annie, 19
Horton, W. T., 33

Howe, Ellic, 32, 214 n. 10
Howorth, Muriel, 225 nn. 11, 13
Huggins, William, 111, 225 n. 16
Hunter, Robert Melville, 116–17, 121, 123, 134, 144, 227 n. 21
Hutchison, Keith, 211 n. 18
Huxley, Aldous, 187
Huxley, Julian, 186
Huxley, Thomas, 70
hyperchemistry, 49, 186. See also Jollivet-Castelot, François

Independent and Rectified Rite, 20
instrumentation
  alchemical, 66
  in chemistry and physics, 66, 73
International Monetary Fund, 141, 159

James, H., and Maurice James, 173
James, William, 21
Jenkins, Philip, 18, 161–62, 212 n. 8
Jennings, Hargrave, 19, 223 n. 5
Jinarajadasa, Curupumullage, 76, 94, 221 n. 16
Jollivet-Castelot, François, 11, 49, 62, 121, 145, 187
Jones, George Cecil, 42, 45
Journal of the Alchemical Society, 51, 52, 54, 59, 63, 129
Journal of the Chemical Society, 60, 119
Jung, Carl, 58, 190–91
  Mysterium Coniunctionis, 191
  Psychology and Alchemy, 190

Kabbalistic Order of the Rose Cross, 19
Karssen, A., 133
Kateley, Walter, 179–80
Kellner, Carl, 20, 46
Kelly, Edward, 62, 164
Kelvin, Lord, 82, 90, 102, 111, 220 n. 12, 225 n. 16
  and vortex atom, 65, 68, 71, 80–81, 91
Kerner, Justinus, 14
Keynes, J. M., 155, 157
King, Francis, 34, 214 n. 14
King, Katie. See Cook, Florence
Kitson, Arthur, 136, 155–56
Knickerbocker Trust, 141
Knights of the Red Cross of Rome and Constantine, 18

Knowledge, 52, 55, 129
Kopp, Hermann, 99, 105, 110
  Geschichte der Chemie, 103

Lancet, 121–22
Lankester, E. Ray, 149–50
Larmor, Joseph, 81, 89, 220 n. 9
Latour, Bruno, 90–91, 94, 199
Lavoisier, Antoine, 103, 110
Lawrence, D. H., 84
Lea, Carey, 104
Leadbeater, C. W., 64, 88. See also occult chemistry
  The Astral Plane, 220 n. 7
  Chakras, The, 74
  Clairvoyance, 75, 78
  Textbook of Theosophy, 79, 221 n. 15
Le Châtelier, Henry, 104
Lemuria, 162
Leucippus, 80
Levere, Trevor, 105
Lévi, Éliphas, 12–13, 18, 23, 38, 41, 210 n. 16
  synthesis of alchemy, kabbalah, and tarot, 18
Lewis, C. S., 28
Lewis, H. K., 51
Lewis, Harvey Spencer, 19
Lockyer, Sir Norman, 54, 71, 100, 104
  and dissociation hypothesis, 40, 60
  ridiculed as "alchemist," 41
Lodge, Sir Oliver, 83, 111, 131, 200 n. 6, 215 n. 21, 220 n. 9
  Ether of Space, The, 80–81
  and Society for Psychical Research, 22
Loring, F. H., 49, 60
  chemistry books by, 54
Lucifer, 67, 71, 72
Lucretius, 48
Lully, Raymond, 34, 48
Lyness, D. D., 94

Machen, Arthur, 192
Mackenzie, K. R. H., 19
Mallard, François Ernest, 104
Manhattan Project, 152–53
Marques, A., 72
Marsden, Dora, 84
Marsh, J. E., 103
Martineau, Harriet, 14
Martinez-Alier, Juan, 157, 175
Masonry, 18

Masson, Irvine, 121, 124, 131–33
Mathers, Samuel Liddell "MacGregor," 19, 32, 41, 45, 47, 165, 186, 212 n. 2
Matin des Magiciens, Le. See Pauwels, Louis, and Jacques Bergier
matter, 10, 23, 29, 47, 54, 107, 110, 148, 158, 171, 180, 191. *See also* ether; occult chemistry; physical chemistry; protyle; ultimate physical atom
   debate over nature of, 4–5, 12, 33, 61, 65–66, 68, 78, 80–83, 90, 97
   in alchemy, 4, 12, 39–40, 61, 63, 68, 101, 114–15, 122, 188
   in occultism, 5, 12, 57, 63–64
   in Theosophy, 65–66, 70, 77–79, 81, 83–90, 91
   radioactive, 33, 63, 89–90, 102
Maxwell, James Clerk, 79
Mayhew, Nicholas, 136, 140, 148
McKay, David, 11
Mead, G. R. S., 72
mediums, 21
Meek, Captain S. P., 172–73
Mellor, Joseph, 49, 54, 55, 60, 109, 129
   chemistry books by, 55
Mendeleev, Dmitrii, 21, 101–2, 109
   and Russian Physical Society, 21
Merricks, Linda, 155, 159, 223 n. 2, 230 nn. 8, 10
Merritt, Abraham, 169–70
Merton, Thomas, 121, 130, 132
Mesmer, Franz Anton, 13
mesmerism, 13–15, 19, 23, 211 n. 19
   and clairvoyance, 14
   and scientific validation, 20
   and spiritual alchemy, 58
Meyer-Abich, Adolf, 29
Meyer, Ernst von, 99–100, 110
Miethe, Adolf, 229 n. 6
   transmutation claims of, 132–34, 143–45, 168–69, 178
Miller, Henry, 186
Miller, Peter Schuyler, "Jeremiah Jones, Alchemist," 177–79
Mitchell, C. Ainsworth, 126
Moore, William R., 57
Morgan, J. P., 176–77
Morning Post, 126
Muir, M. M. Pattison, 99–101, 102
Myers, Frederick, 21

Nathanson, Isaac R., 180–82
National Guilds League, 155
Nature, 52, 54, 55, 114
   and transmutation claims, 50, 60, 67, 118–21, 127–28, 131
Nelson, Robert A., 187
neuroscience, 191
New Age, The, 155–56
Newman, William R., 228 n. 2
Newton, Sir Isaac, 79, 91
New York Daily Tribune
   coverage of transmutation claims, 115–16
New York Times, 172, 224 n. 10, 229 n. 5
   coverage of transmutation claims, 114, 122–23
   coverage of transmutation's threat to gold standard, 142–45, 157
Nye, Mary Jo, 105–6, 204

occult chemistry (of Besant and Leadbeater), 10, 65–96. *See also* Phillips, Stephen
   as bridge between religion and science, 95
   and clairvoyance, 68, 74, 88, 90, 91
   and experimental basis of Theosophy, 68, 72, 195
   The Field of Occult Chemistry, 94
   and image orientation of modern physics, 67, 73
   koilon and Victorian ether physics, 78, 83
   launch of, 67, 72
   and multiplanar Theosophical atoms, 77–79, 91, 192
   Occult Chemistry, 68, 77, 93, 94–95
   as re-enchantment of science, 69
   rhetorical strategy of, 90–96
   as "sanitization" of occultism, 67
   and sexing of sub-atomic world, 83–88
Occult Review, The, 33, 57
occult revival, 5, 12–20, 70
occult science
   as modern science, 25, 41, 44, 46–47
Olcott, Henry Steel, 15–16, 67, 69–70, 72
Old, Walter Gorn ("Sepharial"), 33, 51–52, 59, 128
Oppenheim, Janet, 15, 22, 211 n. 20
Oppenheimer, J. Robert, 186
Orage, A. R., 136, 155
Ordo Templi Orientis (OTO), 20, 46
Ostwald, Wilhelm, 105, 109
Otis, Laura, 75

Ouroboros, 4, 114, 150
Outer Order of the Rosicrucian Order of Alpha + Omega, 20
Owen, Alex, 21
  and "new occultism," 29, 211 n. 21
  The Place of Enchantment, 29, 189
Oxford Phasmatological Society, 21

Paneth, Fritz, 133
Papus (Gérard Encausse), 19
Paracelsus, 4, 34, 39, 42, 43, 70, 100, 129, 144, 239 n. 3
Paracelsus Research Society, 188
particle accelerators, 132, 134, 169
particle physics, 7, 34, 47, 66, 70, 132, 197–98, 222 n. 21
Path, The, 33
Patterson, Hubert, 60, 121, 124, 126, 128, 130–33
Patzer, Sidney, 174
Pauli, Wolfgang, 190–91
Pauwels, Louis, 186–87
Péladan, Joséphin, 19, 210 n. 16
Phillips, Stephen, 92–95, 222 nn. 20–21
  and Buddhist clairvoyant research, 94
  on micro-psi atoms, 93
Philosopher's Stone, 3, 8, 50, 59, 61, 63, 118, 123, 163, 190–91. *See also* radium
Philosophical Magazine, The, 90
physical chemistry
  as borderland between chemistry and physics, 105–11, 120–21, 203–4
  and study of matter, 108–9
  and study of radioactivity, 106
physics, nuclear, 5, 7–9, 49, 64, 97–98, 105, 112, 134, 139, 186–87
Planck, Max, 6
Plato, 161
Poe, Edgar Allan, 169–70
Poisson, Albert, 19
popular press, 5, 41, 49, 128, 131, 198, 200, 210 n. 8. *See also* gold standard
  "alchemical" coverage of atomic physics, 34, 49, 56, 60, 64, 73, 114, 123, 126, 132–33, 139
  occult, 11, 14, 44, 51, 72
Pound, Ezra, 136, 156
Poynting, John, 78
Preiswerk, Emilie, 190
Preiswerk, Helene, 190

prima materia, 3, 4, 65, 68, 82, 88, 104, 115–16
protyle, 40, 59, 60, 65, 68, 71, 114, 218 n. 31, 219 n. 5, 222 n. 1. *See also* Prout, William; Crookes, Sir William
  Theosophical interest in, 40, 81–83, 91
Prout, William, 40, 65, 68, 71, 82, 91, 100, 102, 110
Puységur, Marquis de, 14
Pythagoras, 48

quantum mechanics, 7, 93, 190, 191, 222 n. 20

radioactive transformation, 4, 6, 8, 9, 34, 70, 90, 97, 100
  importance to alchemy of, 9, 11–12, 43, 104
  in occult novels, 24–28
  in science fiction novels, 146
radioactivity
  comparison to alchemy, 4–5, 62
  and Elixir of Life, 4
  and occult novels, 24–28
  and spiritual alchemy, 88–90
radiochemistry, 5, 9, 97, 98, 112, 139, 193
  as "modern alchemy," 5
radium, 89
  as cancer treatment, 63
  discovery of, 6
  as Elixir of Life, 12, 118
  occult powers of, 90
  as Philosopher's Stone 4–5, 12, 61, 63, 118
  in popular fiction, 28
Ramsay, Sir William, 9, 26, 44, 53, 55, 59, 67, 71, 90, 97, 102–3, 226 n. 19, 226 n. 20
  and alchemy, 5, 44–45, 63, 111
  and discovery of helium, 8
  Elements and Electrons, 119
  lectures on alchemy and atomic transmutation, 115–16
  membership in Society for Psychical Research, 22
  and physical chemistry, 108–10, 203–4
  "Radium and Its Products," 117–18
  radium-to-helium transformation, 106, 114
  transmutation claims, 50, 52, 60, 62–63, 67, 115–34, 136, 141
Randolph, Paschal Beverly, 18–19, 191
  Hermes Mercurius Trismegistus: His Divine Pymander, 102, 223 n. 5
Rayleigh, Lord. *See* Strutt, John William

Redgrove, H. Stanley, 11, 49, 51, 54, 60, 216 n. 27
  against spiritual alchemy thesis, 58
  Alchemy: Ancient and Modern, 61, 63, 129
  on alchemy and atomic science, 59, 61, 127–29
  interpretation of alchemy of, 57
  on occult and scientific subjects, 54
  and University of London, 50
Redway, George, 43, 223 n. 5
re-enchantment of science, 29, 34, 59, 63, 69
Regardie, Israel, 43
  The Middle Pillar, 191
  The Philosopher's Stone, 188
  psychoanalytic use of magic and alchemy, 58, 188–89
Repp, Ed Earl, 231 n. 16
Reuss, Theodor, 20
Rider, William, and Son, 11, 33, 51, 54
Rockefeller, John D., 175
Röntgen, Wilhelm, 26, 67
  discovery of X-rays, 5–6, 709
Roosevelt, Franklin D., 174, 177
  and bank holiday, 141, 171, 174
  and confiscation of privately held gold, 142, 171
Rose + Cross University, 187
Rosicrucian Fraternity, 19
Rosicrucianism, 17–20
Rosicrucian Publishing Company, 102
Rosycross (Rosenkreuz), Christian, 17–18
Rowbottom, B. Ralph, 62, 129, 219 n. 32
Royal Society, 12, 22, 41, 82, 92, 115, 125
Royds, T., 129, 130
Ruskin, John, 155, 230 n. 8
Russell, A. S., 227 n. 22
Russell, Bertrand, 186
Rutherford, Ernest, 4, 24, 34, 59, 67, 71, 100, 104, 107, 110, 127, 202–4
  and alchemy, 5, 111
  challenges transmutation claims, 123–24, 129–30
  collaboration with Frederick Soddy (*see* radioactive transformation)
  The Newer Alchemy, 5, 111
  and nuclear model of atom, 6–7, 60
  Radio-active Substances and Their Radiations, 52
  transmutation by, 9, 63, 64, 73, 97, 119, 132, 134, 142, 168

Schachner, Nathan
  "The Revolt of the Scientists," 174–77
Schorlemmer, Carl, 103, 110
Schrödinger, Erwin, 7
Science
  on economic threat of synthetic gold, 142
Science Wonder Stories, 168, 173, 179
Scientific American
  and transmutation claims, 131, 133
Scientific Illuminism. *See* Crowley, Aleister
Sclove, Richard, 209 n. 2, 230 n. 9, 231 n. 14
Scott, Howard, 175
séances, 21
Serviss, Garrett P., 146, 149, 152, 183
  The Moon Metal, 146–48
Severn, Elizabeth, 58
  and psychological interpretation of alchemy, 58, 189, 217 n. 30
Sheldon, H. H., 145
Shelley, Mary
  Frankenstein, 229 n. 3
Shirley, Ralph, 33, 51
Sidgwick, Henry, 21
Silberer, Herbert, 189–90
Sinnett, A. P., 72
Sitwell, Edith, 186
Smith, E. Lester, 92–95
Smithells, Arthur, 124–25, 131–32
Smits, Arthur, 132–33
Social Credit movement, 136, 156–57, 171
Societas Rosicruciana in America, 18
Societas Rosicruciana in Anglia (S.R.I.A.), 18–19, 32
Societas Rosicruciana in Civitatibus Foederatis, 18
Société Alchimique de France, La, 11
Society for Psychical Research (SPR), 21, 92, 102, 109, 149–50
  physicists in, 22
Soddy, Frederick, 4, 5, 8, 9, 34, 42, 59, 67, 71, 94, 97, 100, 104, 187
  alchemy in chemistry education of, 103
  on alchemy and chemistry, 111–12, 230 n. 9
  and Atlantis, 160–67
  on atomic energy, 143, 145
  and Book of Enoch, 160–67
  on chemists' transmutation claims, 131
  collaboration with Ernest Rutherford (*see* radioactive transformation)

criticism of physicists' encroachment on chemistry, 105, 111
on energy as real wealth, 152, 157
"The Evolution of the Elements," 150–51
and Fall and Deluge, 163–65
The Interpretation of Radium, 27, 52, 53, 63, 107, 145, 151, 152, 162–67, 181
The Inversion of Science, 156
lectures on alchemy, 110
monetary theory of, 136, 139, 149–60
and radium-to-helium transformation, 106, 114, 115
"real alchemy" vs. "false alchemy," 138, 158–60
The Story of Atomic Energy, 158–60
"Transmutation, the Vital Problem of the Future," 113, 152
Wealth, Virtual Wealth and Debt, 156, 175
working at disciplinary boundaries, 107, 202–4
South, Thomas, 36
Speaker, David M., 170
spectroscope, 66, 73, 94, 96
spiritualism, 14–15, 69, 70
and "Hydesville knockings," 14, 190
and science, 21
S. R., 90
Stafford-Jerningham, Fitzherbert Edward (Lord Stafford), 11, 43, 100
Stammreich, Hans, 132
Star, Susan Leigh, 196, 199–201
Stella Matutina, 20
Stewart, Balfour
Unseen Universe, 71, 81
stock market crash of 1929. *See* gold standard
Stoker, Bram
Jewel of the Seven Stars, 24–27
Stoney, Johnstone, 6
Strutt, John William (third Baron Rayleigh), 22, 127
Strutt, Robert John (fourth Baron Rayleigh), 120, 130
Sullivan, J. W. N., 131
Szilard, Leo, 152

Tait, P. G., 80
Unseen Universe, 71, 81
Technical Alliance of North America, 176
Technocracy Incorporated. *See* Technocracy movement

Technocracy movement, 157, 174–75, 183
telepathy, 21, 74, 75, 81, 109
Theosophical Quarterly, 71, 72
Theosophical Review, 71, 72, 89
Theosophical Society, 15–16, 42, 51, 64, 109, 160
and boundaries of science and religion, 67, 95
presses of, 11, 72
Theosophist, The, 71, 72
Theosophy, 15–16, 19, 65–96, 101
and boundaries of science and religion, 69–72, 95
compared to Golden Dawn, 69
and evolutionary cosmology, 70
seven planes of, 70, 79, 95
and spiritualism, 70
and transmutation, 69
vitalism of, 83–88, 89
Thomson, John Millar, 53
Thomson, Joseph John, 34, 67, 71, 73, 81, 89, 112, 127
debunking transmutation claims, 60, 120, 124, 128, 130–32
and discovery of electrons, 6, 70
membership in Society for Psychical Research, 22
and "plum pudding" model of atom, 6–7
Thomson, Thomas, 99
Thorpe, T. E., 42, 214 n. 9
Thurschwell, Pamela, 74–75
Times Literary Supplement
alchemy coverage of, 114
Tolkien, J. R. R., 28
Torrens, R. G., 35
transmutation. *See also* Chemical Society...
as goal for chemistry, 40, 97, 110, 119
scientists' claims of: John Norman Collie, 60, 119, 121, 124, 125, 128, 130–33; A. C. G. Egerton, 119–21, 125, 130–34; A. Karssen, 133; Masson, Irvine, 121, 124, 131–33; Merton, Thomas, 121, 130, 132; Miethe, Adolf, 132–34, 143–45, 168–69, 178; Patterson, Hubert, 60, 121, 124, 126, 128, 130–33; Ramsay, Sir William, 50, 52, 60, 62–63, 67, 115–34, 136, 141; Rutherford, Ernest, 9, 63, 64, 73, 97, 119, 132, 134, 142, 168; Smits, Arthur, 132–33; Stammreich, Hans, 132

transmutational gold rush, 10, 45
Travers, Morris, 44, 107
Traweek, Sharon, 55, 196, 198–201, 225 n. 13
Trenn, Thaddeus, 120, 124, 209 n. 2
Trust Company of America, 141
Tyndal, John, 28

ultimate physical atom (UPA, or "anu"), 68, 77–78, 83, 86, 88, 95. *See also* occult chemistry
Unknown World, 11, 33, 38–39, 100, 212 n. 8. *See also* Waite, A. E.
United States Geological Survey, 143

Valentine, Basil, 45, 102
  Triumphal Chariot of Antimony, 100
van't Hoff, Jacobus Henricus, 105, 106, 107, 109
Vaughan, Thomas, 34
Virchow, Rudolf, 29
vitalist biology, 29

Waite, A. E., 11, 20, 33, 47, 100
  on alchemy and radioactivity, 60, 127–28
  against spiritual alchemy thesis, 57–58
  and boundaries of science and occultism, 38–39, 46, 53, 72
  Hermetic and Alchemical Writings of Paracelsus, 43, 100
  The Hermetic Museum Restored and Enlarged, 43
  influence on Golden Dawn's alchemy, 41–43
  interpretation of alchemy, 57–58, 59
  Lives of the Alchemystical Philosophers, 43
  as translator of key alchemical texts, 43
Walden, A. F., 103
Wallace, Alfred Russel, 16
Wallis, Roy, 196
  and "sanitization," 67, 195
Warlick, M. E., 189
Washington, Peter, 15, 68, 88, 219 n. 4

Watts, Alan
  "The New Alchemy," 192, 233 n. 8
Weart, Spencer, 8, 112, 164, 226 n. 18, 230 n. 7, 231 n. 15, 232 n. 2
Weber, Max
  and "disenchantment," 28–29, 34
Wellby, Phillip Sinclair, 59, 61, 137
  as occult publisher, 11, 33
Wells, H. G., 127, 179
  and alchemy, 153–4
  and *Interpretation of Radium* (Frederick Soddy), 152–53
  The World Set Free, 63, 145, 152–54, 167, 179, 180, 230 n. 8
Westcott, William Wynn, 19, 32, 35, 39–41, 46, 47
  Aesh Mezareph or Purifying Fire, 41
  Hermetica Collectanea, 41
Westminster Gazette, 52, 131
Weyer, Jost, 98–99
Whetham, W. C. D., 90
Wilcox, Ella Wheeler, 16
Wilhelm, Richard, 190
Williams, Charles, 20
  War in Heaven, 27–28
Wilson, C. T. R. *See* cloud chamber
Wilson, Robert Anton, 44
Winter, Alison, 20, 210 nn. 7–8, 211 n. 19
Wonder Stories, 173, 174
Woodman, William Robert, 19, 32
Worthington, A. M., 225 n. 15

X-rays, 5–6, 24, 67, 70
  in occult and science fiction, 26, 47–48, 146, 179
  transmutation efforts using, 116, 121, 124–25, 128

Yates, Frances, 17–18, 210 n. 12
Yeats, William Butler, 19, 41, 47, 212 n. 2
  "Rosa Alchemica," 31–32
Young, Thomas, 79

Zosimus, 165